Educational Reform

CRITICAL EDUCATION PRACTICE
VOLUME 10
GARLAND REFERENCE LIBRARY OF SOCIAL SCIENCE
VOLUME 1050

Critical Education Practice

Shirley R. Steinberg and Joseph L. Kincheloe, *Series Editors*

Curriculum Development in the Postmodern Era
by Patrick Slattery

Becoming a Student of Teaching
Methodologies for Exploring Self and School Context
by Robert V. Bullough, Jr. and Andrew D. Gitlin

Occupied Reading
Critical Foundations for an Ecological Theory
by Alan A. Block

Democracy, Multiculturalism, and the Community College
A Critical Perspective
by Robert A. Rhoads and James R. Valadez

Anatomy of a Collaboration
Study of a College of Education/Public School Partnership
by Judith J. Slater

Teaching Mathematics
Toward a Sound Alternative
by Brent Davis

Inner-City Schools, Multiculturalism, and Teacher Education
A Professional Journey
by Frederick L. Yeo

Rethinking Language Arts
Passion and Practice
by Nina Zaragoza

Educational Reform
A Deweyan Perspective
by Douglas J. Simpson and Michael J. B. Jackson

Liberation Theology and Critical Pedagogy in Today's Catholic Schools
Social Justice in Action
by Thomas Oldenski

Educational Reform
A Deweyan Perspective

Douglas J. Simpson and
Michael J. B. Jackson

Garland Publishing, Inc.
New York and London
1997

Library of Congress Cataloging-in-Publication Data

Simpson, Douglas J.
Educational reform : a Deweyan perspective / by Douglas Simpson and Michael J. B. Jackson.
p. cm.
Includes bibliographical references (p.) and index.
ISBN 0-8153-2089-2 (hardcover) (alk. paper)
ISBN 0-8153-2323-9 (paperback)
1. Dewey, John, 1859–1952. 2. Education—Philosophy. 3. Educational change. 4. School management and organization. 5. Education—Social aspects. 6. Teachers—Training of. I. Jackson, Michael J. B. (Michael John Brierley), 1943– . II. Title. III. Series : Garland reference library of social science ; vol. 1050. IV. Series : Garland reference library of social science. Critical education practice ; vol. 10.
LB875.D5S55 1997
370'.1—dc20 96–46530
CIP

Paperback cover design by Eric Brearton.

Printed on acid-free, 250-year-life paper
Manufactured in the United States of America

For
Judy and Geneviève

What the best and wisest parent wants for his own child, that must the community want for all of its children. Any other ideal for our schools is narrow and unlovely; acted upon, it destroys our democracy.

John Dewey, 1900
The School and Society

Contents

Abbreviations

Several kinds of abbreviations appear throughout the text. We are particularly indebted to the editors of Southern Illinois University Press who created a handy reference system we follow here with a minor variation when we cite their collection of Dewey's works. Their *Index* provides references to the early, middle and later volumes by employing, for example, the simple indicators of E5: 289 to refer to the *Early Works*, volume 5, page 289. Our slight modification changes the citation to E5, 289. The scheme affords frequent and accurate references to the SIUP series, a highly desirable feature for a work of this nature. For secondary sources, we follow either house style or the *Publication Manual of the American Psychological Association* (4th edition). An important exception to these practices occurs when we use repeatedly a limited number of well-known primary sources. In these cases, simple abbreviations appear. Each of the sources listed below is either an original work or an edited set of the original works of John Dewey. The abbreviation for each work is at the immediate left. Secondary sources, as well as full details about all primary ones, are included in the Selected Bibliography.

The Southern Illinois University Press Collection:

E: *The Early Works of John Dewey, 1882-1898*. Carbondale: Southern Illinois University Press, 1967-1972. 5 vols.

M: *The Middle Works of John Dewey, 1899-1924*. Carbondale: Southern Illinois University Press, 1976-1983. 15 vols.

L: *The Later Works of John Dewey, 1925-1953.* Carbondale: Southern Illinois University Press, 1981-1991. 17 vols.

Collections of Writings:

Archambault: Archambault, R. D. (Ed.). (1964/1974). *John Dewey on Education: Selected Writings.* Chicago: The University of Chicago Press.

Dworkin: Dworkin, M. S. (Ed.). (1959). *Dewey on Education: Selections with an Introduction and Notes.* New York: Bureau of Publications, Teachers College, Columbia University.

Ratner: Ratner, J. (Ed.). (1939). *Intelligence in the Modern World: John Dewey's Philosophy.* New York: The Modern Library.

Individual Publications:

AE: *Art as Experience* (1934/1980). New York: Perigee Books.

CF: *A Common Faith* (1934/1962). New Haven, CT: Yale University Press.

DE: *Democracy and Education* (1916/1966). New York: The Free Press.

EE: *Experience and Education* (1938/1963). New York: Collier Books.

EN: *Experience and Nature* (1925/1929/1958). New York: Dover Publications, Inc.

FC: *Freedom and Culture* (1989). Buffalo, NY: Prometheus Books.

HWT: *How We Think* (1933/1960). New edition. Lexington, MA: D. C. Heath and Company.

MPE: *Moral Principles in Education* (1909/1936/1975). Carbondale: Southern Illinois University Press.

PN: *The Psychology of Number and Its Application to Methods of Teaching Arithmetic* (1908). New York: D. Appleton and Company.

QC: *The Quest for Certainty* (1929). New York: Minton, Balach and Co.

RP: *Reconstruction in Philosophy* (1920/1948/1957). Enlarged Edition. Boston: Beacon Press.

SSCC: *The School and Society* and *The Child and the Curriculum* (1900/1902/1915/1943/1956/1990). Expanded Edition. Chicago: The University of Chicago Press.

Acknowledgments

We acknowledge with gratitude the assistance of a large number of people who helped with the development of this work. This help came from a variety of people, including those who encouraged us by discussing Dewey and educational reform, others who asked that we teach a graduate seminar, still others who invited us to write a proposal for Garland Publishing Inc., several others who reviewed portions of the manuscript, and others who provided editorial and stylistic advice for the volume. In particular, we thank Arno Bellack, Willard Brehaut, J. W. Bulcock, Joe Burnett, Rodney Clifton, Jim Covert, Jim Garrison, Joe Green, Graham Jackson, J. D. Jefferis, Joe Kincheloe, William Knitter, Phyllis Korper, Marie Ellen Larcada, Kathleen Martin, Joan Netten, John Netten, Jose Alejandro Ramirez, Ron Reed, Sherrie Reynolds, Linda Schamer, Shirley Steinberg, Barbara Stengel, Chipman Stuart, and Andrew Wilson. Our anonymous copyeditor, Betty Taylor, Ian Steinberg and Robin Van Heck merit a special word of thanks for their efforts in helping us create a more readable book. We also express our appreciation to Harvey Neufeldt for writing the Introduction. His comments establish the context for the entire volume. Likewise, we would like to thank *Paideusis*, the Canadian Journal of Philosophy of Education, and its editor, William Hare, for giving us permission to draw copiously upon our article, "Glorious Dreams and Harsh Realities: The Roles and Responsibilities of the Teacher from a Deweyan Perspective" (*8*, 2, Spring, 1995). Geneviève Racette's support for the final preparation of this book deserves particular recognition. Her gracious assistance enabled the authors to bring closure on the project.

Finally, we acknowledge those publishers who granted us permission to quote from their works. Mona Wilson, Southern Illinois University Press, was especially helpful in enabling us to secure permission to use material from *The Collected Works of John Dewey* edited by J. A. Boydston (Copyright © by The Board of Trustees, Southern Illinois University. Published with permission of the publisher, Southern Illinois University Press.). In addition, we would like to thank others who assisted us in obtaining permission to quote from the following publications: *American Education: The Metropolitan Experience, 1876-1980* by L. Cremin (© HarperCollins Publishers. Reprinted with permission. All rights reserved.); *American Teachers: Histories of a Profession at Work* edited by D. Warren (© Simon & Schuster. Reprinted with permission. All rights reserved.); *To Be Our Best: Learning for the Future* edited by J. Downey and D. McCamus (© Corporate-Higher Education Forum. Used with permission. All rights reserved.); *The Common Curriculum* (© Queen's Printer for Ontario, 1993. Reproduced with permission of Ministry of Education and Training, Government of Ontario); *Toward a Critical Politics of Teacher Thinking: Mapping the Postmodern* by J. Kincheloe (Reprinted with permission of Greenwood Publishing Group, Inc., Westport, CT); *Democracy and Education* by J. Dewey (Copyright © 1916 by Macmillan Publishing Company. Renewed 1944 by John Dewey. Reprinted with permission of Simon and Schuster. All rights reserved.); *Dewey on Education* edited by M. S. Dworkin (© 1959 Teachers College Press, Columbia University. Reprinted with permission. All rights reserved.); *Educational Wastelands: The Retreat from Learning in Our Public Schools* by A. Bestor (© 1985 by the Board of Trustees of the University of Illinois. Reprinted with permission. All rights reserved.); *Essays on Educators* by R. Peters (Reprinted with the permission of Routledge & Kegan Paul. All rights reserved.); *Experience and Education* by J. Dewey (© Kappa Delta Pi. Reprinted with permission. All rights reserved.); *Guidelines for the Kindergarten to Grade 12 Education Plan: Implementation Resource* (Reproduced with permission of British Columbia Ministry of Education. All rights reserved.); *How Teachers Taught: Constancy and Change in American Classrooms, 1880-1980* (2nd edition) by Larry Cuban (© 1993 Teachers College Press, Columbia University. Reprinted with permission. All rights reserved.); *Improving the Quality of Education in British Columbia: Changes to British Columbia's Education Policy* (Reproduced with permission of British Columbia Ministry of Education. All rights reserved.); *Intelligence in the Modern World: John Dewey's Philosophy* edited by J. Ratner (© Random House, Inc. Reprinted with permission. All rights reserved.); *The One Best System: A History of American*

Education by David Tyack (© 1974 by the President and Fellows of Harvard College. Reprinted with permission of Harvard University Press. All rights reserved.); *Places Where Teachers Are Taught* edited by J. I. Goodlad, R. Soder, and K. A. Sirotnik (© 1990 by Jossey-Bass Inc., Publishers. Reprinted with permission. All rights reserved.); *Reconstruction in Philosophy* by J. Dewey (© Beacon Press. Reprinted with permission. All rights reserved.); *Teacher as Stranger: Educational Philosophy for the Modern Age* by M. Greene (© Wadsworth Publishing Co. Reprinted with permission. All rights reserved.).

Preface

The challenges, problems and predicaments of schooling, like those associated with politics and religion, seem at times to fall within the expertise of nearly everyone, regardless of experience, preparation or reflection. Most of us seem to know what is right and wrong with schools and how to promote the rights and eliminate the wrongs. By contrast, the enormous body of research and accumulated expertise within the profession itself appears to have had little positive, wide-ranging or sustained effect upon schooling and educator preparation programs, past or present.

Education remains ineffective, according to its critics, because the curriculum has been watered down, the standards have dropped, the students disrupt learning, the preparation of educators is inadequate, school activities are misconceived, parental support is anemic, the concern of educators is limited, the traditions of the profession are entrenched, reform proposals tend to be faddish, educational research is flawed, educational institutions discriminate, administrative structures are authoritarian, central offices are prescriptive, legislatures are intrusive, proposed solutions are simplistic, educational missions are too inclusive, the goals of schools are too narrow, the perspective on education and human nature is Hobbesian, the view of children is romantic, and so it goes. The different voices we hear, marginalized and mainstreamed, at times seem to cancel one another.

"Raise the standards," we hear. Then we hear that the standards should be changed as well as raised. Some advise us to improve schools; others encourage us to reinvent them. Some accuse educators of maintaining a stranglehold on teaching and teacher preparation; others urge us to free educators to use their expertise and professional judgment, to think and act for themselves. Support independent schools, Charter schools, school vouchers and home schools—such frustrating messages as these tempt us to throw out the baby with the bath water, to abandon the entire effort of building and maintaining viable public schools.

In the midst of such conflict and misgivings, experts and novices alike are well-advised to consider what we can realistically do in the area of educational reform and to look for ways to weigh contradictory claims and move beyond them to better-informed decision making and action. One promising way to start is to examine an existing comprehensive philosophy of educational reform and to look for the kinds of questions, arguments and recommendations it raises, develops and proposes. By comparison and contrast, then, we can refine our own thinking about educational reform, seeing issues formerly ignored, understanding complexities for the first time, observing previously unnoticed connections, exploring newly perceived alternatives and abandoning settled beliefs.

Yet, the process of reconsidering our views of schooling and developing a more inclusive philosophy of educational reform is hardly easy. It requires sustained study, reflective thought and open debate about the most important questions that face us. After all, educational reform influences the entire scope of life, including our most highly cherished values, beliefs, goals and practices. Our views of politics, religion, work, leisure and government, to name a few, are influenced by and, in turn, affect our opinions of education and schooling. Given these pervasive influences, we must think carefully and comprehensively about educational reform. Toward this goal, we propose to reexamine in our modern context the reflective, controversial voice of John Dewey. During his life, Dewey earned fame for analyzing conflicting educational claims, attempting to gain insight from all parties and moving beyond partisan thoughts to more coherent, rational positions. He attempted to avoid the either-or and reactive thinking that characterized many of his contemporaries and continues to characterize educational criticism to this day.

The full title, *Educational Reform: A Deweyan Perspective*, suggests the focus, the background, and the relevance of the book for educational reformers. Yet *Educational Reform* addresses more than the reform of schooling and educator preparation programs. Dewey's thought reveals a connectedness in all aspects of education, not just the formal pedagogical settings we call schools and universities. The subtitle then points to one of the major fallacies in the thinking of many current educational reformers: they offer no coherent *perspective* or philosophy that takes into account the multiple and complex issues in educational reform. That is to say, many of us disregard various social, political, economic, philosophical and professional considerations that influence both formal and informal education. Instead of reflecting an understanding of the nature of a democratic society, a reflective conception of education, a balanced view of human nature, an informed understanding of the mission of schooling in egalitarian countries, an interest in building a profession of teaching, a desire to see schools nurture educated people, and a public philosophy of education, our thoughts reflect partisan political, economic, religious or pedagogical perspectives. Many of us lack a *public* philosophy of education. Instead, we often hold a thinly layered and narrowly confined set of beliefs that ultimately indicate that *we want to promote our private, personal agendas in public schools*. Lacking an ability to impose our will on public schools, we often settle for whatever victories we can claim, or turn our allegiance to other institutions that welcome our ideas. In so doing, however, we may leave public schools at the mercy of the strongest local political group, the state legislature, or a disillusioned profession. But even if we retreat to private and home schooling, we probably all realize that public schools are too important to society to leave them adrift on the fluctuating currents of social, economic, religious and political trends.

Accordingly, we encourage broad reflection on how educational reform can help us all meet the educational needs of both children and society. Our suggestions arise largely from a presentation, and occasional critiques, of the writings of John Dewey. Our subtitle alludes to one of his major books, *How We Think.* How we think about educational reform influences both the problems we see and the options we consider. Our thinking opens and—especially if we are unaware of cultural and philosophical lenses—can close windows that look out on the paths to reforming education and society. An examination of our own ideological and pedagogical lenses may help us think more clearly and comprehensively about the topic before us. Even if we already think in Deweyan terms, we can still profit from a reexamination of his work, for this book is one of only a few introductory works that emphasize his basic philosophical position and his pedagogical ideas.

The term *Deweyan* indicates more than the fact that the book focuses predominantly on Dewey's thoughts about educational reform. The volume is also peculiarly Deweyan in that it provides an explication, discussion and synthesis of Dewey's thinking about educational reform. We quote frequently and extensively from his work to convey some of the beauty and power of his style and thought, which have wrongly been labeled obscure and pedantic. With Lovejoy (1936/1964), we have often found paraphrases inadequate or even misleading and prefer "the actual language of authors" (viii). So we hope to entice readers to explore our original sources, along with this book. Except for suggesting that one start with "My Pedagogic Creed" (1897) and *Experience and Education* (1938), we recommend, in no particular order, *How We Think* (1933; new edition), *Moral Principles in Education* (1909), *Reconstruction in Philosophy* (1948; enlarged edition), *Democracy and Education* (1916), *The Quest for Certainty* (1929), *The Sources of a Science of Education* (1929), *Interest and Effort in Education* (1913), *The School and Society* (1915; revised edition), and *The Child and the Curriculum* (1902). We suggest the expanded edition of *The School and Society* and *The Child and the Curriculum* (1990) since it includes the so-called "lost essay" entitled "Three Years of the University Elementary School" (1899), Dewey's explanation of his Laboratory School. Likewise, we recommend a sampling of Dewey's dozens of more popular essays on education and his autobiographical article entitled "From Absolutism to Experimentalism" (1930) for a better understanding and appreciation of the man.

Although Dewey wrote on many other subjects, the twin themes of educational and social reform run through most of his thought and political action. The timeliness of his thinking rests on the fact that his perspective provides a context for appraising the implications, merits and likelihood of success of modern attempts at educational reform. The relevance of his ideas further appears in his emphasis on what he calls "the scientific viewpoint," meaning *a broadly defined thoughtful, reasoned and reflective approach to practical and intellectual problems based on a respect for evidence and argument* rather than a blind loyalty to tradition or the status quo or unthinking acceptance of ill-considered opinions and ideologies.

The issues facing educational reformers today bear striking similarities to those of Dewey's day. The themes of the connection of education with employment and national economic competitiveness arise often in his writings. He also examines the subject of social and personal educational outcomes. He discusses individual opportunity; the kind of society in which we would choose to live; and the kind of moral and civic education that is appropriate in the school, community and home. Like many today, Dewey thought the changed social conditions of his age complicated problems and challenges more than ever before, and he devoted his life to proposing ways of thinking constructively and comprehensively about them. This comprehensive situating of the school in the context of larger social issues makes Dewey's thought more pertinent than ever and its implications remarkably modern. Dewey remains very much alive, studying society and schooling and writing for us as he speaks of the changes occurring in his society and as he calls for drastic changes in education. Indeed, he seems to stride directly into the present when he claims, "It is radical [social] conditions which have changed, and only an equally radical change in education suffices" (M1, 8).

Dewey acknowledged the importance of isolated instructional, curricular and organizational problems and outmoded educational policies and practices facing schools, but he went on to assert that the fundamental question is whether anything that occurs in schools is "worthy of the name *education*." Quickly he added, "What we want and need is education pure and simple, and we shall make surer and faster progress when we devote ourselves to finding out just what education is and what conditions have to be satisfied in order that education may be a reality and not a name or a slogan" (EE, 90-91). This warning against faddish, isolated and particularistic educational change is also timely. Such reforms, Dewey cautioned, are "at the worst transitory fads, and at the best merely improvements in certain details—and this is the plane upon which it is too customary to consider school changes" (M1, 5).

The current cry for systemic change, therefore, is a concept Dewey would have appreciated; however, he would broaden the concept to reach into the fabric of each sphere of society and all its institutions, including the heart of formal educational institutions. He would argue that every facet of society, each aspect of its culture, and all the features of formal and informal education are parts of the picture requiring examination as we embark upon systemic change. An important aspect of changing the formal education schools provide involves rethinking pedagogy. Yet, if acted upon, one of Dewey's many assertions—"Were all instructors to realize that the quality of mental process, not the production of correct answers, is the measure of educative growth" (DE, 176)—would probably start a revolution unlike any experienced in education. Thus a study of Dewey's thought about reforming school and society could have a direct informative and evaluative bearing upon many proposals we hear and read.

Deweyan educational reform, therefore, encompasses all facets of society and its institutions, traditions and customs. It is revolutionary, and according to Dewey, at once simple but difficult. It is difficult and challenging work because it involves the whole of society and demands the attention of all segments of society. But it is rooted in the familiar democratic vision of a reflective and productive citizen who enjoys thinking, working and living. We selected Dewey's lenses, then, because we found them an invaluable prism for viewing contemporary educational problems and for evaluating the proposals of modern reformers.

But we found another compelling reason for selecting Dewey as a filter for rethinking educational reform. Both critics and admirers still refer to him when attempting to discredit or establish specific educational proposals. Some critics see him as the godfather of everything that is wrong with education, past and present. His admirers include many who consider him the neglected messiah of schooling. Unfortunately, on both sides many who invoke Dewey misrepresent his views, strip his comments from their rich context, or repeat misleading slogans. This problem, of course, is not new; as Archambault (1964/1974) overstated decades ago: Everybody discusses Dewey although no one takes the time to read him (ix). Thus, we set out to develop a better contextual understanding of Dewey and to provide a stimulus for reading some of his primary works, and we quote frequently from Dewey's works to give a firsthand experience with the colorful and candid way he often expressed himself. We expect these passages to stimulate reflection on the important task of educating students.

Finally, our book offers a critique of contemporary approaches to educational reform and a perspective for future thought on the subject by examining Dewey's ideas and comparing them directly with ideas influential today. In this endeavor, we based our selection of his ideas on our desire to be both historically accurate and pedagogically current. As a result, we explore generic reform issues rather than focus on the more specific concerns of specialists and theorists. Even so, the implications should be useful to anyone who thinks broadly about educational reform, including educational decision makers and policy makers. In fact, any educated person who wants a clear picture of the questions to ask and to pursue in educational reform should find profit here.

While we believe that understanding Dewey's view of educational reform should help clarify the alternatives educators, teacher educators, school board members, parents and policy makers consider, we acknowledge his controversial philosophical assumptions, occasionally dated curricular proposals, and frequently questioned hypotheses. His more reflective critics and proponents usefully remind us of his shortcomings and weaknesses. Still, many of his views warrant attention even—perhaps, especially—by those who raise profound philosophical objections. A person who does not share many of Dewey's philosophical ideas can still conclude that he offers valuable insights. So we ask those with divergent philosophical and pedagogical views to explore Dewey's thinking about educational reform with an open mind, for even if they end by continuing to reject his major philosophical and educational presuppositions and conclusions, they may well refine their own ideas about the educational reform contemporary democracy requires.

In the Introduction, "School Reform in Dewey's America," Harvey Neufeldt provides an analysis of the historical, social and pedagogical times in which Dewey wrote his major educational works and compares them with selected contemporary situations. The attention he pays to the economic, cultural, institutional and intellectual settings of this period leads to an understanding of why Dewey wrote many of his major works on education and why contemporary educators can find there insights into present-day educational reform.

The chapters that comprise the majority of this volume represent our own research, thoughts, teaching and discussions, now structured to answer a series of questions interwoven in the writings of Dewey and arising in discussions of current educational reform. The chapters fall into four main divisions. The first three provide a political, ethical and philosophical background for understanding Dewey's thought and its educational relevance. Chapters 4 through 6 examine the roles, responsibilities and education of aspiring and practicing educators and describe the complexity and coherence of Dewey's viewpoint. Chapters 7 and 8 examine several different kinds of schools that Dewey believed had played or could play important but not necessarily valuable roles in developing a profession, preparing future educators, educating children and youth, and reforming society. The discussion in Chapter 9 focuses on the kinds of questions we might raise were we to approach educational issues and reform from Dewey's perspective.

Chapter 1, "Thinking about Educational Reform," examines Dewey's scientific approach to thinking about educational problems and reiterates his warnings against dichotomies, reactive thinking and compromise. In order to illustrate these problematic ways of thinking, we discuss his warning to some of his contemporaries (both traditionalists and progressivists), the relevance of historical precedents to current issues, and the kinds of thinking today that illustrate ongoing problems with either-or, reactive and compromissorial thinking. Since Dewey believed that one of the reasons educational practice is "at the mercy of every intellectual breeze that happens to blow" (EE, 51) is that educational planners either lack theories of education or possess inadequate theories, this chapter lays a foundation for future discussion of his thought.

Chapter 2, "The Social Aims of Education," moves from Dewey's conceptual framework and view of reflective or scientific thinking described in Chapter 1 to distinguishing Dewey's approach to school and society from that of many of today's educational and social reformers. Succinctly stated, much contemporary thinking appears to be based upon the supposition that schools can be improved by tinkering with their internal structure or adjusting them to reflect societal and economic interests and needs. In sharp opposition to these viewpoints, Dewey *felt that both society and schools should be reformed by adapting them to a more intelligent understanding of the nature of human beings, education, community and democracy* and by acting upon this understanding to alter the policies and practices of all major economic, political, religious and educational institutions. Thus, his theories of ethics, human psychology and epistemology are connected, with the result that it becomes easier to understand why Dewey turned and continues to turn most educational reform upside down in this sphere.

Chapter 3, "The School and Social Reform," inquires into the role of the school as it nurtures social reform. Chapter 2 focused on understanding how school and society should be adapted to people and education. This chapter examines the other side of Dewey's thinking: how the school should contribute to the reform of society and its cultures, traditions, customs and institutions. The key to understanding Dewey's thought in this domain is recognizing the connection between his views of democracy and education and his understanding of moral education and the social and political ends of schooling. These ideas emerge as part of a conceptual scheme tied to both personal and social growth. As a consequence of this phase of our study, one begins to see the cyclical or reciprocal nature of the relation of school and society:

School and society interact to shape and be shaped by each other.

Chapter 4, "The Roles and Responsibilities of the Teacher," explores the central roles and responsibilities of teachers as Dewey enunciated them. In view of the philosophy of education that he proposed, two questions become paramount. First, what roles and responsibilities does the classroom teacher have and play in pursuing the aims of education? Second, how should prospective teachers be prepared to ensure that they can play these roles and handle these responsibilities? Chapter 4 addresses the first question; Chapters 5 and 6 address the second. Dewey's views of the teacher as "the prophet of the true God and the usherer in of the true kingdom of God" and as "a social servant set apart for the maintenance of proper social order and the securing of the right social growth" are compared with his claim that the "teacher is not in the school to impose certain ideas or to form certain habits in the child, but is there as a member of the community to select the influences which shall affect the child and to assist him in properly responding to these influences" (E5, 95, 88).

Chapters 5 and 6, "The General Education of Teachers" and "The Professional Education of Teachers," analyze Dewey's views of the selection and preparation of future educators, with special attention to the liberal, pedagogical and experiential components of educator preparation programs. This inquiry raises implications for the general education of all students. Furthermore, the chapters pursue a variety of questions from Dewey's perspective. For example: How do we develop the kind of educators and citizens and schools and society we need? How would Dewey's recommendations change educator preparation programs today? Would he support or condemn current policy and program trends in teacher preparation programs? Indeed, does he have anything to say to those who prepare future educators given that he first wrote over a century ago?

Chapter 7, "Schools in Transition," examines principally the transitional roles and deficiencies Dewey saw in both traditional and progressive schools in his day. Though affirming what he thought best in the thinking behind progressive schools and largely criticizing the practices in traditional schools, he appears to have seen both as schools in transition. The traditional school, he believed, represented the philosophy of the leisure or controlling social and economic class and had been imposed upon everyone indiscriminately, including the children of the masses. This school was undemocratic, authoritarian and irrelevant to the new social realities. The progressive school represented a reaction to the traditional school and suffered from such thinking, as well as from a tendency to promote vague principles in pedagogically problematic ways. In Dewey's opinion, both kinds of schools, though differing sharply in their strengths and weaknesses, revealed transitions toward more democratic, reflective and educative types of schools: the school of tomorrow or, ideally, the utopian school.

Chapter 8, "Schools of the Future," investigates several kinds of schools Dewey believed could play a positive role in the future education of a truly democratic country. In particular, the chapter discusses the Laboratory School, the practice school, the school of tomorrow and the utopian school. The mission of each is examined for its importance and relevance in educating children and youth, preparing prospective educators, and promoting educational and social reform. We also note his startling notion that a properly functioning community in a genuinely democratic nation could do without schools as we know them.

Chapter 9, "The Spirit of Deweyan Reform," is devoted first to the identification of key Deweyan thoughts worth remembering as we examine present-day and future educational reform plans and proposals. Second, we note how these ideas may contribute to avoiding common mistakes in reform efforts and to changing education in defensible and desirable ways. In treating this subject, we suggest the importance of connecting the various Deweyan themes regarding educational reform and focusing on social and school conditions and experiences that emerge from a reflective society engaged in continuous growth.

When discussing personal, institutional and social progress, Dewey warned that "all reforms which rest upon the enactment of law, or the threatening of certain penalties, or upon changes in mechanical or outward arrangements, are transitory and futile" (E5, 93). Even so, he claimed, "Man is capable, if he will but exercise the required courage, intelligence and effort, of shaping his own fate" (RP, 49). Yet Dewey knew that this exercise, which requires the use of individual and social intelligence to find and apply truth and to shape personal and group fates, is based upon a critical premise: "There is but one sure road of access to truth—the road of patient, cooperative inquiry operating by means of observation, experiment, record and controlled reflection" (L9, 23). Educational planning, he knew, must draw upon the calm application of intelligence:

> Where is there a school system having a sum of money with which to investigate and perfect a scheme experimentally, before putting it into general operation? And can we expect continuous and intelligent progress in school matters until the community adopts a method of procedure which is now a commonplace with every great industrial undertaking? Is not the existing method of introducing reforms into education a relic of an empirical cut-and-try method which has been abandoned in all other great organizations? And is not the failure to provide funds so that experts may work out projects in advance a pennywise and pound foolish performance (M7, 106)?

Douglas J. Simpson
Fort Worth, Texas

Michael J. B. Jackson
Montréal, Québec

INTRODUCTION

School Reform in Dewey's America

> An admittedly overworked term, *crisis*, has been used to depict any number of situations whose immediate, decisive, and often extraordinary action must halt or reverse the existing condition. When educators speak of crises, they may be referring to test scores, increased illiteracy, dropout rate, deteriorating school buildings, rampant delinquency, or more profoundly, the moral and spiritual vacuity in the schooling powers (Paringer, 1990, 7).

> During all the recurring changes when curriculum reforms have swept through schools and altered master schedules and handbooks of course offerings, teachers have still entered their classrooms, closed their doors, and taught in ways that have endured over decades with few significant alterations in practice (Cuban, 1989, 372).

The persistence of reform, as Cuban points out, characterizes twentieth-century American education. Reformers at various times have assumed that society faced a crisis which necessitated and legitimated a change in school policies or practices. Many reformers in the three decades between 1890 and 1920 called for educational, curricular and administrative reforms to deal with perceived or real crises in urban and rural education. During the 1930s, George Counts and Harold Rugg sought to respond to an economic crisis by daring educators to "build a new social order." In the 1950s, numerous reformers believed that the schools had become "educational wastelands," unable to prepare America's youth to meet the challenges brought on by the Cold War or the space race. By the 1960s critics often depicted the schools as both part of the problem of and a solution for a class-, race- and gender-biased society. Critics of the 1980s and 1990s too, discovering a crisis precipitated by global economic competition and a changing family structure, quickly defined it as an educational problem. In each of these societal and economic crises, advocates of change often called for school reforms that conflicted with or negated a previously recommended reform. Recommendations, for instance, included a call for both more and less government spending on public schools; for more control by experts and less political interference on the one hand and for schools more responsive to "the public" on the other; for more testing, less testing and then again more testing; for teacher creativity but also for a more centralized control of both the content and methods of teaching; and for more stringent certification requirements for education majors while at the same time recruiting university graduates with little or no formal pedagogical training. That these reforms often were contradictory in no way lessened their appeal.

Several generalizations characterize much of educational reform during the twentieth century. One is that societal changes viewed unfavorably by particular segments of society are often called crises and then redefined as educational problems. Another generalization is that much educational reform literature ignores history. Critics of our schools rarely notice when a proposed reform in one crisis was the problem in a previous crisis. In part, Simpson and Jackson seek to address this historical amnesia by bringing a Deweyan perspective to bear directly and indirectly upon contemporary educational reform.

But why go back to John Dewey? In addition to the reasons the authors give, Cornel West suggests another. In his study of American pragmatism, West states:

> As I see it, it will be Dewey, not Ford, not Edison, not Roosevelt, who, when the last word has been said and the last vote has been counted, will figure as the pregnant symbol of what is best in the America of today and most hopeful for the Americanism for tomorrow (1989, 71).

Dewey—unlike Ford, Edison or even Roosevelt—recognized that he lived in a day when social, political, economic and educational problems were constantly changing and so required conceptual tools also constantly refashioned in the light of new experiences and discoveries. Life and understanding are both dynamic. Equally important, Dewey reminded his audiences that education is an ethical enterprise, that the ends as well as the means of education are important in a democratic society. While not dismissing the serious criticisms which critics have raised concerning Dewey's concepts of liberalism and democracy and his accommodation with the corporate state, Flower and Murphey's (1977) conclusion relative to Dewey's impact appears to be warranted: "Certainly no other modern philosopher has exercised so wide an influence on the American scene" (812). Nevertheless, his views have frequently been misunderstood, and thus his so-called influence has been in directions that he himself would have disavowed.

Dewey insisted that knowledge and values are always to be understood contextually. In keeping with this thought, this Introduction provides a context for understanding Dewey by briefly describing the school and society in his America, identifying some of the changes Americans faced in the late nineteenth and early twentieth centuries, and analyzing how these changes provided a context for much that Dewey wrote. Since much current educational reform deals with both public schools and teacher education, the emphasis is on dominant trends in curricular and administrative practices and on the recruitment and education of teachers in the four decades preceding the Great Depression of the 1930s.

To describe schools and society in Dewey's day is, as one might expect, to describe much of modern America. He was born on October 20, 1859, the day after John Brown was jailed for his attack on the federal arsenal at Harper's Ferry. He died on June 1, 1952, while Americans fought with the United Nations in Korea. During his lifetime America was transformed "from a divided, rural entrepreneurial, capitalist country into a consolidated, urban, industrial, multinational capitalist world power" (West, 1989, 77). He was born before the advent of the automobile and lived to see the jet age. His America witnessed the abolition of slavery and the institutionalization of racial segregation. He died just before the Brown decision which declared legally prescribed segregation unconstitutional. Since Dewey's major writings on education span the period from 1890 to 1930—with only a few exceptions, but especially his *Experience and Education* published in 1938—this Introduction focuses primarily on schools and society in what we call the Progressive Era (Dykhuizen, 1973, 278-279, 392n). This America increasingly confronted what Cremin (1988, 2-9, 19) calls "The Metropolitan Experience" and "The Challenge of Modernism."

One aspect of the metropolitan experience was, in Cremin's

phrasing, an "expansion of the Republic, in territory and population" (1988, 2), an expansion in numbers and kind. Two new states, New Mexico and Arizona, entered the Union in 1912; two more, Alaska and Hawaii, were added seven years after Dewey's death. The country's population more than doubled from 1860 to 1900, increasing from 31 to nearly 76 million and to over one quarter billion by 1980. Between 1860 and 1900 some 14 million immigrants entered the country, many from eastern and southern Europe. In 1909, the United States Immigration Commission's study reported that 57.8 percent of the parents of the children in schools of 37 percent of the nation's largest cities were foreign born, representing some 60 distinct ethnic groups (Cremin, 1961, 72; and Cremin, 1988, 4-5).

The influx of immigrants and the rise of the metropolis greatly burdened the schools. In 1893, Joseph Mayer Rice sensationalized the inadequacies of the existing schools in his book *The Public School System of the United States*. On visiting classrooms in several cities, he found "rote learning, mindless teaching, administrative ineptitude, political chicanery, and public apathy" (Cremin, 1988, 227). Dewey's more passionate analyses of schools during the early part of the twentieth century resembled Rice's. Not unlike the critics of the 1980s and 1990s, Rice saw the educational crisis as national in scope. Schools, he argued, would have to assume new tasks. Kliebard points out that "As cities grew, the schools were no longer the direct instruments of a visible and unified community. Rather, they became an ever-more critical mediating institution between the family and a puzzling impersonal social order" (1986, 1).

Although born in rural Vermont, Dewey spent most of his professional life in two of the country's largest urban centers, Chicago and New York City. While in Chicago he came to know Jane Addams and her work with immigrant families at Hull House. Addams' work, part of the settlement movement, was as Cremin observes both a criticism of current educational practices and a "living embodiment" of a view of education "centered in reformed conceptions of the uses of knowledge, the meaning of culture, and the nature of community" (1988, 176). This urban experience and the settlement movement led Dewey toward a culturally pluralistic view of society. While recognizing the need for consensus in the creation of a community, Dewey, nevertheless, called upon educators to recognize the various contributions of different immigrant groups. In 1916 he reminded the National Education Association that unity in America could not be homogenized but "must be a unity created by a drawing out and composing into a harmonious whole the best, the most characteristic which each contributing race and people has to offer" (M10, 204).

While Dewey endorsed this concept of a culturally pluralistic society, many educators followed a more explicitly assimilationist or Americanization model. Feeling threatened by the influx of tens of thousands of immigrants, educators in the early twentieth century redoubled their efforts to Americanize the new immigrants. Bilingual schools, common in many public school systems in the Midwest in the nineteenth century, were no longer acceptable. The rhetoric of Americanization, Tyack points out, "was often messianic, a mixture of fear outweighed by hope, of a desire for social control accompanied by a quest for equality of opportunity for the newcomers under terms dictated by the successful Yankee" (1974, 232). Americanization would, it was thought, bring about a "'modernization' of behaviors and beliefs" (234). Such a modernization, which was linked to a mastery of the English language and evidenced in the willingness of the child to "shed an old culture" (235), even to the point of feeling "a sense of shame at being 'foreign'" (235), would, the Americanizers claimed, help overcome the pernicious influences of the immigrant ghetto. Supporting the Americanization drive were many teachers who were second- and third-generation immigrants themselves (234-235).

The major discussions concerning the creation of community focused on incorporating Caucasian children of different ethnic groups or nationalities. Crossing the race or color line was rarely considered, especially when it came to African-American children. Their experience, as Tyack (1974) describes it, was of "victims without 'crimes'" (217). The exodus of southern African-Americans to the northern urban centers during World War I made race a national issue. Educational testing provided an apparently scientific justification for tracking African-American students and placing them in programs that would train them for those jobs open to them in a white supremacist society. Segregation and industrial training became the dominant response, the latter thought especially suitable for southern Blacks in order, as Anderson (1988) observes, to prepare a work force willing and able to fill the lower-level positions in the New South. But when it came to financing educational programs and combating racist doctrines, the burden of educational reform rested heavily on the African-American community itself (Tyack, 1974, 217-229; and Anderson, 1988, 77-109).

Late-nineteenth-century American society changed from an agricultural to an industrial society. From 1860 to 1900, investments in manufacturing plants jumped twelvefold while the number of workers employed in factories increased threefold. Manufacturing, transportation and commerce became increasingly centralized in larger organizations. Low wages, long hours and poor living conditions led to worker unrest, and the fifteen-year period from 1891 to 1905 witnessed over 38,000 strikes and lockouts involving some 7.5 million workers. American society, Paringer notes, was clearly "stratified along class, race, and gender relations." As industrialization increased, "the relative wealth of the rural sector declined. Agriculture, as a percentage of national income, slipped from 50 percent in 1860 to 20 percent by 1900" (1990, 40).

Along with the rise of urban centers and industry, schools and churches faced what Cremin calls "The Challenge of Modernism" (1988, 19). Modernism questioned the "Thomistic-Aristotelian synthesis of faith and reason," placing instead the "authority of science over reason." Included in the concept of modernism was the faith in an objective researcher "untainted by the world of opinions, perspectives or values" and a belief in progress. Modernism affected, Kincheloe observes, all social relations: "Even familial ties were severed as the new order shifted its allegiance to the impersonal concerns of commerce, industry, and bureaucracy" (1993, 1-3).

Not surprisingly, amid the problems posed by population changes, urbanization, industrialization and modernism, the challenge of building communities encouraged many reform proposals. Central to these proposals in the Progressive Era was the call to reform education. As Fraser (1988) points out, however, there was more than one group of progressives; in the end, the "conservative progressives" or "administrative progressives" won out. Thus Dewey, while in agreement with many progressive pedagogical ideas and practices, was also understandably openly critical of many other progressive pedagogical and administrative beliefs and practices.

American school enrollments increased dramatically after 1890. For example, New York City's school enrollment increased by 60 percent from 1899 to 1914. Moreover, more children were attending school, and they were attending longer. The nation's secondary school enrollment jumped from 202,963 in 1890 to 1,645,175 in 1918, and by 1930 the high school had changed from an institution of the elite to one of mass schooling. Whereas only 6.7 percent of the 14-to-17 age group attended a public or private high school in 1890, nearly 50 percent did so by 1930 (Tyack, 1974, 182-183; and Spring, 1994, 214).

One prominent reform proposal addressed the issue of school administration. Led by a group Tyack and Hansot (1982) call the "administrative progressives," these reformers urged the replacement of the politically based administration then existing with a professional bureaucracy. Administrative progressives called for the centralization of urban school systems, the elimination of the smaller ward or village boards, and the election at large or appointment of school board members. The reconstructed school board would then function like a board of directors of a corporation, and its members, in turn, would select a professional superintendent to carry out school board policies. Merit, it was also presumed, would replace patronage in a "hierarchically stratified and functionally differentiated school structure." It was a reform from the top down, where university-trained men would apply "'scientific management' to all phases of school life" (129).

I chose the noun *men* purposely. Reform from the top down envisioned the female teacher carrying out policy initiated by male administrators trained in the "science" of education. Teachers responded by organizing an activist teachers' organization, the American Federation of Teachers. Dewey found himself in sympathy with the AFT and wrote extensively on the importance of teacher unions. However, other teachers, as Lazerson suggests, "came to identify with middle-class professionals, as they began to equate status and competence with educational credentials.... There was little to be gained by waging war with the hierarchy when one's goal was to join it." Giving up the right to initiate educational policy, teachers were "pretty much left alone in their classrooms. When they shut the door, the classroom was theirs" (1984, 174).

The reform also called for replacing citizen teachers with professionally trained teachers. Tyack points out that

> Throughout most of the nineteenth century, teachers in the common schools of the countryside entered the occupation for a brief time in their early adulthood, were mostly untrained and minimally educated, were paid in rural areas about the same as farm and house workers, and used the occupation as a transition to marriage (for women) or a stepping stone to other jobs (for men) (1989, 417).

The teachers Tyack describes were citizen teachers in several respects. They were often hired locally, reflecting distrust among local residents of the professional or outside expert. As late as 1910, less than two-thirds of American teachers held a high school diploma and only five percent had more than a high school education. Dewey's proposed education for aspiring teachers, described in Chapters 5 and 6, reflects his farsightedness and seems as much a part of the contemporary debate as of his own time.

Salary posed of course a major problem, especially for males who usually viewed teaching as a short-term occupation and considered an extended normal school training a poor investment. Reforms to lengthen the school year and increase teacher training requirements correlated with an increased feminization of the teaching profession except in the case of black male teachers in urban areas who had few alternative employment opportunities (Rury, 1989, 26).

Educating a professional teacher meant increasing the teacher's academic credentials without increasing the teacher's power to determine his or her own activities in the classroom. In fact, Herbst points out, the drive to professionalize education, a drive "that ignored and shut out the teacher began in the early centers of teacher education" (1989a, 228). The nineteenth-century normal schools established to train teachers for the rural elementary schools quickly began to function as peoples' colleges offering both high school and post-secondary work. As the normal schools upgraded to college-level institutions, they increasingly diversified their functions as they undertook also to train high school teachers, educational administrators and other specialists. Training for upward mobility meant training educators to leave the classroom. Herbst calls this abandonment of the elementary classroom teacher the "Treason of the Normal Schools" (229-230). While at the University of Chicago (1894-1904), Dewey argued initially for the importance of the School of Education and the Laboratory School in preparing educational leaders and later in preparing prospective teachers for the emerging school districts. But he obviously valued what he may have believed to be the temporary contributions and transitory value of normal schools. He also argued vigorously for better-educated elementary school teachers and against the prevailing social conditions that forced many teachers to leave the classroom to earn decent salaries. He seems to have had little sympathy with attempts to *professionalize* teaching into an elite group although he was strongly interested in teachers having the formal education and working environment that would encourage them to think and act professionally, make judgments and act upon them.

Dewey's views notwithstanding, the place of teacher education remained secondary at best on college and university campuses. Clifford and Guthrie's (1988) study of education departments and colleges at a select group of prestigious universities demonstrates that the drive to expand graduate programs and specialization in education was increasingly tied to a hierarchically and bureaucratically designed educational system. It served the needs of administrators, test makers and other specialists. These departments followed the lead of Charles Judd at the University of Chicago and Edward Thorndike at Teachers College in promoting a scientific study of education. For Judd, this meant studying the field of education as it existed; ethical questions were to be eliminated. For Thorndike a scientific study meant placing "measurement at the core of emerging problematics of education research" (Lagemann, 1989, 210). By the 1920s, it was clear that such institutions as Harvard, Chicago and Teachers College had "turned their backs on what one might well describe as the education profession's most important and most basic responsibility. They no longer prepared beginning teachers for the classroom" (Herbst, 1989a, 184).

Much of the new science of education, especially the trend toward sorting students scientifically in the name of social efficiency, was antithetical to Dewey's viewpoint and his concern for social renewal and change. Much of the professional educational component in the twentieth century became "oriented toward the values of sorting and classifying children for purposes of efficient mass schooling and ease of entry into the existing economic structure, exemplified by the growth of standardized testing and distinct vocational programs..." (Levin, 1990, 52). This trend, Levin argues, can be traced back at least to the 1920s. Lagemann suggests that when it comes to understanding the history of educational research in twentieth-century America, one must realize "that Edward L. Thorndike won and John Dewey lost" (1989, 185). One cannot help wondering whether the outcome would have been different if Dewey's appointment had been at Teachers College with Thorndike instead of in the Department of Philosophy at Columbia University and these two educational giants had conferred regularly.

Henry Holmes, Harvard's dean of education during the 1920s and 1930s, sought for a time to focus on educational reform and decrease the emphasis upon research. But even during Holmes' day, Harvard focused more on experienced teachers engaging in part-time study than on training preservice teachers. Holmes' proposed two-year graduate program for inexperienced teachers failed to gain the support of his Harvard colleagues, and identifying Holmes' name with teacher education reform has been seen as ironic (Herbst, 1989a, 175-180; and Johnson, 1987, 221-240).

Progressivism in education also included curricular reform. Kliebard (1986) identifies four curriculum categories that have competed for dominance in the public schools: humanism, social efficiency, developmentalism and social meliorism. As one would expect, these topics, though not necessarily under these names, commanded Dewey's attention during the early part of the twentieth century. The movements often overlapped as did social efficiency and developmentalism in the 1920s. Humanism, evident in the 1892 Committee of Ten Report, stressed the transmission of what many considered to be high-brow culture. But its focus on a literary curriculum and a faculty or mental-discipline psychology became increasingly problematic once the public high school changed from an elite to a mass institution. Developmentalism, rooted in part in the "child study movement," called upon educators to organize the curriculum around the interests and needs of children. Some of the proposals of the advocates of developmentalism, however, "amounted almost to a denigration of intellect in favor of a sentimentalization of childhood and especially adolescence" (50). By 1920, the social efficiency movement had become the most influential. These experts assumed that education was for an adult's, not the child's, life. Invoking science to legitimatize their curricular theory, the defenders of social efficiency "held out the promise of social stability in the face of cries for massive social change" (89). Theorists like John Franklin Bobbitt advocated a differentiated curriculum and the sorting of children so as to prepare them "specifically and directly for the role they would play as adult members of the social order" (Kliebard, 1986, 90; see also 30-31, 98-99).

By the first decade of the twentieth century, the supporters of humanism had reached an accord with the advocates of social efficiency. Unlike Dewey, both groups accepted the need to test and sort students. Both came to terms with the high school as an institution for mass education. The literary curriculum of the humanists became the curriculum for the intellectual elite (Kliebard, 1986, 123-124). Both groups accepted the concept of objective knowledge, which Cohen points out, viewed truth as "objective systems of fact and knowledge, not as human construction.... Humans were portrayed as discoverers and accumulators of knowledge, not as constructors and reconstructors." Unlike Dewey, advocates viewed "knowing as a relatively passive process," a process where "children learned because man and nature taught them" (1989, 399).

Vocational education proved to be the most successful curricular innovation during the period. Replacing the nineteenth-century concept of manual training, vocational education included industrial and agricultural education for urban and rural youth respectively (Kliebard, 1986, 128-152). But while Dewey advocated organizing the curriculum around occupations, he warned against a vocational training that "breeds and perpetuates a class structure whose rigidities are alien to democracy" (M10, xvi). For Dewey, the issue was "whose concerns" received primary consideration in industrial education (M10, 145). He argued that much vocational education was misdirected, designed not to add to the child's intelligent understanding "but rather to the earnings of others [industrialists]" (M10, 145). He warned that the "method...most likely to be resorted to in an unintelligent industrial training" was "habituation in various specialized modes of skill, methods of repetition and drill, with a view to getting automatic skill" (M10, 141).

Along with reforms in teacher education and the school curriculum, critics also called for innovations in teaching and learning. Citing Finklestein, Cuban (1993) describes three types of teachers in the elementary school during this general period of time:

> The "Intellectual Overseer" assigned work, punished errors, and made students memorize. The "Drillmaster" led students in unison through lessons requiring them to repeat aloud. A third pattern, "Interpreter of Culture," she found only occasionally. Here the teacher would clarify ideas and explain content to children (25).

As for high school teachers, anecdotal evidence suggests that "teacher talk dominated verbal expressions" (Cuban, 1993, 37). Student recitations, textbook assignments, and teacher questions and explanations constituted the most common form of classroom activity. The teacher-centered classroom, the dominant form of the social organization in the schools, included "students sitting in rows of bolted-down desks...rising to recite for the teacher" (37). The "academic organization of the classroom hinged upon the whole class's moving as one through the course of study, text, recitation, and homework" (37). As the authors of this volume later point out, Dewey vigorously criticized these practices and the philosophy upon which they rested.

Critics of the study, textbook, recitation and homework learning model, including Dewey if one rightly understands his distinctive position, called for a shift from teacher-centered to student-centered instruction. For Dewey, however, so-called student-centered instruction —better labeled *community-centered learning* as the authors note—included group activities, joint experiences, development of social imagination, cooperative rather than competitive learning and "teachers' encouragement of student expression" (Cuban, 1993, 45).

Reform, Dewey observed at mid-century, occurred more in talk than in "actual alterations in classroom teaching and learning" (Cuban, 1993, 145). Constancy rather than change characterized most classrooms before 1940. Nevertheless, more changes in teaching occurred in elementary than in high school classrooms, and teachers there incorporated some aspects of "pedagogical progressivism" (143) that did not threaten their authority or undermine a prescribed curriculum (142-146). Dewey himself viewed many of the advances toward progressivism as simply pedagogical instead of philosophical steps, resulting in an unhealthy educational mixture or compromise. He condemned the practical excesses and pedagogical abuses of progressivism as serious mistakes.

Analysts offer several explanations for the persistence of constancy rather than the embracing of change in classroom teaching practice. One suggestion contrasts the complexity and skill required of teachers in a student-centered—or in Dewey's formulation a community-centered —classroom with the limited educational background of many teachers, especially rural elementary teachers. Such teachers found themselves unable to use even the simpler pedagogical ideas advocated in the progressive educational movement. Needing to keep control of their students, they relied on "time-killing 'busywork'" (Clifford and Guthrie, 1988, 92-93). This pattern was especially true of poorly paid, undereducated teachers instructing large classes in poor facilities with few supplies. The lack of education alone, however, does not adequately explain teachers' resistance to change, for the better-educated high-school teachers of the time were even less likely than their counterparts to implement changes (Cuban, 1993, 120-128, 146).

A second suggestion is that progressive educational reform proposals failed to match the dominant models of knowledge and theories of learning. In contrast to Dewey's conception of knowledge as evolutionary, naturalistic and social, the dominant academic conceptions viewed knowledge in Cohen's words as "objective systems of facts and knowledge not as a human construction." The reigning theories in psychology "portrayed knowing as a relatively passive process" and assumed that students "learned because man and nature taught them, not because they imaginatively and originally made sense of their surroundings" (1989, 399).

Preservice teacher education programs at major universities promoted few of those changes in teaching Dewey envisioned. In their drive to make education more professional and scientific, the education professors often emphasized testing and a mechanistic psychology. Furthermore, the faculty in colleges of education often lacked any direct experience with the schools. By the early 1930s, some 73 percent of the education faculty members in major universities had never taught in an elementary school and over 50 percent had never taught in a secondary school. Teacher behavior had never been their primary concern (Clifford and Guthrie, 1988, 97), which limited their impact.

In any event, most teachers and administrators differed with Dewey when it came to fundamental or what Cuban (1989) calls "second-order changes" in the classroom. Instead, they concentrated on first-order changes or "intentional efforts to enhance *existing* arrangements while correcting deficiencies in policies and practices." For many teachers and administrators in Dewey's day, the major concern was to make the existing system "more efficient and effective without disturbing the basic organizational features and without substantially altering how adults and children perform their roles" (374, italics added).

Dewey's second-order changes entailed a pedagogy based on a vision of children as active learners, of a curriculum rooted in experience, and of knowledge as something children "need to discuss and create...rather than to only absorb" (Cuban, 1989, 374-375). He urged a new or different kind of education. While administrators sometimes sought some second-order administrative changes like the consolidated school, they rarely sought to alter either teaching practices or the hierarchical relationship between students and teachers and between teachers and administrators. Teachers, in turn, usually incorporated only those aspects of pedagogical reform that maintained their authority in the classroom and enabled them to manage large numbers of students.

Much of the rhetoric of reform in the 1980s and 1990s focused again on first-order changes, but this time a broad strain of reform literature has urged the reinvention of schools and educator preparation programs. Still, teacher accountability, testing, the career ladder, certification requirements and longer school years leave the relationships between students and teachers and between teachers and administrators unchanged. The same can be said for many of the recommendations related to effective schools and teaching research. The Holmes Group describes a professional teacher with an expertise based on knowledge that resembles the science of education university-based educators sought in Dean Holmes' day. But as Johnson (1987) observes, the assumption that "the promise that a science of education is about to be achieved" is problematic at best (227-228). Like the teacher educators at major universities in the pre-1930 era, the Holmes Group privileges the knowledge of university-based researchers over that of classroom practitioners. By contrast, Dewey urged that the experiential knowledge of administrators and teachers become an important part of the science of education, a view significantly different from those of the majority of his colleagues throughout the twentieth century. The position is only now finding a voice in practitioner-based, narrative and action research.

Educational critics in the 1980s and 1990s, like many of their predecessors, believe they have seen crises in society and the schools. In Dewey's day, the crises brought on by demographic changes and economic consolidation were defined in part as educational problems. In the 1980s and 1990s the crises, brought on by the globalization of economics, changes in family structure, and the demands and opportunities new technologies introduce, once again have become educational problems. In both eras, critics found teachers, the curriculum and student learning problematic. In both eras most critics—with some exceptions in the late twentieth century—called for a top-down approach to educational reform.

When it comes to educational research in the late twentieth century, as in the early part of the century, Lagemann's observation still holds true: "Edward L. Thorndike won and John Dewey lost." By default, he won many other battles as well without really entering the field. The kinds of questions Thorndike's quasi-experimental research paradigm cultivated still profoundly influence assessment and evaluation models. In turn, the paradigm itself influences curriculum, instruction and school experiences. First-order reforms, measures for improving existing schooling and educator preparation programs, therefore, characterize much educational reform, ensuring that beneath appearances things remain much the same.

An important question remains, of course, regarding the value of the two positions: Is Dewey's viewpoint a more defensible one than Thorndike's? But lest we engage in either-or thinking, perhaps we should look for something worthwhile in each. On the other hand, we seem well-advised to avoid the kind of compromise against which Dewey also cautioned. At a minimum it would be interesting to hear the question—and related ones—debated and won on relevant, public grounds. But, then, that suggestion no doubt sounds too Deweyan.

Harvey Neufeldt
Cookeville, Tennessee

Educational Reform

CHAPTER ONE

Thinking about Educational Reform

> It is the business of an intelligent theory of education to ascertain the causes for the conflicts that exist and then, instead of taking one side or the other, to indicate a plan of operations proceeding from a level deeper and more inclusive than is represented by the practices and ideas of the contending parties (EE, 5).

> Any significant problem involves conditions that for the moment contradict each other. Solution comes only by getting away from the meaning of the terms that is already fixed upon and coming to see the conditions from another point of view, and hence a fresh light. But this reconstruction means travail of thought (M2, 273).

> The better way of thinking...is called reflective thinking: the kind of thinking that consists in turning a subject over in the mind and giving it serious and consecutive consideration (L8, 113).

John Dewey (1859-1952) remains a widely misunderstood writer on education, and many attribute this fact to his writing style. So perhaps the best start for a discussion of his ideas about education and educational reform is his little book *Experience and Education* (1938) based on a series of Kappa Delta Pi lectures conceived expressly to address common misunderstandings of his educational ideas and the innovations he proposed. This book, however, was less than entirely successful in clarifying the controversial issues even in educational circles; and academic critics and public figures, as well as the general public, continue to attribute to him positions and ideas—or at least responsibility for developments in educational practice—that many sympathetic readers find puzzling and even amazing. In the United

States, Arthur Bestor and Admiral Hyman Rickover immediately come to mind as in Canada does Hilda Neatby. In addition to maintaining that Dewey's thought dominated the most influential colleges of education in North America at the time she wrote, Neatby claimed his educational theory suggested that the classroom should be a natural environment in which

> children should be allowed and encouraged to grow, with no distinction of mind and body, and certainly with no discrimination of the soul. They learn by shared activities, by doing things together, and they should be encouraged to grow and learn and plan and share with no thought of the future, living always in the present (Neatby, 1953, 24).

Perhaps even more amazing is Neatby's claim that in the Deweyan classroom, "There is no conscious preparation for the future, there are no ultimate 'aims', there is no abstract thought, no external discipline or stimulus, and, of course, no moral teaching" (24). Moreover, she asserted that the Deweyan teacher would have no responsibility to "open to his pupils the heritage of his own and of other civilizations" and that Dewey's method and discipline were "ferociously amoral" (26).

Dewey was, of course, an outspoken critic of the prevailing educational practices in his time, and he did support substantial and fundamental rethinking of educational ideas and far-reaching reforms of educational practices. He even made some comments, used some words, and expressed a few thoughts similar, to varying degrees, to those Neatby expressed. Neatby, in fact, is sometimes accurate in her interpretations of Dewey. But she commingles her accuracies with many inaccuracies, and her writing illustrates a common problem among Dewey's supporters and detractors. They cite texts and interpret them plausibly except in the context of the larger corpus of his writings and the spirit and overall direction of his intentions. Compare, for instance, his comments about the "problem" of Polish immigrants and his action in Trotsky's case. To answer Neatby, apart from the traditional academic content in the curriculum Dewey proposed, moral and civic education are in fact central to his thinking, and it is difficult to imagine any growth, planning, education or reform movement that is not oriented to the future.

We repeat, however, that Dewey was a reformer, a strong advocate of both educational and social change, and an outspoken critic of education from within the ranks of teaching and teacher education (Westbrook, 1991). He held views about how we might understand social and educational problems and how, on the basis of this understanding, we might improve customs, practices and institutions generally—education in its widest sense—and the quality of life in schools and the social and academic outcomes of schooling in particular. Nowadays we talk of life-long learning, but for Dewey education was inherent in the life of an involved citizen—part of what others might talk of as "the good life" or a full and rich participation in life, a life of growth. Nor was he merely an abstract thinker about these issues, for he involved himself in social welfare projects and civil liberties and union movements. Moreover, his experiences with and his observations about ethical conflicts, social experiments, strikes, elections, and the movement to outlaw war all influenced his reflection.

Beginning our discussion with Dewey's thinking about educational reform in *Experience and Education* offers several advantages. A brief, popular work, it addresses a variety of misunderstandings in a discussion of the major concepts that form the conceptual underpinnings of Dewey's philosophy of education: experience, subject matter, authority, continuity, interaction, habit, and means and ends. Behind these conceptions lies his new way of thinking, especially about purpose in life and education. Typical of his close attention to the idea of evolutionary and social change and correspondingly individual and social growth, Dewey also proposed a new way of thinking about philosophical, social and educational problems. This way of approaching problems he called both reflective and scientific thinking. In either phrasing, he meant a broad, thoughtful and evaluative approach to thinking about everyday and theoretical problems based upon a respect for public evidence and reasoned argument.

Dichotomous Thinking

Taking seriously educational disputes and conflicts—the genuineness of the disagreements, the sincerity of the proponents, and the value of their experience and insights—Dewey reflected as follows on our way of thinking about such disputes:

> Profound differences in theory are never gratuitous or invented. They grow out of conflicting elements in a genuine problem—a problem which is genuine just because the elements, taken as they

> stand, are conflicting. Any significant problem involves conditions that for the moment contradict each other. Solution comes only by getting away from the meaning of terms that is already fixed upon and coming to see the conditions from another point of view, and hence in a fresh light (M2, 273).

Just rejecting another opinion offers no solution to controversy, he insisted. In fact, rejecting another's viewpoint as manifested in dichotomous or either-or thinking often leads to adopting "the opposite extreme," and the real problem is not even recognized, much less addressed (EE, 22). One result of this either-or thinking is that those who observe or are involved in the dispute often recoil at "the extreme character" of the logical outcomes and resort to a common-sense approach that "vibrates back and forward in a maze of inconsistent compromise" (M2, 277). Just as likely, the result is "an eclectic combination of points picked out hither and yon from all schools [of thought]," also producing a smorgasbord of intellectual, moral and practical compromise (EE, 5). Compromise of this sort was a major concern of Dewey's, leading him to refer to it as "the Great Bad" and "the mixing together of things that are contrary and opposed" (L15, 261). Nothing illustrates the Deweyan perspective on educational disputes better than his typically dualistic titles: *The Child and the Curriculum*, *The School and Society*, *Democracy and Education* and *Experience and Education*. For him, two or more pieces of the pedagogical picture were necessary, both to be evaluated, both to be critically considered, but neither to be compromised in any justifiable educational synthesis.

Educational reform naturally seems to be a matter of replacing one practice or way of thinking with another—putting something else, something better, in the place of the obsolete, unethical, inefficient or ill-founded. The original "Editorial Foreword" to *Experience and Education* provides us with the key to one of Dewey's central ideas, indicating how to approach educational reform:

> Where the traditional school relied upon subjects or the cultural heritage for its content, the "new" school has exalted the learner's impulse and interest and the current problems of a changing society. Neither of these sets of values is sufficient unto itself. *Both* are essential (EE, 9-10).

Dewey began with precisely the same point, emphasizing our preference for dichotomous thinking:

> Mankind likes to think in terms of extreme opposites. It is given to formulating its beliefs in terms of *Either-Ors*, between which it recognizes no intermediate possibilities. When forced to recognize that the extremes cannot be acted upon, it is still inclined to hold that they are all right in theory but that when it comes to practical matters circumstances compel us to compromise. Educational philosophy is no exception (EE, 17).

Whether the question involves subject matter, methods of teaching, the teacher's authority in the classroom, the interests of the student, or some other topic, addressing this either-or attitude in Dewey's view provides a basis for successful educational thinking. Failure to abandon this attitude is more than just a problem; it can lead to educational disaster. For example,

> When external control is rejected, the problem becomes that of finding the factors of control that are inherent within experience. When external authority is rejected, it does not follow that all authority should be rejected, but rather that there is need to search for a more effective source of authority. Because the older education imposed the knowledge, methods, and rules of conduct of the mature person upon the young, it does not follow...that the knowledge and skill of the mature person has no directive value for the experience of the immature (EE, 21).

What is needed instead of either-or thinking is to return to the problem itself and to think again about the insights underlying each of the contending points of view, asking, for instance, "What does freedom mean and what are the conditions under which it is capable of realization" (EE, 22)? If we assume that the parties to the dispute are neither completely misinformed, simply stupid, nor just being difficult—and usually educational and practical disagreements take place between people of good will talking from their experience—then we need to find a way to take their insights into account, however partial or one-sided we may eventually conclude them to be. For in seeing them as partial or one-sided, we can also see them as partially true. Similarly, we may come to see our own views as partial, incomplete, (now and then) largely incorrect or (ideally) largely correct.

This consideration of conflicting positions may suggest, wrongly in Dewey's mind, that some form of compromise is in order. If each side is "onto something," as we say, then each should have a piece of the solution. This reasoning seems consonant with our notions of democracy and fair play: Each player has a kind of entitlement to "his or her place" or "a turn." Moreover, at a time when values seem problematic and at least somewhat relative to culture and situation, it must appear all the more dogmatic to talk of a correct solution. But of course, if the disagreement is genuine, dividing up the field does nothing other than hold the contending parties apart. Like a United Nations peace-keeping force, it does nothing to address the issue, though it may restore some calm or make possible further discussion. The peace-keeping force satisfies none of the participants precisely because it fails to solve the problem. But that is not its purpose; it is to keep the contending armies apart while the issue is resolved. The parties understandably may feel "compromised" or resentful, a sense of injustice, for their grievances remain unremedied or even unaddressed. Even if the problem is merely a practical one involving the sharing of limited resources, some principle is needed to justify the actual distribution or redistribution. And it is this point that Dewey makes: If the dispute is genuine, putting the contending parties together or merely holding them apart is hardly a solution. In fact, lacking a rational foundation, it must be arbitrary or dogmatic.

If a solution is to be possible, one must find a new way of thinking about the problem, a way of conceiving it that transcends the different points of view. This new way of conceiving the problem is Dewey's Hegelian insight: Partial truths that we can see as conflicting, and so recognize as incomplete, suggest the possibility of another, transcendent viewpoint—a point of view that recognizes their partiality. What is required is a reconception or a new way of thinking "from a level deeper and more inclusive than is represented by the practices and ideas of the contending parties [or] a new order of conceptions leading to new modes of practice" (EE, 5). To use this kind of thinking successfully, we must develop a more comprehensive understanding of the concept of education and with it appropriate conceptions of experience, growth, habit, discipline, freedom and order. In our initial example, the problem is not whether authority and discipline in education should stem from traditional subject matter or the child's experience but rather how to incorporate both into a fuller, richer understanding of education so that each has its rightful place and plays its rightful role. This is easily said, Dewey admitted, but not so easily done, for the mind falls readily into habitual ways of thinking (EE, 28).

But to resist transcending our traditional modes of thought is to risk being trapped into defining our views in terms of those of our opponents, to limit our ways of thinking to categories defined by others, and to reduce our statements to claims about what we are not. Since this behavior limits any chance to create a new way of thinking, we come to a second Deweyan principle: It is a mistake to think in terms of either-or dichotomies, but it is also a mistake in educational debate not to return to fundamental educational considerations. Returning to fundamental considerations means that we think "in terms of Education itself," not in terms of some *ism* (EE, 6). Thinking in terms of an ism, regardless of the label, produces a reactionary kind of thought "unwittingly controlled" by the people and ideas being opposed (EE, 6). The problem of being or becoming an ism and the accompanying reactionary thinking was what Dewey saw facing, for example, progressive education or progressivism. Custom and habit, he observed, lead us to conceive of education in certain ways, and it is not enough simply to criticize the conventional curriculum or traditional discipline. What is required is a positive new theory: "The problem for progressive education is: What is the place and meaning of subject matter and of organization *within* experience" (EE, 20)?

Traditional and Progressive Schools

The "Editorial Foreword" to *Experience and Education* contains some amusing and eerily prescient language, even if the questions now may have more to do with ethnic, religious, racial, gender, cultural, ideological and paradigmatic differences than with the merits of progressive education:

> the Executive Council of Kappa Delta Pi requested Dr. Dewey to discuss some of the moot questions that now divide American education...and thereby weaken it at a time when its full strength is needed in guiding a bewildered nation through the hazards of social change (EE, 9).

The issues have, of course, changed. We argue now more about accountability, quality indicators, conflict resolution, cooperative learning, whole language, learning styles, educational outcomes, district benchmarks, national standards, nation-wide testing, authentic evaluation, school vouchers, school choice, applied learning, religious schools and home schooling. But with only slight changes, the editor's words might have come from any recent issue of *Educational Leadership* or *Kappan*. Dewey's thinking, then, appears as relevant today as it ever has been, for the type of thinking he feared seems as prevalent now as ever.

Traditional education, Dewey went on to suggest, gets to claim the field in educational debate for two reasons. First, we seem psychologically reluctant to question the familiar. If we see schools doing what they always did, nothing strikes us as odd, nothing needs an explanation. By contrast, change "means the necessity of the introduction of a new order of conceptions leading to new modes of practice" (EE, 5). Retaining the old or simply making first-order adjustments to the status quo rather than fundamental second-order innovations is easier than initiating the new. Thus, "those who adhered to the established system needed merely a few fine-sounding words to justify existing practices. The real work was done by *habits* which were so fixed as to be institutional" (EE, 29, italics added). The psychology of the familiar and the habitual, therefore, prevails in discussion and wins most educational arguments.

Second, a logical point supports the traditional: People are born without an education and subsequently acquire it from others. Perhaps this is why we so readily think of education in the traditional terms of a teacher who has something to transmit to learners who will, if successful, "master it" and "give it back" or "apply it"—a traditional, subject-matter-centered conception. Thus, the newcomer, progressive education, faces a second challenge. This opposition in ideas and practices during Dewey's life was hardly new in the history of education. For instance, he noted that

> The history of educational theory is marked by opposition between the idea that education is development from within and that it is formation from without; that it is based upon natural endowments and that education is a process of overcoming natural inclination and substituting in its place habits acquired under external pressure (EE, 17).

Similar or overlapping controversies appear in nearly every age, including the present. Generally speaking, Dewey thought one could summarize traditional education as follows:

> The subject matter of education consists of bodies of information and of skills that have been worked out in the past; therefore, the chief business of the school is to transmit them to the new generation. In the past, there have also been developed standards and rules of conduct; moral training consists in forming habits of action in conformity with these rules and standards. Finally, the general pattern of school organization (by which I mean the relations of pupils to one another and to the teachers) constitutes the school a kind of institution sharply marked off from other social institutions. Call up in imagination the ordinary school-room, its time-schedules, schemes of classification, of examination and promotion, of rules of order, and I think you will grasp what is meant by "pattern of organization" (EE, 17-18).

Traditional education enjoys the advantage of being in place, familiar and accepted; and consideration of an alternative suggests the simultaneous existence of discontent, criticism or a questioning of conventional practices (EE, 18). What is important is that we be precise about that discontent with traditional education, about its pedagogical and, we might add, ethical significance. The problem was not that traditional educators created an environment in the school; it was that in creating that environment "they did not consider the other factor in creating an experience; namely, the powers and purposes of those taught" (EE, 45). Dewey explained that

> It is not the subject per se that is educative or that is conducive to growth. There is no subject that is in and of itself, or without regard to the stage of growth attained by the learner, such that inherent educational value can be attributed to it. Failure to take into account adaptation to the needs and capacities of individuals was the source of the idea that certain subjects and certain methods are intrinsically cultural or intrinsically good for mental discipline. There is no such thing as educational value in the abstract (EE, 46).

Thus understood, however, the adherents of the new education—the progressivists—can more easily identify what they disagree with than state a positive conception of education. The failure to explicate a positive view of education led to another problem: Progressive educators were likely to fall prey to either-or thinking.

> To imposition from above is opposed expression and cultivation of individuality; to external discipline is opposed free activity; to learning from texts and teachers, learning through experience; to acquisition of isolated skills and techniques by drill, is opposed acquisition of them as means of attaining ends which make direct vital appeal; to preparation for a more or less remote future is opposed making the most of the opportunities of present life; to static aims and materials is opposed acquaintance with a changing world (EE, 19-20).

But a positive philosophy is possible, one based on a clear conception of education, as Dewey's position required, and an understanding of the concept of experience (EE, 20). Notably the new philosophy of progressive education needed its own positive account of subject matter and its organization, of authority, freedom, order and discipline, and so of habit and growth in light of its underlying conceptions of education and experience. Put more positively, in Dewey's opinion, "the true meaning of preparation [is] that a person, young or old, gets out of his present experience all that there is in it for him at the time in which he has it" (EE, 49). This full learning from present experience does not happen spontaneously. It calls for planning and organization—planning and organization which, being tied to the particularities of the present moment, cannot be fixed and settled entirely in advance. For experience "is always the actual life-experience of some individual" (EE, 89). Thus, in contrast to traditional education, which largely ignored the student in the design of curricular experiences, progressive education, when it is positive rather than reactive, considers the student in curricular matters, for

> It is a cardinal precept of the newer school of education that the beginning of instruction shall be made with the experience learners already have; that this experience and the capacities that have been developed during its course provide the starting point for all further learning. I am not so sure that the other condition, that of orderly development toward expansion and organization of subject-matter through growth of experience, receives as much

> attention (EE, 74).

In grasping this thought, we have at least a first step toward the new philosophy Dewey supported and some insight into a fundamental responsibility of the teacher:

> It is...essential that the new objects and events [in the curriculum] be related intellectually to those of earlier experiences, and this means that there be some advance made in conscious articulation of acts and ideas. It thus becomes the office of the educator to select those things within the range of existing experience that have the promise and potentiality of presenting new problems which by stimulating new ways of observation and judgment will expand the area of further experience (EE, 75).

This conception of education seems strikingly different from Neatby's caricature which included "no conscious preparation for the future,...no ultimate 'aims',...no abstract thought, no external discipline or stimulus, and, of course, no moral teaching" (1953, 24). Dewey allows only one source of insight into the future: what we already know. But this knowledge gives us the subject matter of education and reveals the partial truth in the traditionalist view of the importance of the curriculum:

> the sound principle that the objectives of learning are in the future and its immediate materials are in present experience can be carried into effect only in the degree that present experience is stretched, as it were, backward. It can expand into the future only as it is also enlarged to take in the past (EE, 77).

Critics who accuse Dewey of ignoring traditional subject matter and the established academic disciplines simply ignore such strong declarations as this.

This view of progressive education or, better, new conception of education correlates with the need to avoid either-or thinking and return to fundamental educational considerations by incorporating the best insights of both traditional and progressive education into a synthesis that transcends the limits of either in a principled way and ensures that we have more than just "a bit of both," an inconsistent compromise, or an eclectic combination of incoherent pieces. It is also a conception of education that sounds remarkably modern. The definition could fit comfortably with notions of authentic tasks and authentic evaluation, with success understood in terms of outcomes rather than objectives, with cooperative learning and portfolios, with talk of accountability and quality, and with concerns about values in education. Yet, in saying this, we must avoid exactly what Dewey warned us to shun: borrowing or blending in an unprincipled way and so ending with a philosophical and pedagogical smorgasbord that lacks clarity, consistency and coherence.

Educative Experience

If education is the first concept in understanding the basis of Dewey's philosophy, the second is experience. Dewey thought it odd that educational disputants would bother questioning whether experience should inform education. Education itself is an experience; it cannot be otherwise; and so the only possible questions concern which experiences, what sorts of experiences, and how they can best be organized or applied. To summarize his view, while students in traditional schools had experiences, those experiences had a "defective and wrong character—wrong and defective from the standpoint of connection with further experience" (EE, 27). Consequently, he stressed that "the belief that all genuine education comes about through experience does not mean that all experiences are genuinely or equally educative. Experience and education cannot be directly equated to each other. For some experiences are mis-educative" (EE, 25).

Some experiences do seem complete, with a kind of unity or integrity; and to talk of "an experience" is to talk as though the experience were a self-contained entity. But such usage, though understandable and often appropriate, can also mislead if it encourages us to forget that experiences do not occur in a vacuum or to ignore the continuity of our experiences. We experience in the context provided by our past experience, and our new experiences affect what we will experience in the future. This realization partly explains parents' concern with the kind of education their children receive: Present experiences can have lasting effects. This point is also critical to understanding Dewey's notion of an educative experience: The educational value of an experience depends on what it makes possible, particularly the quality or value of the other experiences it permits. So Dewey thought it more helpful to imagine a continuum than discrete, isolated experiential units.

Nothing Dewey has said illustrates this notion of the continuity of experience better than his conception of *habit*. We get into the habit of doing things in a certain way—that is, we learn habits (as a consequence of our past experiences). They affect how we react and behave in unfamiliar situations (our present experiences). That is the nature of a habit. Habits tend to become settled (determining our future experiences) and are hard to break though we can break them if circumstances change or new experiences warrant. In each of these examples, we see that the habit is anything but a self-contained entity. We can neither understand nor explain it without reference to past, future or present circumstances. Even though we speak of habit "as a more or less fixed way of doing things" (EE, 35), this isolation is an artificial and often unhelpful way of thinking in education, for it invites us to forget that the habit comes from somewhere and is exemplified in future instances. The habit represents, more accurately, the *continuity* between past and future; indeed, the habit is one way we link our past experiences with the future. Rightly then, we often think of education in terms of developing the right habits or dispositions, acting now to create habits over time by which we will live and from which we expect to benefit.

But what are those "right" habits and dispositions? For Dewey, they are those that make further growth possible: "*[O]nly* when development in a particular line conduces to continuing growth does it answer to the criterion of education as growing" (EE, 36). Notice the apparently simplistic assumption concealed in the idea of a particular line of growth—the assumption that growth can be clearly, precisely and unambiguously specified along a single identifiable line. Today we would probably be more sensitive to open-ended possibilities and therefore less certain about specifying which experiences lead to educational growth. But so was Dewey. In fact, his conception of ends, particularly his criticism of fixed ends, was influenced by a close attention to the notion of social and biological evolution and its open possibilities. Still, the underlying point remains: Some experiences seem to be stifling or even likely to lead into dead ends. Dewey talks of the positive values of "decency and kindliness" (EE, 34) but also of arresting or distorting experiences, those that engender callousness and a lack of sensitivity and responsiveness. He talks of falling into a rut, of a slack and careless attitude, and of disconnectedness and not being linked cumulatively. In short, he recognized those experiences that prevent us from getting from future experiences all they have to offer (EE, 25-26).

We often say that we want "a better life" for our children or at least a chance for them to lead "the good life." This is often what we think their education should help them to achieve. We want to be sure that they really are "growing," not withering or becoming stifled. This hope explains much of our concern with the quality of education. Notwithstanding Sizer's observation that "any education is outcome-based. The whole point of education is to have outcomes" (cited in O'Neil, 1995, 7), the immediate quality and enjoyment of the experience remains important along with our students' comfort and physical and psychological security. But we would be concerned about too much immediate enjoyment if it came at the expense of long-term value (EE, 27). So we are not always surprised or troubled if education proves difficult, challenging or unpleasant—even something to be "got through" for the sake of the good to "come of it." We want our children to "grow up" not just physically but also emotionally and intellectually. Much of that growing may, in fact, involve learning the ways of our community and adapting to them, but we also expect our children to grow in such a way that their lives are enriched and that new opportunities open for them. This notion of a growth that enriches and opens opportunities is Deweyan in spirit; this is Dewey the educational thinker articulating a common sense, parental notion, preserving one side of a traditional dichotomy. Unlike many educational thinkers, Dewey took pleasure in identifying with the aspirations of parents, for he saw in their common concerns a noble spirit: "What the best and wisest parent wants for his own child, that must the community want for all of its children" (M1, 5).

A problem with traditional education, Dewey could then explain, was its indifference to this continuity in experience. Apart from vague references to "preparation for life," "when you are out working" or just "you'll need this later" (perhaps only in still further studies), he found little or no linking of learning experiences to past or future ones. People did learn habits of action and thought but in isolation—habits which, having no obvious value or interest, rendered students callous to the pursuit of ideas, destroyed their motivation, discouraged the development of judgment and independent thought, and led them to see school as something apart from life (EE, 26-27). Students could have had experiences that aroused their curiosity, strengthened their initiative, and cultivated more helpful desires and purposes (EE, 38). Instead, they learned that large parts of their lives, not least the time spent in school, were irrelevant and meaningless—criticism with a decidedly contemporary ring.

Ironically, the only way in which students could have had those experiences, though this is hardly how it appears to generations of students, was through the insights and ways of thinking that constitute our cultural heritage, for we have found or devised these ways for understanding and making meaningful our experiences, for distinguishing the important and significant. The traditional disciplines embody our ways of pursuing and recording such understanding; they are bodies of knowledge together with modes of inquiry and research that make their pursuit possible. Phenix (1964) calls them "realms of meaning" or "ways of knowing." About this, the educational traditionalists were right. Here we see the real Dewey, who talked of those disciplines as "funded experience," not the fabricated Dewey, who is supposed to have denied the importance of traditional academic subjects. But to teach these disciplines as though they were remote and static bodies of information, unrelated to the past, present and future experiences of living people, is more than just boring; it does an injustice to their nature as ways of thinking: "That which we call a science or study puts the net product of past experience in the form which makes it most available for the future" (M2, 284).

Dewey liked to insist that science infuses all the technology we see around us and that chemistry is in everything that happens in the kitchen. At this juncture, Dewey said the progressive educator made a valuable, if incomplete, contribution to pedagogical practice: Children's experiences are at the center of education. To miss either of the two points—the value of the traditional subject matter or the place of the student's experience—is to resort again to either-or thinking. In addition to using "the formulated wealth of knowledge that makes up the course of study" to create an educative environment (M2, 291), the teacher can discover "the real child" who explores this wealth and manifests emerging and passing interests and abilities (M2, 281). Similarly, the goals or outcomes become significant to the educator when funded experience is viewed in this way:

> To see the outcome is to know in what direction the present experience is moving, provided it move normally and soundly. The far-away point, which is of no significance to us simply as far away, becomes of huge importance the moment we take it as

> defining a present direction of movement. Taken in this way it is no removed and distant result to be achieved, but a guiding method in dealing with the present (M2, 279).

Along with *continuity*, then, a second feature, *interaction*, characterizes experience for Dewey: An experience is an individual interacting with an environment. So an experience has both a subjective and an objective side, the learner's experience and the learning experience, both of which can affect the planning of an educational experience. In fact, experience can be acquired collectively by the group as well as individually; there is continuity in both, thus making possible and encouraging the growth of a way of life over generations and the accumulation of intellectual and practical insights and advances, a cultural heritage. The richness of the environment in which a student interacts partly ensures experiential quality, but a rich environment is wasted unless the interaction is genuine:

> The trouble with traditional education was not that it emphasized the external conditions that enter into the control of the experiences but that it paid so little attention to the internal factors which also decide what kind of experience is had. It violated the principle of interaction from one side. But this violation is no reason why the new education should violate the principle from the other side—except upon the basis of the extreme *Either-Or* educational philosophy which has been mentioned (EE, 42).

In short, individuals are not *in* situations in the same way that pennies are in a pocket or paint is in a can (EE, 44). They are more like fish *in* a stream where both the fish and the stream act upon one another and where the past, present and future of the fish and the stream remain important considerations. Consider a person "in a predicament": The predicament has precisely the links with past and future that continuity emphasizes and is a predicament because of the problems our present interaction with the situation poses. Approached from this angle, "The two principles of continuity and interaction are not separate from each other. They intercept and unite. They are, so to speak, the longitudinal and lateral aspects of experience" (EE, 44). The trick is to develop "the kind of present experience which has a favorable effect upon the future" (EE, 50), balancing the reality and power of the present interaction with the potential offered by its continuity. How then are we to choose subject matter that respects *continuity*, *interaction* and *quality*?

A Curriculum of Human Problems

Having urged us to abandon dichotomous thinking about the curriculum and the child, Dewey also argued that the notion of subject matter and children's experience as permanent distinctions should be forsaken. Rather, experience occurs with each child and each child is a dynamic being; therefore, "we realize that the child and the curriculum are simply two limits which define a single process" (M2, 278). Such language and thinking reflect continuity and interaction in experience; they talk of method but not content, offering opportunities but making no judgment about the quality of a particular experience, telling us about means but providing no direction. But Dewey does, in fact, also offer direction: "[A]t every level there is an expanding development of experience if experience is educative in effect" (EE, 88). Moreover, he affirmed that an educative experience must meet two criteria, one regarding facts and ideas, and the other their orderly arrangement:

> No experience is educative that does not tend both to knowledge of more facts and entertaining of more ideas and to a better, a more orderly, arrangement of them. It is not true that organization is a principle foreign to experience. Otherwise experience would be so dispersive as to be chaotic (EE, 82).

Even so, the teacher's point of view concerning organized knowledge differs from that of the scientist who thinks "the subject-matter represents simply a given body of truth to be employed in locating new problems, instituting new researches, and carrying them through to a verified outcome" (M2, 285). The perspective and challenge are different:

> what concerns him, as teacher, is the ways in which that subject may become a part of experience; what there is in the child's present that is usable with reference to it...with the subject-matter as a related factor in a total and growing experience (M2, 286).

The curriculum, therefore, must "be derived from materials which *at the outset* fall within the scope of ordinary life-experience" (EE, 73, italics added). Identifying material in the experiences of each child is, while a necessary first step, insufficient by itself. The second step is

> the progressive development of what is already experienced into a fuller and richer and also more organized form, a form that gradually approximates that in which subject-matter is presented to the skilled, mature person. That this change is possible without departing from the organic connection of education with experience is shown by the fact that this change takes place outside of the school and apart from formal education (EE, 74).

As elsewhere, Dewey advises us to examine how the child learns naturally—that is, outside the school setting. But this informal learning is usually unplanned and need not contribute to the child's growth: It is not necessarily educative and not typical of school learning. *Learning* and *education* are not synonyms, and unplanned learning is not typical of school learning. So Dewey must choose his examples carefully. One can usually expect the family, for example, to have at least an informal plan or commitment to a child's education. Dewey was alert to the neglect of the "orderly development toward expansion and organization of subject-matter through growth of experience" in progressive schools (EE, 74). As if to answer later critics, he explicitly told the teacher that "connectedness in growth must be his constant watchword" (EE, 75).

Dewey's position so far appears to be essentially conservative, as much backward-looking as forward-looking. It looks forward to account for the child's future needs and development, "but the achievements of the past provide the only means at command for understanding the present" (EE, 77). In this sense, all knowledge and all growth (academic, moral and social) are historically rooted; and, *in this sense,* cultural history supplies the only possible basis for the curriculum—the psychology of the learner suggesting what and perhaps how to draw upon this rich pool of funded knowledge. But at the same time it shows why no single curriculum can be devised to suit all students (SSCC, xxiii ff). Meanwhile, all this insight puts to rout the claim that

> no student of Dewey will be led to believe that one great duty of the teacher is to open to his pupils the heritage of his own and of

> other civilizations. He will be much more likely to consider contemplation of the past as at best a harmless form of escape, and at worst an undemocratic operation (Neatby, 1953, 26).

That Dewey considered our historical heritage the basis for a curriculum geared to growth and inquiry should surprise no one. He realized that *we develop social conventions and academic subjects as responses to problems as we search for better ways of living and understanding*. They provide, in short, modes of inquiry and insights.

Two principles govern the selection from that heritage—an inescapable problem for every educator—the first consonant with the nature of experience and the second consistent with Dewey's frequently misunderstood advocacy of the importance of children:

> First, that the problem grows out of the conditions of the experience being had in the present, and that it is within the range of the capacity of students; and, secondly, that it is such that it arouses in the learner an active quest for information and for production of new ideas (EE, 79).

Dewey made yet another suggestion regarding this problem of selection: "It is a sound educational principle that students should be introduced to scientific subject-matter and be initiated into its facts and laws through acquaintance with everyday social applications" (EE, 80). Thus we find him approaching science through cooking and technology and social studies through the study of the local community and its problems. We also find a common thread linking these domains to the scientific study of human problems, a favorite theme in Dewey's crusades for social reform (EE, 81). Today we see some educational reform efforts based at least in part on aspects of this emphasis in Dewey's thought, sometimes called "applied learning" or learning rooted in the application of what is learned to the everyday affairs of life. To be Deweyan, however, we may not tear the point from the context of Dewey's other ideas. Rather, we must focus on human problems in a rich and generous sense, not in a narrow, mechanical, skill-dominated manner.

Though he may gradually have come to regard the role of the school in social reform as limited (Burnett, 1979, 192-210; and Pratte, 1992, 140-142)—limited, that is, to influencing the thinking of the next generation of citizens, if that is such a great limitation—Dewey, the social reformer, lurks just below the surface here, accompanied by the school as a potential agent for social reform and, in particular, an agent of critical reflection through the scientific study of social problems and their origins. The sources of the curriculum may be conservatively rooted in the cultural heritage; but change is at times in order, and that change must be based, like the best in the tradition, on thoughtful, informed (that is, "scientific" for Dewey; we might say "educated") reflection about current social needs. Not all the cultural heritage, therefore, is unquestionably acceptable. This point Dewey drove home in several different ways. A scientific knowledge of "how things got to be that way," in society as much as in medicine, in ecology as much as in physics, is the only reasonable basis for using that knowledge to ensure that things do not have to remain that way. The past imposes a kind of authority, but it has its limitations to be cautioned against:

> Failure to give constant attention to development of the intellectual content of experiences and to obtain ever-increasing organization of facts and ideas may in the end merely strengthen the tendency toward a reactionary return to intellectual and moral authoritarianism (EE, 86).

Dewey offered no apologies for his position on the nature of the curriculum and scientific inquiry. He saw the need for and identified a number of different kinds of school laboratories. He saw each, however, as scientific in nature:

> The final justification of shops, kitchens, and so on in the school is not just that they afford opportunity for activity, but that they provide opportunity for the kind of activity or for the acquisition of mechanical skills which leads students to attend to the relation of means and ends, and then to consideration of the way things interact with one another to produce definite effects. It is the same in principle as the ground for laboratories in scientific research (EE, 85).

The key to Dewey's thinking about subject matter, like education in general, appears then to be the idea that an intellectual thread runs through all experience, linking seemingly isolated and individual events, facilitating the continuity of all development, enhancing each present and future learning opportunity through reflective interaction with the environment (including disciplined forms of inquiry), and allowing human problems to be studied and solved scientifically. We may say that the thread of early experience runs through us throughout life (continuity of experience). It is partially transformed (reconstruction of experience) as it joins with other threads of worthwhile experience (interaction of experience and disciplined organization of experience). These then broaden, extend, organize and refine themselves as they meet later threads of experience, enabling us to apply a fabric of experience to the scientific study and amelioration of human problems. In ideal development, therefore, the intelligent habits of the past combine with currently forming ones to promote ways of behaving in the future that are conducive to scientific reflection and rational action and so to solving personal and social problems.

The Nature of Freedom and Authority

Returning to our preliminary discussion of authority, we can now add a further dimension to Dewey's prohibition of either-or thinking: the erroneous conception of authority as either external or internal, either present or absent. Typical of Dewey's approach, and a necessary and natural outgrowth of his avoidance of dichotomous thinking, is his care to make distinctions. Hence we read: "When external authority is rejected, it does not follow that all authority should be rejected, but rather that there is need to search for a more effective source of authority" (EE, 21). About the relationship experience bears to authority and personal involvement, Dewey concluded that

> basing education upon personal experience may mean more multiplied and more intimate contacts between the mature and the immature than ever existed in the traditional school, and consequently more, rather than less, guidance by others. The problem, then, is: how these contacts can be established without violating the principle of learning through personal experience (EE, 21).

Moreover, if freedom is thought of as simply the opposite of authority, Dewey said, a similar dichotomy arises and leads to a dogmatism as unreflective as traditional education:

> It is not too much to say that an educational philosophy which professes to be based on the idea of freedom may become as dogmatic as ever was the traditional education which is reacted against. For any theory and set of practices is dogmatic which is not based upon critical examination of its own underlying principles. Let us say that the new education emphasizes the freedom of the learner. Very well. A problem is now set. What does freedom mean and what are the conditions under which it is capable of realization (EE, 22)?

Dewey's account of authority, freedom and rules sounds remarkably modern and well within the traditions of linguistic analysis. The existence of rules does not necessarily infringe upon freedom; quite the contrary, they actually provide opportunities for freedom. Consider, he suggested, children's games, a felicitous example of a shared social activity. Without rules, no game can be played, and children happily accept them (EE, 51ff). So the game generally runs smoothly enough in accordance with the rules, with relatively few appeals to the umpire who normally serves only to ensure that the rules are respected. Dewey attributed this functional peace to the fact that children see the rules as part of the game. New games call for new sets of rules, and in this sense rules are arbitrary. But in another important sense they are not arbitrary. They are essential to the group activity, and they arise from that activity rather than being imposed from outside. In this sense they are natural. Freedom thrives within the rules essential to the activity. By contrast, the traditional school

> was not a group or community held together by participation in common activities. Consequently, the normal, proper conditions of control were lacking. Their absence was made up for, and to a considerable extent had to be made up for, by the direct intervention of the teacher, who, as the saying went, "kept order." He kept it because order was in the teacher's keeping, instead of residing in the shared work being done (EE, 55).

More generally, the fact that people are social beings leads them to work naturally in groups—communities—with common purposes. In this crucial way, Dewey's theory of education was not child-centered in any individualistic sense; it was community-centered, an education focused upon children who compose a community with rules and common goals.

Problems, therefore, arise from the arbitrary imposition on group activities of purposes unnatural to the activity. The bossy child who disrupts everyone's enjoyment is Dewey's example of an external imposition. That rules are natural is not to say, however, that the best ones will always be obvious or that they will need no revision from time to time. But they do have a natural and inherent justification. They facilitate the activity of the group or the achievement of its ends. To avoid either-or thinking, we can consider rules as neither imposed from without nor simply subjective whims.

The key to unlocking Dewey's conception of legitimate and natural rules lies in the idea of *getting one's priorities straight*. That is, the appropriate set of rules, and the rules people will naturally accept and readily follow, contribute to or form part of the point of the activity in the first place. Such rules, we might say, are *reasonable* rather than *arbitrary*. They respond to a genuine social need, and we can understand and accept them on this basis. The issue is in principle an objective question, a matter of whether the rules proposed do or do not further the group ends, a point Dewey would state in terms of its being a *scientific* matter. The word *scientific* has for us perhaps unhelpful, value-neutral connotations, but he used it to emphasize the objective and reasoned basis of ethical decisions (and so ethics in general). One of the services an education performs for us is to help us to see the likely consequences of our actions, to understand whether either behavior or rules promote our ends. Ironically this knowledge of the necessary, inevitable or likely outcomes of behavior and rules is what frees us from their tyranny. To be free, then, is to live by rules that result in consequences consistent with the ends we desire and to be able to foresee and choose those ends.

In the case of a school, we might reasonably inquire what its raison d'être is, and any answer will presumably involve facilitating the learning of certain worthwhile material. Under Dewey's formulation, rules that derive from this purpose should win a natural and willing acceptance from all participants. They promote desirable learning outcomes, growth, and the opportunity for future development. This identification of purpose, then, defines the kinds of questions legitimately asked and their appropriate answers. There may, of course, be more than one possible or desirable way of structuring learning situations or schools. We might learn to do better and so want to reform schools, or we might call existing structures into question from time to time. But we still face the very real contemporary problem of the child who does not share the purposes for which the school exists. Dewey (EE, 56-57) recognized that this situation called for an intensive study of the individual and the teacher's professional judgment rather than the application of a specific rule. He advised, as well, that intermediate responses, even when necessary, rarely produce ultimate solutions.

If we believe a school should foster rational inquiry, the question of freedom and of rules and authority acquires perplexing but also promising educational implications: The structures can and in principle must be reasonable, and reasonable questions can be posed and reasonable answers expected and provided. Such an approach would provide a mandate for a reflective moral—and social, political and civic—education, an education, Dewey thought, worthy of the name. In fact, we see emerging the idea of the school as a *community*, a community because its members share the purposes and processes, including reason and democracy, that define it.

Within this Deweyan vision, then, a school—even an orderly and apparently well-run school—may go wrong and can expect discipline problems when some authority outside the purposes, processes and people of the school imposes its rules arbitrarily and illegitimately. We use the term *arbitrarily* in the sense that the rules bear no relation to the purposes for being in school and the word *illegitimately* in the sense that no such purposes exist. At the opposite extreme, the school may go wrong when all are left to do as they please with no thought to the promotion of the common purpose. Traditional schools are often accused of the former and progressive schools of the latter. In addressing the latter criticism, Dewey emphasized the need for teacher planning rooted in a pedagogy (and a good understanding of the principles of continuity and interaction in experience) that avoids arbitrarily imposed conditions and activities. In essence, the teacher needs

> to arrange in advance for the kind of work (by which I mean all kinds of activities engaged in) which will create situations that of themselves tend to exercise control over what this, that, and the other pupil does and how he does it (EE, 57).

This kind of planning may well be harder than drafting the traditional lesson plan, though its implementation may be easier—a circumstance that might remind us of recent claims about cooperative learning.

In fact, planning is one aspect of the teacher's role as a member of the group, and the other members would be justified in complaining if a teacher exercised it incompetently. So too, teachers' greater experience (including formal education and preparation) qualifies them for this position of leadership; to deny this, for Dewey, would be to deny the facts of the situation. The situation itself implies a duty to plan the learning environment of the classroom learning community:

> I have heard of cases in which children are surrounded with objects and materials and then left entirely to themselves, the teacher being loath to suggest even what might be done with the materials lest freedom be infringed upon. Why, then, even supply materials, since they are a source of some suggestion or other? But what is more important is that the suggestion upon which pupils act must in any case come from somewhere. It is impossible to understand why a suggestion from one who has a larger experience and a wider horizon should not be at least as valid as a suggestion arising from some more or less accidental source (EE, 71).

One interesting feature of this analysis is that *it defines the teacher's authority*—and that of the principal, the school and the board—*and its legitimate exercise in pedagogic terms* rather than terms imposed on the school from outside its educational mandate—in, for example, economic, psychological or political terms. What we need, Dewey believed, is

> first, for the teacher to be intelligently aware of the capacities, needs, and past experiences of those under instruction, and, secondly, to allow the suggestion made to develop into a plan and project by means of the further suggestions contributed and organized into a whole by the members of the group (EE, 71-72).

Yet "the essential point [of this understanding of students and allowing a suggestion to develop into a plan and a project] is that the purpose [of the individual and group] grow and take shape through the process of social intelligence" (EE, 71-72). The intensive and extensive prior preparation and planning of the teacher is to be used to guide intelligent discussion with students and the formulation of learning projects.

Anything less is to undervalue the knowledge and role of the teacher and the potential and needs of students, of present and emerging members of a community and of citizens of a democracy.

Thus for Dewey, the purpose of an institution or an activity is crucial. But the fact is that purposes do change and evolve, and people do have competing agendas. How then do we establish the legitimacy of a purpose? The sin in traditional discipline is the arbitrary, the imposition of what is irrelevant to the purposeful functioning of the group or the institution. The essence of that sin lies in the imposition of the illegitimate, what there is no inherent reason for imposing. As a result, a certain legitimacy resides in the child's question, "Why do I have to?" even if it is naive to suppose that the child will always naturally and spontaneously understand and accept the reason.

The Student's Formation of Purposes

When he talks of the purposes of schooling, we can expect that Dewey will wish to incorporate both the subject matter and the child's past, present and future experiences into a conception of the school as a community with shared purposes, thus giving his notion of social and individual growth educational content. In fact, the social component of education plays a second role in education, as it does in knowing: As we have seen, children are to be introduced to subject matter through its social applications and knowledge itself is to be understood as the scientific study of human problems (EE, 80-81). This orientation in turn forms the basis of his approach to social reform and involves the better use of what we know and our ability to know in recognizing social problems and improving the lot of humankind. As a result, we find Dewey asserted, "The fundamental factors in the educative process are an immature, undeveloped being; and certain social aims, meanings, values incarnate in the mature experience of the adult" (M2, 273).

While thinking about educational reform, we should note that Dewey found one of the assumptions underlying traditional education to be that the experiences which would make up the bulk of the child's later adult life would resemble those his parents and grandparents had known (EE, 19). Thus a view of education as initiating the child into the traditional ways of living, thinking and working seemed natural and appropriate. Consequently, the aims and purposes of education, and ends in life generally, were largely settled. But while this approach had worked more or less satisfactorily for generations, class divisions, particularly in the nineteenth and twentieth centuries, and economic crises, notably in the 1830s and 1930s, showed that traditional education had not always served the good of the whole community. Nor had it produced people who could recognize and understand these class and economic problems, let alone propose and implement solutions. Dewey felt that in his time, a time of change, the traditional assumption of stability could no longer be taken for granted. His rejection of the traditional belief in stability is the key to his reconsideration of the nature of education: The old conception of education had proven inadequate, and a better understanding, truer to the nature of genuine education and better suited to the present times, particularly the social context, was needed. His assumption that his society had entered a period of significant change resonates today and helps validate for us his ways of thinking about educational reform.

During a time of change, however, we cannot always see clearly "where things are going" or be sure of our own goals. This lack of clarity makes discussions of goals and precise explanations of growth all the more important but all the more problematic; it requires an open-mindedness unencumbered by hesitancy or paralysis (Hare, 1979). We do not know exactly what to expect or, therefore, how to prepare people precisely for what will come. So we naturally talk, for instance, of life-long learning or of learning to learn as an educational goal, but without necessarily giving these terms Dewey's full sense of growth.

The concept of radical, profound social change suggests then that, in addition to rethinking our actual purposes, aims and goals, we may have to reformulate our understanding of the very nature of purposes, aims and goals. In serious change the nature of aims and not just the actual aims or conditions, and certainly not just the means for achieving ends, may be changing. In fact, we may need a conception of goals that allows us at least to imagine goals that are not static but evolving. For Dewey this possibility was more than an idle reflection, for he was among the first educational thinkers to take seriously and see fully the implications in this realm of the novel notion of natural evolution. Thus it is significant that Dewey talked of forming, formulating and constructing ends rather than finding, discovering or identifying them as though they already existed. The challenge in education, as far as he was concerned, is to prepare people who can form or construct ends, who can imagine ends in this manner, and who can act on this conception and live with the uncertainty that the position entails.

Thus Dewey devoted two chapters in *Experience and Education*,

Chapters 5 and 6, to the ability to formulate purposes—intelligent purposes—as one way of conceiving the aim of education:

> There is, I think, no point in the philosophy of progressive education which is sounder than its emphasis upon the importance of the participation of the learner in the formation of the purposes which direct his activities in the learning process, just as there is no defect in traditional education greater than its failure to secure the active co-operation of the pupil in construction of the purposes involved in his studying (EE, 67).

Indeed, the ability to formulate purposes for oneself is part of living well or being a mature adult. Today we might talk of freedom or "empowering" people through education or enabling them to think for themselves. So, Dewey concluded,

> It is, then, a sound instinct which identifies freedom with power to frame purposes and to execute or carry into effect purposes so framed. Such freedom is in turn identified with self-control; for the formation of purposes and the organization of means to execute them are the work of intelligence. Plato once defined a slave as the person who executes the purposes of another, and, as has just been said, a person is also a slave who is enslaved to his own blind desires (EE, 67).

It is a long step—an idea seldom contemplated by zealous progressive educators—from an initial impulse, which may be vague, ill-defined or blind, to a consciously thought-out, reflectively considered purpose. But this work of moving from an initial impulse to a reflective purpose falls naturally to education: "A purpose is an end-view. That is, it involves foresight of the consequences which will result from acting upon impulse" (EE, 67). Dewey's point is important: One may be driven by an impulse, but when one has a purpose in mind it is "a plan and method of action based upon foresight of the consequences of acting under given observed conditions in a certain way" (EE, 69). *Purpose* can be both a verb and a noun.

Like an experience, a purpose arises from somewhere and has potential connections with the future; it is informed by what we know and what we make of what we know. The key educational terms in this context for Dewey are *observation*, *knowledge* of what has happened in similar situations, and *judgments* of significance. These ideas reflect Dewey's belief that ends are not fixed or predetermined but rather open to change and reformulation, to evaluation and appraisal, particularly as we come to know their sources and the consequences of acting on them. They also reflect his tendency and desire to talk of moral questions in terms of objective conditions and consequences, like questions of science. Individuals have ends as purposes, ends-in-view; objects do not (EE, 67). Even those objects that have been made for a purpose may at times be used for another end if we so choose.

This way of seeing ends, Dewey clearly understood, differed markedly from how they had traditionally been understood in philosophy, and certainly in classical realism, where the nature of an object was understood by knowing its end or purpose, an end that was fixed. Similarly, the major western religions customarily conceived of human beings as having a certain unchangeable quality or spirit or self destined to pursue at least a general purpose, like loving and serving the creator and the created. Accepting the theory of biological evolution, Dewey appears to have concluded that these older ways of thinking could no longer be assumed. The consequences of this conclusion are radical in two ways particularly pertinent to thinking about educational reform. First, what is now required is a way of choosing or determining the ends worth pursuing, rather than discovering them or learning what they are, and of re-evaluating them when appropriate and knowing when that time is. Second, in the continuum of experience, what is an end at one time will later become a means or contribute to defining a further end. The risk is that, if reasonable ways of reevaluating ends remain undetermined, fundamental social commitments and personal values may be left to unreason or war, and schools may become victims of the tides of anger that wash across communities. Dewey knew this threat from experience, and we believe it characterizes the dilemma facing social and educational reformers today, particularly educational leaders charged with responding to new demands, needs and situations in the face of competing pressure groups. Old goals and values and old ways of thinking about goals and values no longer seem workable or realistic or, at a minimum, they work for only segments of society, not for everyone. While they may gain consideration out of respect for particular members of the community, they cannot be allowed to dominate or paralyze educational reform.

Dewey's thought here remains open-ended, complementing a conception of life as evolutionary and a view of education as growth.

Philosophical and educational circles had always kept a place for discussion and debate about means in relation to achieving ends. This discussion would benefit, Dewey believed, from more scientific and better informed thinking. What he now required of himself and others was a way of conceptualizing ends as something also to be determined and as something that could change over time. This required a logic of choice about objects—purpose and ends—other than means. In this way his approach speaks directly to the problems that confront educational reform movements today: Dewey never considered such choices arbitrary, personal preferences or a matter for political compromise. For him, the challenge was to find how to make objectively better choices about what is worth pursuing in life, what will encourage individual and social growth.

Central to such a conception of the world is the idea that it is contingent, unfinished and open to new possibilities. For Dewey, this idea involved taking means—and causality—seriously, not downplaying them as if they were of little consequence next to infinitely worthwhile, fixed and eternal ends. He wanted us to recognize that means bring about the ends we choose—as we see in the arts, most obviously the practical applied arts—and will bring about their consequences whether or not we choose or foresee them (EN, 89ff).

This understanding of means explains the importance of knowing their potential and the consequences we can expect them to occasion, one role of science in ethics. It also reflects the parental hope that children will acquire a common wisdom about life and be able to make choices while foreseeing the likely results of their actions, whether in money matters, sexuality, study habits or the workplace. To repeat, this way of considering means, for Dewey, involved associating them with their potential, and their inevitable consequences, rather than thinking of them as instruments chosen only to reach predetermined ends. Moreover, this stream of events—these means—is on-going. Life is never static, and we are forever thinking about the consequences of our actions—those consequences in their turn becoming means and defining future options. The alternative is idleness and irrelevance, ends which are "empty castles in the air unless they are translated into the means by which they may be realized" (EE, 70). This position implies recognizing causality in human affairs rather than postulating transcendent ends whose value carries over neither to means nor to consequences. So it is interesting to read the opinion of at least one critic that Dewey's philosophy itself "was not a workable plan of political action, which is a major irony in Dewey's work" (Pratte, 1992, 148; see also Smith, 1994, 200, 208).

Dewey believed his emphasis simultaneously brought morality down to earth and gave our choices cosmic significance. At the very least, it inevitably colors our way of thinking about ends: "Outcomes of desire are also beginnings of new acts and hence are portentous" (M14, 174). So, "the genuine implication of natural ends may be brought out by considering beginnings instead of endings. To insist that nature is an affair of beginnings is to assert that there is no one single and all-at-once beginning of everything" (L1, 83). Weaned of "eulogistic connotations" and given such a "neutral interpretation" (L1, 83), ends no longer seem fixed and so become serious matters of choice and a proper subject of education and the cultivation of judgment. What kind of community, what kind of life, we might ask, are we building from our beginnings? For the means we choose determine the ends we achieve, the decisions we make today determine the opportunities and the further decisions—the means—we will have tomorrow. We may act wisely, with foresight and judgment, or in ignorance. Ends that are fixed or natural and part of a pre-established order lead away from reflection, from the cultivation of choice, from "reflective appraisal as more worthy to be striven for" (L1, 89). Thus we find Dewey saying of the distinction of ends and means,

> "End" is a name for a series of acts taken collectively—like the term army. "Means" is a name for the same series taken distributively—like this soldier, that officer. To think of the end signifies to extend and enlarge our view of the act to be performed. It means to look at the next act in perspective, not permitting it to occupy the entire field of vision (M14, 28).

Without his conception of ends and the attitude and education it implies, Dewey believed we are likelier to work with "a fancy...a phantasy, a dream, a castle in the air" than even "an ideal" (M14, 161), let alone a practical, realizable aim. Thus, he argued that while a desire or interest satisfied does not necessarily produce a complete calm, there is "that kind of quiescence which marks the recovery of unified activity: the absence of internal strife among habits and instincts" (M14, 173).

Such thinking was typical of social reform movements in the 1930s, and Dewey certainly participated in them. He envisioned clearly better and worse ways of living, better and worse choices in the realm of educational and social policy. These choices related to individual and social flourishing and waning, to power and weakness, that is, to both individual and social growth. The considerations that made those choices better or worse were the objective personal and social conditions to which they contributed or failed to contribute. This is why Dewey saw a danger in making too much of basing choices upon natural instincts and felt compelled to attend to the differences between "original impulse and desire" and "a plan and method of action based upon foresight of the consequences" (EE, 69). He warned that

> Desire for something may be intense. It may be so strong as to override estimation of the consequences that will follow acting upon it. Such occurrences do not provide the model for education. The crucial educational problem is that of procuring the postponement of immediate action upon desire until observation and judgment have intervened (EE, 69).

On the other hand, he had faith in "the potentialities of education when it is treated as intelligently directed development of the possibilities inherent in ordinary experience" (EE, 89-90). One might even think of the aim of education, then, as the ability to formulate purposes and to pass from the "immediate execution of impulses and desires" to "intelligent activity," together of course with the requirement that this foresight become a motivation or a "moving force" (EE, 69).

In the light of these thoughts, it came naturally to Dewey to adopt a language of science—a science of social, economic and political consequences and objective conditions—in discussing such decisions. Given this orientation, we have no more reason to believe that political pressure groups or the negotiation of compromises among competing interests, for instance, are likely to produce the right answers in education than we have in science. What matters in educational reform, as in day-to-day teaching, are the actual consequences—the objective facts—in the particular lives of individual children, notably the effects on their futures and their life chances. In this conclusion, Dewey reflected the commitments of all well-meaning teachers and school administrators.

It takes now but a short step to imagine that the ends worth seeking in society are those that promote growth, opening and enriching possibilities rather than narrowing and stifling them and so making intelligent choices possible. For Dewey, the aim of genuine education can be nothing less than such growth and the continued capacity for growth. Growth, in turn, requires both the capacity and the disposition to reflect thoughtfully and critically on our knowledge and experience.

Education for Freedom and Power

Dewey concluded one lengthy discussion of competing conceptions of education and educational reform by reaffirming the view that the fundamental considerations in educational reform are educational, not a matter of arguing for one *ism* or another: "The basic question concerns the nature of education with no qualifying adjectives prefixed" (EE, 90). While he had, as we shall see, a much larger social agenda for the school, concerned in part with its role as an agent in social reconstruction, we have now identified at least some *individual aims of education*, those pertaining to the individual's ability to formulate and reconsider aims and the appropriate means for achieving them, aims that can be expressed in terms of both cognitive and motivational educational growth and in terms of the life appropriate for an adult member of a community, a free citizen in a democratic society.

The two realms of social and individual aims remain linked despite the many misinterpretations of his "disciples." Careful reading quickly dispels any dichotomy of individual and social in Dewey's work. For example, following a discussion of authority, he made a striking claim about freedom, striking in that we might be inclined to think that adult freedom consists in the right to do as one pleases without interference, to be free rather than a slave subject to the will of another. Yet he made no such pronouncement, preferring instead to claim that "the only freedom that is of enduring importance is freedom of intelligence, that is to say, freedom of observation and of judgment exercised in behalf of purposes that are intrinsically worth while" (EE, 61). He held that the dichotomy of negative and positive freedom, freedom from restraint and freedom to act on one's wishes, arises out of either-or thinking, just like the dichotomy of freedom and authority.

Even so, power is a legitimate individual, social and educational concern, for without it growth is impossible. Four expressions here—*intelligence*, *observation*, *judgment*, and *purposes that are intrinsically worth while*—allude to the crucial role for knowledge and education in the good life. Moreover, given the nature of legitimate authority as an expression of the purposes of the group, the good life must be social.

Certainly freedom, either as a lack of restraint or as the power to get one's way, while indispensable, is worthless without the additional freedom bestowed by the power to choose wisely or the ability to determine what is worth choosing:

> freedom from restriction, the negative side, is to be prized only as a means to a freedom which is *power*: power to frame purposes, to judge wisely, to evaluate desires by the consequences which will result from acting upon them; power to select and order means to carry chosen ends into operation (EE, 63-64, italics added).

In fact, only this freedom to choose purposes and to evaluate options wisely provides self-control; without this power, "a person...has at most only the illusion of freedom. Actually he is directed by forces over which he has no command" (EE, 65).

Taking the common sense adage "Stop and think," Dewey explained why and how the "ideal aim of education is the creation of power of self-control" (EE, 64). While natural inclinations provide a beginning point in education, they need "some reconstruction, some remaking" (EE, 64). This reconstruction involves inhibiting an impulse by means of reflection or thinking

> until that impulse has been brought into connection with other possible tendencies to action so that a more comprehensive and coherent plan of activity is formed. Some of the other tendencies to action lead to use of eye, ear, and hand to observe objective conditions; others result in recall of what has happened in the past. Thinking is thus a postponement of immediate action, while it effects internal control of impulse through a union of observation and memory, this union being the heart of reflection. What has been said explains the meaning of the well-worn phrase "self-control" (EE, 64).

Education properly understood then has among its individual aims power, freedom, growth and self-control.

In addition, only by first recognizing these educational considerations—by seeing education as *empowering the student*—can we, second, make real, meaningful school reform, rethinking ends as well as means. For "effects [or outcomes] are not ends unless thought has perceived and freely chosen the conditions and processes that are their conditions" (L1, 275), transforming them into ends-in-view or "*means* in present action" (M14, 156). In other words, only educational outcomes that result from students perceiving and choosing the conditions and the means of their accomplishment are really their ends. The pedagogical means are steps taken toward the educational ends, and the educational ends consequently are the pedagogical means that collectively constitute the ends. Only this conception of ends, Dewey believed, truly empowers by truly giving people control over their lives and the changes they wish to make by providing them with realistic means for achieving their goals. Only this concept of means and ends empowers students to control their experiences.

As Dewey put it, the problem with most reform movements is that

> moral and spiritual "leaders" have propagated the notion that ideal ends may be cultivated in isolation from "material" means, as if means and material were not synonymous. While they condemn men for giving to means the thought and energy that ought to go to ends, the condemnation should go to them. For they have not taught their followers to think of material and economic activities as really means (L4, 224).

Thinking about educational reform, then, entails ultimately thinking about education, on the one hand, and about means and ends, on the other. One of the tragedies of present-day educational reform is that so much discussion depends on the false assumption that both the discussants and other interested parties understand or share an understanding of the nature of education. Few assumptions seem less accurate and more costly. If we are to make progress in educational reform, we need some common understanding about what we want to reform.

Furthermore, an interesting paradox of contemporary educational reform is that many policy and decision makers who have been highly prescriptive concerning both the means and the ends of education in past decades now proclaim themselves unconcerned with the means educators select; they are concerned only with the outcomes or ends. In taking this stance, they ignore nearly everything Dewey had to say about both ends and means. To say that we are the better for the half-ounce of freedom from prescribed means while still receiving the full pound of prescribed ends is to misconceive the connection between means and ends and the dual nature of each.

Conclusion

This chapter has explained Dewey's conception of educational reform, by exploring his understanding of change and the open-ended nature of ends; his views about the relations among education, society and the individual; his conceptions of education and society in terms of growth, power, freedom and self-control; and his idea of experience in terms of continuity, interaction and habit. We used the historic debate between traditional and progressive education and the problems of subject matter in the curriculum and authority in schools to illustrate his intellectual approach as well as his ideas about education generally and the role of schools in particular. Along the way, we also dispelled some misconceptions of specific Deweyan views and raised doubts about certain aspects of his thought. This approach to rebutting misconceptions and raising doubts characterizes the remainder of the work.

Dewey's understanding of social and educational problems and how to do something about them led him into crusades for reform in which education, growth and life-long learning became central ideas. Westbrook (1991) argues that Dewey moved from general philosophical concerns in his early career to a consideration of educational questions and then, particularly in his retirement, to an involvement in more general social and political problems, a development reflecting his belief that the school had a limited but important *educational* role to play in social reform. Reform—with its connotations of change, opposition and replacement—seems a natural focus for Dewey's concern with dichotomies, particularly people's tendency to think in terms of opposed extremes and thereby to ignore the very insights that lead others to different beliefs. What he opposed was the arbitrary and dogmatic, and the unprincipled compromise. Accordingly, he proposed returning to fundamental concepts of community and education in order to derive from them accounts of related concepts (authority, discipline, freedom, order, experience, growth, knowledge, habit and learning) and so to develop solutions with rational, empirical and moral legitimacy gained by reflecting fundamental priorities and purposes.

A key to Dewey's thinking, then, is that the value of an experience (or an institution or a social organization) lies in its instrumental significance or what it makes possible, and particularly the other experiences it opens up and the capacity to use those experiences to enrich human life. That is, the value of an experience lies in its service as a beginning, not an end. Growth for him expressed this idea of enrichment; by contrast, some experiences, some schools and some social arrangements stifle, limit or lead to dead ends, denying future experiences what they have to offer. Schooling divorced from the real concerns of the community and the experiences of students fails this test. It is irrelevant, meaningless, boring, unpleasant and apart from "real life"—a hurdle rather than a resource or a guide to understanding and power—regardless of the latent educational potential of its curriculum.

The school so divorced from reality tends to be traditional and overly academic. But its curriculum is not its real problem and may even be its strength, for modes of inquiry arise in our attempt to understand the world and to cope with our problems of living in it. Thus understood, the resources of the culture and the traditions of the community are empowering; so presented, they become a more useful and accurate initiation into an on-going tradition of inquiry. The challenge is to build a better social and intellectual order by participating in these human endeavors. The legitimate purpose of school then is to promote such learning, not rote acceptance; and the purpose of society is to make it possible for us to live in accordance with what we know and to create the conditions for its realization. Properly understood, then,

> A society is a number of people held together because they are working along common lines, in a common spirit, and with reference to common aims. The common needs and aims demand a growing interchange of thought and growing unity of sympathetic feeling. The radical reason that the present school cannot organize itself as a natural social unit is because just this element of common and productive activity is absent (M1, 10).

These purposes or aims are natural, being in the nature of knowledge and living together, and the resulting social and educational order is then reasonable rather than arbitrary. We can always test their legitimacy by asking what we know of these aims and ends, particularly their functioning and their likely consequences. As we shall see later, these shared purposes build a community, not just a society. Viewing means as beginnings, we can ask what kind of community we are building with our choices—and particularly whether it promotes or stifles growth, whether it allows us to derive from future experiences what they have to offer.

In education, then, legitimate purposes are centrally educational, deriving from the school's educational mandate rather than being imposed from without. They imply an education concerned with learning to formulate and construct aims, with knowing when and how to reevaluate them, with exercising open-mindedness and life-long learning, and with discovering and acting on what we know to be best from an objective, "scientific" study of the facts and the choices. They imply a freeing, empowering, liberating education, because it encourages the formulating of purposes. Here, for Dewey, is the basis for educational reform: to construct schools that remain true to their educational mandate. Such schools will produce individuals who can inquire and choose purposes and who, in turn, will reconstruct society or at least the spheres of it they touch.

This approach to educational and social reform reflects a pragmatic (or perhaps, better, an experimental) conception of knowledge and its goals and of experience and values that Dewey articulated in *The Quest for Certainty*. If Bertrand Russell was obsessed with a quest for certainty (Madigan, 1993, 11), Dewey's concern is better expressed in terms of a search for reasonable belief, control and security: "Man who lives in a world of hazards is compelled to seek for security" (L4, 3). But this is more than a search for only temporary security. It is a quest for meaning, for a knowledge and an understanding of the connectedness of experience and of that which renders it problematic (QC, 234), a pursuit of unity and harmony. This meaningfulness is partly aesthetic, suggesting a completeness or integrity in our experience. And a moral component, a peace and harmony, accompanies the unity and integrity (QC, 235).

While, in explaining a Deweyan way of thinking about problems of educational reform, we include moral, aesthetic and intellectual perspectives that give them deeper meaning, we realize that such perspectives must themselves change as problems change, as what we take to be issues evolve, as our ways of thinking about them mature, and as what we know changes (QC, 236). But particular changes rarely come every day and are rarely inevitable, beyond our control, or all equally worthwhile. Nor are we mere spectators; rather we are judges and agents. As Dewey remarked, "Thus we are led to our main proposition: *Judgments about values are judgments about the conditions and the results of experienced objects; judgments about that which should regulate the formation of our desires, affections and enjoyments*" (L4, 212). So we believe Dewey's approach holds promise for contemporary educational reform—for just the reason that it is not static or stagnant but "pragmatic," taking change seriously and so challenging us to rethink our ideas and to remain intellectually alive and morally responsible.

CHAPTER TWO

The Social Aims of Education

> [T]he ultimate aim of education is nothing other than the creation of human beings in the fulness of their capacities. Through the making of human beings, of men and women generous in aspiration, liberal in thought, cultivated in taste, and equipped with knowledge and competent method, society itself is constantly remade, and with this remaking the world itself is re-created (L5, 297).

> The best guarantee of collective efficiency and power is liberation and use of the diversity of individual capacities in initiative, planning, foresight, vigor and endurance. Personality must be educated, and personality cannot be educated by confining its operations to technical and specialized things, or to the less important relationships of life. Full education comes only when there is a responsible share on the part of each person, in proportion to capacity, in shaping the aims and policies of the social groups to which he belongs. This fact fixes the significance of democracy (RP, 209).

If Dewey considered some of the aims of education individual—that is, expressed in terms of individual growth, liberation, transformation, self-control, independent thinking and empowerment—others, perhaps those for which he was best known and most distrusted, are social. Given his understanding of human nature and human life as social, the school as a social institution, and the classroom as a learning community, we should expect this side to his thinking, especially if we understand growth as the capacity to extract from future experiences all they have to offer. Yet, as we have suggested, he may have come to view education and schools as having a more limited role in social reform, a role beginning with the transformation of individuals through their ability to form and act on purposes.

Today we hear educational reforms proposed for a variety of levels in the school system: in classroom practices, for example, with the introduction of computers, cooperative learning, applied learning, contracting, effective teaching strategies, or engaged learner arrangements; at the school or district level, perhaps with the introduction of site-based management or district-wide testing; at state, provincial, or national levels, with new curricula in, for instance, mathematics or science, or national benchmarks and expectations. Proposed reforms also address the school's relation to the home and the community. We see, for example, revised reporting procedures or parent and community involvement in committees concerned with school decision- and policy-making. Sometimes we hear these proposals stated in terms of goals or the aims of education or schooling: for instance, preparing students for work or leisure, for citizenship, for advanced study, for family life, for healthy living, or for living a full life.

When reform efforts gain expression—for example, in a mission statement or as a commitment to quality, to serving the client, or to a new respect for cultural differences or an acceptance of different abilities—their implications often cut across several different levels. On rare occasions the proposals take the form of a complete, explicit mandate for the schools, perhaps representing a whole philosophy or orientation to life, as can happen with Charter schools, private schools, quasi-military academies or religious schools. But generally, even when they involve the community, such proposals involve designing schools which either respond better to community expectations or utilize better community resources. They emphasize conforming or using rather than reforming or transforming. Almost never do they envision a transformed community (U.S. Department of Education, 1994). Roughly speaking, much contemporary educational reform appears to assume that schools should be aligned with societal interests and needs. Dewey, by contrast, believed that both society and schools should be reformed by coming to a better understanding of people, education and democracy and by acting upon this understanding to alter the policies and practices of all major institutions, economic, political, educational, and so forth. This chapter undertakes to explicate this basic difference and to clarify Dewey's way of thinking.

Reform in Perspective

Because so many present-day educational proposals present themselves as reforms, departures from existing or common practices, the changes proposed appear to be new, often innovative, and often (except when based on a return to enduring religious or perennialist philosophies) to respond to new or changing social conditions. In fact, however, many proposals envision a return to earlier suggestions and practices, including at times a return to Deweyan ideas (Darling-Hammond, *The Current Status of Teaching,* 1994, 25). On this point some historical perspective is both instructive and amusing. In the medieval university, certainly closer to the "good old days" than we are, regular complaints arose about the low standards of achievement and poor academic preparation of the arriving students, notably their deficiency in Latin, the language of instruction. As a result, many students had to spend their first two years perfecting their knowledge of prerequisite subjects (Curtis and Boultwood, 1970, 93). This problem sounds contemporary; its solution resembles our current developmental and remedial work; and the medieval professors might have welcomed a junior college system. Reforming schools, then, is hardly a novel idea or cause.

On the other hand, concerns with vocational education and employment skills; comparative national or regional test scores; declining standards of achievement; the global economy, national competitiveness, and a national economic strategy; the media, the service industries, and the information revolution; the breakdown of the home; changing social structures; and the attitudes of the young seem to be more recent concerns, the structure of society, the economic order and the training required for jobs being different than they were in the days of Abélard and Aquinas. Yet a century ago Dewey discussed the impact of social, scientific, political, demographic and industrial changes—notably problems of immigration and migration from rural to industrial settings—and the critical requirement for schools to change so as to meet these new circumstances and needs. While he enumerated the familial, urban and rural transformations that beset children, he insisted that a return to the so-called good old days was impossible. Instead, he advocated looking on the positive side of the ledger and moving forward:

> We must recognize our compensations—the increase in toleration, in breadth of social judgment, the larger acquaintance with human nature, the sharpened alertness in reading signs of character and interpreting social situations, greater accuracy of adaptation to differing personalities, contact with greater commercial activities. These considerations mean much to the city-bred child of today. Yet there is a real problem: how shall we retain these advantages, and yet introduce into the school something representing the other side of life—occupations which exact personal responsibilities and which train the child in relation to the physical realities of life (M1, 8-9)?

An appreciation of the importance and value of meaningful learning, authentic tasks, and cooperative approaches, along with the ironies in the inappropriateness of current practices, appears in Dewey's writings a century ago. He described differences that occur when "occupations are made the articulating centers of school life," including but not limited to "a difference in motive, of spirit and atmosphere" and a passage "from more or less passive and inert recipiency and restraint to one of buoyant out-going energy" (M1, 10). He observed a new community emerging in more progressive schools:

> Helping others, instead of being a form of charity which impoverishes the recipient, is simply an aid in setting free the powers and furthering the impulse of the one helped. A spirit of free communication, of interchange of ideas, suggestions, results, both successes and failures of previous experiences, becomes the dominating note (M1, 11).

Despite some of the intractable problems that plagued his day, he kept a positive outlook, for he saw in classrooms "people held together because they are working along common lines, in a common spirit, and with reference to common aims" (M1, 10). Even so, the educational reform he occasionally observed was typically not being

> done "on purpose," with a full consciousness that the school must now supply that factor of training formerly taken care of in the home, but rather by instinct, by experimenting and finding that such work takes a vital hold of pupils and gives them something which was not to be got in any other way. Consciousness of its

> real import is still so weak that the work is often done in a half-hearted, confused, and unrelated way. The reasons assigned to justify it are painfully inadequate or sometimes even positively wrong (M1, 9).

Dewey offered a similar account of vocational education in his day. While he acknowledged that most people work at a job in order to earn a living, he dismissed the need for job training as a justification for including it in the curriculum. Likewise, he made no argument that the school should ensure the nation's economic viability. Indeed, the real justification for vocational education was not even motivational, though that certainly could be a benefit, providing "a genuine motive...experience at first hand...contact with realities" (M1, 15). More important to Dewey was the notion that vocational education was "liberalized throughout by translation into its historic and social values and scientific equivalencies" (15). In turn, he added,

> It is not only that the occupations, the so-called manual or industrial work in the school, give the opportunity for the introduction of science which illuminates them, which makes them material, freighted with meaning, instead of being mere devices of hand and eye; but that *the scientific insight thus gained becomes an indispensable instrument of free and active participation in modern social life* (M1, 15-16, italics added).

More bluntly, Dewey thought that occupations taught in school should be "freed from all economic stress. The aim is not the economic value of the products, but the development of social power and insight" (M1, 12). He would have little patience with contemporary reform endeavors that attempt to motivate students to learn merely by introducing them to modern-day job skills and the world of work. Nor would he support the position that schools must help a country become or remain economically competitive. More recently, like Dewey, Peters (1981a, 47-48) noted that the sorts of jobs at which many people work, being "labor" rather than fulfilling "work," tend to be menial, trivial, boring and often unpleasant. In a word, this labor alienates workers and, at best, produces objects of extrinsic value rather than providing intrinsically valuable experience. It is hardly the activity around which an educationally meaningful curriculum or valuable experiences could or should develop, unless the covert aim is subversion of the status quo.

Neither our educational problems nor their proposed solutions are particularly new. The trouble is that we have yet even to begin to solve them. In fact, we have an inadequate understanding of those problems and of education itself. We also follow inadequate routes to thought about the aims of education and about the relation of the school to the community. To replace such wrong-headed thinking, we need a new way of thinking and a different perspective on educational reform. For Dewey, however, as for such educational reformers in the 1930s as the social reconstructionists and for such educational thinkers as Rousseau, the solution lay not in aligning schools more closely with the expectations of society—making a commitment, for example, to produce graduates who meet the expectations of employers or consulting the community about its vision for its schools. Rather the solution lay in a fuller understanding of education and the genuine needs of society and people, then revamping both social and educational practices and institutions so as to do justice to the fundamental nature of both. As with problems caused by dichotomous thinking, it becomes necessary to return to a reconsideration of underlying concepts and what they mean or should mean today—notably of education, schools, the person, and society and, for Dewey, the values expressed in democracy and growth.

Definitions of Education

The ideas of the English philosopher R. S. Peters have influenced thought about the nature of education in the last half of the twentieth century. Peters turned from questions of psychology and ethical and social philosophy to the study of education, and his concerns and commitments often parallel those of Dewey. The author of *Authority, Responsibility and Education*; *Ethics and Education*; and *Moral Development and Moral Education* as well as the editor of *John Dewey Reconsidered*, Peters' initial and best-known statement of his general views of education, though subsequently modified (1981a), was his Inaugural Lecture, "Education as Initiation" (in Archambault, 1965), on his appointment to the Chair of Philosophy of Education at the University of London Institute of Education. This account of education produced three criteria now widely accepted as characterizing education: that it is of intrinsic value, that it implies understanding and commitment to what is worthwhile, and that accordingly only certain methods that respect the conditions of genuine understanding and voluntary commitment are properly educational. In Peters' words,

> 'Education' involves essentially processes which intentionally transmit what is valuable in an intelligible and voluntary manner and which create in the learner a desire to achieve it, this being seen to have its place along with other things in life (in Archambault, 1965, 102).

Two elements in this conception of education immediately command attention: The process is essentially one of transmission, and the content is essentially intellectual. To many, this account may sound old-fashioned, other-worldly, removed from the practical realities which lead people to pursue an education, and frankly elitist—a fascinating claim given Peters' life-long moral and social commitments to democracy. For the moment, we note that a study of Peters would demonstrate that one should interpret neither "transmission" nor "intellectual" too narrowly.

By contrast, the contemporary American philosopher Maxine Greene propounded a broad, multidimensional conception of education that matches its diverse, daily and familiar usage:

> Education, in one perspective, is a process of initiating young people into the ways of thinking and behaving characteristic of the culture into which they were born. In another perspective, it is the development of a person from innocence to experience, from the confines of childish immediacies to the open plains of conceptual thought. In still another, it is the effort of a community to recreate itself with the rise of each new generation and to perpetuate itself in historic time (1973, 3).

These views of education in turn contrast with more starkly "realistic" and "practical" economic and vocational objectives defined in terms of employability and national economic competitiveness that have recently appeared. The aptly named Secretary's Commission on Achieving Necessary Skills (U. S. Department of Labor, n.d.), concerned with the transition from school to work, talks of "workplace know-how" in terms of foundation skills and the competencies all employees need to perform well on the job. Still others take a more client-centered view of education, talking of choice and Charter schools, schools whose mandates reflect the values of the local community or the parents or even the students—views that complicate notions of a common school or a common curriculum and conceptions of national norms, national testing and national standards.

A more comprehensive overview of educational aims came recently from Mark Holmes who lists them as follows:

> 1) an intellectual/academic purpose including the basic skills, introduction to the disciplines of knowledge, and the development of the aptitude for and inclination toward intellectual inquiry;
> 2) a cultural (aesthetic) purpose involving the induction of young people into our heritage of literature, music, history and general culture;
> 3) a social purpose involving the development of skills, habits and attitudes helpful for everyday life in our society as a family member, worker and citizen;
> 4) an expressive purpose involving the development of the ability and will necessary for self-expression in a variety of media for a variety of purposes;
> 5) a vocational and economic purpose involving the development of abilities and skills necessary for active, productive, independent adulthood;
> 6) a moral and spiritual purpose involving the cultivation of a sense of right and wrong and the development of transcendent goals (such as a sense of duty) which lie beyond material advantage (1990, 4).

Some may see this list as a sociological catalogue of the roles schools have come to play. But certainly, it broadens our way of thinking about education. We have come a long way from a conception of an education defined by its academic content and its concern with the fundamental questions of human existence—the meaning of life and the nature of truth, beauty and goodness.

Mentioning Dewey while revising his initial views, Peters (1981a, 32-34), argues that education is inherently associated with learning but that, over the centuries and for good reasons, the term evolved from a general sense of *upbringing* (applied even to animals) to—in contrast with *training* in some specific skills or for a specific occupation or role—the cultivation of the understandings, beliefs, and so values characteristic of the well-rounded person. On this account, the cognitive element remains central, and awareness becomes a key term, as the creation of meaning does for Phenix (1964). The advantage of this analysis, Peters suggests, is its insistence that serious disputes about education have essentially to do with what is to be learned, not just with factual information but with the kind of understanding and awareness to be cultivated. It has to do with the way a person thinks about life and the way a person lives. This purpose underscores a distinction between education and mere training and explains the traditional importance of liberal education and our concerns with indoctrination, with the teaching of religion and values, and with the possible teaching of false theories and positions regarding, for example, the Holocaust or evolution. Peters, like Dewey, reflects a concern that schools develop ways of thinking in their students. Dewey, however, concerned himself with developing a broadly conceived scientific way of thinking while Peters encourages different ways of thinking tied to relatively distinct forms of inquiry and knowledge.

Crucial from both educational and social perspectives is the matter of *how we are to settle* controversial questions. Problems of moral or character education must be close at hand, and concepts of authority and intellectual, institutional and parental legitimacy will surely be invoked. Pluralist, multicultural and democratic societies serve only to place these questions in relief.

A Democratic Foundation for Reform

For Peters as for Dewey before him, the key questions focus on the values at the base of educational reform, and for both, those values are democratic though Peters insists that this choice is a choice and others might choose differently. His statement of what those values entail is revealing:

> stress is placed on the social principles presupposed by the use of reason in social and personal life and the intellectual virtues implicit in the elimination of prejudice, superstition and error. Democracy is concerned more with principles for proceeding than with a determinate destination and aims of education in a democracy should emphasize the qualities of mind essential for such a shared journey (1981a, 49).

With the rise of fascist régimes in the first half of the twentieth century, the conformist pressures of the McCarthy era, a belief in laissez-faire capitalist policies, the subtle coercion of popular and mass culture, and questions about the influence of the media, we might well expect both of these philosophers to be concerned with such democratic values and ways of making decisions. Moreover, the two shared a commitment to individual well-being, a dedication to the growth of society, and a concern about the possible manipulation of society by special-interest and power groups, notably economic interests.

Two ideas emerge in Dewey's discussion of democracy. His first thought presents democracy as, more than a form of government, a means for developing human personality and relationships.

> Democracy is much broader than a special political form, a method of conducting government, of making laws and carrying on governmental administration by means of popular suffrage and elected officers. It is that, of course. But it is something broader and deeper than that. The political and governmental phase of democracy is a means, the best means so far found, for realizing ends that lie in the wide domain of human relationships and the development of human personality (Ratner, 400).

His second notion is that freedoms are guaranteed in order to ensure the growth of individuals and the possibility of their contributing to society:

> The modes of freedom guaranteed in the Bill of Rights are all of this nature: Freedom of belief and conscience, of expression of opinion, of assembly for discussion and conference, of the press as an organ of communication. They are guaranteed because without them individuals are not free to develop and society is deprived of what they might contribute (Ratner, 404).

Dewey made no secret of his commitment to socialist candidates in the 1930s and connected his position with a set of social values, notably equality and participation, embodied in a set of procedures making possible free, rational inquiry. As such, he like Peters saw democratic principles and procedures as "the best means that human wit has devised up to a special time in history" and asserted that "no man or limited set of men is wise enough or good enough to rule others without their consent" (Ratner, 401). He maintained, therefore, that

> The foundation of democracy is faith in the capacities of human nature; faith in human intelligence and in the power of pooled and cooperative experience. It is not belief that these things are complete but that if given a show they will grow and be able to generate progressively the knowledge and wisdom needed to guide collective action (Ratner, 401-402).

Dewey would almost certainly expect a renewed concern with schooling in difficult social or economic times, like those he experienced in the 1930s, when major political decisions must be made. As he noted, "The great movement for tax-supported public education had its strong impetus in the thirties of the nineteenth century, a time of general economic depression," and

> now, a century later, in the midst of a still greater economic crisis, there is again a period of a new educational demand and unrest. It is a time to take stock and to consider why and how the existing educational system has failed to meet the needs of the present and the imminent future (Ratner, 683-684).

In such situations, education and the social order become linked in an immediate and practical way—"The method and the aim of education corresponded to the conditions" (Ratner, 685). That way might express itself merely in terms of the need for jobs or vocational training or welfare programs but has more significant implications in the possible use of the schools as an agent of social criticism and reform, if not actual revolution. In these unsettling circumstances, an opportunity arises:

> When social life is in a state of flux, moral issues cease to gather exclusively about personal conformity and deviation. They center in the value of social arrangements, of laws, of inherited traditions that have crystallized into institutions, in changes that are desirable (Ratner, 761).

School, as we often say, forms future citizens. Literate, educated voters may question more than just their immediate economic problems: When a person begins thinking, Dewey once said, there is no knowing where it may end.

Without much change in the argument, we might also be talking now of the requirements of the information age, the information highway, the world wide web, the global economy, or national economic competitiveness. These topics well illustrate Dewey's notion of the sense in which lessons can be learned from history to help solve present-day social problems (SSCC, 14ff). Historical understanding can be a tool in an inquiry that uses what we know of past changes, especially the processes and forces that have produced current social and economic conditions, for they are processes and forces whose mastery would enable us to change or control their current effects (Ratner, 688-690).

So it is significant that Dewey's key educational suggestion for such uncertain and changing times is epistemological: "The real alternative to settling questions [and to stability] is not mental confusion, but the development of a spirit of curiosity that will keep the student in an attitude of inquiry and of search for new light" (Ratner, 689). That is, we need to understand social problems and use intelligence and what we know of past changes to frame, choose and implement possible solutions. For him, this educational challenge is a task appropriate to and worthy of the school. It is also an inherent part of the democratic commitment to dealing with social problems through discussion, thought and decision rather than force or blind allegiances (Ratner, 700-702). His underlying reasons are close at hand: "[D]emocracy is so often and so naturally associated in our minds with freedom of action, [we are prone to keep] forgetting the importance of freed intelligence which is necessary to direct and to warrant freedom of action" (L11, 220).

Though both Dewey and Peters make democracy a central value in their accounts of education, Peters suggests that Dewey offered a more sophisticated, fuller and richer, but also strange and nebulous account of the concept (1981a, 36, 73-75). Yet Peters' sparer account also embodies both procedural considerations of obvious epistemological and educational relevance and substantive considerations:

> To decide things by discussion requires truth-telling, respect for persons and the impartial consideration of interests as underlying moral principles. But it also requires the institutional underpinnings of a system of representation, public accountability and freedom of speech and assembly. If these are to

> be more than a formal façade that can be manipulated by interest groups, something approaching Dewey's passion for 'shared experiences', together with concerns for the common good, is also required to encourage widespread participation in public life. This suggests a revival of the almost forgotten ideal of *fraternity* to vitalise public projects as well as the ability to discuss and criticise public policy. Such criticism should be well informed and a rational attitude is required toward authority and its exercise (1981a, 37).

Freedom, commitment to the truth, respect for persons, impartiality and consideration of interests, being well informed, and a rational attitude—all of these are familiar educational values. Interestingly, though, they are rooted in (and perhaps then confined to) procedural considerations, the logical requirements of inquiry. One is not serious about pursuing the truth (that is, deciding on the basis of the evidence) if one fails to promote free inquiry (by providing access to relevant knowledge, information and arguments, and treating the reasons, evidence and arguments impartially) and actions needed for and based on the results of that inquiry. Neither, we might add, is one treating people as capable of thinking, choosing and deciding things for themselves ("respecting them as persons," we might now say) if one does not make free inquiry possible for them. The epistemology evident here may be based on an unstated account of human nature.

But what then do Dewey and Peters add to this seemingly formal, procedural conception? *Nothing less than a restructuring of society.* If we follow their arguments closely, we see that freedom becomes a central value, first as the grounds for intellectual inquiry and second in the social conditions required to support it.

Oddly enough, critics have accused Dewey of favoring a monolithic conception of society as reflected in a melting-pot view of the adaptation, absorption or "Americanization" of immigrants. Certainly Peters' criteria, rooted in the nature of inquiry and reflecting more explicitly recent constructivist views of epistemology, lead him to stress the value of tolerance—which we might extend to an acceptance of a multicultural society—and an openness to other points of view. If truth is the goal, one would want to open one's mind to ideas that might be true or insightful. But that is not all. Peters' precise wording is interesting:

> In a democracy this liberal view of the role of aesthetic and religious values in education is taken because of the importance ascribed to freedom and toleration and because of the reluctance to deprive the individual of possible ways of making something of himself provided by his cultural heritage (1981a, 41-42).

Dewey's wording is equally interesting, and it tends to undermine his critics. For him equality in a democracy means

> In short, each one is equally an individual and entitled to equal opportunity of development of his own capacities, be they large or small in range. Moreover, each has needs of his own, as significant to him as those of others are to them (L11, 219-220).

The extent to which the criticism of harboring a monolithic conception of society is consistent or inconsistent with Dewey's pragmatist epistemology makes for an interesting debate. But this aspect of Peters' position too needs to be seen in the context of his stress in moral education on the importance of initiating the child into the moral code and conventions of the society. Without this initiation, Peters, following Aristotle, believes the child will lack a genuine understanding of what a society is and a source of experience on which to exercise serious moral reflection. Similarly, Dewey maintained that as children learn to function in groups they learn important moral values that enable them to grow individually and contribute productively to society.

Dewey and Peters consider it a sham to mouth such values in social conditions that make their exercise unrealistic. Moreover, they agree that the likeliest cause of these undesirable conditions is economic. For Peters, the reasoning at root appears to be epistemological. It is insincere to talk of free inquiry if people are denied access to the understanding they need or the opportunity to act on their conclusions. But the ideas of insincerity and human needs suggest a moral foundation (indeed, an underlying conception of human nature) as well. Here we begin to gain insight into Peters' concern with respect for persons as an educational value. We see his interest in treating people as endowed with such characteristic traits or capacities as the ability to think, inquire, and know but also to feel, to be enriched by certain relationships and settings, and as Dewey might say, to grow.

This discussion of Peters becomes still more interesting if we think of preparation for democratic citizenship as one of the possible aims of education, a fairly conventional if often imprecise aim in Western societies. First, it complements a long-standing belief that the realm of ideas is or constitutes a democracy encouraging—indeed requiring—the open and free exchange and play of ideas, and so of the players (even those in school). Second, it suggests, as Dewey also did, an epistemological rationale based on the nature of inquiry for educational values and practices—the pursuit of knowledge also being a familiar educational value. Third, it leads us to inquire into the moral and social implications of these commitments, to ask what is the right or best or appropriate way for people to live. This brings us to moral education and to a conception of education as more than acquiring factual knowledge.

Dewey and Peters come into their own here, but they appear to separate on one major point: Dewey's idea of education as growth. Dewey, of course, thought of education as making growth possible. Despite his commitment to respect for persons and potential for each person to make something of herself or himself, Peters finds this idea too individualistic and, as the single end of all education, insufficiently cognizant of the fact that values are choices: "All such concepts of education are contestable, for what has happened is that an aim of education has been taken as the aim and incorporated into the concept of 'education'" (Peters, 1981a, 49). Given Dewey's extensive discussion of ethics and his view of ends as emergent, not fixed, this latter charge that Dewey seems insufficiently aware of the nature of value judgments is startling. A complete rebuttal requires a study of Dewey's conception of ends, a notion we must reexamine soon; here our concern is with the former charge that Dewey's notion of growth is too individualistic.

This much is clear: Dewey and Peters agree that human beings are by nature social. This explains for Peters the importance of learning social conventions and customs in moral education and presumably the importance of the moral, social and political ramifications of education. Here, though he links democracy to the conditions that make possible inquiry, Dewey is the more explicit social reformer, the more articulate exponent of a social democracy that is more than just formal or procedural and more than just a matter of occasionally voting for delegates charged with solving social problems. In thinking about school reform, we notice that democracy contains implicit suggestions about the principles that should govern the conduct of schools, notably about their nature as democratic communities, and about the underlying intellectual and moral aims of education. We will encounter these ideas later.

A Democratic Community of Individuals

Dewey and Peters are committed to similar epistemological and resulting social values, "the ancient democratic liberties of free inquiry, free assembly, and freedom of voluntary association" (Ratner, 426). In an essay written expressly for Ratner's collection of his writings, Dewey repeated an earlier argument for a right to work; insurance against accidents, illness and old age; and increased worker control of industry as "the essential minimum elements of an intelligent program of social reorganization." Suggesting a fairly rich conception of his ideal society as one rooted in the values of liberalism, Dewey wrote:

> The urgent and central question at the present time is whether the needed economic-social changes (with which legal and political changes are bound up) can be effected in ways which preserve and develop what was fundamental in earlier liberalism, or whether social control is to be instituted by means of coercive governmental control from above in ways which destroy for a time (a time whose length cannot now be measured) all that was best worth conserving in older democratic ideas and ideals: intellectual and moral freedom; freedom of inquiry and expression; freedom of association in work, recreation and for religious purposes; the freedom of intercourse among nations (Ratner, 422).

No doubt reflecting the economic and political realities of the 1930s, Dewey felt compelled to define those economic and social conditions that bestow dignity and security upon individuals and to advocate an openness in social decision making and the use of power or authority that places a premium on democratic civil liberties. He showed here a deep interest in the principles of dignity, security, power and authority, all of which schools typically share. While pragmatically appropriate for school principals, the implicit values of freedom and pluralism in this discussion have an epistemological justification for Dewey: Intelligent or scientific inquiry requires access to information, a free exchange of ideas, and a commitment to acting on what is known. These commitments encourage individual and collective growth and in turn imply a sense of community, a community of shared interests which for Dewey defined a *public*. The lasting, extensive and serious consequences of associated activity bring into existence a public, and "publics are constituted by recognition of extensive and enduring indirect consequences of acts [where the] only constant is the function of caring for and regulating the interests which accrue as the result of the complex indirect expansion and radiation of conjoint behavior" (Ratner, 375).

For his part, Peters espouses deeply Christian commitments which in his later writings Dewey shared, if at all, only in a faint way. In this light, consider Dewey's assertion that

> the divergence of philosophic systems instead of being a reproach (as of course it is from the standpoint of philosophy as a revelation of truth) is evidence of sincerity and vitality. If the ruling and the oppressed elements in a population, those who wished to maintain the status quo and those concerned to make changes, had, when they became articulate, the same philosophy, one might well be skeptical of its intellectual integrity (Ratner, 252).

Accordingly, for Dewey the object of moral inquiry like the pursuit of ends was not to discover pre-established, absolute moral truths, "as if there might be in the processes of human life meanings which are wholly cut off from the actual course of events" (Ratner, 252). Indeed, the door is at least open, in Dewey's opinion, to the possibility that moral truths might vary with historical or cultural contexts. We will examine this notion further when we discuss whether Dewey's ethical position is better described as utilitarian or instrumental.

This suspicion of absolute moral truths also appears to invite the element of choice that Peters wishes to emphasize. But the choice is to be intelligent and informed—limited, that is, by the facts, by what we know from past experience and inquiry, and by what we can reasonably foresee. The method of inquiry then need not guarantee fixed, settled and unchanging outcomes even though it may yield secure and reasonable results. So Dewey talked of "the only method by which alterations of political forms might be directed: the use of intelligence to judge consequences" (Ratner, 74). Thus, Dewey concluded "that temporal and local diversification is a prime mark of political organization, and one which, when it is analyzed, supplies a confirming test of our theory" (Ratner, 375).

In a democracy, we can presumably accept the diversity of states and of moral views generally. Even moral absolutists recognize this, though perhaps rather as the problem than as evidence of its solution. But what are we to make of the constant "function of caring for and regulating the interests which accrue"? Why is Dewey not simply guilty of some version of absolutism or the "naturalistic fallacy," an attempt to pass off some state of affairs as immune to moral question or a self-justifying basis for other moral conclusions—the very absolutism in morals he seemed to oppose? After all, he stated that the primary objective of "philosophic discourse" was to "clarify, liberate and extend the goods which inhere in the naturally generated functions of experience" and that its business was "to accept and to utilize for a purpose the best available knowledge of its own time and place." Conversely, he stated that business was also to "appraise values by taking cognizance of their causes and consequences; only by this straight and narrow path may it contribute to expansion and emancipation of values" (Ratner, 269-270).

The answer must lie in his epistemology, in the supremacy accorded to the method of inquiry—in short, in *the discovery in experience of what is genuinely good*. As implausible as this might at first sound, it does seem to be Dewey's position:

> Empirically, the existence of objects of direct grasp, possession, use and enjoyment cannot be denied. Empirically, *things are poignant, tragic, beautiful, humorous, settled, disturbed, comfortable, annoying, barren, harsh, consoling, splendid, fearful* [italics added]; are such immediately and in their own right and behalf. If we take advantage of the word esthetic in a wider sense than that of application to the beautiful and ugly, esthetic quality, immediate, final or self-inclosed, indubitably characterizes natural situations as they empirically occur. These traits stand in themselves on precisely the same level as colors, sounds, qualities of contact, taste and smell....*Any* quality as such is final; it is at once initial and terminal; just what it is as it exists (Ratner, 778).

Thus we can understand Peters' belief that Dewey placed less weight on choice than he would.

Like science, intelligent inquiry or the method of intelligence involves exploring the nature of these immediate experiences and notably—since improvement, responsibility, and control are our objective—their causes and consequences. But it also involves exploring what has happened in similar situations—elements derived from past experience, from history, which, in telling us at what price an enjoyment is bought, tell us much about it, and even about its enjoyment. "It is a matter of frequent experience that likings and enjoyments are of all kinds, and that many are such as reflective judgments condemn" (Ratner, 786). They are the subject matter of a body of knowledge about experience but not automatically or unreflectively to be pursued. At one point, Dewey even claimed that the immediate appeal of an experience often proves to be a reason to distrust it: "Not stern moralists alone but everyday experience informs us that finding satisfaction in a thing may be a warning, a summons to be on the lookout for consequences" (Ratner, 784).

Our exploration of the moral realm, then, is an exploration of the consequences of our choices and their effects on our lives. But in our exploration of the moral we are not alone any more than individuals work alone in science. Moral knowledge is no more a private matter than are other forms of scientific knowledge. In every domain, as advocates of the social construction of knowledge also point out,

> Knowledge is a function of association and communication; it depends upon tradition, upon tools and methods socially transmitted, developed and sanctioned. Faculties of effectual observation, reflection and desire are habits acquired under the influence of the culture and institutions of society, not ready-made inherent powers (Ratner, 390).

Epistemology, therefore, must refer to a social context, for knowledge itself is socially constructed, not the single achievement of an individual however gifted or insightful. It takes place within a tradition of inquiry, a tradition committed to the use of intelligence and to "getting it right." In ethics and social philosophy, Dewey felt that we really have yet to begin the quest:

> But some of the conditions which must be fulfilled if it is to exist can be indicated. We can borrow that much from the spirit and method of science even if we are ignorant of it as a specialized apparatus. An obvious requirement is freedom of social inquiry and of distribution of its conclusions (Ratner, 391).

To be human, to be social, and to be intelligent all go hand in hand, and all three are more like unfinished, on-going projects:

> To learn to be human is to develop through the give-and-take of communication an effective sense of being an individually distinctive member of a community; one who understands and appreciates its beliefs, desires and methods, and who contributes to a further conversion of organic powers into human resources and values. But this translation is never finished (Ratner, 389).

To be successful, these three projects—being human, social and intelligent—must also respect certain epistemological and ethical values that make possible growth rather than stagnation. They enable us to profit from experience by learning from it, seeing what it has to offer us rather than being blinded by or blind to it. For Dewey, these values are those that define a society:

> a number of people held together because they are working along common lines, in a common spirit, and with reference to common aims. The common needs and aims demand a growing interchange of thought and growing unity of sympathetic feeling (M1, 10).

We may see here, as well, a second important epistemological foundation for Peters' (1981a, 37) emphasis on fraternity and the role in moral education of initiation into the traditions of the group or the community—that is, for enculturation.

Talk of common aims, however, reminds us that aims may not be common. They could be individual and in conflict, they could be incoherent, or they could even be destructive of the society. These conditions prevailed, Dewey believed, in the society around him in the 1930s. Talking of the individual pursuit of private advantage and power in corporate capitalism as he perceived it, he observed that

> while the actions promote corporate and collective results, these results are outside their intent and irrelevant to that reward of satisfaction which comes from a sense of social fulfillment. To themselves and to others, their business is private and its outcome is private profit. No complete satisfaction is possible where such a split exists (Ratner, 408).

Worse still, the split produces not a public or a genuine society, a moral community or a community of interests, or even a genuinely rewarding situation for those who profited from it. Rather it produces a destructive "situation in which individuals do not find support and contentment in the fact that they are sustaining and sustained members of a social whole" (Ratner, 408). This kind of inconsistency or incoherence in society and in individual lives might be said to be irrational. The society cannot do what it exists to do: enable its members to work together at some common, shared project. In fact, they do not form a genuine society at all.

To some, Dewey's thought might seem again to suggest a society or an ideal of a society which is unrealistically harmonious, perhaps even devoid of inspiration for growth or new ideas. Not so for him, for diversity is crucial, as we have seen, and uniformity is neither a synonym for society nor a necessary feature of it (Ratner, 412). Moreover,

> The future is always unpredictable. Ideals, including that of a new and effective individuality, must themselves be framed out of the possibilities of existing conditions, even if these be the conditions that constitute a corporate and industrial age. The ideals take shape and gain a content as they operate in remaking conditions (Ratner, 415).

We might rather think, and talk, then, of a community of individuals, a community of shared interests and activities, rather than uniform ideas and conclusions—an ideal perhaps, but not an unrealistic one. In fact,

> the mental and moral structure of individuals, the pattern of their desires and purposes, change with every great change in social constitution. Individuals who are not bound together in associations, whether domestic, economic, religious, political, artistic or educational, are monstrosities (Ratner, 410).

The two elements—community and individuality—are essential, and it is fundamental that this community respect certain conditions, for

> it would be difficult to bring any more severe indictment against anything that calls itself a civilization, than the fact that it is not able to utilize the energy, physical, intellectual and moral, of the

> members who are desirous and anxious of rendering some kind of service (Ratner, 417).

These conditions help to give substance to Dewey's democratic ideal, especially the condition that society's ends not be fixed or permanent. As he indicated:

> When social "planning" is predicated on a set of *"final"* truths, the social end is fixed once for all, and the "end" is then used to justify whatever means are deemed necessary to attain it. "Planning" then takes place only with respect to means of the latter sort, not with respect to ends, so that planning with respect to even means is constrained and coercive. The social result is that the means used have quite other consequences than the end originally set up (Ratner, 432).

In summary, the concept of community, a community of genuinely individual members, looms large as an ideal in Dewey's account of democracy. There is an *epistemological community* of fellow inquirers and a *moral community* of fellow citizens. This account, then, raises questions about the status particularly of the moral community but also of ideals or ends generally. Clearly for Dewey moral knowledge, just like any other realm of human inquiry, is a matter of knowing causes and consequences, for these give us the possibility of intelligent control over our actions. In the case of morality, the causes and consequences flow from our actions and institutional arrangements, some of which we know facilitate group purposes and solidarity—that is, growth—while others frustrate them. This dual possibility seems to suggest the importance of two components of moral education: participation in the group's activities (as befits a social being) and critical reflection about them (facilitated only by our experience with others) and notably their success in achieving their ends.

But those ends are not fixed in advance. We learn the consequences of our actions as we experience the success of others as well as our own. That is to say, we experience ends as either fulfilling or not, promoting or frustrating growth or the ability to get from experience what it has to offer. In particular, we are concerned with promoting human understanding; with dignity, security, a decent way of living for individuals (Dewey talks of protection against illness, accidents and the consequences of poverty); and with our arrangements for reflecting on and, if necessary, amending our living conditions and institutions. Here we see the importance of the moral and epistemological commitments of the democratic community to "the ancient democratic liberties of free inquiry, free assembly, and freedom of voluntary association" (Ratner, 426) of individuals (civil liberties that Dewey saw enshrined in the American Constitution) and control over one's life. We see as well that the frustrating life results from an incoherence among ends or of means chosen and ends sought.

If these traits define any healthy community, then from them we can identify appropriate principles for guiding the reform of school communities, particularly since both the community as a whole and the school in particular aim for growth. In fact, we could test Dewey's ideas by asking if we as a community find these traits acceptable. A healthy school community, then, ought to promote four values: a sense of fraternity among its members; respect for their dignity, security, and well-being; respect for knowledge and so conditions that facilitate inquiry, reflection, discussion, and a disposition to action on the basis of knowledge; and a willingness to reconsider ends and means in light of new knowledge—in short, a commitment to a shared goal of learning and a life based on understanding and control, the central traits of a democratic community. The community's authority and the legitimate exercise of its power, therefore, rest with its claim to being genuinely educational rather than limiting and narrowing. Educational reform and the exercise of authority and power, then, must focus upon establishing an authentically growing, educative community.

A Scientific Ethics

We have already raised the question of whether Dewey is committed to some kind of naturalistic fallacy: the attempt to present some state of affairs, perhaps the nature of scientific inquiry or intelligence, as the basis for all moral judgments, itself immune to moral question, or a self-justifying basis for other moral conclusions, notably in this case the values of liberalism. We have also considered a reply in terms of human understanding, power and growth. Having considered Dewey's conception of the democratic society, individuality and growth, a more specific form of the question suggests itself: whether Dewey was a utilitarian, for ethical reasoning is in part a kind of instrumental thinking and the good community, the one that promotes growth, is good because it promotes states that are recognized to be rewarding. In fact, at one point we read:

> The problem of bringing into being a new social orientation and organization is, when reduced to its ultimates, the problem of using the new resources of production, made possible by the advance of physical science, for social ends, for what Bentham called the greatest good of the greatest number (Ratner, 449- 450).

Yet if we identify utilitarianism with the promotion of the greatest *happiness* of the greatest number, one would certainly be hard pressed to find passages in which Dewey avows anything of the sort. Further, as we have seen, he is clear that happiness, or at least pleasure, may be misleading: "It is a matter of frequent experience that likings and enjoyments are of all kinds, and that many are such as reflective judgments condemn" (Ratner, 786). As well,

> There remains a difference between narrow and partial ends and full and far-reaching ends; between the success of the few for the moment and the happiness of the many for an enduring time; a difference between identifying happiness with the elements of a meagre and hard life and those of a varied and free life. This is the only difference between materialism and idealism that counts (Ratner, 497-498).

Citing Mill, he asserted as well that the quality of a pleasurable experience is central to its assessment, suggesting at least a second or ultimate criterion other than pleasure itself, possibly culture: "The only test and justification of any form of political and economic society is its contribution to art and science—to what may roundly be called culture" (M10, 198). Thus,

> Everything depends upon the quality of the experience which is had. The quality of any experience has two aspects. There is an immediate aspect of agreeableness or disagreeableness, and there is its influence upon later experiences. The first is obvious and easy to judge. The [long-term] effect of an experience is not borne on its face. It sets a problem to the educator (EE, 27).

The likelihood that an experience will produce or facilitate further growth is sure to be one of Dewey's criteria of the quality of an experience.

While the instrumental element in his reasoning remains strong, his account of judgment is the key to understanding the injustice of ascribing utilitarianism to him:

> If enjoyments *are* values, the judgment of value cannot regulate the form which liking takes; it cannot regulate its own conditions. Desire and purpose, and hence action, are left without guidance, although the question of regulation of their formation is the supreme problem of practical life. Values (to sum up) may be connected inherently with liking, and yet not with every liking but only with those that judgment has approved, after examination of the relation upon which the object liked depends (Ratner, 786-787).

Likings and the experience of enjoyment, the immediate qualities of experience, then are *the subject matter of ethics*, not its ultimate test: *"Judgments about values are judgments about the conditions and the results of experienced objects; judgments about that which should regulate the formation of our desires, affections and enjoyments"* (Ratner, 787). The immediately satisfying is not necessarily ultimately satisfactory. We need a knowledge and understanding of the conditions that accompany these satisfactions, and especially of causes and consequences and what experience has shown us of their fulfillment. But the utilitarian question may seem to remain open. Surely all this shows is that not all pleasures are equally good; pleasure or a more lasting happiness may still be the ultimate good (when intelligently realized without undesirable consequences). But Dewey's point persists. Some other criterion is then needed to assess these pleasures even if the good life for human beings presumably in some sense satisfies. Such a judgment, then, is based in a conception of human (and so social) needs and fulfillment—conditions of growth, for "the ultimate place of economic organization in human life is to assure the secure basis for an ordered expression of individual capacity and for the satisfaction of the needs of man in non-economic directions" (Ratner, 453).

The conception of growth does the work in this system, together with, to give it content, human nature—for example, "the creative capacities of individuals" (Ratner, 454)—and society—in the creation of those interpersonal contacts and so those shared interests and relationships that generate a public, and with it just those problems ethics is to settle (Ratner, 371-372). These interests, rather than pleasure, help us understand which satisfactions are worthy of pursuit; we do not make decisions a priori, and we cannot develop them independently of experience of concrete situations. We may base decisions on previous experience, social science, and general knowledge of human relationships, but they are inevitably particular and distinct.

Only thus can the epistemological and social values of liberalism that express the interests of human beings—values central to Dewey's ethical writings and social commitments—bear concrete meaning. "Temporal and local diversification is a prime mark of political organization, and one which, when it is analyzed, supplies a confirming test of our theory" (Ratner, 375). Even the cherished value of liberalism itself (or at least its manifestations) seems to be historically conditioned, despite the fact that in a general way "liberation of the capacities of individuals for free, self-initiated expression is an essential part of the creed of liberalism" (Ratner, 454). The task of liberalism, therefore, is the "mediation of social transitions" as long as classes exist in a society, for

> The direct impact of liberty always has to do with some class or group that is suffering in a special way from some form of constraint exercised by the distribution of powers that exists in contemporary society. Should a classless society ever come into being the formal *concept* of liberty would lose its significance, because the *fact* for which it stands would have become an integral part of the established relations of human beings to one another (Ratner, 451).

This orientation also provided Dewey with the basis of an account of duty in spite of criticism that he was interested only in the individual (Neatby, 26). So we read,

> we have an interest in the peace of the world deeper and broader than that which self-interest dictates. We are bound by the history and spirit of our position in the world, and the law of *noblesse oblige*—the law that urges that every human being shall use his advantages and privileges not for his own enjoyment alone, but as well for the aid and service of his neighbors—lies more heavily upon us than it does upon any other nation that has ever existed

(Ratner, 512).

For Dewey, rather than happiness or personal interest taking the central place in ethical reasoning, emphasis should be on the process of judgment, the use of intelligence in making moral decisions—that is, on assessing the satisfactoriness of proposed solutions to objective public problems that arise because of the conditions of community living and their potential for frustrating or promoting human growth. Thus, Dewey believed there exists "no value except where there is satisfaction," but that "there have to be certain conditions fulfilled to transform a satisfaction into a value (Ratner, 790). These conditions involve using what we have learned about past experience as hypotheses to anticipate, plan and control future experiences and are the antithesis of dogmatism, conforming to established rules or the blind pursuit of previously established ends. They place the emphasis in ethics on intelligent practice rather than abstract ends or obedience—taking means, our present actions, seriously as beginnings, determinants of the future course of events—and so emphasize our responsibility for future events (Ratner, 790ff). In this way, morality becomes "scientific," despite our likely initial distrust of this suggestion. Dewey understood science here to signify "the existence of systematic methods of inquiry, which, when they are brought to bear on a range of facts, enable us to understand them better and to control them more intelligently, less haphazardly and with less routine" (Ratner, 632).

Can science then be said to pursue a fixed end? In a sense, yes. That end is truth or knowledge. But truth or knowledge has no precise definition—in the sense of a settled, established content—other than in terms of the methods used for its establishment. Instead, truth represents the best understanding available. Any other commitment to truth constitutes dogmatism or blind loyalty, holding to particular conclusions in spite of the evidence. So in morality one may dogmatically hold to a particular end however bizarre or perverse the consequences. As in science, there can be an end; the end may be said to be justice, the good or the right thing to do—for Dewey, growth or individual and social human well-being—but what these will be or entail depends at any given time on the circumstances, the reliability of prior understanding, and the quality of our inquiry, not on some a priori conclusion. Dewey, then, can be no more a utilitarian than an adherent of any other a priori moral system, and commitments to the pursuit of "the good" or "the truth" turn out to lack any definite content. Thus, the fundamental concerns for Dewey must become reliable knowledge, its use, and a reliance on intelligent methods of inquiry. His view of ethics may be said to be instrumental in its emphasis, but certainly not utilitarian.

Neither, then, could Dewey be said to think that all morality is *situational* in the sense of events being totally unique or without reference to funded knowledge and to the experiences of others (RP, 206). Similarly, if there is an element of "conscious meaning and hence of thought" in moral discourse, then it cannot be purely a matter of personal whim, "blind and arbitrary" (L8, 177). So, too, wisdom suggests the need

> to compare different cases, to gather together the ills from which humanity suffers, and to generalize the corresponding good into classes. Health, wealth, industry, temperance, amiability, courtesy, learning, aesthetic capacity, initiative, courage, patience, enterprise, thoroughness and a multitude of other generalized ends are acknowledged as goods (RP, 169).

"[T]he *value* of this systematization" lies in its shaping the way we think, suggesting "traits" that should be observed and "methods of action" that may help solve problems. In short, our learning and these concepts are "tools of insight," not "a catalogue of acts nor a set of rules to be applied" (RP, 169). They provide "a rule for the conduct of observations and inquiries, not a rule for overt action" (Ratner, 638), "because generalized science provides...questions to ask, investigations to make and enable...[a person] to understand what he sees" (RP, 168). Dewey declined to attribute moral deficiency and defeat to an abandonment of ethical absolutes. On the contrary, he observed that

> Our moral failures go back to some weakness of disposition, some absence of sympathy, some one-sided bias that makes us perform the judgment of the concrete case carelessly or perversely. Wide sympathy, keen sensitiveness, persistence in the face of the disagreeable, balance of interests enabling us to undertake the work of analysis and decision intelligently are *the distinctively moral traits*—the virtues or moral excellencies (RP, 164, italics added).

Indeed, without at least this much content, neither reasoned inquiry in science or any other domain nor any sort of moral education would be possible. We can learn from experience but we should learn intelligently, not blindly conform to it, merely repeating past practices, or supposing that we must begin anew in each situation. The challenge of education, which always carries moral import, is found in cultivating autonomous but responsible individuals who learn experientially, reflect comparatively, reason carefully, think sympathetically, analyze impartially, and judge wisely—people who live and think "scientifically." In later chapters, we shall see that the challenge applies just as directly to teacher preparation, demanding everything that education does plus the professionally specific abilities and understandings that enable a person to live and think scientifically in the classroom and school as well as in the neighborhood and broader communities.

In a summary that expresses the spirit of his approach to knowledge, including moral knowledge, and the significance he attached to all means, Dewey noted,

> It is usual to condemn the amount of attention paid by people in general to material ease, comfort, wealth, and success gained by competition, on the ground that they give to mere means the attention that ought to be given to ends, or that they have taken for ends things which in reality are only means. Criticisms of the place which economic interest and action occupy in present life are full of complaints that men allow lower aims to usurp the place that belongs to higher and ideal values. The final source of the trouble is, however, that moral and spiritual "leaders" have propagated the notion that ideal ends may be cultivated in isolation from "material" means, as if means and material were not synonymous. While they condemn men for giving to means the thought and energy that ought to go to ends, the condemnation should go to them. For they have not taught their followers to think of material and economic activities as really means. They have been unwilling to frame their conception of the values that should be regulative of human conduct on the basis of the actual conditions and operations by which alone values can be actualized (Ratner, 793).

The issue for Dewey was not abstract ends like happiness, the general good, or even growth. It involved considering the actual consequences of particular actions in concrete situations with the realization that the ends we achieve are the result of our actions and that we can make intelligent choices about them and take informed action. That the words *instrumentalist* and *pragmatic* should have been widely applied to his views is then hardly surprising. Because the instrumentality this morality emphasizes is intelligent inquiry, it has a particular appropriateness for education. Furthermore, it introduces into our lives an openness appropriate to a notion of growth, a flexibility broadening our interests and horizons. Thereby it avoids a "preoccupation with attaining some direct end or practical utility [that] always limits scientific inquiry" [and] "restricts the field of attention... [to] those things that are immediately connected with what we want to do or get at the moment" (Ratner, 637).

A Natural Community

Central to Dewey's thinking about philosophy, society and education, as we have seen, is his conception of the democratic community of individuals. In keeping with the rhetoric that civilization and civilized ways of living had become endangered in the build-up to the Second World War, but also because Dewey valued such ends as a "contribution to art and science" (M10, 198); culture, "the creative capacities of individuals" (Ratner, 454); growth, the quality of experience (EE, 27); "a varied and free life" in contrast with "a meagre and hard life" (Ratner, 498); "the needs of man in non-economic directions" (Ratner, 453); and even "what Bentham called the greatest good of the greatest number" (Ratner, 450), we might ask what community Dewey would consider civilized. We have already seen that such a community ought to be able to build on the capacities of its members and their willingness to contribute; that it ought to provide dignity and security, for example in the form of guarantees of employment (if only as a protection against poverty), some protections against life's misfortunes, and participation in planning its key activities; and that it should promote growth and a sense of fraternity among its members. Beyond these thoughts, Dewey affirmed that "the ultimate place of economic organization in [civilized] human life is to assure the secure basis for an ordered expression of individual capacity and for the satisfaction of the needs of man in non-economic directions" (Ratner, 453).

The really critical issue for Dewey, though, arose in the contrast between the social or political state and the state of nature:

> The distance which separates the code of intrigue and conquest permissible to nations from the code exacted of persons measures the significance for morals of social organization. The nations exist with respect to one another in what the older writers called a state of nature, not in a social or political state (Ratner, 509).

The constitution of the community is crucial, both in its fact and in its nature; for Dewey this made it imperative to establish as well a league or "federation of nations not merely in order that certain moral obligations might be effectively enforced *but in order that a variety of obligations might come into existence*" (italics added). He explained that

> "Conscience," that is the aggregate of the moral sentiments and ideas of man, is not the author and judge of social institutions, but the product and reflex of the latter.... They reflect criticism of the existing social order as well as approval of it.... The notion that it is possible to get bodies of men to act in accord with finer moral sentiments while the general scheme of social organization remains the same is not only futile, it is a mark of the subtlest form of conceit, moral egotism (Ratner, 510).

The establishment of the right democratic social order, then, calls for the use of intelligence and the principles of liberalism that make possible its exercise. It also creates the conditions or environment that make possible its exercise, or at least within which it can be exercised with a reasonable prospect of success. Not all social orders facilitate these conditions, nor is the task done once and for all, which makes it necessary for

> knowledge and habits...to be modified to meet the new conditions that have arisen. In collective problems, the habits that are involved are traditions and institutions. The standing danger is either that they will be acted upon implicitly, without reconstruction to meet new conditions, or else that there will be an impatient and blind rush forward, directed only by some dogma rigidly adhered to. The office of intelligence in every problem that either a person or a community meets is to effect a working connection between old habits, customs, institutions, beliefs, and new conditions. What I have called the mediating function of

liberalism is all one with the work of intelligence (Ratner, 452).

This effort to establish democratic social order also, in Dewey's view, calls for a knowledge of sociology, of social truths and principles, and a frank courage in acting on that knowledge—qualities the society, through its spirit but also its education system, can either encourage or not. To do less is to lose the opportunity to control one's living conditions and to build a better way of living:

> Needs, wants and desires are always the moving force in generating creative action. When these wants are compelled by force of conditions to be directed for the most part, among the mass of mankind, into obtaining the means of subsistence, what should be a means becomes perforce an end in itself. Up to the present the new mechanical forces of production, which are the means of emancipation from this state of affairs, have been employed to intensify and exaggerate the reversal of the true relation between means and ends (Ratner, 453).

In understanding the nature of a community, notably a rational and intelligible organization of its affairs, Dewey found it helpful to look back to an earlier era, believing that work and its purposes and results could be more clearly seen and understood then. This search of the past complements the claim that modern labor (unlike a craft) alienates, that it is unfulfilling as Peters put it, and thus has limited educational value. Dewey saw factories in contrast with the typical community or neighborhood since the latter were "the center in which were carried on, or about which were clustered, all the typical forms of industrial occupation" (M1, 7). Accordingly, he argued that one could learn discipline and character in these latter settings, including "training in habits of order and of industry, and in the idea of responsibility, of obligation to do something, to produce something, in the world" (M1, 7-8). But when the work changed, this learning disappeared, becoming mere vocational training in skills sought by employers:

> The entire industrial process stood revealed, from the production on the farm of the raw materials till the finished article was actually put to use. Not only this, but practically every member of the household had his own share in the work. The children, as they gained in strength and capacity, were gradually initiated into

> the mysteries of the several processes. It was a matter of immediate and personal concern, even to the point of actual participation (M1, 7).

The image that Dewey suggested is that of a transparent natural, organic, functioning whole, a social and not just an economic order—a process which, in its transparency and so comprehensibility, is educational. This was a tempting model for the school for it taught understanding, productive skills, and personal and social roles and responsibility and also revealed and questioned their justification, their raison d'être. Dewey's concept of growth remains inherent here.

Moreover, Dewey drew from the home, neighborhood, and factory a message for schools and for civic education, contending that school activities in "wood and metal, of weaving, sewing, and cooking" must be conceptualized "as methods of life, not as distinct studies." In other words, he believed that

> We must conceive of them in their social significance, as types of the processes by which society keeps itself going, as agencies for bringing home to the child some of the primal necessities of community life, and as ways in which these needs have been met by the growing insight and ingenuity of man; in short, as instrumentalities through which the school itself shall be made a genuine form of active community life, instead of a place set apart in which to learn lessons (M1, 10).

Furthermore, he argued that in the traditional school "the motive and the cement of social organization are alike wanting" and that

> The radical reason that the present school cannot organize itself as a natural social unit is because just this element of common and productive activity is absent. Upon the playground, in game and sport, social organization takes place spontaneously and inevitably (M1, 10).

As in the school, so in the community at large, Dewey saw otherwise no apparent reason to be involved, to be committed. There was no "society," no group of "people held together because they are working along common lines, in a common spirit, and with reference to common aims" (M1, 10), no fraternity or community spirit, no sense of belonging. As the teacher had to "keep" school and to keep order in it, to use the phrasing Dewey considered evocative (EE, 55), so then society keeps or imposes—or tries to keep or impose—order among its members. In so doing, it either ceases to be a genuine society or a community or shows it has already ceased to be one. Its members are alienated, we might say, or rather the state has become alien to them and their lives and interests. Similarly, its members cease to be free in just the sense that they no longer govern themselves, for their own understandings, ideas, purposes and imaginations no longer determine their actions (M1, 15ff). Instead, they must now show obedience or conformity to some external, imposed order just as at work they become "mere appendages to the machines which they operate" (M1, 16). Thus, life itself becomes artificial.

Dewey thought that the artificiality of life had affected every aspect of schooling and, therefore, suggested a

> change in the attitude of the school, one of which we are as yet far from realizing the full force. Our school methods, and to a very considerable extent our curriculum, are inherited from the period when learning and command of certain symbols, affording as they did the only access to learning, were all-important. The ideas of this period are still largely in control, even where the outward methods and studies have been changed (M1, 17).

This change of attitude surely leads to an equally profound and far-reaching reconceptualizing of society as well, a transformation from "the division into 'culture' people and 'workers'" whom they lead (M1, 18) into a democratic community. Dewey's conclusion is clear:

> It remains but to organize all these factors, to appreciate them in their fulness of meaning, and to put the ideas and ideals involved into complete, uncompromising possession of our school system. To do this means to make each one of our schools an embryonic community life, active with types of occupations that reflect the life of the larger society and permeated throughout with the spirit of art, history, and science. When the school introduces and trains each child of society into membership within such a little community, saturating him with the spirit of service, and providing him with the instruments of effective self-direction, we shall have the deepest and best guaranty of a larger society which

is worthy, lovely, and harmonious (M1, 19-20).

Conclusion

The public, we are told, looks to its schools for a variety of services, including, first and above all, the provision of safety and order. Then follow instruction in the basics, higher standards of achievement and traditional teaching methods ("What the Public Wants," 1995). And very likely we might add, a preparation for work and a sense of values. Only after a substantial reworking could we call these public desires the values Dewey espoused. For him a healthy school community ought to promote a sense of fraternity among its members; respect for their dignity, security, and well-being; respect for knowledge and the conditions that facilitate inquiry, reflection, discussion; a disposition to action on the basis of knowledge; and a willingness to reconsider ends and means in light of new knowledge. In short, the school community should nurture a commitment to a shared goal of learning and thinking and a life based on understanding and control, the central traits of a democratic community.

In Dewey's philosophy, then, we find an explicit project for school reform which takes as its basis the idea of the school as a community and a mirror of the larger community. But the school is more than a simple reflection of that larger community. It is a reflection of some of its possibilities and ideals, a reflection that highlights some features, brings them into relief, and subjects them to closer examination. The school community might even criticize that larger community and propose its reform.

As a community with a spirit of caring and fraternity, the school is concerned with the well-being and dignity, the quality of life, of its students. It also seeks to meet the parents' basic ethical (not to mention familial) concerns about providing a safe and secure setting—for example, a drug-free, abuse-free, supportive, welcoming and nurturing setting. It is concerned as well with fundamental educational values, the cultivation of knowledge and understanding, intelligent methods of inquiry, and wise ways of living. Dewey's challenge to other school reformers, then, posits two criteria: one concerned with the ethical treatment of children, the other with their educational growth. Both are relevant, as we have seen, to the exercise of authority within the school.

Dewey would also apply his two criteria to such specific programs as proposals for student work placements. But experience of the workplace alone would not qualify despite all that Dewey says about linking the school and the community and the school and work. British Columbia is explicit about the educational importance of assignments outside of school: "Work experience placement must have educational value and should relate to the goals and aspirations identified in a student's SLP [an individually developed Student Learning Plan]" (Province of British Columbia, 1994, 7). These criteria characterize a democratic community for Dewey, defining for the school a clear role in civic education in providing both socialization or initiation into democratic practices and critical reflection and—through its educational commitment to reasonable inquiry and action—making place for a program of social reform.

CHAPTER THREE

The School and Social Reform

> It is not whether the schools shall or shall not influence the course of future social life, but in what direction they shall do so and how. In some fashion or other, the schools will influence social life anyway. But they can exercise such influence in different ways and to different ends, and the important thing is to become conscious of these different ways and ends, so that an intelligent choice may be made, and so that if opposed choices are made, the further conflict may at least be carried on with understanding of what is at stake, and not in the dark (L11, 411).

> All education which develops power to share effectively in social life is moral. It forms character which not only does the particular deed socially necessary but one which is interested in that continuous readjustment which is essential to growth. Interest in learning from all the contacts of life is the essential moral interest (DE, 360).

Dewey described democracy in terms of epistemology, ethics and community—as an epistemological community and a moral community—including the fundamental values of liberalism as conditions in both communities that, as in schools, promote growth. Democracy thus becomes a central concept in Dewey's account of education, embodying its basic values. Indeed, one of his major educational works was entitled *Democracy and Education*. There is then a certain perceptive truth and an irony in Peters' characterization of Dewey's conception of democracy in *Democracy and Education*:

> [It] is a puzzling book, for there is plenty about education in it but

> very little about democracy—no proper discussion of liberty, equality and the rule of law, no probing of the problems of representation, participation and the control of the executive. The explanation of this is that Dewey viewed democracy mainly as a way of life; he was not particularly interested in the institutional arrangements necessary to support it. This way of life, he claimed, had two main features. First, it was characterised by numerous and varied *shared* interests and concerns. These play an important role in social control. Second, there is full and free interaction between social groups, with plenty of scope for communication. This is surely a strange characterisation of democracy (1981a, 73).

Actually, Dewey's volume does offer an account of legitimacy in the exercise of power and authority and of the purposes for which both schools and other social groups exist. Free and informed participation, the traditional values of political liberalism, are also key concepts.

Martin Buber also talked of community, voicing concerns about the impossibility of a genuine community if its size grew beyond certain fairly strict limits imposed by the restraints of face-to-face contact (Cohen, 1980, 335-356). Dewey (and Peters too at least by implication) was also concerned by the social problems created by depersonalization in modern industrial societies, notably the alienation of work. Indeed, *community* might be a better word than *society*, with interesting echoes of communication (DE, 4), though the idea of participatory democracy comes readily to mind too. In any case, the cultivation through education of the abilities and dispositions and in society of the conditions that make meaningful participation possible are certainly a key to both Dewey's and Peters' conceptions of democracy. Democratic values then imply not just provisions for voting but a commitment to a certain kind of social order— "a way of life," as Peters puts it. In Dewey's view, that way of life meant also a commitment to the "institutional arrangements necessary to support it" and to criticizing and reforming social conditions that prevent people from living such a way of life. School and society (another of his titles) cannot be separated: They are indeed school *and* society, not school *or* society or school *versus* society.

This partnership adds to Dewey's educational views by turning the thoughts of Chapter 2 upside down, then moves beyond them. That is, Chapter 2 examined aims the way many others like to talk about them:

What are the aims of education? What are the aims of schooling? What are the aims, objectives and goals of studying mathematics, music, gardening, history and so forth? Far from dismissing all aspects of these questions, Dewey knew he had to address the way others think about educational aims. Hence he discussed the aims or goals of "reflective thinking" (L8, 125ff); "self-control" (EE, 64); "the organized subject matter of adults" (EE, 83); and initiating the young into "the interests, purposes, information, skill, and practices of the mature" (DE, 3). Nor should we conclude that Dewey gainsaid what he wrote. For him as well as others, insights came from examining the aims of education from a traditional perspective. But much, he believed, could also be lost if aims were not developed along the lines he preferred.

He agreed with certain features of traditional thinking about educational aims and goals, but they required reinterpretation if they were to be understood properly—that is, contextually, fully and richly. Two results appeared. First, Dewey often wrote of the aims of education through the eyes of others but with his own distinctive flavor or content, and, second, he frequently wrote of the aims of education hoping to encourage others to reconstruct their perceptions of education.

When encouraging others to reconsider their views of education, Dewey sometimes went on to transform modes of thought and at other times to invert the form of the discussion while keeping his content and creating new categories of understanding. We can see where he turned the conversation in his direction as he spoke of the aims and goals of enabling the young to "share in a common life" (DE, 7), the aim of "an added capacity of growth" at each stage of moving toward the goal of growth (54), "the process and the goal of education...[being] one and the same thing" (100), and "all the aims...in education...[being] moral" (359). He moved beyond these thoughts, however, to claim that it is futile to attempt to "establish *the* aim of education" (111) and even that "education as such has no aims" (107). Yet since we already understand his concepts of experience, community, growth, continuity and education, we are not surprised to read that "a philosophy of education must make the social aim of education the central article in its creed" (L9, 203).

Dewey preferred to think of life not as fragmented but as a democratic whole with people, communities and institutions which nurtured it. Consequently, this chapter raises questions and proposes answers more in keeping with his way of thinking than with the way others thought. But it also develops ideas about what it means to educate for democracy, promote moral education, nurture the social and political ends of schooling, and pursue growth as an end. Each of these topics had in Dewey's mind a bearing upon the role of the school in social reform. He wove together these pieces of his philosophical fabric as he sought to show how "the school may be connected with life," how "all studies arise from aspects of the one earth and the life upon it," and how "all studies grow out of relations in the one great common world" (M1, 54). Concluding, he mused about how the personal and social and the various ways of examining different so-called educational aims all led to the subject of growth:

> Moreover, if the school is related as a whole to life as a whole, its various aims and ideals—culture, discipline, information, utility—cease to be variants, for one of which we must select one study and for another another. The growth of the child in the direction of social capacity and service, his larger and more vital union with life, becomes the unifying aim; and discipline, culture, and information fall into place as phases of this growth (M1, 55).

The Democratic End

Because Dewey became so closely associated with social and educational reform movements, we might expect at least some difference, perhaps chiefly in emphasis, with Peters when it comes to school organization and the conception of civic and moral education, notably in terms of what Peters calls—conservatively, it seems—learning my "station and its duties" (1981a, 39), or an initiation into the existing social order including the learning and practice of traditional social roles and conventions. But Dewey seemed to have recognized the potential of such claims for both good and ill, noting this possibility in school structures: "the ways in which activities are carried on for the greater part of the waking hours of the day [constitute] a highly important factor in shaping personal dispositions; in short, forming character and intelligence" (Ratner, 717). Importantly, however, this potential for shaping "attitudes, dispositions, abilities, and disabilities" exists in all institutions, including the school (717).

Thus democracy is needed for education as well as education for democracy. Children and adults cannot learn democratic living without experiencing it, and democracy depends upon education for its survival: "The best way to produce initiative and constructive power is to exercise it. Power, as well as interest, comes by use and practice" (Ratner, 719). School organization then is crucial in education to forming attitudes, dispositions, and abilities, both moral and intellectual, not just as an instrument for keeping order. In words Peters might have used, Dewey spoke of "initiation into the tradition [being]...the means by which the powers of learners are released and directed" (621). Exclusion from this initiation means what we might now call disempowerment or alienation and reduces an individual and social "sense of responsibility for what is done and its consequences" (719).

Moreover, recalling his notions of community, Dewey believed that "the democratic idea itself demands that the thinking and activity proceed cooperatively" (L11, 225). Talking of "freedom of belief, of speech, of the press, of assembly, and of petition...aspects of what I have called intellectual freedom, but which perhaps would better be called moral freedom," he added, "The ultimate stay and support of these liberties are the schools. For it is they which more than any other single agency, are concerned with the development of free inquiry, discussion and expression" (Ratner, 723). Thus, in school as in society, "In ultimate analysis, freedom is important because it is a condition both of realization of the potentialities of an individual and of social progress" (725). The school itself, in fact, is a society. The only question is of what kind, and the answer explains the appropriate structure and discipline of the institution.

Education for civic purposes, for citizenship or for making possible meaningful participation in society is hardly a new or surprising educational objective. But it is rarely the sole objective and could never be for Dewey. In part, Dewey resisted a reductionist view of education and democracy because such schooling risked being shallow and devoid of the intellectual content the freedoms of a democracy should make possible. He argued that "schools have also the responsibility of seeing to it that those who leave its walls have ideas that are worth thinking and worth being expressed, as well as having the courage to express them." He added,

> It is quite possible that in the long run the greatest friend of censorship, whether public and explicit or private and insidious, and the greatest foe to freedom of thought and expression...is the triviality and irrelevance of the ideas that are entertained, and the futile and perhaps corrupting way in which they are expressed (Ratner, 723-724).

The contemporary fear might be that without those "ideas that are worth thinking and worth being expressed" such a curriculum would become insufficiently academic.

We might also be concerned—and certainly in the domestic and international political context of the 1930s, we would have been—about losing the important values of individuality and self-realization. So we may be surprised by Dewey's thoughts on these latter values:

> it is said the end of education may be stated in purely individual terms. For example, it is said to be the harmonious development of all the powers of the individual. Here we have no apparent reference to social life or membership, and yet it is argued we have an adequate and thoroughgoing definition of what the goal of education is. But if this definition is taken independently of social relationship we shall find that we have no standard or criterion for telling what is meant by any one of the terms concerned. We do not know what a power is; we do not know what development is; we do not know what harmony is; a power is a power with reference to the use to which it is put, the function it has to serve. There is nothing in the make-up of the human being, taken in an isolated way, which furnishes controlling ends and serves to mark out powers. If we leave out the aim supplied from social life we have nothing but the old "faculty psychology" to fall back upon to tell what is meant by power in general or what the specific powers are. The idea reduces itself to enumerating a lot of faculties like perception, memory, reasoning, etc., and then stating that each one of these powers needs to be developed. But this statement is barren and formal (E5, 60).

Indeed, as we saw when he discussed communities, Dewey had no interest in creating a dichotomy of the individual and the social. This would be contrary to the entire spirit of his philosophy and his explicit claim that "individuals who are not bound together in associations, whether domestic, economic, religious, political, artistic or educational, are monstrosities" (Ratner, 410). Social problems of modern life result from the isolation of individuals from their institutions, from the isolation of individuals from one another, and from the incoherence that results. Dewey thought he saw in corporate capitalism a facet of social incoherence: the tendency of people to find "reward...not in what they do, in their social office and function, but in a deflection of social consequences to private gain" (408). Unfortunately, even when their

> actions promote corporate and collective results, these results are outside their intent and irrelevant to that reward of satisfaction which comes from a sense of social fulfillment. To themselves and to others, their business is private and its outcome is private profit. No complete satisfaction is possible where such a split exists (Ratner, 408),

and there is little true promotion of "inner contentment" (408) since such people's "beliefs and ideals...[are] not relevant to the society in which they outwardly act and which constantly reacts upon them" (409).

Thus Dewey's emphasis on democracy and his conception of it become central. For Dewey, the social and educational reformer, clearly dismissed the idea that the work of the school was simply to transmit the established and received values of a society he thought rife with economic, social, political and moral difficulties. Indeed, he dismissed even the idea that the school should transmit an uncritical, unreflective conception of its underlying values—among them democracy—and of its desirable features. This kind of unreflective schooling would defeat his educational aims of power and control, so it would be no substitute for a genuine education or for moral education. Moreover, the practice of democratic values or any other moral values is an inherent requirement of moral education. So, for Dewey, education for democracy and in a democratic setting was a way of engaging in moral education, academic education, individual self-fulfillment, and—ultimately and indirectly—social reform. These engagements are all expressions of the inevitable and natural educational mandate of the school.

The Moral End

Though some educational thinkers and reformers see a role for the school in socialization, cultural preservation or vocational preparation, schools are more commonly thought to have two possible major educational responsibilities: academic education and moral education (Goodlad, Soder, and Sirotnik, 1990a). These responsibilities may even (as we sometimes say of a liberal education whose immediate end is "to broaden the mind") subsume other possible roles.

The latter responsibility, moral education, may take the form of religious education, and in some jurisdictions like Québec, students or their parents can choose moral education as an alternative to religious education. People often consider academic and moral education separate domains, apparently because they see values as different from facts. So some jurisdictions excuse students from class during religious instruction and distinguish religious education from teaching about religion. Even so, while some claim moral education as the preserve of the home, others, perhaps concerned with building a common culture or a political community, see it as an important function of public schooling. In a multicultural setting, the very title *The Common Curriculum* reveals the latter concerns in Ontario, and we read that

> While schools do not have the predominant role in the development of values in children and youth, they do have a clear responsibility to address the values implicit in all curriculum. Schools cannot be value-neutral. The values that form the foundation of the curriculum described in this document are those that the majority of Canadians hold and regard as essential to the well-being of their society. These values transcend cultures and faiths, reinforce democratic rights and responsibilities, and are based on a fundamental belief in the worth of all persons and a recognition of the interdependence of all human beings and the environment (Ministry of Education and Training, 1993, 4).

The British Columbia School Act, as amended in 1993, on the other hand, is much briefer on the subject, stating that the purpose of the "school system is to enable all learners to develop their individual potential and to acquire the knowledge, skills, and attitudes needed to contribute to a healthy, democratic, and pluralistic society and a prosperous and sustainable economy" (Province of British Columbia, 1993).

In contrast to a common desire to separate an understanding and teaching of facts and values, religious schools and those with a commitment to programs of moral education argue that moral and religious values do and should permeate the entire curriculum and indeed the entire life of the school. The separation of values and facts was equally alien to Dewey's way of thinking about moral education, perhaps in the spirit of his opposition to either-or thinking and because he believed that "morals are as broad as acts which concern our relationships with others" (DE, 357). He found equally alien the notion that moral education could take place by learning to think about morality or studying the nature of moral reasoning, "ideas about morality," as he puts it, in contrast to "moral ideas." Crediting an unnamed contemporary philosopher, he observed, "'Moral ideas' are ideas of any sort whatsoever which take effect in conduct and improve it" (M4, 267). For him, as for certain right-wing and religious critics of some current attempts to achieve a moral neutrality in schools and to develop there discrete moral education programs, moral education pervades the curriculum; it is not and cannot be taught as a separate subject at school or anywhere else simply because neither values nor knowledge stand apart from the rest of life. Ultimately, he said, "the problem of moral education in the school is one with the problem of securing knowledge" (DE, 356). Hence, Dewey insisted that teachers were right in holding that they conduct moral education "every moment of the day, five days in the week" (M4, 268), and he proclaimed,

> The business of the educator—whether parent or teacher—is to see to it that the greatest possible number of ideas acquired by children and youth are acquired in such a vital way that they become *moving* ideas, motive-forces in the guidance of conduct (M4, 267).

Moreover, what we value and what we should value remain related to the objective, factual consequences of our actions, as we saw in Dewey's discussion of means and ends. So too they are related to what we do know and what we could know about consequences, and how we reflect. These points are part of the key to appreciating his scientific approach to the study of values and to understanding his conception of the evolving nature of ends. In the light of his scientific approach and its emphasis on consequences of behavior, Dewey's theory cannot involve a morality confined to intentions either: "The kind of character we hope to build up through our education is one that not only has good intentions, but that insists upon carrying them out" (M4, 287). It is inevitable on epistemological grounds, as far as Dewey was concerned, that thought and knowledge should influence action and it is morally and practically important since "the influence of direct moral instruction, even at its very best, is *comparatively* small in amount and slight in influence" (M4, 268). But when we realize that "all the aims and values which are desirable in education are themselves moral" (DE, 359), we see that moral education is effective to the degree that education is educative.

Morality and moral education, like other realms of interest, then inevitably become part of living (and, thereby, intrinsically a part of what schools do), more than a matter of intentions, and very much a matter of what we know. Education and moral education are of a piece, having to do with acquiring the right ideas, attitudes and habits as a basis for our actions. In fact, he asserted, "the qualities of mind...are all of them intrinsically moral qualities," including but not limited to "open-mindedness, single-mindedness, sincerity, breadth of outlook, thoroughness, [and the] assumption of responsibility for developing the consequences of ideas which are accepted" (DE, 356-357). Dewey obviously considered these important ideas about moral education, but he also considered moral education explicitly a legitimate and inescapable function of the school—at least of a public school, publicly established, publicly funded, and supported by the community:

> The moral responsibility of the school, and of those who conduct it, is to society. The school is fundamentally an institution erected by society to do a certain specific work —to exercise a certain specific function in maintaining the life and advancing the welfare of society. The educational system which does not recognize that this fact entails upon it an ethical responsibility is derelict and a defaulter. It is not doing what it was called into existence to do, and what it pretends to do (M4, 269).

Now it might seem that this statement would legitimatize a role for the school only in social or political aspects of moral education, notably civics. But for Dewey this is impossible, for moral development is also all of a piece. Moreover, all morality for us essentially social beings is, of course, social. As we saw in his remarks about developing the child's powers, "The child is one, and he must either live his social life as an integral unified being, or suffer loss and create friction" (M4, 269). Furthermore, each person is

> an organic whole, intellectually, socially, and morally, as well as physically. We must take the child as a member of society in the broadest sense, and demand for and from the schools whatever is necessary to enable the child intelligently to recognize all his

> social relations and take his part in sustaining them (M4, 270).

All of our roles are social, and every aspect of our education that contributes to our own development or growth—personal or vocational, intellectual or emotional, familial or civic, as leaders or as followers—contributes also to our expression of ourselves in these roles. In reality, however, the moral role of the school enjoys preeminence: It defines the school's very purpose. Consequently, Dewey believed that "apart from participation in social life, the school has no moral end nor aim" (M4, 271). Yet he cautioned that aiming too intently at developing moral children and youth, and thereby adults and citizens, and overlooking the relationship of character to knowledge and understanding could lead to harm:

> Moral education in school is practically hopeless when we set up the development of character as a supreme end, and at the same time treat the acquiring of knowledge and the development of understanding, which of necessity occupy the chief part of school time, as having nothing to do with character (DE, 354).

These strong claims—that morality is intrinsically connected to the knowledge, understanding, and sociality of schooling—so inhere in the conception of persons as social beings that an independent notion of individual development is impossible. Thus, Dewey discussed the school in terms also of social reform, the kind of society worth constructing or living in. For although persons are social, it does not follow that the existing social relationships in a society determine the kind of person one ought to be. But what then is the basis for the ideal by which social relationships are to be judged? How do we know life in one society or one set of social structures is preferable to another or whether, historically, reform movements have led to improvements in the human condition?

Dewey would advise us to look around at what has resulted, at the causes and consequences of our acting as we do. This is the scientific aspect of his ethics. With a sufficiently strong "impulse toward justice, kindliness, and order," he became convinced that both formal and informal education could reduce "the disorder, cruelty, and oppression" that existed in his lifetime (L9, 32). What then is the role of society and schooling in reducing these undesirable features of society? As Dewey observed,

> Ours is the responsibility of conserving, transmitting, rectifying and expanding the heritage of values we have received that those who come after us may receive it more solid and secure, more widely accessible and more generously shared than we received it (L9, 57-58).

Here again we might expect notions of growth and so personal fulfillment to be lurking in the background. Are people's lives, we should ask, growing and being enriched in society?

THE GOAL AND TEST OF GROWTH. Dewey's conception of the person as a social being, a member of a community, is not out of keeping with his organic orientation and denies legitimacy to the metaphysical question, "What entity enters into these social relations?" or the linguistic question, "What meaning has this attribution of the social to human beings if it has no contrast?" or the pseudo-historical question, "What was man like earlier in the pre-social state of nature?" Moreover, Dewey believed that "the self is not something ready-made, but something in continuous formation through choice of action" (DE, 351). Thus we have seen his concern to preserve an account of individuality within his ideas of self and society. Interestingly enough, Dewey talked of one whose education has failed in the social respect: "Instead of caring for himself and for others, he becomes one who has himself to be cared for" (M4, 271), someone whose life is still social but who plays no active or full social role. The language (reminiscent of his description of the social incoherence of the capitalist whose privately held selfish and publicly articulated altruistic values conflict) suggests that education does not create our social roles but only how we will play them. Education, in other words, decides how we will act within our roles, how well we will live, and whether that life will be rich and fulfilling.

By way of illustration, we can return to the common educational objective of the full and harmonious development of the individual, noting with Dewey that it seems to make no reference to the social and so is deficient:

> But if this definition be taken independently of social relationship we have no way of telling what is meant by any one of the terms employed. We do not know what a power is; we do not know what development is; we do not know what harmony is. A power is a

> power only with reference to the use to which it is put, the function it has to serve (M4, 271).

Yet within the Western tradition, human powers of contemplation, worship, or self-perfection only occasionally include this social interpretation—this notion of social service, an "interest in community welfare" (M4, 274). It is an idea that, nevertheless, loomed large in Dewey's social conscience and political actions, perhaps reflecting his early religious experience. Today, on the other hand, such service need not have religious connotations, being a common orientation for some who enter certain professions or vocations.

Continuing the theme of potential incoherence or harmony in one's way of living (Ratner, 408) and thinking of society as "a number of people held together because they are working along common lines, in a common spirit, and with reference to common aims" (M1, 10), we find two key values emerging: habits of service and healthy growth. Both of these values are reflected in Dewey's general comment that we accept "the child as a member of society in the broadest sense, and demand for and from the schools whatever is necessary to enable the child intelligently to recognize all his social relations and take his part in sustaining them" (M4, 270).

We notice here how Dewey resisted considering these as independent values introduced extraneously. The crucial point in any justification of values is his contrast of the formal, the arbitrary, the ad hoc, and the merely conventional to the functional, that which, like the rules of a game, facilitates the activity. Even the traditional school virtues—"promptness, regularity, industry, non-interference with the work of others, faithfulness to tasks imposed"—came in for Dewey's criticism, not because he opposed these virtues per se but because the traditional school had stripped learning and values from life and had concocted a system of discipline apart from the family and the neighborhood, apart from social living in the real world: "Just in so far as the school system is itself isolated and mechanical, insistence upon these moral habits is more or less unreal, because the ideal to which they relate is not itself necessary" (M4, 273-274). Connected to the life of the child as a future voter, subject, husband, wife, mother, father, worker and neighbor, many of these virtues, when translated from the formal to the functional, help develop and manifest "habits of serviceableness" (270). Thus, life duties and related virtues "flow from the very nature of the social life" (274).

> Interest in community welfare, an interest that is intellectual and practical, as well as emotional—an interest, that is to say, in perceiving whatever makes for sociál order and progress, and in carrying these principles into execution—is the moral habit to which all the special school habits must be related if they are to be animated by the breath of life (M4, 274).

But we must wonder whether this position is enlightening or circular. Is there, for instance, any independent test of whether an established social activity (say, traditional school practices and their associated virtues) is worth supporting? Is there any way of identifying an authentic, thriving, healthy community whose values are "animated," in Dewey's religious metaphor, "by the breath of life" (M4, 274)? The answer cannot be simply a reference to the quality of life of individuals within the community, for they are by nature essentially social beings. But this is part of the answer nevertheless, for the goal of "growth" is both social and individual:

> I can only say that the introduction of every method that appeals to the child's active powers, to his capacities in construction, production, and creation, marks an opportunity to shift the centre of ethical gravity from an absorption which is selfish to a service which is social (M4, 277).

The clue to Dewey's answer, however, lies in the words "flow from the very nature of social life" (M4, 277) for they suggest for him concepts of thriving and dying—that is, growth. It would be tempting to add richness, that quality of life which goes beyond immediate enjoyment. Dewey certainly had in mind such an ideal of society. The model here is the family, "the very nature of the social life in which the family participates and to which it contributes" (274); the contrast is the traditional school régime. Reading aloud, a traditional enough school activity, Dewey suggested, is typically a pointless activity (since everyone has the text and can read it perfectly well alone), and it encourages destructive motives and habits (watching for others' errors and taking advantage of them) and destroys or marginalizes the central and inherent interest of the activity (in this case, reading aloud or even reading). In short, this reading aloud is counter-productive. The only thing worse than the extrinsic and mechanical means required to keep children at this task is the possibility that they may eventually come to take it, or such tasks generally, as normal and reasonable both in school and in life.

Now what does this argument show? Dewey hoped it would show that such reading aloud is inherently inconsistent or contradictory. Here we have a negative test of the viability of an activity or a custom or a practice, and this example of teaching fails it. The teaching does not flow from the nature of social life and fails to add to its richness, including the growth of individual students and the class. But what if we consider an activity that is not inherently contradictory but just trivial or silly, or one that might be though we are not sure? In view of his commitment to the democratic way of life, Dewey resisted any suggestion that there is one narrow, single best way of living for every person. Thus the list of characteristics of a desirable or healthy social life, his conception of growth, is both important and interesting in its form, its variety, and its flexibility for both students and teachers.

At various points in discussing this theme, Dewey made the following five assertions about the desirable features of social life, including life at school. Each child (1) develops "an appreciation, for its own sake, of the social value of what he has to do, because of its relations to life" rather than thinking that what he does is important because of the external rewards received (M4, 276); (2) learns to rejoice in his strengths rather than in the fact that he is stronger than others in some respects (276-277); (3) learns that something "is worth doing in itself" rather than thinking that everything is always a preparation for something else or for the future (277); (4) acquires an "enlightened and trained capacity to carry forward those values which in other conditions and past times made those experiences worth having" rather than developing an emotional readiness to assimilate uncritically the surrounding environment (278); and (5) enjoys a personal "power [and] opportunity for reciprocity, cooperation, and positive personal achievement" rather than experiencing "a training infected with formality, arbitrariness, and an undue emphasis on failure to conform" (278).

What have these assertions in common? What do we learn from them about a desirable or healthy life in any social setting? The ideas that come to mind are again richness of experience, thriving and growing—and not comparatively but intrinsically. The reference point seems to be the nature of healthy growth, which happens to be precisely Dewey's position. He concentrated on human nature and the use of human reason, the resulting morality passing beyond obedience to an imposed, external code to self-realization and self-fulfillment—the realization of the self without selfish-realization, for this would only lead to a further "lack of cultivation of the social spirit [and to] individualistic motives and standards" (M4, 276). So, the child's "natural desire to give out, to do, to serve" (275) needs to be cultivated and "flow from the very nature of social life in which the family participates and to which it contributes" (274). Directly or indirectly, and most successfully, it appears, many institutions today draw upon this "natural desire" and channel it into service learning projects and the learning of habits that manifest themselves in additional service.

In order to open doors to growth and to keep them open for students, the teacher must be something of "a true psychologist," "a true moralist" and, thereby, possess "the essential qualifications of the true educationist" (PN, 5). These qualities and abilities need to come together in the educator since everyone

> grants that the primary aim of education is the training of the powers of intelligence and will—that the object to be attained is a certain quality of character. To say that the purpose of education is "an increase of the powers of the mind rather than an enlargement of its possessions"; that education is a science, the science of the formation of character; that character means a measure of mental power, mastery of truths and laws, love of beauty in nature and art, strong human sympathy, and unswerving moral rectitude; that the teacher is a trainer of mind, a former of character; that he is an artist above nature, yet in harmony with nature, who applies the science of education to help another to the full realization of his personality in a character of strength, beauty, freedom—to say this is simply to proclaim that the problem of education is essentially an ethical and psychological problem. This problem can be solved only as we know the true nature and destination of man as a rational being, and the rational methods by which the perfection of his nature may be realized (PN, 4).

In this overall philosophical context, Dewey made two critical comments concerning pedagogy and the pedagogue. First, regarding the positive test for developing the fullest potential of the student he observed:

> To the educator, therefore, the only solid ground of assurance that he is not setting up artificial or impossible aims, that he is not using ineffective and perverting methods, is a clear and definite knowledge of the normal end and the normal forms of mental action (PN, 4-5).

By contrast, he asserted,

> Every aim proposed by the educator which is not in harmony with the intrinsic aim of human nature itself, every method or device employed by the teacher that is not in perfect accord with the mind's own workings, not only wastes time and energy, but results in positive and permanent harm; running counter to the true activities of the mind, it certainly distorts and may possibly destroy them (PN, 4).

These ideas, as significant as they appear, take on even greater importance as we discuss the preparation of future teachers and the schools of the future in later chapters.

THE SOCIAL AGENDA IN THE CURRICULUM. As a social reformer, Dewey kept his social objectives in education always in evidence, frankly describing the educational potential he saw for reforming society through the thoughtful reflection that characterizes education. He publicly urged educators and others to use their offices to help society find "a better way." As we noted when we discussed "the human problems curriculum," this interest in problematic social questions defines a natural starting point for the curriculum, combining student interest with important content while providing a reason and a plan for drawing on the collective wisdom of the traditional disciplines. Of these disciplines or the subject matter, he said,

> *A study is to be considered as a means of bringing the child to realize the social scene of action.* Thus considered it gives a criterion for selection of material and for judgment of values. We have at present three independent values set up: one of culture, another of information, and another of discipline. In reality, these refer only to three phases of social interpretation. Information is genuine or educative only in so far as it presents definite images and conceptions of materials placed in a context of

> social life. Discipline is genuinely educative only as it represents a reaction of information into the individual's own powers so that he brings them under control for social ends. Culture, if it is to be genuinely educative and not an external polish or factitious varnish, represents the vital union of information and discipline. It marks the socialization of the individual in his outlook upon life (M4, 279).

Each of the various disciplines then "represents materials arranged with reference to some one dominant typical aim or process of the social life" (M4, 280).

In geography, for instance, "the ultimate significance of lake, river, mountain, and plain is not physical but social; it is the part which it plays in modifying and directing human relationships" (281). The significance of history was still more obviously social to Dewey; thus he stated that "everything depends, then, upon history being treated from a social standpoint" and added,

> the study of history can reveal the main instruments in the discoveries, inventions, new modes of life, etc., which have initiated the great epochs of social advance; and it can present to the child types of the main lines of social progress, and can set before him what have been the chief difficulties and obstructions in the way of progress (M4, 282-283).

Such a position evidently presupposes a way of identifying at least "great epochs," the "main lines of social progress," and "the chief difficulties and obstructions." Dewey's criteria require the identification of social problems and solutions that influence the ability of community members to live fulfilling lives and to grow. His examples (influenced in part by the Depression and preparations for the Second World War) include war as a way of solving disagreements and the health and social consequences of poverty. His theme remains our capacity but unwillingness to find and make use of a better way through the serious study of causes and consequences. Today, too, we might usefully consider proposals for new curricula concerned with war and conflict resolution, health issues and economic inequities. We could also consider curricula that address racial and gender inequities, multiculturalism, employability, the environment and, most Deweyan of all, sustainable growth.

Such topics, Dewey would say, cannot be taught or discussed without raising value questions. This is what makes education moral education: "When a study is taught as a mode of understanding social life it has positive ethical import" (M4, 283), filling it with "moral ideas," developing "habits of social imagination and conception" (rather than "ideas about morality" or the preaching of specific virtues) and developing, as well, character and disposition. While one could take this social approach to subject matter narrowly to mean that business arithmetic is more educationally important (or more motivating) than number theory, given Dewey's emphasis on "funded knowledge" and especially in the context of his examples from history and geography, this is clearly far from his intention. Even though he criticized teaching a mathematics extracted from social life as "unduly abstract, even upon the purely intellectual side [and as being] an end in itself" (284), he did not discourage the study of any field of mathematics and stressed only that the "social realities" and "sociological" features of the field need to be recognized and brought into the study (284).

On the other hand, his program of social reform through moral education did include an argument for expanding our conception of the moral, for he believed it did "not designate a special region or portion of life [or a single subject in the curriculum]. We need to translate the moral into the conditions and forces of our community life, and into the impulses and habits of the individual" (M4, 291). We also need to abandon those views of moral education that have been "too narrow, too formal, and too pathological" (284). Further, he urged that people understand the simplicity and the significance of the moral by understanding that "ultimate moral motives and forces are nothing more or less than social intelligence—the power of observing and comprehending social situations —and social power—trained capacities of control—at work in the service of social interest and aims" (285). All things considered, it is no wonder Dewey largely dismissed traditional instruction in the virtues and the instilling of moral sentiments as "goody-goody" and ineffectual in contrast to the "moral trinity" of the school: "social intelligence, social power, and social interests" (285). Moral education extends beyond a mere subject; it is a process of living, learning, thinking and behaving wherever life is educative. So in his mind the school that engages in education pure and simple is on the right track in moral education and social reformation:

> In so far as the school represents, in its own spirit, a genuine community life; in so far as what are called school discipline, government, order, etc., are the expressions of this inherent social spirit; in so far as the methods used are those that appeal to the active and constructive powers, permitting the child to give out and thus to serve; in so far as the curriculum is so selected and organized as to provide the material for affording the child a consciousness of the world in which he has to play a part, and the demands he has to meet; so far as these ends are met, the school is organized on an ethical basis. So far as general principles are concerned, all the basic ethical requirements are met. The rest remains between the individual teacher and the individual child (M4, 285).

If it is to be successful, of course, this ethical education must direct the educator's understanding of child psychology and development: "[T]he true moralist" and "the true psychologist" must come together and form "the true educationist." We require a system of schooling (and so a preparation for teachers) that allows children to develop their powers; to channel their spontaneous impulses and instincts into a "*force* of character" (M4, 287); and to cultivate rather than an abstract intellectual understanding, the judgment, discrimination, and intelligence through practice that encourages them to direct their powers wisely. The system must also demonstrate a sensitive, flexible, sympathetic and tactful responsiveness, together with a base of accurate, relevant, practical knowledge of social forces.

This curriculum for moral education, Dewey believed, leads to social reform which is neither arbitrary and unfounded, lacking in legitimacy and intellectual rigor, nor transcendental, sectarian, private or removed from the world's daily concerns. His explanation for the value of moral education is his explanation of education generally. Morality, the question of how we should live, continually influences our daily life which is by nature social; nor can our answers separate themselves from what we know about our choices and their consequences. His positive arguments—concerned with "social intelligence," our knowledge of the conditions that promote individual and social growth, and our disposition to act on what we know—duplicate those we found in his account of discipline, authority and freedom. We are to use this same social intelligence in planning the structure of the school community as a caring, inquiring, learning democracy and "to make each one of our schools an embryonic community life" (M1, 19).

Dewey called his first major book on education *Democracy and Education* and it is easy to see why. In his conception of democracy, intellectual education, moral education, self-fulfillment and social reform come together in an account of human growth. In his account, moral values permeate the curriculum. They do not compete with intellectual values, but they anchor those intellectual values in the concerns of daily life, transforming their usual intrinsic value. Here Dewey offered a further test for proposed school reforms: Do they address significant social problems in a way that makes use of our collective moral wisdom, encourages critical and informed reflection about their causes, consequences, and possible solutions, and then leads to plans of action?

We find ourselves now better able to see that those critics who accused Dewey and his disciples of undermining traditional academic values were not completely off the mark. Dewey's arguments did, in fact, diminish the importance of the disciplines. Despite his stress on funded knowledge, he refused to value knowledge for its own sake. Instead, he valued it for the kind of beings we are, social beings who live by what we know and with others engaged in the same adventure. While his critics often tend to imprecise analyses, they draw attention to a debate that helps us focus more clearly and accurately on a central feature of his thinking.

The Social and Political Ends

Dewey's conceptions of democracy, community, morality and education and their inter-relationships led logically to his interest in social reform, school authority and cultural achievement as an outgrowth of promoting the ends of the school. Here we find him viewing education through a socio-political lens and showing how education forms the thinking and habits of students as they interact in their epistemological and ethical communities and understand more fully that they are potentially if not yet full members of a larger social and political community.

SOCIAL REFORM. One can expect any curriculum that sets out to reflect on existing social problems and the search for alternatives to disturb the community. But for Dewey such disturbances were beside the point. First, he found no separate, non-social notion of individual self-fulfillment, development or growth which would make possible an alternative to social involvement. Second, in any case,

> It is not whether the schools shall or shall not influence the course of future social life, but in what direction they shall do so and how. In some fashion or other, the schools will influence social life anyway. But they can exercise such influence in different ways and to different ends, and the important thing is to become conscious of these different ways and ends, so that an intelligent choice may be made, and so that if opposed choices are made, the further conflict may at least be carried on with understanding of what is at stake, and not in the dark (L11, 411).

A school is, of course, part of its community, not a community apart, and changes in the school are changes in the community. Children's lives, therefore, do not begin and end at the school door.

Third, Dewey mentioned another consideration pertinent to any educational mandate concerned with promoting understanding: "There is much that can be said for an intelligent conservatism. I do not know anything that can be said for perpetuation of a wavering, uncertain confused condition of social life and education" (Ratner, 695). In short, in social and political education as in moral education, Dewey saw the question not as whether schools should be involved but as how.

Dewey knew that people invariably argue over their schools. Some want them merely to mirror prior social changes; others want them to mirror current social trends; still others want them to be conscious contributors to the development of society. In the latter group, some support indoctrinating students in valued ideas and dispositions while others resist this approach because they consider it anti-educative (L11, 408ff). Here Dewey faced, as we do today, one persistent dilemma confronting the public school, especially when it is conceived as the common school, one made worse in the absence of social consensus. As a public institution, publicly funded and publicly supported, to what extent can it—should it, dare it—do other than explicitly transmit the conventions and values of its society? What is its mandate? What are its moral responsibilities? This dilemma also faces every teacher, Dewey believed. Yet Dewey long resisted the objections and pessimism or realism of many of his contemporaries. Instead, he chided them for their lack of confidence in the power of education:

> But I am surprised when educators adopt this position, for it shows a profound lack of faith in their own calling. It assumes that education as education has nothing or next to nothing to contribute; that formation of understanding and disposition counts for nothing; that only immediate overt action counts and that it can count equally whether or not it has been modified by education (L11, 412).

Dewey's solution seemed all the more objectionable when critics read it as a radical approach, stressing dispositions and action as much as understanding. His own words seem at times to invite this criticism:

> The problem will be to develop the insight and understanding that will enable the youth who go forth from the schools to take part in the great work of construction and organization that will have to be done, and to equip them with the attitudes and habits of action that will make their understanding and insight practically effective (L11, 411).

Yet, on closer examination, Dewey's ideas are less radical than those of the social reconstructionists who surrounded him in the 1930s, for he talked of the importance of tradition and funded knowledge and the inevitability that "schools do follow and reflect the social 'order' that exists [and] tend to lag behind" (L11, 409, 408). In fact, citing Burnett (1979; 1988), Pratte (1992) thinks that

> Dewey gradually lost faith in both the motivation and the ability of teachers to change the character of American schooling. He saw clearly that teachers were docile, under the control of school boards and school managers, and expressed little or no desire to become formidable agents committed to a radical reform of education. By the end of the 1920s, Dewey would admit, if pressed, that he was no longer optimistic about pedagogical reform per se or that he believed [sic] in the power of schools and schooling to reform society (142).

In any case, immediately following the seeming radical call to action above, Dewey observed, "What is suggested does not mean that the schools shall throw themselves into the political and economic arena and take sides with some party there" (L11, 412). But he clung to his belief that the school should be "a necessary [but] not a sufficient condition [of] forming the understanding and the dispositions that are required to maintain a genuinely changed social order" (L11, 414). While he agreed that "the school cannot by itself alone *create or embody this idea* [for example, "equality of opportunity for all, independent of birth, economic status, race, creed, or color"]," he stressed that "the least it can do is to *create individuals* who understand...[and] who cherish it warmly in their hearts" (L11, 416; italics added). If we are to create individuals with warm hearts for the liberal values, we must first create schools that are "the constant nurse of democracy" (L11, 416).

More precisely, Dewey said, in the American democratic context, schools have been given a special responsibility because the faith Americans have in "education has been grounded in the belief that without education the ideal of free and equal opportunity is an idle fantasy; that of all the guarantees of free development, education is the surest and the most effective" (Ratner, 722). This faith, Dewey felt, imposed "a great responsibility upon the schools and upon the educators who conduct them. What have the schools done to bring the social-economic goal of freedom nearer to realization? What have they failed to do? What can and should they do to combat the threats which imperil freedom" (723)?

If, for Dewey, education for democracy, meaning the fullest possible sense of democratic community, constituted something other than a change in the goals of schooling, how is the purpose to be accomplished? What did he mean when he said that schools should be "the constant nurse of democracy"? We know that he saw the inevitable involvement of the school and the special responsibilities it has in American democracy as presupposing an initiation into the customs, practices, beliefs and understandings of that society, participation that makes possible further participation—a conservative start, but necessary to understanding community questions and problems and to effective action if it is required. This initiation, then, opens the doors of the mind and the corridors of action for students during their regular education, which is social and moral and political. Dewey drew a parallel between this initiation and learning a trade:

> If we generalize from such a commonplace case as the education of artisans through their work, we may say that the customs, methods and working standards of the calling constitute a "tradition," and that initiation into the tradition is the means by which the powers

> of learners are released and directed (Ratner, 621).

A critical question, of course, is how this initiation is to take place and how we can ensure that real "powers...are released and directed" so that initiation does not produce uncritical "true believers," slaves to an authoritarian system rather than free and thoughtful participants in a democracy. Indeed, Dewey's treatment of authority, in addition to his conception of education, offers once again the answer to this question. Rather than residing in "antagonism of methods and rules and results, [the problem lies] in the hard and narrow way and...uneducated habits and attitudes of teachers who set up as authorities, as rulers and judges in Israel" (Ratner, 622-623). The teacher who has these habits and attitudes goes on to offer

> himself as the organ of the voice of a whole school, of a finished classic tradition, and arrogates to himself the prestige that comes from what he is the spokesman for. Suppression of the emotional and intellectual integrity of pupils is the result; their freedom is repressed and the growth of their own personalities stunted. But it is not because of any opposition between the wisdom and skill of the past and the individual capacities of learners; the trouble lies in the habits, standards and ideas of the teacher (Ratner, 623).

Although it is hard to imagine a school without authority—both the authority of knowledge and experience and some control over student behavior—it seems plausible that a submissive attitude to authority could frustrate the empowering, liberating and questioning values of an education.

SCHOOL AUTHORITY. If authority then is the key, how should we understand it? Dewey suggested that our conception of freedom developed historically from a rebellion against repressive, authoritarian institutions and grew into a rebellion against the very idea of authority. We tend, therefore, to treat any exercise of authority—by parents, the community, or the school—as an intrusion or an imposition, an infringement needing justification. But for him, as we might expect given his concerns about the dangers of either-or thinking, "The genuine problem is the relation between authority and freedom" rather than the more conventional definition of separate domains for each (L11, 131). Two such notions, both concerned with the exercise of power in society, naturally resist compartmentalization. They require a judicious, thoughtful and complementary balance. The linchpin then becomes the legitimate, rationally defensible exercise of such power, in contrast to arbitrary, pointless, even despotic, authoritarian regimes.

Indeed, reminiscent of my "station and its duties" and the importance of initiation, he held that one cannot simply overthrow authority in the name of freedom, for authority represents "stability of social organization by means of which direction and support are given to individuals; while individual freedom stands for the forces by which change is intentionally brought about" (L11, 131). We need some stability, therefore, as a basis for change or even intelligent action, even if that stability and the authority it implicitly claims, as much as the changes that might be proposed, need to be justified. In fact, freedom might seem to be something that needs to be secured—or so we could conclude from Dewey's advocacy of a planned economy including employment, protection against life's misfortunes, and influence over major social and so economic ventures. Freedom cannot be a given any more than any other value, for the moment it moves into the realm of the unquestionable it also moves into the realm of dogma (EE, 22, 58-59).

The legitimacy of the order and authority in any institution—as we saw in the case of the teacher who "kept school"—depends on whether the structures created serve the purposes for which the institution exists, whether they serve that public the shared practices created and the legitimacy of its purposes: Does the discipline of the school, for instance, encourage or hinder students' learning and learning the right kinds of things, notably intellectual and moral attitudes? We might think then of authority in science founded on advances based on and facilitating innovation, individual creativity and freedom of inquiry—an epistemological notion. This idea comes close to Dewey's conception of legitimate authority, a conception that goes hand in hand with "the kind of individual freedom that is both supported by collective, organic authority and that in turn changes and is encouraged to change and develop, by its own operations, the authority upon which it depends" (L11, 143). Thus we have Dewey's "thesis that the operation of cooperative intelligence as displayed in science is a working model of the union of freedom and authority," that the basis of freedom is something "deeply rooted in the constitution of human beings" (L11, 143-144) and, by way of clarification, society and its publics.

This account of freedom and authority provides richer conceptions of the matter than a spare, negative account of freedom as the lack of constraints. For, as Dewey observed, "Removal of formal limitations is but a negative condition; positive freedom is not a state but an act which involves methods and instrumentalities for control of conditions" (Ratner, 392). This idea Dewey, more understandably now, wished to associate with

> one phase of freedom, a fundamental one—Intellectual Freedom. The Bill of Rights in the federal Constitution...guarantees, as far as law can guarantee anything, freedom of belief, of speech, of the press, of assembly, and of petition. These are aspects of what I have called intellectual freedom, but which perhaps would better be called moral freedom (Ratner, 723).

Moreover, as democracy cannot be learned except by participating in its institutions (for example, in the school), so intellectual freedom can be learned no other way. That is, it must be exercised if it is to be learned. And, he continued, "The ultimate stay and support of these liberties are the schools" (Ratner, 723). But there is more to Dewey's account, related to the school's other mandate, understanding, but important to the exercise of democratic structures. The exercise of inquiry, observation, experimentation and judgment are essential experiences:

> It is indeed necessary to have freedom of thought and expression. But just because this is necessary for the health and progress of society, it is even more necessary that ideas should be genuine ideas, not sham ones, the fruit of inquiry, of observation and experimentation, the collection and weighing of evidence. The formation of the attitudes which move steadily in this direction is the work and responsibility of the school more than of any other single institution. Routine and formal instruction, undemocratic administration of schools, is perhaps the surest way of creating a human product that submits readily to external authority.... It is idle to expect the schools to send out young men and women who will stand actively and aggressively for the cause of free intelligence in meeting social problems and attaining the goal of freedom unless the spirit of free intelligence pervades the organization, administration, studies, and methods of the school itself (Ratner, 724).

Thus, reminiscent of the inherent incoherence or contradiction between selfish private values and public expressions of concern for community welfare Dewey thought characteristic of capitalist societies, and returning to his earlier discussion of teachers who "set up as authorities, as rulers and judges in Israel," we read, "This suggests that the proponents of freedom are in a false position as well as the would-be masters and dictators" (Ratner, 622-623). In other words, we should be wary of confusing freedom with a lack of planning or direction rather than contrasting it with inappropriate planning or direction. Freedom and growth are unlikely to develop without being cultivated or nursed systematically and sequentially. What makes planning and direction appropriate is precisely the likelihood of developing genuine freedom and growth rather than blind conformity, aimless meandering or harmful thrashing about.

The identification of genuinely educational priorities defines *the professional competence of an educator*. Thus we return to the question of the justification of educational reforms and the nature of ends, for professional competence ensures that someone who has acquired a genuine education is not someone who has reached an end but a person capable of beginning or continuing, forming ends, and making decisions and growing. So, we find in Dewey expectations for the teacher's own qualities and attitudes: "The fuller and richer the experience of the teacher, the more adequate his own knowledge of 'traditions,' the more likely is he, given the attitude of participator instead of that of master, to use them in a liberating way" (Ratner, 626-627). But this objective requires knowledge and an understanding both of content and of the methods of intelligent reflection. It comes of an initiation into the traditions reflecting the best of our intellectual heritage, its real authority (DE, 76).

Genuine and worthwhile educational reform then promotes and capitalizes on the best and richest professional preparation of teachers, respects their exercise of these competencies, and so promotes central educational values. To ignore or slight professional educators, a perennial stance of policy and decision makers, is to attempt to change a profession without enlisting its support. Such a change could actually destroy the only real means to bring about subsequent change. In these conditions, authentic reform or change is about as promising as forcing a gifted artist to stay within the lines of a coloring book.

CULTURAL ACHIEVEMENT. In brief, traditional academic and intellectual roles of the school reemerge in Dewey's treatment of the ends of schooling. Knowledge and knowledge of the means of intelligent reflection and inquiry are central, but they are not ends in themselves, for we must keep sight of the purpose of schooling in the larger society and the larger life of man. But if these ideals motivate professional teachers and promote reform, Dewey's America surely needed it, for they certainly did not for him reflect the realities in the schools. In fact, practice contradicted belief. "While the critics are all wrong," Dewey concluded, "about the conscious attitude and intent of those who manage our educational system, they are right about the powerful educational currents of the day" (M10, 197). Nothing less than a program of social reconstruction was required:

> Political and economic forces quite beyond their [superintendents'] control are compelling these things. And they will remain beyond the control of any of us save as men honestly face the actualities and busy themselves with inquiring what education they impart and what culture may issue from their cultivation (M10, 199).

This reconstruction, for all that the school may contribute to its realization, is essentially larger than the school because, even though the "old culture is doomed...because it was built upon an alliance of political and spiritual powers, an equilibrium of governing and leisure classes, which no longer exists" (M10, 199-200), the new culture was still "something to achieve, to create" (198). Yet we know that we need to transform "a society built on an industry which is not yet humanized into a society which wields its knowledge and its industrial power in behalf of a democratic culture" (198). More precisely,

> It is for education to bring the light of science and the power of work to the aid of every soul that it may discover its quality. For in a spiritually democratic society every individual would realize distinction. Culture would then be for the first time in human history an individual achievement and not a class possession. An education fit for our ideal uses is a matter of actual forces not of opinions (M10, 200).

Some of Dewey's language may sound quaint to us now, but the commitments he expected from every segment of society are clear:

> Government, business, art, religion, all social institutions have a meaning, a purpose. That purpose is to set free and to develop the capacities of human individuals without respect to race, sex, class or economic status. And this is all one with saying that the test of their value is the extent to which they educate every individual into the full stature of his possibility. Democracy has many meanings, but if it has a moral meaning, it is found in resolving that the supreme test of all political institutions and industrial arrangements shall be the contribution they make to the all-round growth of every member of society (RP, 186).

But learning of such epistemologically based attitudes and community values requires their exercise if they are to live in the habits of individuals and the culture. Ironically perhaps, the wrongful use of authority to present intellectual history as a set of settled conclusions rather than the record of a shared and continuing collective human enterprise, a quest for meaning and better ways of living, undermines the very resource before us. Instead, the skills of that inquiry are to be practiced. They develop gradually, and they are abilities and dispositions as much as intellectual understandings. This process was, for Dewey, the passage to genuine educational reform: the reconstruction of the school as a democracy based on the traditional principles of freedom and participation in political liberalism, a reconstruction that promotes the growth of all its members—especially students, teachers and administrators—initially and most importantly their intellectual and moral growth.

The implications for school organization or community life, a topic we revisit in Chapter 8, "Schools of the Future," are clear and best exemplified in learning in the family and on the job:

> Within this organization is found the principle of school discipline or order. Of course, order is simply a thing which is relative to an end. If you have the end in view of forty or fifty children learning certain set lessons, to be recited to a teacher, your discipline must be devoted to securing that result. But if the end in view is the development of a spirit of social co-operation and community life, discipline must grow out of and be relative to such an aim.... But out of the occupation, out of doing things that

> are to produce results, and out of doing these in a social and co-operative way, there is born a discipline of its own kind and type. Our whole conception of school discipline changes when we get this point of view. In critical moments we all realize that the only discipline that stands by us, the only training that becomes intuition, is that got through life itself (M1, 11-12).

The General End

We often think of education as having either an intrinsic or an extrinsic end in the form of a state or goal, an accomplishment or achievement. We "have an education," as we say, or we "get an education" either in order to "be educated" (to have the qualities of an educated person—knowledge, understanding, a sense of priorities and values, and a way of looking at life perhaps) or in order to "have the qualifications" for a job or in some other way "be prepared" for life. Though we talk sometimes of "life-long education," we also think of education as a stage, something to be gained or even "got through," finished, early in life, a part of childhood, or part of growing up. But education, being growth, was itself an on-going process for Dewey, not just some future or realized state. Hence, although we may have immediate ends in view while involved in educating, he talked of education itself as having no fixed end. In being open-ended, education resembles life itself. To express this idea he needed a different way of discussing ends: ends as evolving, as completions of beginnings that then become new beginnings, and immediate objectives achieved perhaps for the moment but in turn leading on to other possibilities and making them possible. He seized then upon the idea of growth as process: We may grow, but we are never completely grown, as it were, or grown up (DE, 76). In this open-endedness, growth shares a characteristic of all moral questions, for "such questions...cannot be settled by deduction from fixed premises, and...the attempt to decide them in that fashion is the road to the intolerant fanaticism, dogmatism, class strife, of the closed mind" (Ratner, 763).

Processes, nevertheless, are governed by the laws of nature and tend toward certain ends, some preferable to others, some likelier than others to be rewarding or fulfilling. Education is equally growth that has—and so requires from the teacher—direction: a better understanding of life, notably our social milieu, and an increased ability to know what to do and how to act effectively. It is progress we can measure or at least evaluate: People do cope more or less well in their lives. In contrast to experiences that help us to grow, other ways of developing are stifling and stultifying: *Ungrowth* is a word we might create, if Dewey had not, to describe those experiences teachers and parents try to help us avoid.

Two problems arise in any discussion of growth as the general end of education. First, we have the general question of how to understand growth as an end in Dewey's biological sense of ends as evolving. With this phrasing, as we have seen, he deliberately challenged conventional thinking about values and indeed an entire philosophical tradition in ethics, stressing the importance of processes like formulating and reformulating rather than finding, discovering or accepting. Second, we find the problem of Dewey's conception of educational growth as growth appropriate to evolving and formulating ends, for no less a critic than Peters objects that "what he needed was other criteria by reference to which desirable and undesirable forms of growth could be distinguished" (1981a, 74; see also Archambault, 1965, 91-92, 94-95).

This latter comment seems odd if we remember Dewey's emphasis on connectedness and his contrast with ungrowth, and Peters himself notes that later in *Democracy and Education* Dewey "reached what he called a 'technical definition' of 'education' as 'that reconstruction or reorganization of experiences which adds to the meaning of experience, and which increases ability to direct the course of subsequent experience'" (1981a, 74). Peters also considers the possibility that autonomy is the real value at issue but he concludes, "I doubt whether it completely fits Dewey with his continued emphasis on 'shared experiences' and communication" (1981a, 75). But in *Experience and Education*, Dewey did offer an account of educational growth—growth that is, first of all, individual, linked to the conditions of intelligent reflection and inquiry, and yet social in nature:

> the question is whether growth in this direction promotes or retards growth in general. Does this form of growth create conditions for further growth, or does it set up conditions that shut off the person who has grown in this particular direction from the occasions, stimuli, and opportunities for continuing growth in new directions? What is the effect of growth in a special direction upon the attitudes and habits which alone open up avenues for development in other lines (EE, 36)?

Taken by itself, that account may seem strange and ambiguous. Growth that makes possible further growth does seem at first singularly lacking in content and direction and may even be circular. But to adopt this interpretation would be to take Dewey's conception of growth out of its context of inquiry and knowledge and their application to the problems of social living. So, too, it would ignore his observations that "no experience is educative which does not tend both to knowledge of more facts and entertaining of more ideas and to a better, a more orderly, arrangement of them" (EE, 82) and that "growth in judgment and understanding is essentially growth in ability to form purposes and to select and arrange means for their realization" (EE, 84).

Growth in the ability to form and to achieve wise purposes does not, of course, tell us which specific purposes will be called for in as yet unknown circumstances. But we can expect the context of those purposes and actions to be pluralistic. People are social; and so real growth, second, must make possible genuine and meaningful participation in the individual's social setting, helping the individual form and realize ends. This kind of growth complements the openness of ends and makes meaningful personal and social freedom possible by enabling people to formulate, evaluate and reformulate realistic projects and to envision the means for realizing them—in short, to know how to be in control of their lives rather than helplessly buffeted by outside forces (M14, 209-210). Still, we need the guidance and direction community life and learning communities provide, for no one "was ever emancipated merely by being left alone. Removal of formal limitations is but a negative condition; positive freedom is not a state but an act which involves methods and instrumentalities for control of conditions" (Ratner, 392).

Power and freedom go hand in hand in Dewey's view; they also accompany growth, as do order in nature and a knowledge of the laws of nature and the social world (M14, 215). Implicit also is a social order that either tolerates or fosters this self-realization. Knowing what it takes to achieve one's ends, though necessary, is not enough to achieve them: "What we want is possibilities open in the *world* not in the will, except as will or deliberate activity reflects the world" (M14, 214). When we explain democracy in terms of the epistemological and moral community, then, *Democracy and Education* is not an infelicitous title for a book that posits growth, knowledge and freedom as connecting links.

This conception of human freedom in choosing ends and

marshaling the means for achieving them accomplishes something else. It lays the basis for a possible account of causal and moral responsibility. We are responsible for choosing intelligently, and choosing intelligently, in turn, is a useful basis for moral education in that it stresses its educational basis, its links with understanding and thinking rather than with obedience or conformity to custom (L13, 221-222). Most of us hope that an education will provide just this kind of knowledge so that we can identify and analyze problematic situations and understand what to do about them. We hope our educations, in other words, provide us with efficacious judgment.

Revealingly, Dewey's way of thinking about moral questions allowed Ratner to group a series of selections concerned with ethics into a chapter entitled "Intelligence in Morals." Four ideas seem central to an understanding of Dewey's approach. First, moral thinking is always practical and takes place in a particular situation. Second, perhaps derivatively, moral theory has a role to play for

> it is *not* the business of moral theory to provide a ready-made solution to large moral perplexities. But...while the solution has to be reached by *action* based on personal choice, theory can enlighten and guide choice and action by revealing alternatives, and by bringing to light what is entailed when we choose one alternative rather than another (Ratner, 762).

Third, moral thinking is as scientific as any other domain of inquiry and helps us know how to go about addressing problematic moral situations by putting

> before us situations where the moral struggle is not just to be kept from departing from what we know already to be good and right, but where we need to discover what is good and right, and where reflection and experimentation are the sole means of discovery (Ratner, 763).

Fourth, there remain criteria of growth to guide such decisions. Therefore, moral education, if not all education, becomes essentially the application of intelligence to the problems of daily life, the question of how to live wisely and well.

Conclusion

Given Dewey's instrumental and situational conception of morality and the kind of decision making it calls for, we now understand why participation—initiation into the traditions of a democratic epistemological and moral community—looms so large in Dewey's account of education. *Morality, in fact, is simply the question of how we should live an essentially social life.* Moral education is the cultivation of the abilities and dispositions associated with participation in community life at school, coupled with reflective inquiry and action in the context of choosing, notably about social questions. Moral education is a practical matter, not an application of grandiose, abstract theories. We learn it through experience as much as reflection. The success of the endeavor determines the quality of individual and community life; its epistemological and moral success also determines and is determined by the quality of school life, not least the quality of a school as an educational community. The experience of schooling thus is empowering, making possible the recognition and realization of potential for the individual and the community. For such recognition and growth, we need the full resources of the intellectual and moral culture, not an uncritical transmission of the status quo or even its professed ideals but a recognition of its potential.

But we should avoid the idea that potentiality, especially the potential of a way of life, is predetermined, something that inevitably will come about or something simply to be recognized and then realized without human choice and intervention. In this sense ends remain open and are better understood in terms of beginnings that define for the school as for its students an almost existential responsibility for choices. The central idea is of creating a culture and a world, again imparting meaning to the notion of cultivating the individual's powers (as always, for Dewey, in a social context). Here, the idea of a democracy as an epistemological and moral community gives a rich conception of the nature of the school as a learning community as well as a direction for educational reform based on the richness of the learner's experience, not merely on the fact or the amount of learning.

This conception also gives meaning to the slogan of life-long learning—learning prior to, during, and after school hours and years—and it places a priority on educational values, notably educational learning. In so doing, it also provides criteria for judging the school's appropriate response to other social problems, particularly those which like poverty impinge on its work. For example, some encourage a greater attention in the schools and the teaching profession to poverty and its impact upon society, schools, homes and children. They further urge that the educational reform agenda include an attack on a poverty which, in our time, has become too pervasive and influential to ignore. Yet, in the spirit of Dewey, we must be cautious:

> Schools are not primarily responsible for poverty's existence, nor can they eliminate it; other economic and social structures and policies are much more influential in both regards. There is a danger that schools will be blamed for problems not of their making, just as there is a danger that schools will blame parents and children. We can usefully focus on things that can be done in schools even knowing full well that schools are only one part of the struggle for a more humane world (Levin, 1995, 211-212).

Levin suggests four lines of approach, very much in the spirit of Dewey's analysis: (1) making teaching in school more appropriate to the needs of poor students; (2) strengthening preschool education; (3) building mutually advantageous links, particularly political links, with the community; and (4) undertaking the straightforward educational task of helping people to understand poverty, its causes, consequences and alternatives. Such strategies could certainly strengthen education, community and participatory democracy. They also seem consistent with Dewey's view of the democratic end, the social and political ends, and the general goal of growth.

The strength and value of Dewey's account, in addition to its stressing the practical importance of inquiry and participation, lies then in its identifying the underlying moral values that would justify such a program, values like achievement, reciprocity, capacity, recognizing the worth of what one is doing and fraternity—self- but not selfish realization and fulfillment—as opposed to pointless, limiting and frustrating experiences that lead to an incoherent way of living. This position, in turn, implies school reform, a transformation, that affects both the school and the larger community. This position gives the school a mandate also for social reform, an educational mandate which in preparing future citizens, it cannot avoid in any case. The key values then become Dewey's "moral trinity of...social intelligence, social power, and social interests" (M4, 285) and the traditional political and intellectual values of liberalism found in the U. S. Bill of Rights.

What we see, finally, is the importance for Dewey of conceiving of the school as a democratic community in which participation makes possible further participation, an institution that is the "ultimate stay and support" (Ratner, 723) of democratic and intellectual liberties. This is the richness which understanding education in terms of Dewey's democratic, moral and epistemological communities adds.

Most interesting in these proposals is the fact that the underlying principles stress the central place of educational values in schooling and school reform and, taking that concern one step further, draw attention to the professional competence and autonomy of teachers. This emphasis brings us directly to questions of the reform of education through a better understanding of the roles and responsibilities of teachers, of how good teachers should be selected and educated and, after they have been selected and prepared, of the kinds of schools they should help create for the well-being of children and society and for the preparation of aspiring educators.

Chapter Four

The Roles and Responsibilities of the Teacher

> Everything the teacher does, as well as the manner in which he does it, incites the child to respond in some way or other, and response tends to set the child's attitude in some way or other (L8, 159).

> What will happen if teachers become sufficiently courageous and emancipated to insist that education means the creation of a discriminating mind, a mind that prefers not to dupe itself or to be the dupe of others? Clearly they will have to cultivate the habit of suspended judgment, of scepticism, of desire for evidence, of appeal to observation rather than sentiment, discussion rather than bias, inquiry rather than conventional idealizations. When this happens schools will be the dangerous outposts of human civilization. But they will also begin to be supremely interesting places (M13, 334).

If one thing characterizes education in the last decade or so, it is the belief that it must be reformed and that schooling and teaching must either improve or be reinvented. The idea that schooling and teaching should be reformed is, of course, hardly new; what is new is the extent of discontent among parents, voters, board members, administrators and teachers and the range of their reform proposals. Popular disenchantment expresses itself in endless discussion, publications and legislation concerning classrooms, schools, districts and programs. Proposals range from Charter schools based on the Paideia program to customer-oriented models imported from business. What many educators find discouraging about these proposals is their fragmented, incoherent, and often contradictory conceptions of education and teaching and related problems and their identification of single causes and simple panaceas like site-based management, national testing, a common curriculum, privatization, skills for employment and national economic advantage, and cooperative learning styles. Both intuition and experience tell us that all this breast beating is counterproductive. Education and schooling are embedded in a multiplicity of complex and seemingly conflicting contexts. The problems are not simple, and so we need a comprehensive conception of them and of the activities of education.

Accordingly, we begin to see reactions to simplistic criticisms in the form of dramatic, radical, sweeping but equally single-minded reconceptualizations of the solution to the so-called educational problem. These newer proposals insist, for instance, on the importance of rethinking the roles of educational technology, the nature of knowledge, our conception of intelligence, the nature of society, the relationship of schools to parents and the community, and the responsibilities of principals and supervisory staff. They urge as well alternative licensing programs and accrediting associations, and new roles for teachers as reflective practitioners, researchers and professionals. Sometimes these two simplistic approaches, single panaceas and radical rethinking, go hand in hand: they combine the information age and the learning society, for example, to advocate a computer for every child.

Surprisingly, we find almost no attention devoted to the day-to-day roles and responsibilities of the person whose daily activities ultimately determine whether any reform succeeds—the classroom teacher or, in Dewey's words, *"the only real educator"* (M1, 272, italics added). Except for research that comes from effective teaching sources and the study of classroom processes (Buchmann and Floden, 1993; and Hawley, Rosenholtz, with Goodstein and Hasselbring, 1984), general educational renewal projects (Fullan, with Stiegelbauer, 1991; and Goodlad, 1990), pedagogic thoughtfulness (van Manen, 1991) and ethical interpretations of the traits desirable in a teacher (Hare, 1993), we find reformers making few contributions to a better understanding of the actual roles and responsibilities of the classroom teacher. Of course, discussions of how teachers should be prepared in university (Dill, 1990), how they should set the stage for students to create their own knowledge (Perkinson, 1993), why they should have a differentiated set of career options (Holmes Group, 1986) and whether they should become professionals (Covert, 1993; and Socket, 1993) abound. Occasionally we also find practical proposals for specific behavior management, conflict resolution, and cooperative learning strategies and techniques, among others, which appeal to many because they are said to "work."

But despite the merits of this reform literature, most remarkable is its lack of attention to the roles and responsibilities of teachers, the kinds of activities they should engage in as professionals, and the considerations pertinent in making pedagogical decisions. It is as if we are so familiar with the roles of teachers that we find them simple and unproblematic—until, that is, we try to explain our reactions to complicated or controversial incidents (Hare, 1990). Then we are left wondering where to turn for a careful analysis of what teachers do, ought to do, or might be expected to do or refrain from doing. In short, where do we turn for an analysis of the roles and responsibilities of the teacher? Once again it is helpful to review the work of Dewey. Specifically, Dewey's notion of community, his concept of the experiential continuum, and his analogies for teaching help clarify the point of reform and emphasize the inappropriateness of simple reforms by drawing attention to the complexity of the teaching context and the need to reconcile potentially conflicting demands hidden in the familiarity of both the teacher's role and the school, elements pertinent to teaching and educational reform today.

The Teacher and the Community

As we have seen, the concept of community dominates Dewey's educational and social thinking, playing several roles and inevitably raising perplexing questions about the community's control of its schools and the use of schools as a vehicle for social criticism and social reconstruction or at least educational reform. Central to this discussion we find Dewey's account of educational communities as constantly expanding and shrinking, depending upon the movements of the teacher or the student within the school and in the environments that influence it in so many ways. Our discussion here centers on a set of four overlapping educational communities: the class, the school, the neighborhood, and the larger social environment. Meanwhile, we should keep in mind that emerging and fading communities or subcommunities occur in each of the four basic communities we discuss. Dewey's idea of community, therefore, is much more complex and richer than that found in most contemporary theories of school and community cooperation and collaboration. Several ideas help us to understand the complexity and richness of his thinking.

First, we should avoid viewing the teacher in Dewey's educational philosophy as an isolated entity either in conception or in practice: She is not an island, either personally or educationally. She cannot, or at least should not, hide herself in a cubicle. Instead, she is or becomes a member of an informal educational community composed of parents, neighbors, students and others. Indeed, she is a part of a community or environment that includes factories, businesses, parks, streets, houses, vehicles, trees and so on—or "whatever conditions interact with personal needs, desires, purposes, and capacities to create the experience" a child has (EE, 44).

This greater educational community is unusually important because "every place in which men habitually meet, shop, club, factory, saloon, church, political caucus, is perforce a schoolhouse, even though not so labeled" (M7, 304). Thus, Dewey maintained, the "teacher should become intimately acquainted with the conditions of the local community, physical, historical, economic, occupational, etc., in order to utilize them as educational resources" (EE, 40). In one sense, then, professional preparation in what may be termed "school specific environmental understanding" begins only when a person accepts a teaching assignment in an identifiable school and community. Once the contract has been signed, the teacher begins expanding her professional knowledge base in a way that was previously impossible: she learns about the "schoolhouses" scattered throughout the informal educational community. This aspect of the teacher's post-university studies may also include answering what was for Dewey a fundamental, central social and philosophical question that formal studies may overlook: Each teacher—and ultimately each school and district—must decide whether "to use industry for education or let industry use education for its own purposes" (M7, 385).

Dewey's thoughts on this broader community contain elements that we today might consider at once both conventional and unconventional, repugnant and acceptable, radical and commonplace. For example, he addressed the economic impact of an environment or community:

> the life which men, women and children actually lead, the opportunities open to them, the values they are capable of

> enjoying, their education, their share in all the things of art and science are mainly determined by economic conditions. Hence we can hardly expect a moral system which ignores economic conditions to be other than remote and empty (L4, 225).

This quotation reflects Dewey the social activist, who worked at Hull House in Chicago and for the election of socialist candidates in the 1930s. He considered economic conditions both a moral and an educational issue. Thus he formed the theory that economic factors and social class are major determinants of much else in society and broaden the social and educational responsibilities of teachers rather than limit the effect of educational institutions and personnel. Rather than wanting to use socio-economic circumstances to explain why some children make less educational progress than others, he wanted educators to become involved in improving society for the well-being of children and youth. He had no interest in blaming either background or parents for the educational inadequacies of children.

Dewey thus tempered his reform proposals with a "realism" born of practice and involvement, believing that in the spread of defensible educational ideas and practices teachers needed the support of the broader community: "Without the support of the progressive and enlightened forces of the community,...all their best plans and ideas would have... little or no effect on the education system" (Dworkin, 129).

But the teacher should be more than just an observer of this broader community that partially educates children. As part of the larger society, teachers should be involved in the "proper protection and... proper nurture" of the young because these two responsibilities constitute "the most fundamental care of society." Educators then should "bear a responsibility as *leaders,* as *directors* in the formation of public opinion" (M7, 110, italics added). He thought, at least in 1913, that teachers should be aggressive advocates in the community for the needs of children and youth, but he sensed their general ineffectiveness in this advocacy role:

> The larger questions about the protection of childhood, the movements for the abolition of child labor, movements for playgrounds, for recreation centres, even for the adequate use of the school plant, these and the thousand and one problems relative to children that have come forward with the great congestion of population in cities in the last generation—the initiative in the

> agitation of these questions and the formation of public opinion has to a surprisingly small extent proceeded from teachers (M7, 110).

We might well think that this kind of talk foreshadows critical pedagogy and commitments to teacher empowerment. Yet, when he discussed the topic of professional responsibility, Dewey appears to have been concerned that the influence of teachers be neither underestimated nor overestimated—even within the school, much less in the external community:

> It is absurd to say...that the teachers are responsible for the evils, the backwardness, the overscholasticism of the present system; that they are exclusively responsible. Of course, we teachers must bear our share of the blame; we are partly to blame, but we are far from being exclusively or mainly to blame. *The teachers are not in control of the schools.* The schools are in the control of the community, and if they have carried out an overacademic and an overscholastic policy, it is because that is as far as the average public sentiment of the average community has advanced up to this time (M7, 89, italics added).

Dewey's belief that communities controlled schools may now seem quaint, timid, or even conservative except to those recently embroiled in a controversy that excited the parents in a school neighborhood. But Dewey also believed that teachers should be actively involved in shaping the views of the larger community that controls the schools:

> I know there are some who think that the implications of what I have said point to abstinence and futility.... But I am surprised when educators adopt this position, for it shows a profound lack of faith in their own calling. It assumes that education as education has nothing or next to nothing to contribute; that formation of understanding and disposition counts for nothing; that only immediate overt action counts and that it can count equally whether or not it has been modified by education (L11, 412).

From Dewey's perspective, then, social activism of a sort is a teacher's professional as well as moral responsibility.

Moreover, by extrapolation at least, especially considering his own involvements and his views on the role of economic factors in determining social conditions, that responsibility extends to another larger environment or community: the province or state and the nation that affect cities, neighborhoods, schools and classrooms. While we focus our attention here on the immediate community that surrounds the school, the school itself as a community and the classroom as a learning community, in an important sense Dewey recognized only one community or environment:

> As an individual passes from one situation to another, his world, his environment, expands or contracts. He does not find himself living in another world but in a different part or aspect of one and the same world. What he has learned in the way of knowledge and skill in one situation becomes an instrument of understanding and dealing effectively with the situations which follow. The process goes on as long as life and learning continue (EE, 44).

To appreciate it fully, we should place this point within the context of Dewey's account of habit and his principles of continuity, the experiential continuum, and pedagogical interaction—these being vital to a teacher's ability to select and use environments that promote growth rather than stifle it (EE, 17ff).

But here we find inevitable ambiguity. Since people are social beings, any social setting becomes a kind of community or a society. Dewey's term *environment* may be better here, for some environments are more like true communities than others. We might comment on the presence or lack of "community spirit" in a town or a group, asking "Is that a community you would wish to live in?" or "Is that a group you would like to be part of?" or even "Is that a real community?" A town then that is "not much of a community" still remains a community in some minimal sense of being a social environment just as a school, no matter how bad, remains in some sense a learning community. But it is not a particularly full, authentic community. *Community* then may function on occasion as an evaluative term, as in a "real community" with "real community spirit," caring and concern for the "neighbors" and "the neighborhood." Such neighbors are more than just the people who live next door.

Dewey moved from the larger community surrounding the school to identify two additional learning communities important to the teacher: the school as a unit (EE, 55) and the individual class as a social group (EE, 59). He often spoke of the business of the school and the teacher's contributions to the overall educative environment of the unit, contrasting some types of school organization with more natural groups and activities where the appropriate structure and order were spontaneous, natural and genuine, as in matters of discipline. But as we have seen earlier,

> The [traditional] school was not a group or community held together by participation in common activities. Consequently, the normal, proper conditions of control were lacking. Their absence was made up for, and to a considerable extent had to be made up for, by the direct intervention of the teacher, who, as the saying went, "*kept* order." He kept it because order was in the teacher's keeping, instead of residing in the shared work being done (EE, 55).

The challenge in each community, if it is interested in being healthy and educative, is to make that community genuine—one that recognizes and responds to the genuine needs of its members—or natural rather than alien, external or arbitrary. The problem then is less gaining commitment to the community than designing a community to which commitment is spontaneous and natural rather than enforced. The challenge for Deweyan teachers, then, is to create learning communities that exist for the genuine growth and enrichment of the lives of their members, and in this respect all genuine communities are also educational.

Given his view of the teacher, Dewey paid even more attention to the classroom community or, more precisely, "the social group" or "the particular set of individuals with whom" (EE, 58) an individual teacher interacted. Meanwhile, he carefully distinguished those schools where, since "pupils were a class rather than a social group, the teacher necessarily acted largely from the outside, not as a director of exchange in which all had a share" (EE, 59). This analysis of the dynamics of a class shows how central the concept of social group or community is to his educational theory and how decisive the shared purposes of the group are. A teacher, as a member of a smaller learning community or class, is a member of a group designed and held together by an intention to learn together; the teacher is, therefore, an insider, not an "external boss or dictator" (EE, 59).

While such a claim might be misunderstood as an abdication of the teacher's authority, Dewey's concern, as we have seen, is with neither overestimating nor underestimating the teacher's role. Nor would he have it misconceived. The teacher is neither "a negligible factor [nor] an evil" (L8, 337). Her powers are not unlimited or arbitrary, concepts to be understood in terms of their appropriateness to the group's purposes. "In reality," Dewey maintained, "the teacher is the intellectual leader of a social group. He is a leader, not in virtue of official position, but because of wider and deeper knowledge and matured experience" (L8, 337). This is not then to say that a group may choose any purposes it wishes. Instead, a school group is designed for the particular kind of learning that encourages genuine educational growth.

Within the larger community the teacher becomes an informed, educated and thoughtful participant, a member who as a social being has a legitimate interest in the nature of that community and who is a potential leader in forming public opinion. So it is within the school and classroom communities. From this participation also come insights of pedagogic and curricular value. Within the school and the classroom, the teacher is also a community member, but again a more knowledgeable and experienced member and therefore a leader.

Yet, with the phenomenal growth of secondary and higher education and rapid changes in society, the teacher now rarely enjoys so influential a role in her community. Neither, with a better-educated public and more fluid social roles nowadays, is the teacher's expertise so clearly distinct. Of course, social and economic problems still abound along with in-school pedagogical challenges. Indeed, they may be more pronounced than ever before in the larger community. And Dewey might consider the role he described abidingly relevant. But if the role is as relevant as ever, the fact that many teachers no longer live in the communities where they teach presents at least two obstacles. First, Dewey's notion of a voice within the community advocating for the well-being of everyone seems at least altered: Teachers must speak to the communities where they live regardless of their association with the communities where they teach. Second, teachers may have to make more concerted efforts to understand those communities from which their students come if they do not themselves live in them. At any rate, in a mobile society Dewey's idea of the community school takes on new meaning and raises new questions.

Distinguishing communities then helps us identify and explain the teacher's central role, clarify questions about it, and understand its conflicts. For Dewey, the teacher has an essential and partially prescribed role, but we can offer no simple, context-free answer to the question, What is the teacher's role? The role is not one in the sense that the context is not one, and the interactions are complex and often difficult to understand: Multiple roles exist in multiple contexts. This complexity explains in part why Dewey stressed that teachers need to be skilled in making sophisticated professional judgments, a topic that now enjoys considerable attention in teacher education circles but has yet to gain the sympathy of many policy and decision makers.

One question, however, often goes neglected in Dewey's conception of different communities: the possibility that the goals of educational communities may simply be in opposition to those of the larger community. For instance, the larger community may favor teaching employment-related competencies and using national assessments and standards even though they may not be helpful in promoting critical thinking or in evaluating the broad general culture (M14, 91). Here, nevertheless, the strength of Dewey's analysis lies in helping us identify the locus of the dispute: Different communities, defined by different purposes, may come into conflict. To the degree that conflict exists, the school may be a counter-culture in either a positive or a negative sense, promoting or resisting reform, nursing or negating growth. Whatever role the school may take in conflicting community settings, these considerations make it easier to understand the concepts of growth and experiential continuum in Dewey's educational theory.

The Experiential Continuum

In understanding the roles and the responsibilities of the teacher, we can recall two of Dewey's educational principles, both related to the continuity of experience. First, unlike many educational thinkers who separate pedagogical responsibilities from as many as three of the overlapping communities, Dewey was wary of dichotomies and saw education as a seamless fabric that contained all of these participants. Second, Dewey was similarly wary of separating subjects into discrete domains for the young, mainly because he saw them as foreign to the way children (and to a lesser degree others too) usually learn. For him, though academic disciplines have their usefulness—indeed they have their fundamental, epistemological and so educational place as "funded experience"—school learning should be an integrated continuum of experience that flows out of informal learning experiences enjoyed at home and in the neighborhood. His accounts of interaction and habit explain the basis for his thinking and inform his idea that a teacher is much like a wise parent, an idea to which we will return:

> The needs of a baby for food, rest, and activity are certainly primary and decisive in one respect. Nourishment must be provided; provision must be made for comfortable sleep, and so on. But these facts do not mean that a parent shall feed the baby at any time when the baby is cross or irritable, that there shall not be a program of regular hours of feeding and sleeping, etc. The wise mother takes account of the needs of the infant but not in a way which dispenses with her own responsibility for regulating the objective conditions under which the needs are satisfied. And if she is a wise mother in this respect, she draws upon past experiences of experts as well as her own for the light that these shed upon what experiences are in general most conducive to the normal development of infants. Instead of these conditions being subordinated to the immediate internal condition of the baby, they are definitely ordered so that a particular kind of *interaction* with these immediate internal states may be brought about (EE, 41-42).

Dewey's use of the term *interaction* signals a critical feature of his overall learning philosophy, for it connotes "the second chief principle for interpreting an experience in its educational function and force. It assigns equal rights to both factors in experience—objective and internal conditions" (EE, 42). Relating his ideas of continuity and interaction to habit, he explained that

> At bottom, this principle rests upon the fact of habit, when habit is interpreted biologically. The basic characteristic of habit is that every experience enacted and undergone modifies the one who acts and undergoes, while this modification affects, whether we wish it to or not, the quality of subsequent experiences. For it is a somewhat different person who enters into them. The principle of habit so understood obviously goes deeper than the ordinary conception of *a* habit as a more or less fixed way of doing things.... It covers the formation of attitudes... it covers our basic sensitivities and ways of meeting and responding to all the conditions which we meet in living (EE, 35).

Thus he believed that the idea of continuity of experience "means that every experience both takes up something from those which have gone before and modifies in some way the quality of those which come after" (EE, 35); and he stressed the wisdom of the teacher helping students to form habits "which are more intelligent, more sensitively percipient, more informed with foresight, more aware of what they [the students] are about, more direct and sincere, more flexibly responsive than those now current" (M14, 90). Thus, Dewey saw all effective educational reform as necessarily based upon a "study of the educative effect, the influence upon habit, of each form of human interaction" (M14, 103). Of particular importance to the teacher, then, is the human interaction that occurs within a learning community and the impact that the interaction has upon students and the formation of habits.

Dewey also associated habit formation with education, with growth, and with the continued capacity for growth. He summarized his position this way:

> from the standpoint of growth as education and education as growth the question is whether growth in this direction promotes or retards growth in general. Does this form of growth create conditions for further growth, or does it set up conditions that shut off the person who has grown in this particular direction from the occasions, stimuli, and opportunities for continuing growth in new directions (EE, 36)?

Terms like *integrated, interaction*, *continuum* and *flows out* should alert us to the presence of more than one element in learning and growth: That which flows out flows also *into* something else. Dewey's notion of experiential quality nicely expresses the ethical and educational point to be made at this juncture and amplifies why he believed that "man is a creature of habit, not of reason nor yet of instinct" (M14, 88). The important decision before teachers is not between habit and reason but between developing habits that are "unintelligent" and those that are "intelligent" (M14, 55):

> The quality of any experience has two aspects. There is an immediate aspect of agreeableness or disagreeableness, and there is its influence upon later experiences. The first is obvious and easy to judge. The *effect* of an experience is not borne on its face. It sets a problem to the educator. It is his business to arrange for

> the kind of experiences which, while they do not repel the student, but rather engage his activities are, nevertheless, more than immediately enjoyable since they promote having desirable future experiences. Just as no man lives or dies to himself, so no experience lives and dies to itself. Wholly independent of desire or intent, every experience lives on in further experiences. Hence the central problem of an education based upon experience [and, we might add, for the teacher] is to select the kind of present experiences that live fruitfully and creatively in subsequent experiences (EE, 27-28).

If these two principles of continuity in experience frame a context and if we think of growth as a measure of the quality of an educational experience, Dewey's pedagogical analogies help us understand the teacher at work in the smallest of the communities, the classroom, and appreciate her attempts to understand her appropriate roles and responsibilities.

Ten Analogies of Teaching

In addition to presenting insights into the roles and responsibilities of the teacher as a member of the school community, a student of its workings, a protector of the young, a director of public opinion and a community leader, Dewey described the teacher from other perspectives. He described many of these perspectives in explicit analogies; he implied others. In either case though, each perspective reveals important features of the roles and responsibilities of the professional educator actively involved in the affairs of the four kinds of communities: the small learning group or class within the school, the school itself, the immediate school environment, and the greater environment that influences the other three.

Ten of these analogies seem particularly helpful: the teacher (1) as learner, (2) as intellectual leader, (3) as partner and guide, (4) as wise parent, (5) as social servant, (6) as prophet, (7) as physician, (8) as engineer, (9) as pioneer and (10) as artist. While these analogies occasionally overlap and while Dewey meant us to take none of them literally, all cast light upon teaching. That Dewey employed so many different analogies to describe the roles and responsibilities of the teacher suggests the enormous complexity of the teacher's roles and responsibilities. Unlike many other reformers, Dewey understood this complexity and thus illuminated teaching in ways others seldom envisioned. In fact, their failure to understand this complexity helps explain the inflexibility, prescription, and dogma we still find in the thinking of some reformers, leaders, legislators, administrators and practitioners.

THE TEACHER AS LEARNER. For Dewey and for us (especially with current talk about the teacher as a life-long learner, about the importance of in-service education and professional growth and development, and about requirements for periodic recertification or relicensing) the concept of the teacher as learner takes on central importance. It contributed to every other idea of the teacher Dewey expressed and continues to lend precision to slogans and clichés. First, as a concerned citizen, the teacher studies interactions and problems of the larger community and considers possible solutions and courses of action. So, too, as an educated, reflective person, the teacher observes and is curious about what goes on at school. Of observation, Dewey stated, "all that the wisest man can do is to observe what is going on more widely and more minutely and then select more carefully from what is noted just those factors which point to something to happen" (DE, 146). He also emphasized that "observation alone is not enough. We have to understand the *significance* of what we see, hear, and touch. The significance consists of the consequences that will result when what is seen is acted upon" (EE, 68). But these are simply the marks of any educated citizen, a person genuinely alive and genuinely participating in the community.

These qualities also characterize the teacher as a professional. Within the school, the teacher is both citizen and student—an involved, committed, and caring student sharing the common goal of establishing an educational context, an environment conducive to growth. Meanwhile, the teacher should understand that the student is also a teacher and that "upon the whole, the less consciousness there is, on either side, of either giving or receiving instruction, the better" (DE, 160). Within a class, both explore the subjects, one however with more experience. With that greater experience comes a responsibility for a special commitment to the success of the pedagogical enterprise. Beyond knowing the subject and learning from the students as they raise questions and suggest answers to problems, the teacher should study the students as both learners and members of the learning group as they engage in their free-time activity (EE, 62). In this way, we can view the teacher as a researcher or investigator though not in any esoteric or mysterious sense. The teacher looking and thinking as a learner searches, inquires and analyzes the behavior of students, seeking for clues in order to understand them better and so to teach them better: "The act of looking" [is] "an act of research" (L8, 121); indeed "all thinking is research" (DE, 148). Dewey believed that professional educational researchers neglected this looking and thinking which was so fundamental to developing a science of education. For the views of reflective classroom teachers, rightly studied, could provide both a source of information for a science of education and a deterrent to the tendency of many other teachers to "convert scientific findings into recipes to be followed" (L5, 23-24).

In the role of an experienced, committed member of the group, the teacher becomes a professional keeping current in her field, recognizing "the responsibility for constant study of school room work, [and] the constant study of children, of methods, of subject matter" (M7, 109). This behavior represents in-service and professional development at its best and helps us recognize more typical requirements for course work and periodic recertification for what they are: policing measures substituting for an effective sense of professional community. Dewey himself intensely disliked any view of teaching that emphasized students' "rehearsing material in the exact form in which the older person [the teacher or an adult] conceives it" (DE, 304), and he abhorred "a diet of predigested materials" (EE, 46). He immediately saw the implication of his first remark for the teacher as learner, for "teaching then ceases to be an educative process for the teacher" (DE, 304).

THE TEACHER AS INTELLECTUAL LEADER. Talk of the teacher learning along with her students may seem to some an abdication of the instructional role and the teacher's authority, even if Dewey's analogy acknowledges her greater experience and knowledge. Indeed, some see this analogy as responsible for the various anti-intellectual disasters attributed to progressive education and, thereby, to Dewey. Yet we know he approved an active, involved role for the teacher as a community leader helping to shape an informed public opinion, create consensus, and initiate progressive social reform in the larger community. As an intellectual leader in the classroom, she has a similar social role. She is more than simply "in charge"—in authority, and in a position to impose her will, to keep order; she is an authority with the resources, the experience and the expertise to promote a common cause. In fact, the very purpose of her "classroom research" is to facilitate the ends for which she and the students are present. This is why occasions to learn are opportunities: "The problem of educators, teachers, parents, the state, is to provide the environment that induces educative or developing activities, and where these are found the one thing needful in education is secured" (M7, 197). In the light of this responsibility to provide an educative environment, "the fuller and richer the experience of the teacher, the more adequate his own knowledge of 'traditions' the more likely is he, given the attitude of participator instead of that of master, to use them in a liberating way" (Ratner, 626-627).

It is in this sense, within the environment the teacher is helping to create, that she takes "a positive and leading share in the direction of the activities of the community" (EE, 58), being in this role both an active selector and a thoughtful arranger of stimuli or conditions with educative potential. The teacher as intellectual leader helps create a learning environment because her responsibility for "selecting objective conditions carries with it...the responsibility for understanding the needs and capacities of the individuals who are learning at a given time" (EE, 45-46).

In addition to selecting and arranging propitious educative conditions, the teacher should shield her students from noneducative and miseducative stimuli:

> The teacher has to protect the growing person from those conditions which occasion a mere succession of excitements which have no cumulative effect, and which, therefore, make an individual either a lover of sensations and sensationalism or leave him blasé and uninterested. He has to avoid all dogmatism in instruction, for such a course gradually but surely creates the impression that everything important is already settled and nothing remains to be found out. He has to know how to give information when curiosity has created an appetite that seeks to be fed, and how to abstain from giving information when, because of a lack of a questioning attitude, it would be a burden and would dull the sharp edge of the inquiring spirit (L8, 144).

As a result, the teacher as an intellectual leader has much greater responsibilities for planning the learning activities of the learning group:

> He must survey the capacities and needs of the particular set of individuals with whom he is dealing and must at the same time arrange the conditions which provide the subject-matter or content for experiences that satisfy these needs and develop these capacities. The planning must be flexible enough to permit free play for individuality of experience and yet firm enough to give direction towards continuous development of power (EE, 58).

This planning is necessary because "no experience is educative that does not tend both to knowledge of more facts and entertaining of more ideas and to a better, a more orderly, arrangement of them" (EE, 82). Planning, then, combines the old and the new, reaching into the students' past for meaningful understandings and drawing the students into the future so they will continue to grow. Incidentally, it also gives the lie to those who accuse Dewey of advocating a watered-down curriculum. We see here no abdication of intellectual leadership, for it is clear that Dewey saw instincts and interests merely as "starting points for assimilation of the knowledge and skill of the more matured beings upon whom he [the student] depends" (M14, 68). Even so,

> It is essential that the new objects and events be related intellectually to those earlier experiences, and this means that there be some advance made in conscious articulation of facts and ideas. It thus becomes the office of the educator to select those things within the range of existing experience that have promise and potentiality of presenting new problems which by stimulating new ways of observation and judgments will expand the area of further experience. He must constantly regard what is already won not as a fixed possession but as an agency and instrumentality for opening new fields which make new demands upon existing powers of observation and of intelligent use of memory. Connectedness in growth must be his constant watchword (EE, 75).

THE TEACHER AS PARTNER AND GUIDE. We have seen that the teacher as leader (or remembering Dewey's democratic orientation, a leading member of the learning community) cares about nurturing children's growth, protecting them from the noneducative and miseducative. Yet it is worth our while to note the novelty in Dewey's conception of educational leadership and the extent to which he thought it rooted in epistemology, in a better understanding of the new scientific method, and in a better articulation of what makes thinking successful—and for that reason progressive in orientation and capable of success. Dewey expected the teacher as an intellectual leader to use the scientific method, this new understanding of effective thinking, in her own educative affairs "as the pattern and ideal of intelligent exploration and exploitation of the potentialities inherent in experience" (EE, 86). He expected her to exemplify it and to adapt it to students learning to engage in "the formation of ideas, acting upon ideas, observation of the conditions which result, and organization of facts and ideas for future use" (EE, 88). In an important way, and harking back to our discussion of authority, this kingdom of reason, this free exchange of ideas, is democratic, not autocratic; and, in the process of assisting students in their development, the teacher is "not a magistrate set on high and marked by arbitrary authority but...a friendly co-partner and guide in a common enterprise" (L9, 200). Moreover, the teacher as "a guide and director," Dewey insisted, should not be misunderstood, for even though she "steers the boat ...the energy that propels it must come from those who are learning" (L8, 140); she cannot overcome that force or steer squarely into the wind. Thus, Dewey thought it possible

> to abuse the office [of teacher], and to force the activity of the young into channels which express the teacher's purpose rather than that of the pupils. But the way to avoid this danger is not for the adult to withdraw entirely. The way is, first, for the teacher to be intelligently aware of the capacities, needs, and past experiences of those under instruction, and, secondly, to allow the suggestion made to develop into a plan and project by means of the further suggestions contributed and organized into a whole by the members of the group. The plan, in other words, is a co-operative enterprise, not a dictation. The teacher's suggestion is not a mold for a cast-iron result but is a starting point to be developed into a plan through contributions from the experience of all engaged in the learning process. The development occurs through reciprocal give-and-take, the teacher taking but not being afraid to give. The essential point is that the purpose grow and take shape through the process of social intelligence (EE, 71-72).

Many of the communitarian traits inherent in this shared, cooperative study advocated by Dewey characterize methods more recently proposed in some forms of cooperative learning, turning the so-called school sin of helping your neighbor back into a productive and natural act and making the school a democratic learning community. In the process, the teacher who acts as a partner and guide helps each person in the learning community become a partner with and guide for others.

THE TEACHER AS WISE PARENT. Seeing the teacher again as concerned with the child's growth and with protecting the child from noneducative and miseducative influences, we turn naturally to one of Dewey's favorite analogies, the teacher as a wise parent motivated by the concern of all good parents that their children receive the kind of education each parent thinks best for her or his own child (SSCC, 7). A teacher like this would be inclined to temper a detached professional attitude with caring and the establishment of rapport with a child's parents and the home. In this analogy, the teacher is more than simply a parent. She is a wise parent. The teacher has the discernment, the sensitivity, and the courage to interact with and act for the student and in the student's best interests. She refrains from acting, especially on a regular basis, when the child wishes simply to be amused or entertained (M7, 153). The wise parent is interested in developing "*persistency, consecutiveness*...[and] endurance against obstacles and through hindrances" (M7, 174). Continuing, Dewey maintained that the judicious parent can distinguish between "mere strain," "excessive fatigue," and a wish for "some easier line of action" (M7, 174). We feel the greater force of his thought when we understand the context:

> The wise parent tries to protect the child from mere strain; from the danger of excessive fatigue, of damaging the structures of the body, of getting bruises. Effort as mere strained activity is thus not what we prize. On the other hand, a judicious parent will not like to see a child too easily discouraged by meeting obstacles. If the child is physically healthy, surrender of a course of action, or diversion of energy to some easier line of action, is a bad symptom if it shows itself at the first sign of resistance. The demand for effort is a demand for *continuity* in the face of difficulties (M7, 174-175).

Beyond describing learning generally as it occurs in the home (RP, 92), a natural learning community, Dewey presented the ideal home as the pattern for the ideal school and indirectly threw light on the teacher as a wise parent:

> we find the child learning through the social converse and constitution of the family. There are certain points of interest and value to him in the conversation carried on: statements are made, inquiries arise, topics are discussed, and the child continually learns. He states his experiences, his misconceptions are corrected. Again the child participates in the household occupations, and thereby gets habits of industry, order, and regard for the rights and ideas of others, and the fundamental habit of subordinating his activities to the general interest of the household. Participation in these household tasks becomes an opportunity for gaining knowledge (M1, 23-24).

In these examples of learning in the home, interest and motivation pose no problem; the learning is spontaneous though directed, and it is child-centered in this way but only in a socially healthy manner, keeping in mind "the general interest of the household." When the educator realizes the important points of home learning or discovery,

> There is no mystery about it, no wonderful discovery of pedagogy or educational theory. It is simply a question of doing systematically and in a large, intelligent, and competent way what for various reasons can be done in most households only in a comparatively meager and haphazard manner (M1, 24).

Dewey compared the teacher to the parent in other revealing ways. For instance, we have seen that he implied that the teacher, like a wise mother, should draw upon "past experiences of experts as well as her own for the light that is shed upon what experiences are in general most conducive to the normal development of infants" (EE, 42). So too he saw it as the teacher's responsibility to arrange learning conditions and utilize "the funded experience of the past"—our traditions and intellectual heritage—as she goes about her duties (EE, 42). But she is not to make "a fetish" of advice and directions so that she abandons "personal judgment" (EE, 43); rather "she draws upon past experiences of experts as well as her own for the light that these shed" (EE, 42) as a wise parent would in establishing a baby's feeding schedule, neither responding to the baby's every cry nor slavishly following a pre-established pattern.

We see here a teacher able to make informed professional judgments—an important ability for Dewey, for he wanted any reflective person to be such a prudent thinker, as he put it (HWT, 125)—and form intelligent habits (EE, 35). He noted that this capacity for judgment distinguishes the artist from the "intellectual bungler" (L8, 214). Moreover, this ability to make professional judgments distinguishes the artistic educator from the pedagogical bungler. But paradoxically, it is one of the last qualities many people seem willing for a teacher to employ regularly.

These parallels and this analogy illustrate and explain the ideal Dewey had in mind. Yet the teacher is not the child's parent, and the school is not the home. We must make important distinctions between the two institutions. And for all the similarities, the distinctions become more problematic now that family structures are changing and the schools assume responsibilities once considered proper for the home. Dewey thought his a time of profound social change, but this may be one area in which he did not foresee the extent of those changes.

THE TEACHER AS SOCIAL SERVANT. Given the limited influence a school and its teachers can exert in view of their restricted involvement in social reform movements, we might naturally think of the teacher as a social servant even if we had never heard the expression. But if a teacher is a leader who identifies community problems, helps build a social consensus, and initiates progressive reforms, she can hardly see herself as simply an employee obligated to espouse the ideas of an institution, district or board, province or state. She seems rather to be employed by the community for the purpose of improving it, "a social servant set apart for the maintenance of proper social order and the securing of the right social growth...engaged, not simply in the training of individuals, but in the formation of the proper social life" (E5, 95). She is then engaged in moral education and the encouragement of critical thought. Accordingly, we are rightly interested in knowing what Dewey understood by "proper social life," "proper social order," and, standing behind the other two, "right social growth."

In fact, his educational and political philosophy interact here. Like a genuine education, a genuine community promotes growth. For Dewey, that genuine community, made genuine in its concern for the growth of its members, is democratic. A democracy represents one way people might choose to live together, and the choice of growth as the fundamental value—a democratic philosophy of life committed to voluntary association, shared interests, communication, and participation rather than externally imposed authority—has profound implications for education. Dewey explained these implications in *Democracy and Education*:

> The devotion of democracy to education is a familiar fact. The superficial explanation is that a government resting upon popular suffrage cannot be successful unless those who elect and who obey their governors are educated. Since a democratic society repudiates the principle of external authority, it must find a substitute in voluntary disposition and interest; these can be created only by education. But there is a deeper explanation. A democracy is more than a form of government; it is primarily a mode of associated living, of conjoint communicated experience. The extension in space of the number of individuals who participate in an interest so that each has to refer his own action to that of others, and to consider the action of others to give point and direction to his own, is equivalent to the breaking down of those barriers of class, race, and national territory which kept men from perceiving the full import of their activity (87).

Listing what he considered the fundamental values of American democracy as reflected in the Constitution, "freedom of belief, of speech, of the press, of assembly, and of petition...aspects of what I have called intellectual freedom, but which perhaps would better be called moral freedom," he added, "The ultimate stay and support of these liberties are the schools. For it is they which more than any other single agency, are concerned with the development of free inquiry, discussion and expression" (Ratner, 723).

Democracy may be a desirable social order, even a natural one in the sense that it encourages a genuine community and human fulfillment, but people are not born committed to it or knowing how to participate in it. Thus Dewey concluded,

> The best guarantee of collective efficiency and power is liberation and use of the diversity of individual capacities in initiative, planning, foresight, vigor and endurance. Personality must be educated, and personality cannot be educated by confining its operations to technical and specialized things, or to the less

> important relationships of life. Full education comes only when there is a responsible share on the part of each person, in proportion to capacity, in shaping the aims and policies of the social groups to which he belongs. This fact fixes the significance of democracy (RP, 209).

Thus understanding the school and the classroom as communities assumes both pedagogic and civic importance; in fact, civic education, moral education and general education become all part of one process: "the educative process is all one with the moral process, since the latter is a continuous passage of experience from worse to better" (RP, 183). In a genuine community, as Dewey defined it, civic growth and educative growth go hand in hand. The attitudes central to educational learning are also moral qualities, including open-mindedness, sincerity, breadth of outlook, thoroughness, and responsibility (DE, 356-357). From teachers who understand the importance of these ideas and who have "a genuine faith" in them, Dewey thought we had secured

> the only condition which is finally necessary in order to get from our education system all the effectiveness there is in it. The teacher who operates in this faith will find every subject, every method of instruction, every incident of school life pregnant with ethical life (E5, 83).

As we noted earlier, these moral and intellectual principles inhere in the democratic community; moral education is not a separate subject. Learning about morality and about moral reasoning does not automatically translate into "good character or good conduct" (M4, 268) if we fail to see these ideas for what they are. Values accompany the rest of life: We act on what we know, and our values concern what we do and the consequences. What we know is active rather than inert. At a minimum, the curricula we teach should be learned in "such a vital way that they become *moving* ideas, motive forces in the guidance of conduct" (M4, 268).

So Dewey found an unusually important sense in which the teacher is a social servant: The school is fundamentally an institution erected by society to do the work of building a moral society. This is its natural function. Consequently, the school is

> a form of social life, a miniature community and one in close interaction with other modes of associated experience beyond school walls. All education which develops power to share effectively in social life is moral. It forms a character which not only does the particular deed socially necessary but one which is interested in that continuous readjustment which is essential to growth. Interest in learning from all the contacts of life is the essential moral interest (DE, 360).

Believing as he did, Dewey reasonably thought that any "educational system which does not recognize that this fact entails upon it an ethical responsibility is derelict and a defaulter. It is not doing what it was called into existence to do, and what it pretends to do" (M4, 269). Educational ideas that promote growth can hardly be inert in either the individual or the community. Thus, money "spent on education is a social investment—an investment in future well being, moral, economic, physical, and intellectual, of the country" (L9, 123). As a result, he felt free to claim that "teachers are simply means, agents in this social work. They are performing the most important public duty now performed by any one group in society" (L9, 123).

THE TEACHER AS PROPHET. Understanding the teacher as a social servant illuminates in many ways Dewey's concept of the teacher as prophet, notably his explicit assertion that "the teacher is always the prophet of the true God and the usherer in of the true kingdom of God" (E5, 95). But if teachers have historically played only a limited role in introducing progressive social change and if they and schools can expect to play only a restricted role, how do we understand this bold conception? Dewey, of course, wrote under the influence of his evolving Christian beliefs when he published these words in "My Pedagogic Creed" in 1897, and as we have already noted, he later revised to some extent his opinions about both Christianity and the social efficacy of schooling. As early as 1916, he admitted that while the school is "one important method of the transmission which forms the dispositions of the immature...it is only one means, and, compared with other agencies, a relatively superficial means," an important consideration in moral education (DE, 4).

To begin, we need to return to the distinction between, on the one hand, the teacher as one citizen among many and the school as one institution among many (where power is indeed limited) and, on the other, the school as a major former of the ways of thinking and the experience of a future generation (Ratner, 694). Of teachers as citizens, Dewey said in 1937 that what they do

> may also contribute, even more than usual classroom practices, to the realization of a better society and a consequently better education. Teachers may, however, play a more understanding and more enthusiastic part in the contemporary social struggle if they appreciate the kind of education which may result from the victory of democracy (L11, 547).

Keeping in mind the school as a major former of ways of thinking and the idea that the teacher as citizen may contribute even more in the political arena and the community than in the classroom, the classroom and the school sound somewhat more robust when Dewey asserted in 1938 that

> The school is the essential distributing agency for whatever values and purposes any social group cherishes. It is not the only means, but it is the first means, the primary means and the most deliberate means by which the values that any social group cherishes, the purposes that it wishes to realize, are distributed and brought home to the thought, the observation, judgment and choice of the individual (L13, 296).

As this quotation suggests, the prophet—either one who sets forth truth or one who predicts the future—rested uneasily in Dewey. Indeed, within several months in 1934, he wrote three essays, recommending in the first caution regarding what we should expect of schools, stressing that they form character but that their influence is neither "constant nor intense" (L9, 187). In the second, he asserted that "unless hearts and minds are prepared with education" the world will not be able to deal with the "mad, often brutal, race for material gain by means of ruthless competition" (L9, 203). Going even further back toward his former and stronger view of the potency of schooling, both the prophetic "forthteller" and the "foreteller" (and a little of the scientific thinker) appear to combine in the following words:

> The other especially urgent need is connected with the present unprecedented wave of nationalistic sentiment, of racial and

> national prejudice, of readiness to resort to force of arms. For this spirit to have arisen on such a scale the schools must have somehow failed grievously. Their best excuse is maybe that schools and educators were caught unawares. But that excuse is no longer available. We now know the enemy; it is out in the open. Unless the schools of the world can unite in effort to rebuild the spirit of common understanding, of mutual sympathy and goodwill among all peoples and races, to exorcise the demon of prejudice, isolation and hatred, they themselves are likely to be submerged by the general return to barbarism, the sure outcome of present tendencies if unchecked by the forces which education alone can evoke and fortify (L9, 203-204).

In the third essay he acknowledged that schools cannot "in any literal sense be builders of a new social order [but that they] *share* in the building of the social order...as they ally themselves with this or that movement of existing social forces" (L9, 207). Again it is just as important to avoid underestimating the importance of the teacher and the school, and then to fail to make use of them, as it is to avoid overestimating them and then to be disappointed by the outcomes. The potential power of teacher and school may be enormous—and dangerous if not subject to the requirements of thinking well. Schooling is purposeful, not just the learning of a prescribed curriculum, and the voice of Dewey echoes the voice of Jesus in Matthew 16:

> What avail is it to win prescribed amounts of information about geography and history, to win ability to read and write, if in the process the individual loses his own soul: loses his appreciation of things worth while, of the values to which these things are relative; if he loses desire to apply what he has learned and, above all, loses the ability to extract meaning from his future experiences as they occur (EE, 49)?

Education is a process with the goal of growth, and as growth is the goal of education so is it the goal of life and the good society. Thus are education and democracy linked, so linked that Dewey saw them as being inseparable:

> Government, business, art, religion, all social institutions have a meaning, a purpose. That purpose is to set free and to develop the

> capacities of human individuals without respect to race, sex, class or economic status. And this is all one with saying that the test of their value is the extent to which they educate every individual into the full stature of his possibility. Democracy has many meanings, but if it has a moral meaning, it is found in resolving that the supreme test of all political institutions and industrial relations shall be the contribution they make to the all-round growth of every member of society (RP, 186).

If teachers and schools, encouraged and assisted by other habit-creating institutions, could succeed in that mission and realize that vision they would indeed usher in a new era. And whether indirectly or directly or both, this must be the work of both society and education. Here we see the teacher as more than a prophet but as the creator or artist, an analogy that we address again shortly.

THE TEACHER AS PHYSICIAN. In one of Dewey's earliest discussions of the teacher's roles and responsibilities, he claimed that the teacher must be "a wise physician of the soul" in order to secure the results she wants (E1, 88). This analogy arose during Dewey's discussion of the value of teaching psychology in high school. He maintained that the study of psychology helped students come to a better understanding of themselves as persons and, when combined with literary studies, helped transform "the reading of literature from a pastime with incidental revenue of instruction into sincere, critical and fruitful appreciation" (E1, 85). In keeping with a later emphasis upon observing and understanding the mind of each student, Dewey went on to say that the "teacher's function must be largely one of awakening, of stimulation" (E1, 86), for

> The mind of the average pupil will reject this awakening if it can, and will ask anything rather than to be led out of the fields of authority into intellectual regions where it is itself responsible for results. But the test of the teaching will after all be the degree in which the mind is awakened and is given ability to act for itself (E1, 86).

The teacher as physician must, however, caution against fostering "undue or morbid introspection" (E1, 87) as students are engaged in the personal responsibility of pursuing "the end of education [or] intellectual freedom, in its various factors of openness of mind, hospitality to ideas, and ability to move among them unconstrainedly" (E1, 87). Only by a personal engagement in the pursuit of this goal, then, can students hope to avoid becoming "monuments of blank and bland helplessness when a new idea" arises later in university (E1, 87). This physician must, therefore, like "Socrates, the founder of scientific psychology," judiciously question and direct the conscious ideas of students as they move toward intellectual freedom (E1, 87). So the teacher comes into "the most intimate relations with the minds of students [as] a wise physician of the soul" (E1, 88).

Some may argue that Dewey abandoned this general orientation to teaching. When his mildly negative opinion of students changed, he no longer stressed so heavily their responsibility in learning, he rejected the Socratic notion of innate ideas, and he abandoned his advocacy of the teacher's need to stimulate or awaken the student's mind. Even if this reasoning is correct—and it appears to be only partially so—Dewey actually increased the attention he paid in this analogy to the teacher's need for a sympathetic understanding of the life and mind of the student and thus for individualizing her instruction.

Dewey's views of teaching did change as he aged; certain ideas became more complicated and he approached others differently. But in the case before us, it appears, first, that his assumptions about students became more positive but he always remained aware of the potentiality of people to reject a life of reflection especially if environmental and institutional conditions were miseducative (L9, 202ff). Second, he modified his view of the responsibility of students but retained an emphasis on the duty of adults to create learning environments that would both stimulate and facilitate personal responsibility (L6, 109). Third, his early view of Socratic questioning never implied that he subscribed to the idea of drawing innate ideas from students (E1, 87).

THE TEACHER AS ENGINEER. The concept of the teacher as engineer lacks immediate appeal, for we tend to consider engineering a mechanical and standardized profession. But Dewey found social engineering (L5, 20) and constructive engineering (M13, 324) suitable ways of viewing the work of the teacher as a professional. The reference to social engineering occurs in *The Sources of a Science of Education*, where he argued that teaching is both a science and an art. Like engineering, teaching arises out of a matrix of sciences—biology, psychology, social psychology and sociology. The selection of relevant information from these sciences should be "organized to bring about more effective solution in practice of the difficulties and obstructions that present themselves" to both engineers and teachers (L5, 17). Even so, Dewey considered both engineering and teaching to be arts. That is to say, the actual *doing* of either engineering or teaching is more art than science (L5, 17-20). In this analogy—especially considering the word *social*—we may see Dewey adding thoughts of the teacher as social servant, prophet and intellectual leader as well as artist.

Discussing the teacher as a constructive engineer, Dewey may have made the case for the teacher as a school reformer, modifier or creator stronger than in any other analogy. In his brief discussion of educators as engineers (M13, 323-328), he stressed the importance of their proceeding beyond the creation of new ideas about schools to making these ideas concrete. Moreover, he believed that the creation of different kinds of schools would require educators to move ahead of the science of education into the domain of the "art of educational engineering" (M13, 325). Educational practitioners, in essence, must move from "pale, remote, vague, formal" ideas about schools to developing them into "concrete life-experiences" for themselves and students (M13, 324). But in order to fulfill the function of a constructive engineer, educators must have qualities we find in pioneers and artists. These qualities, however, are neither highly valued by nor frequently seen in the profession and are neither desired nor encouraged by decision and policy makers—until, that is, economic, social, and educational crises arise.

THE TEACHER AS PIONEER. As we approach our final two analogies, we see Dewey—decades before the rise of the break-the-mold theory or get-out-of-the-box stimulus—nudging educators to become more than they were fully prepared to become and urging them to encourage society to move closer to its democratic ideals. As pioneers of pedagogy, he urged them to employ their present "dependable knowledge" to reach beyond the bondage of "what was already familiar" (M13, 325). To cross the chasm of existing educational inadequacy to reach the edge of a liberating new kind of schooling, Dewey believed that educators would have to employ "imagination," be "daring," have "the courage to think out of line with convention and custom," reflect "inventiveness," and manifest "intellectual initiative" (M13, 325). In addition, teachers had to have "the courage of a creative mind," a mind not satisfied merely to think: They must take the responsibility of creating their own thoughts

(M13, 325). In this setting, Dewey insisted that educators need an experimental attitude rather than a hit-or-miss approach:

> would-be pioneers in the education field need an extensive and severe intellectual equipment. Experimentation is something other than blindly trying one's luck or mussing around in hope that something nice will be the result. Teachers who are to develop a new type of education need a more exacting and comprehensive training in science, philosophy and history than teachers who follow conventionally safe lines (M13, 326).

Viewing teachers also as pioneers for democracy, Dewey said that their responsibilities remain "forever, a frontier task," referring to the their role in helping to create a society better characterized by democratic ideals and individuals who embody these ideals. Together "students and teachers [in Dewey's hypothesized ideal democratic school and society] must create what is to be" (L11, 547). Dewey also believed that "teaching will continue to be an adventure on the social frontier, where each new generation presses its advance toward an ever-growing American dream" (L11, 547).

THE TEACHER AS ARTIST. As a larger sense of community looms over the three narrower senses of immediate concern in education, so does a larger sense of teaching and education we may express in terms of *Art as Experience* (or, perhaps better, both experience and education as art) and the teacher as artist. The fact is that we talk of *an experience*, seeing it as possessing an integrity. We see a flow and a continuity to our experience, and it is part of a larger whole. But some ways of grouping elements or breaking up this flow of components in our experience give meaning and significance to it and to our lives. Revealingly, we say that we can "*make* something" of it, revealingly because it is *we* who are *making* and it is a formulation we make. Like the artist creating, we create an integrity in the flow of experience. This is what education enables us to do: create order, meaning and significance out of chaos—or rather, it equips us through a knowledge of the implications of our actions to create and control our lives. So we read that

> the teacher is a trainer of mind, a former of character; that he is an artist above nature, yet in harmony with nature, who applies the

> science of education to help another to the full realization of his personality in a character of strength, beauty, freedom (PN, 4).

But we also read that "nature is an artist that works from within instead of without. Hence all change, or matter, is potentiality for finished objects" (L1, 79).

We feel no surprise, therefore, when we learn that Dewey could say and mean that "Knowledge is power and knowledge is achieved by sending the mind to school to [study] nature and learn her processes of change" (RP, 49). That power and its wise and proper exercise depend, for the teacher as artist as for the sculptor, on knowing, understanding and making use of the laws of nature to produce change and to anticipate and choose among the consequences of our contemplated actions. Like the artist—or, we would say, like *other* artists—the educator faces "the problem of creating something that is not the exact duplicate of some previous creation" (L9, 198) and must understand that

> a large part of the art of instruction lies in making the difficulty of new problems large enough to challenge thought and small enough so that, in addition to the confusion naturally attending the novel elements, there shall be luminous familiar spots from which helpful suggestions may spring (DE, 157).

The artistry of the teacher, Dewey believed, is thus the supreme art and involves "giving shape to human powers and adapting them to social service" (E5, 94). By "giving shape to human powers," Dewey meant far more than copying from nature or imposing a predetermined design. Like an artist, we learn the consequences and possible consequences of our actions, but we also choose and control our actions. Nature, including students, is not, after all, mere chaos in the face of which no intelligent action is possible. As we might expect, Dewey saw a connection between the past, the present and the future in artistry, claiming that "the artist is controlled in the process of his work by his grasp of the connection between what he has already done and what he is to do next" (L10, 52).

The reason for Dewey's respect for the child's free activity becomes apparent in this context. He saw nature in the child as the spirit of an artist naturally seeking meaning, significance and order and so making education possible. Thus while resisting the temptation to pamper, a teacher can guide the interests, impulses and needs of the child into new experiences and understandings. Guided by an artist who is above nature into worthwhile experiences, a child proceeds toward genuine growth. In typical style, Dewey concluded that "the teacher's own claim to rank as an artist is measured by his ability to foster the attitude of the artist in those who study with him, whether they be youth or little children" (L8, 348). Teaching as an artist, therefore, involves more than "arousing enthusiasm" for a field of inquiry and developing a "mastery of technique of subjects"; it also effects an "enlargement of mental vision, power of increased discrimination of final values, a sense for ideas, for principles" (L8, 349) that, sadly enough, rarely concern the educational policy maker and bureaucrat.

In an extended discussion of the teacher as artist, Dewey drew together several thoughts on the subject, including the teacher's artistic use of technique, her artistic insight into and sympathy with the child, and the personal sensitivity and skill required for helping a student develop the attitude of an artist. Administrators, policy makers, bureaucrats and aspiring and practicing teachers may well find reassurance and challenge in Dewey's words during times of educational reform, disappointment and crisis:

> Now, there is a technique of teaching, a technique of the management of the schoolroom, keeping order, treating children, of asking questions, even of giving out, assigning lessons; assigning the different school work and so forth, is just as much a part of the art of teaching as the particular technique of the artist is a part of the calling of the artist, but over and above that is the need for that sense of the purpose and meaning of it that results in sympathy with a development of the life of the children, what is going on not in their more outward motions, in the things they do, but what is going on in their feelings, their imagination, what effect the schoolroom is having on the permanent disposition, the side of their emotions and imagination, without which the teacher cannot be an artist, no matter how complete and adequate the teacher's command is of the technique of teaching, that is, of the various forms of outward skill which are necessary to make the successful teacher. The teacher as an artist needs to be one who is engaged in getting the pupils as much as possible into the attitude of the artist in their relations in life, that is, solve what is after all the great problem, the moral, the intellectual problem of everyone, to get habits of efficient action, so that the person

> won't be a mere day-dreamer or theorist, or a wasteful or incompetent person, but to get that unity with certain affections and desires and sympathies and with power to carry out intellectual plans. That can be got only when we give as much attention to the thinking side of the life of the pupils from the first day as we give to their forming these good outward habits (L17, 81-82).

Conclusion

As corollaries of his understanding of democracy and education as growth, Dewey's ten analogies of the teacher together with his four conceptions of the educational community provide a rich, comprehensive and coherent context in which to locate, and so to understand and assess, claims made about the roles and responsibilities of teachers and schools and their relationships with families, other institutions and larger social groups. His contributions respond to our intuitive sense of the complexity of such discussions and the competing claims on a teacher's time, loyalties and commitments. But above all, they draw attention to the educational criteria that deserve to be made central, justifying an optimism in teaching based on the belief that the right reasons are educational reasons when we understand them correctly. This is the point of Dewey's observation that "the fundamental issue is...a question of what anything whatever must be to be worthy of the name *education*." If, as Dewey claimed,

> the educational system must move one way or another, either backward to the intellectual and moral standards of a pre-scientific age or forward to ever greater utilization of scientific method in the development of the possibilities of growing, expanding experience (EE, 89),

then an understanding of both the duties of the four related communities and the ten overlapping sets of responsibilities can be immeasurably helpful but also more demanding for the teacher. Dewey warned:

> I gladly admit that the new education is simpler in principle than the old. It is in harmony with principles of growth....But the easy and the simple are not identical. To discover what is really simple and to act upon the discovery is an exceedingly difficult task (EE, 30).

Dewey hoped that the task would become easier, however, after years of diligent pursuit and cooperation among like-minded educators, for when the simple is new, not widely understood, open to misunderstanding and not ingrained in our conventional ways of thinking and traditional practices, advancement comes slowly (EE, 90). Always skeptical of the quick fix or the instant panacea, Dewey knew that not even well-prepared teachers could completely transform schools. Still less did he think a new principal, a new curriculum, a new school structure, a new collaboration, or a new vision could provide a cure-all. The problem of reform is still more complex and complicated; the "reorganization of education so that learning takes place in connection with the intelligent carrying forward of purposeful activities is slow work [and] can only be accomplished piecemeal, a step at a time" (DE, 137). Even so, the complexity and difficulty of the task of reform is no reason to delay action; it is "a challenge to undertake the task of reorganization courageously and to keep at it persistently" (DE, 137).

If we examine many contemporary educational reform efforts, we now have a way of situating and assessing them from a Deweyan perspective. For instance, we find it difficult to judge the merits of Charter schools without looking at the educational provisions of the particular charters proposed; but as with privatization, any commitment to the larger senses of community would seem to be at risk. Paideia proposals risk generalizing the importance of funded experience as the ultimate basis for the curriculum and then confusing it with theories of learning and the design of promising classroom experiences. Customer-oriented models and more generally those borrowed from business, like those stressing employability and national economic growth, often fail to make central the educational ideals of growth, expanded experience and increasing capacity for growth. They may rightly appeal to a recognition of the important influence of economic factors in educational policies, practices and goals; and they may appeal to the need for education to provide a realistic, practical preparation for the lives students lead after their schooling is complete. But they often fail to provide the context for discussing the difference between genuine and felt needs and short-term and long-term interests. On the other hand, some philosophies or views of site-based management, cooperative learning styles, local community involvement, and a common curriculum, if implemented in the right spirit, might have the potential for building classroom and school, local and larger communities in which the appropriate kinds of growth could occur.

But Dewey's insights suggest that reconceptualizations and reorientations of education based on a single factor—be it the information age and the changing nature of knowledge, the changing nature of society, or a new conception of intelligence—are almost certain to be misleading. Yet the last of these, the nature of intelligence, reminds us of the central place of epistemology in Dewey's thinking and forces us to ask about the appropriateness of Dewey's conception of the scientific method (Greene, 1994), its reflection of the nature of thought, and then the epistemological basis of his conception of education. In a word, Dewey's perspective enables us to bring much recent research, thinking and common sense to the consideration and, perhaps, solution of complex social and educational problems.

CHAPTER FIVE

The General Education of Teachers

> Teachers who are to develop a new type of education need a more exacting and comprehensive training in science, philosophy and history than teachers who follow conventionally safe lines (M13, 326).

> The real course of study must come to the child from the teacher. What gets to the child is dependent upon what is in the mind and consciousness of the teacher, and upon the way it is in his mind (M1, 273).

To educate rather than merely to instruct in a skill or a particular topic commonly implies a larger involvement of the teacher and the student, a concern with the kind of person each is and will become. This breadth of responsibility may be part of the point of calling school teachers *educators*. The school teacher then ought at least to be an educated person who shares the qualities of an educated person with her students. Hence Dewey linked the teacher's own education to what we might more narrowly call teacher preparation and to professional responsibilities.

Moreover, for Dewey, simply by virtue of being an educated person, a teacher becomes an active and involved member of several communities. She cannot but reflect on her observations and experiences and, as a result of that reflection, attempt to influence the communities and the world around her in what she sees as desirable directions. If this is so in general, it is more clearly and explicitly so in her specific work of helping to form students' thinking, attitudes and experiences. Thus, unlike critics who would restrict teachers' professional responsibilities, Dewey linked education and teaching to social and educational reform—to looking continually for a better way within both the school and society. Indeed, "any adjustment," Dewey maintained, "which really and permanently succeeds within the school walls must reach out and be an adjustment of forces in the social environment" (M1, 285). So, as a professional responsibility, he expected the teacher to have a life-long disposition toward personal growth, toward educational reform, and—because personal and educational problems are embedded in social problems and a social context—toward social reform. He based this duty on a day-to-day disposition to reflect and on an inclination toward thoughtful and informed scientific analysis of experience. But perhaps because of this emphasis on reflection, in contrast to the emphases of some social reconstructionists, his commitment to educational and social reform precluded the use of schools for propaganda or as platforms to promote specific programs of social reform. He opposed indoctrinating students (L11, 415) and advocated instead a school and university education that would help them be "reborn into the life of intelligence" (M15, 7) by learning to think for themselves and, thereby, "cut loose as far as possible" from the dogmatic positions and attitudes of both conservatives and reformers (M15, 198).

Talk of on-going reform and life-long learning, then, came naturally to Dewey, though he attached specific educational meanings to these terms. The education of professional teachers begins and continues in the home, neighborhood and community. Then it grows in school and university environments and progresses through the influence of prior and on-going educational experiences into an expanding universe of educative experiences. Dewey's observation from *Experience and Education* is informative:

> As an individual passes from one situation to another, his world, his environment, expands and contracts. He does not find himself living in another world but in a different part or aspect of one and the same world. What he has learned in the way of knowledge and skill in one situation becomes an instrument of understanding and dealing effectively with the situations which follow. The process goes on as long as life and learning continue (EE, 44).

But if teachers are to be more than just generally well-educated individuals, if there is something more for them to learn specifically about teaching and some sense of professional expertise to gain, then we must weave from scattered threads of Dewey's writing a tapestry that includes many current issues: the selection of prospective teachers, their appropriate general education, the knowledge they need of the content and subject matter to be taught, the requisite professional knowledge (including the kinds of knowledge and the place of theory and practice), the nature of their field experiences, and some account of on-going education and professional development. In fact, while we can separate out these elements of teacher preparation for discussion, they overlap and inter-link, and all together, they form a relatively consistent philosophical theory.

Modern educational reformers openly address the question of the appropriate components of teacher preparation programs, and we can now choose from a plethora of competing and conflicting recommendations and prescriptions for improvement. They include proposals for attracting outstanding candidates and raising admission standards, requiring fewer education courses and more arts and science courses, designing subject matter courses especially for prospective teachers, developing alternative routes to certification, increasing practice teaching and offering more field-based courses, collaborating with associate or professional development schools, working with business and other community groups, or better defining and developing the competencies required of teachers. We have, as well, those who consider teacher preparation—or at least its teacher education component—unnecessary; all we need, they say, are people who know their subjects.

Almost as if he were anticipating our quandary, Dewey addressed many of these issues explicitly or implicitly, though not exactly as we might expect or for the reasons we might think. Unlike many who focus on a single problem or remedy, Dewey tried to tie the various elements of educational reform into a dynamic and coherent theory of education, society and experience. He considered these connections obvious since he conceived of philosophy of education as "a branch of the theory of social ideals and the institutions by which the ideals may be realized" (L11, 177). The idea that philosophy of education is a branch of the field of inquiry that studies social ideals and how social institutions help us reach these ideals represents an interesting and understandable twist in Dewey's thought. He saw philosophy of education not as an isolated discipline but as one facet of a broader investigation into social ideals or ends and the means of achieving them. From this perspective, philosophy of education becomes a part of the human problems curriculum Dewey urged upon elementary and secondary public schools.

We hasten here to mention two related or overlapping caveats. As Neufeldt's Introduction makes clear, Dewey developed his ideas from issues, circumstances and options specific to his time. But as well, because we can hardly dismiss Dewey's social and educational concerns as old-fashioned and because we use a similar language in somewhat different ways, we risk reading into Dewey our own preconceptions. We see then the double danger of recruiting Dewey to some current educational reform movement. In fact, he would ask us all to go beyond the understandings and conceptions that grew out of the problems of his time or that we take for granted and to reframe and so rethink our questions and suggested answers. So we should neither *read into* Dewey's ideas the issues we wish he had addressed nor *stay within* his ideas and fail to seek insight beyond that which he offered. Ideally, then, Dewey's thinking, far from an intellectual refuge, is a reflective pause on our way to improving our own thinking. As Johnson (1995) implies, we should see ourselves as philosophical pilgrims rather than as Dewey's disciples.

The Selection of Prospective Teachers

Many interested in educational reform throughout history have noted the importance of selecting carefully those who become teachers and administrators—often going so far as to propose restricting admissions to educator preparation programs. Contemporary educational reformers often share a concern that only well-qualified people be allowed to teach although few have dealt extensively with the problem of selection and many seem to view it as a shortcut to improving or altering the teaching profession and, thereby, schooling. Dewey characteristically placed this single consideration of teacher selection within a larger, more realistic context of social problems possibly more devious and prevalent in his time. He saw, for instance, that "personal intrigue, political bargaining, and the effort of some individual or class to get power in the community through manipulation of patronage" (M1, 276) influence hiring, school policies and reform, not to mention the very attractiveness of the profession. Intolerable teaching environments of this sort, Dewey claimed, drive the better teachers from the profession, and "the best class of minds" (PN, 8) are reluctant to enter it.

We can, therefore, supplement our consideration of the problem of selecting candidates with excellent potential for teaching with a consideration of several other factors, including the existing respect for the profession, the image and practices of specific school districts, and the reputations of particular schools. Who, indeed, we might ask, would be attracted or repelled by a

> system which makes no great demands upon originality, upon invention, upon the continuous expression of individuality, [but] works automatically to put and to keep the incompetent teachers in the school[?] It puts them there because, by a natural law of spiritual gravitation, the best minds are drawn to the places where they can work effectively. The best minds are not especially likely to be drawn where there is danger that they may have to submit to conditions which no self-respecting intelligence likes to put up with; and where their time and energy are likely to be so occupied with details of external conformity that they have no opportunity for free and full play of their own vigor (M3, 234).

If we want to select talented and well-prepared future teachers, then, Dewey believed we must address these problems. The options that remain are clear: Select nearly anyone willing to suffer the conditions the school board and administration creates or allows. As Dewey concluded,

> It is the mediocre and the bungler who can most readily accommodate himself to the conditions imposed by ignorance and routine; it is the higher type of mind and heart which suffers most from its encounter with incapacity and ignorance (PN, 8).

Moreover, unlike some unrestrained contemporary proponents of selecting only "the best and the brightest" aspiring teachers, Dewey recognized that the profession of education requires large numbers of practitioners and that while attracting and retaining some of "the best minds" may be desirable, "genius in education is as rare as the genius in other realms of human activity. Education is, and forever will be, in the hands of ordinary men and women" (PN, 8). Apparently he thought we must be satisfied for the most part with so-called average or ordinary men and women, a disconcerting position given the flood of literature that suggests a major part of the problem of schooling is the intellectual inadequacies in the profession. Two circumstances require clarification, however, if Dewey's position is to be correctly understood. First, he argued that many of the more capable would-be teachers and practicing teachers were repelled by school conditions that could be remedied. So he expected the more naturally talented to be both attracted to and retained in the profession. Second, he appears to have had a higher opinion of the potential and capabilities of "ordinary men and women" than do those who want to enlist only the most capable people.

Precisely how did Dewey view the "ordinary men and women" in whose hands education was destined to remain? The presence of a nearly universal trait and skill (PN, 8) in ordinary people, sympathy and natural aptitude (among those qualities we, perhaps, should look for in prospective teachers), encouraged him:

> Fortunately for the race, most persons, though not "born" teachers, are endowed with some "genial impulse," some native instinct and skill for education; for *the cardinal requisite* in this endowment is, after all, *sympathy with human life and its aspirations*. We are all born to be educators, to be parents, as we are not born to be engineers, or sculptors, or musicians, or painters. Native capacity for education is therefore much more common than native capacity for any other calling (PN, 7, italics added).

Even though Dewey saw sympathy—a quality we noticed earlier in his concept of the teacher as artist—or "the instinct to help others in their struggle for self-mastery and self-expression" (PN, 7) as an indispensable quality, he did not see the trait as necessarily and naturally maturing or permanent. He may have been thinking of some burned-out or embittered teacher he had observed. Only those teachers, Dewey said, "who have it in themselves to stay young indefinitely and to retain a lively sympathy with the spirit of youth should remain long in the teaching profession" (L13, 344).

There is another important trait or particular manifestation of sympathy, perhaps implicit in our typical question, Why do I wish to be a teacher? And it reflects his view of learning as more than rote and recitation. It involves understanding the mental processes of students. Without specifying whether this specific feature was instinctive, he observed that

> The teacher is distinguished...by interest in watching the movements of the minds of others, by being sensitive to all the signs of response they exhibit; their quality of response or lack of it, to subject-matter presented. A personal sympathy...does its best work, however, when it is in sympathy with the mental movements of others, is alive to perplexities and problems, discerning of their causes, having the mental tact to put the finger on the cause of failure, quick to see every sign of promise and to nourish it to maturity (L13, 345).

In a word, Dewey believed an intending teacher must show signs of and the practicing teacher must possess a special kind of sympathy that results in wanting to "help others in their struggle for self-mastery" (PN, 7) and that manifests itself in "sympathetic understanding of individuals as individuals [and] which gives...an idea of what is actually going on in the minds of those who are learning" (EE, 39). If Dewey was correct, the ordinary person has a native sympathy that motivates her to help others and gives sympathetic insight into the minds of the students she guides.

Moreover, reflecting common experience, Dewey noticed some "extraordinarily good teachers" who had never completed formal teacher preparation programs (L13, 345), people who (in part through luck, intuition, circumstances, solitary reflection, or a combination of matters) have—largely because of their developed sympathetic sensitivities—proved capable of effective teaching. They have a highly developed, "quick, sure and unflagging sympathy with the operations and process of the minds they are in contact with. Their own minds move in harmony with those of others, appreciating their difficulties, entering into their problems, sharing their intellectual victories" (L12, 345-346).

Despite the routine, ignorance, obstruction and belittlement found in segments of the profession and the occasional naturally or culturally gifted teacher, in the interests of widespread educational reform and uniformly good teaching, Dewey still wanted to attract the right people; to make room for reflection, originality, invention and individuality in districts and schools; and to create school and district environments that would prize genius. Accordingly, he stressed that

> native endowment can work itself out in the best possible results only when it works under right conditions. Even if scientific

> insight were not a necessity for the true educator himself, it would still remain a necessity for others in order that they might not obstruct and possibly drive from the profession the teacher possessed of the inborn divine light, and restrict or paralyze the efforts of the teacher less richly endowed (PN, 8).

Having attracted appropriate people to the profession, Dewey recognized a need for carefully planned teacher preparation programs since "training and native outfit, culture and nature, are never opposed to each other." He also recognized that would-be teachers are unequally endowed with abilities or sympathy and need to have their capacities and sympathies nourished since "in most people this native sympathy is either dormant or blind and irregular in its action; it needs to be awakened, to be cultivated, and above all to be intelligently directed" (PN, 7). Teacher education, then, should build on these capacities, as school learning builds on what students bring to school.

Yet another important trait sharply distinguishes the successful educator from others, and separates mindless drill and recitation from the excitement of inquiry: the love of knowledge and of learning, which enlivens teaching and so often explains the success of great teachers who have had no significant teacher preparation. Each of us can recall

> that the teachers who left the most enduring impression were those who awakened...a new intellectual interest, who communicated... some of their own enthusiasm for a field of knowledge or art, who gave...desire to inquire and find out a momentum of its own. This one thing is most needful. Given this hunger, the mind will go on (L8, 329).

But however important intellectual depth and excitement may be, Dewey cautioned about selecting teachers on the basis of an unbalanced intellectual and theoretical orientation. Quite apart from the additional considerations of sympathy, a desire to help others, youthfulness and an understanding of learners' ways of thinking, teachers need a sound understanding of society and its functions, institutions and vocational expectations—including the social purposes of schools—if they are to provide the kind of education that results in citizens prepared to live in a democratic community and contribute to its well-being and growth (M15, 158-169).

Thinking of the subject matter to be taught, one always finds a temptation to stress academic success, notably marks or grades, in selecting "the best minds" and "the best and brightest." One tends naturally to be inclined toward those for whom school has been a successful, enjoyable, rewarding experience—an experience not, however, typical of all students. But, as Dewey explained, choosing *all* prospective teachers on the basis of an academic mind-set may alienate students of a practical bent:

> The prevalent overestimation of value, for mind training, of *theoretic* subjects as compared with practical pursuits, is doubtless due in part to the fact that the teacher's calling tends to select those persons in whom the theoretic interest is specially strong and to repel those in whom executive abilities are marked. Teachers sifted out on this basis judge pupils and subjects by a like standard, encouraging an intellectual one-sidedness in those to whom it is naturally congenial, and repelling from study those in whom practical instincts are more urgent (L8, 160).

Teacher education candidates who know something about the complexities of life, who have grown through their non-academic educational experiences—and perhaps their own difficulties in school—and who can share their insights with their colleagues and students may have important and relevant experience to contribute. Perhaps this experience explains why many second career and late-entering teachers receive praise today for their ability to "relate to" all students, not just those attracted by the more esoteric dimensions of schooling. Linking school learning to out-of-school life and work was hardly a strange idea to Dewey. Ironically, many teachers today need programs that are designed to provide them with some experience in real life businesses, enterprises and corporations as much as their students. Teachers fresh from university preparation programs often have had little experience in other places of employment.

Finally (recalling the question, Why do I wish to be a teacher?) we see Dewey drawing attention to the need for explicit self-selection. Aspiring educators and those continuing in the profession should thoughtfully examine the field of education and the personal qualities they themselves possess. Wanting potential educators to have chosen their career responsibly, intelligently and reflectively, he suggested three topics for contemplation: the advantages to be derived from teaching, the match of one's personal traits with employment opportunities, and the difficulties and disappointments of teaching.

Dewey recognized that teaching offers a variety of potential rewards from "cultural development" and "intellectual, moral, [and] social" growth to "material rewards" and "opportunities for usefulness." He also understood that considerations involved in the selection of teaching as a career are complicated (L13, 342). Personal preferences as well as circumstances, for instance, influence the decision; and the latter, among them professional conditions, vary from one school, region, state or province, and country to another. But one constant for the intending educator Dewey insisted on was mental inquisitiveness, another reflection of the kind of learning he valued: "No one can be really successful in performing the duties and meeting these demands [of teaching] who does not retain his intellectual curiosity intact throughout his entire career" (L13, 342). But even the material benefits of teaching or their absence cannot be simply assessed, and they certainly depend in part on temperament and circumstances:

> The material or pecuniary rewards of the calling are not the chief reason for going into it. There are no financial prizes equalling those to be obtained in business, the law, or even, if we take the exceptional physician as the measure, in medicine. On the other hand, there are not the great disparities and risks which exist in most other callings. The rewards, if not great, are reasonably sure. Until the depression they were, moreover, pretty steadily increasing. If we include vacation periods as part of the material reward of teaching, the profession ranks high. There is no other calling which allows such a prolonged period for travel, for study, and recreation as does the educational. To many temperaments, this phase of teaching counterbalances all the material drawbacks (L13, 343-344).

Despite increasing awareness of the problems of burnout and the need to screen persons unsuited for the profession, we hear less today of mental and physical fitness as explicit conditions for teaching or for excluding people from teacher preparation. Dewey, however, was explicit and adamant:

> Those persons who are peculiarly subject to nervous strain and worry should not go into teaching. It is not good for them nor for

> the pupils who come under their charge. One of the most depressing phases of the vocation is the number of care-worn teachers one sees, with anxiety depicted on the lines of their faces, reflected in their strained high pitched voices and sharp manners. While contact with the young is a privilege for some temperaments, it is a tax on others, and a tax which they do not bear up under very well (L13, 344).

Added to "all-round health" and "nervous balance" is "a natural love of contact with the young" (L13, 344) and "a natural love of communicating knowledge." A teacher had to have the former love, Dewey thought, to avoid being bored, perfunctory and mechanical with children and to promote an encouraging approach to learning. We have seen the importance for him of sympathy, enthusiasm and love of learning and knowledge (HWT, 263; L13, 344-345). The latter love reminds us of a further element in the love of knowledge:

> There are scholars who have...[a love of knowledge] in a marked degree but who lack enthusiasm for imparting it. To the "natural-born" teacher learning is incomplete unless it is shared. He or she is not contented with it in and for its own sake. He or she wants to use it to stir up the minds of others. Nothing is so satisfactory as to see another mind get the spark of an idea and kindle a glow because of it (L13, 345).

So what finally can we conclude about an aspiring or practicing teacher's academic background and preparation? Failing to master the subject to be taught risks missing educative opportunities or actually misleading students. For those few possessing the other appropriate pedagogically relevant dispositions—the self-made or natural teachers—an excellent academic preparation may be enough. On the other hand, there is always more to learn and no teacher can be an expert in all she teaches. Dewey proposed a modern-sounding solution reminiscent of such current phrasing as "the structure of the discipline" and "the mode of inquiry" in debates about the possibility of education in the face of the knowledge explosion: depth in one field together with the appropriate spirit of inquiry and the ability to foster this curiosity in others (L13, 345). He could make this proposal in part because of his belief in a structure common to all disciplines, each with a key set of concepts whose interlinking makes possible webs of meaning. He also spoke from his belief in a common model of thinking, the "scientific" method of inquiry:

> Every branch of science, geology, zoölogy, chemistry, physics, astronomy, as well as the different branches of mathematics, arithmetic, algebra, calculus, etc., aims at establishing its own specialized set of concepts that are keys to understanding the phenomena that are classified in each field. In this way there is provided for every typical branch of subject matter a set of meanings and principles so closely interknit that any one implies some other, according to definite conditions, that, under certain other conditions, implies another, and so on (L8, 261).

So in Dewey's opinion,

> the teacher should combine an active and keen interest in some one branch of knowledge with interest and skill in following the reactions of the minds of others. I would not say that a teacher ought to strive to be a high-class scholar in all the subjects he or she has to teach. But I would say that a teacher ought to have an unusual love and aptitude in some one subject; history, mathematics, literature, science, a fine art, or whatever. The teacher will then have the *feel* for genuine information and insight in all subjects; will not sink down to the level of the conventional and perfunctory teacher who merely "hears" recitations, and will communicate by unconscious contagion love of learning to others (L13, 345).

Finally then we turn to "the discouragements and...the difficulties connected with the vocation" (L13, 342). Neither wishing to turn away the would-be teacher nor wanting anyone to venture into the profession unprepared, Dewey specified the challenges, problems, obstacles and difficulties that stimulate some and overwhelm others. "Few things," he said, "are more disastrous than the round peg in the square hole" (L13, 346). For example, some aspiring teachers look down on the young; for others the profession is too safe and protected, not challenging enough; still others are intimidated or crushed by the political forces in the outside community. This third point should alert intending teachers attracted by the passivity and docility of the traditional school. Should "the most docile among the young...who [want to] become teachers when they are adults" exercise a special caution about both whether and where they should be teachers (M13, 327)? Such people no doubt should carefully consider their options; but for others, those "who are fitted for the work, the calling of the teacher combines three rewards, each intense and unique. *Love of knowledge; sympathy with growth, intellectual and moral; interest in the improvements of society through improving the individuals who compose it*" (L13, 346, italics added).

Implicit in this discussion, and explicit elsewhere in Dewey's writing, are ideals of both individual teachers and the profession, schools and communities. Above all, Dewey wanted to attract creative, nurturing, gifted, and learning people by identifying and encouraging those with educationally valuable dispositions and qualities—people with a sympathetic interest in and insight into human beings, a love for and depth of understanding in a branch of knowledge, a sense of excitement about inquiry, a passion for communicating a field of knowledge, a balanced interest in the practical and the theoretical domains of life, the personal health and understanding of themselves that enable them to succeed in educational settings, and a fondness for and attachment to children and youth. And he wanted them to choose to come to the profession freely, to be selected by its representatives, and, having made an informed and thoughtful choice, to stay.

Such people, Dewey believed, would create a profession that merits and gains public respect, as the best in the profession now do. They require preparation programs that identify, encourage and nourish these qualities. They also require schools, school systems and communities that allow them to exercise their professional competencies, commitments and judgments.

The Education of Teachers

We see clearly at this juncture that for Dewey every educative experience contributes to the general education of aspiring teachers and, though one can make a theoretical distinction between the two realms, helps form part of their professional teacher preparation program. He differed from many in this emphasis on the continuity of education, which begins virtually at birth and ends only in death, an emphasis reflecting his belief that educative experience begins with our earliest experiences. It occurs in the family, the neighborhood and the broader environment. It continues in elementary and secondary school, through and beyond university studies, and on throughout life. What we observed earlier concerning dichotomous thinking, traditional and progressive schools, a scientific ethics, and a community of individuals—and especially concerning a human problems curriculum, cultural achievement, and the democratic, moral, social and political ends of schooling—all bear upon the education of future teachers. In essence, the early educative experiences and learning communities a future teacher enjoys have a profound impact upon her living and thinking and teaching.

This philosophy of experience, society, learning, inquiry, growth and education represents Dewey's "attempt to apply a single social philosophy, a single educational philosophy, to a single problem manifested in forms that are only outwardly diverse" (M1, 259)—that is, to show a seamless unity in the diversity of experience. It forced him to question past theories of general education, rejecting those rooted in the classics and liberal studies, despite his recognition of the importance of the academic disciplines, on the grounds that they served essentially only certain class interests and promoted undemocratic occupational and social divisions. It led him as well to argue for a new general education suited to the needs of contemporary democratic societies. Where we might today hear talk of industry, technology, business, communications, the information highway, or the world wide web, he maintained that

> The first thing which has to be done...is to study the most important processes of today in farming, manufacturing, and transportation to find out what are the fundamental and general elements which compose them, and thereby develop a new kind of *general education* on top of which the more special and technical training for distinctive vocations may be undertaken (M10, 14, italics added).

Dewey's social philosophy, his social commitments, and his theory of learning coincide at this point. The old social order or an elite class that serves the interests of a few has failed to produce the kind of democratic community responsive to the needs of the greater society. It has also enshrined a false theory of what is worth learning and why and has prized a way of learning and kinds of learning, a curriculum, leading neither to intellectual and social progress nor to a scientific attitude of openness and inquiry. The new education then must find a new starting point in experience, a new attitude to learning and correspondingly a new approach to teaching.

Because of the intertwining and overlapping of general education with a teacher's education, much of what we say about the teacher's education will reflect the larger concept of education and indicate the kind of learning environment she should help create particularly for her students and in her school. Setting aside initial explicitly identified professional preparation and on-going study in the form of both professional development and in-service training and even general personal educational growth, we focus here on these four topics: socialization, elementary education, secondary education, and university study.

INFORMAL EDUCATION. Dewey believed that everywhere children and others sleep, play, eat, cook, read, mix, observe, talk, argue, fight, sing and dance is a place where learning experiences occur and can be either educative, noneducative or miseducative. Given the breadth of Dewey's conception of education and learning, socialization or informal education is a key part of his account of the general education of aspiring teachers. Some settings, notably those that are true and democratic communities, foster a genuine informal education. Thus anyone concerned with experiences that promote the growth of children, youth or adults (and particularly parents with their own children) can be thought of as an educator:

> Good teaching of this kind will be done in doctors' offices, in museums, newspaper plants, farms, forests, steamboats, buses, art studios, factories, stores, government offices, civic concerts, theaters, public discussions, and in the thousand other enterprises of living. The community itself...can become cooperative and educative. All of the agencies which investigate, invent, produce, distribute, inform, cure, build, entertain, or govern will have the additional function of helping every one directly involved and all of the youth of the community to understand how their work is done and why it is done as it is (L11, 541).

With this philosophical and pedagogical backdrop, Dewey spoke of the ideal home, an ideal learning environment that educates the child before school, during the school years and after school hours:

> If we take an example from an ideal home, where the parent is intelligent enough to recognize what is best for the child, and is able to supply what is needed, we find the child learning through the social converse and constitution of the family. There are certain points of interest and value to him in the conversation carried on: statements are made, inquiries arise, topics are discussed, and the child continually learns. He states his experiences, his misconceptions are corrected. Again the child participates in the household occupations, and thereby gets habits of industry, order, and regard for the rights and ideas of others, and the fundamental habit of subordinating his activities to the general interest of the household. Participation in these household tasks becomes an opportunity for gaining knowledge. The ideal home would naturally have a workshop where the child could work out his constructive instincts. It would have a miniature laboratory in which his inquiries could be directed. The life of the child would extend out of doors to the garden, surrounding fields, and forests. He would have his excursions, his walks and talks, in which the larger world out of doors would open to him (M1, 23-24).

Good parents—and by implication good hospitals, museums, businesses and factories—can plan the experiences of children and their influences so as to become models for the school and the community: "What the best and wisest parent wants for his own child, that must the community want for all of its children. Any other ideal for our schools is narrow and unlovely; acted upon, it destroys our democracy" (M1, 5). The complexities and relationships of the home also establish an ideal for the school and other learning communities characterized by multi-aged groupings of children and adults:

> Mother and nurse, father and older children, determine what experiences the child shall have; they constantly instruct him as to the meaning of what he does and undergoes. The conceptions that are socially current and important become the child's principles of interpretation and estimation long before he attains to personal and deliberate control of conduct. Things come to him clothed in language, not in physical nakedness, and this garb of communication makes him a sharer in the beliefs of those about him. These beliefs coming to him as so many facts form his mind;

> they furnish the centres about which his own personal expeditions and perceptions are ordered. Here we have "categories" of connection and unification (RP, 92).

Three sorts of opportunity and obligation emerge from such an account: one for the practicing teacher, the second for the prospective teacher, and the third for the community. The experiences that contributed to the teacher's education, particularly if she applies them in an informed way, help her gain valuable insights into how children learn and so, especially if she knows the community well, into creating environments that encourage students to have similar educative experiences. Reflection on how learning takes place and some preparation for the study and understanding of communities then form part of the teacher's initial preparation. But if Dewey is right about the importance of understanding the particular community, much of this learning becomes possible only after the teacher has secured a position, which obligates schools, districts and communities to assist their teachers as they grow in their understanding of the lives and interests of their students. In view of this point, Dewey might be disappointed that so much of the planned professional development of contemporary practicing teachers occurs in schools and in universities. No doubt, he would support some of these kinds of professional growth, but he also would strongly support a genuine understanding of the histories, cultures, economies, homes and communities that shape and reshape the children who inhabit schools only five or six hours a day.

We mentioned three opportunities and obligations. The first is the teacher's opportunity and obligation to learn from and about the community. The second is the community's opportunity and obligation to support the learning of the teacher and the school about the community itself. The third is the prospective teacher's or the child's opportunity to have informative and useful educative experiences provided by families and the community that present chances to appraise the value the community places upon personal and community growth, education and the education profession. This third opportunity seems inextricably tied to the first two. The prospective teacher or the child who grows up in a family and a community that highly values and supports local educative experiences and professional educators will undoubtedly see, think and value differently than someone who does not. As difficult as this model sounds, Dewey's social and educational philosophy demands no less. It also demands an imaginative and determined school and community to conduct such a human experiment. But evidence from certain ethnic communities suggests that his model can succeed.

Dewey's disappointment with the profession today would be natural from yet another perspective since learning about the peculiar resources and particular problems of the community helps teachers fulfill their roles as leading community members, enabling the profession to become

> a body of self-respecting teachers and educators who will see to it that their ideas and their experience in educational matters shall really count in the community; and who, in order that these may count, will identify themselves with the interests of the community; who will conceive of themselves as citizens and as servants of the public, and not merely as hired employees of a certain body of men (M10, 171).

Such a community-oriented professionalism—whether the community be the classroom learning group, school, neighborhood, town or nation—goes hand in hand with a narrower, more immediate sort of professionalism: a teacher's obligation to continue learning from students and colleagues and from reflection on experience in ways that contribute to personal and professional growth and so to better teaching. If there is any truth to the assertion that modeling facilitates learning, we can only guess what children would learn from parents, teachers, citizens and civic leaders in truly educative families and communities of the sort Dewey envisioned. In such a community, schooling as we know it today might virtually disappear. In fact, as we shall see in a later chapter, Dewey made this very claim.

ELEMENTARY EDUCATION. The kinds of experiences that occur before schooling continue outside school once the child enrolls. Dewey wanted these ordinary experiences of daily life to be part of the school and the classroom, believing that this continuity of experience was the only way at the elementary level to make sure of the relevance and applicability of school learning to the life of the child. This continuity also eases the transition to school learning and focuses on its point, inquiry into and understanding of life. So he saw elementary schooling, including kindergarten, as a place where stories, biographies, drama, history, drawing, music, nature study, excursions, gardens, language, manual training, sewing and cooking weave the fabric of the educative environment. The teacher, however, must utilize these immediate experiences in the classroom in order to initiate children into "the symbols of the intellectual life" of society (M1, 266-267).

The curriculum Dewey envisioned then is neither narrowly "traditionalist" nor strictly "progressive" in a simple child-oriented sense:

> The real course of study must come to the child from the teacher. What gets to the child is dependent upon what is in the mind and consciousness of the teacher, and upon the way it is in his mind. It is through the teacher that the value even of what is contained in the text-book is brought home to the child ...just in the degree in which the teacher's understanding of the material of the lessons is vital, adequate, and comprehensive, will that material come to the child in the same form; in the degree in which the teacher's understanding is mechanical, superficial, and restricted, the child's appreciation will be correspondingly limited and perverted. If this be true, it is obviously futile to plan large expansions of the studies of the curriculum apart from the education of the teacher (M1, 273-274).

The "reality of education" then "is found in the personal and face-to-face contact of the teacher and the child" (M1, 268). The teacher is in a sense the curriculum. Her knowledge of the subject matter and her understanding of children and their growth are central. In essence, the teacher needs "insight into the relation of...studies to one another and to the whole of life...[and the] ability to present them to the child from the standpoint of such insight" (M1, 275). These extracts make it clear that while the teacher is not the only important person in the learning community, she is an indispensable contributor. No lesser interpretation of the role fits with what Dewey wrote.

Thus, for Dewey the basic issue in education is not about the relative importance of different subjects in the curriculum (be they the three Rs, history and science; art, music and drawing; or manual training, gardening and nature study) but about reconciling "our professed ends and the means we are using to realize those ends" (M1, 277). That is, the elementary curriculum, the choice of subject matter and its best organization, depends on our purposes; and those purposes have to do with how we understand knowledge (as a body of truths to be accepted and contemplated, for instance, or as an on-going process of inquiry and a search for meaning) and its use in everyday life and the organization of society. For Dewey, then, those student aims and means—"personal appropriation, assimilation and expression"—are the key to the intellectual organization and practical application of the curriculum and to "sanity, steadiness, and system in the mental attitude of the instructor" (M1, 269-270, 275).

Vocational studies illustrate his point. For him, they should be liberalizing experiences, and liberal studies should be vocationally important. Professional studies later in life should be less technical and more liberal, and professional preparation itself can be a form of liberal education if it is "informed by an adequate recognition of its human bearing and public purpose" (M10, 157). Behind these claims lies Dewey's way of thinking about society and social reform: Professional preparation needs to be "less narrowly professional—less technically professional" (M10, 154), and industrial education should *not* be designed to prepare skilled workers for the present system but to develop "human beings who are equipped to reconstruct" industry to meet the needs of society (M10, 147-148). More precisely,

> To charge that the various activities of gardening, weaving, construction in wood, manipulation of metals, cooking, etc., which carry over...fundamental human concerns into school resources, have a merely bread and butter value is to miss their point. If the mass of mankind has usually found in its industrial occupations nothing but evils which had to be endured for the sake of maintaining existence, the fault is not in the occupations, but in the conditions under which they are carried on. The continually increasing importance of economic factors in contemporary life makes it the more needed that education should reveal their scientific content and their social value. For in schools, occupations are not carried on for pecuniary gain but for their own content. Freed from extraneous associations and from the pressure of wage-earning, they supply modes of experience which are intrinsically valuable; they are truly liberalizing in quality (DE, 200).

This idea of occupation as education reveals Dewey's scientific attitude both to knowledge and to the resolution of social problems; as well, it draws attention to effective teaching by educators and learning by children during the elementary school years, for this

> scientific attitude of mind might, conceivably, be quite irrelevant to teaching children and youth. But this book also represents the conviction that such is not the case; that the native and unspoiled attitude of childhood, marked by ardent curiosity, fertile imagination, and love of experimental inquiry, is near, very near, to the attitude of the scientific mind (L8, 109).

The aim of cultivating a reflective disposition is also then the means of education: "*Active, persistent, and careful consideration of any belief or supposed form of knowledge in the light of the grounds that support it and the further conclusions to which it tends* constitutes reflective thought" (L8, 118). This is hardly a startling or original educational aim, although making it an aim for children distinguishes Dewey from many other educational thinkers. The reason Dewey considered reflective thinking so important to children, youth and adults, including those preparing to be teachers, is that

> it emancipates us from merely impulsive and merely routine activity. Put in positive terms, thinking enables us to direct our activities with foresight and to plan according to ends-in-view, or purposes of which we are aware. It enables us to act in deliberate and intentional fashion to attain future objects or to come into command of what is now distant and lacking. By putting the consequences of different ways and lines of action before the mind, it enables us to know what we are about when we act. It converts action that is merely appetitive, blind, and impulsive into intelligent action. A brute animal...is pushed on from behind; it is moved in accordance with its present physiological state by some present external stimulus. The being who can think is moved by remote consideration, by results that can be attained perhaps only after a lapse of years—as when a young person sets out to gain a professional education to fit himself for a career in years to come (L8, 125).

With education so directly tied to the community and to social uses, we need some account of a democratic society. It too functions as both a means and an end, and at least in a democracy, the elementary school should operate in the form of a democratic community where

> it is assumed that the aim of education is to enable individuals to continue their education—or that the object and reward of learning is continued capacity for growth. Now this idea cannot be applied to all the members of society except where intercourse of man with man is mutual, and except where there is adequate provision for the reconstruction of social habits and institutions by means of wide stimulation arising from equitably distributed interests. And this means a democratic society (DE, 100).

This thought reveals Dewey's larger sense of democracy as more than a form of government—as educational and as a social, political and personal environment permeated with a common moral meaning. As we have seen before, "Government, business, art, religion, all social institutions have a meaning, a purpose. That purpose is to set free and to develop the capacities of human individuals without respect to race, sex, class or economic status" (RP, 186). Just as Dewey saw democracy as a moral endeavor, so is "every incident of school life pregnant with moral possibility" (M4, 291). And moral education, being concerned with our actions and the reasons for acting as we do, is an appropriate part of anything we can call education, elementary or secondary, formal or informal. Thus the need of the child is to acquire "*moving* ideas, motive-forces in the guidance of conduct" (M4, 267).

In view of this thinking, we can easily understand why Dewey believed that "Democracy has to be born anew every generation, and education is its midwife" and ultimately that education, including elementary education, should bring society's values and purposes "to the thought, the observation, judgment and choice of the individual," future teacher or not (M10, 139; L13, 296). Schooling during the elementary years, therefore, contains at least in part the entire scope of learning as founded upon the life of the child and the communities that shape and are shaped by the child. As a result, the elementary education of the future educator is crucial; it provides information and experiences that nurture attitudes and habits that distinguish an educated, reflective person from the individual who has merely been socialized. In an important sense, therefore, elementary school teachers are teacher educators, contributors to the next generation of professional educators. But they are more; they are builders of a community, nation and world—albeit in a supporting role.

SECONDARY EDUCATION. We talk today of the secondary school (and now the middle school) in terms of transition from the more integrated, personal and protective elementary school and to work or university study. Much earlier in the century, Dewey recognized that high schools faced the difficult problems of how to mediate between the realities of the elementary schools, the expectations of the universities, and the prospects of the workplace while appropriately fulfilling their own educational mandate. In his day, curricular debate pitted the older, traditional subjects (modern and classical languages, the natural sciences, history, economics, literature and composition, the social sciences, and civics) against newer studies (notably manual training, technological, commercial and secretarial studies, and the fine arts)—a dichotomy Dewey considered misconceived. Rather than manufacture curricular dichotomies, he wished to distinguish or separate several legitimate considerations so as to assign them to their appropriate place.

He first recalled two favorite principles of progressive education. First, he enunciated the principle that a "single course of studies for all progressive schools is out of the question [because] it would mean abandoning the fundamental principle of connection with life-experiences" (EE, 78). An inflexible and prescribed national curriculum, then, would seem to countermand this principle. Second, he recommended the principle of the uniqueness of the individual student in curriculum planning:

> There can be no difference of opinion...as to the necessity of a more persistent and adequate study of the individual as regards his history, environment, predominant tastes and capacities, and special needs...[or] of the effect of particular school studies upon the normal growth of the individual, and of the means by which they shall be made a more effective means of connection between the present powers of the individual and his future career (M1, 292-293).

A further consideration was the consequent change in the university curriculum and so its admission requirements: "The college course will be so broad and varied that it will be entirely feasible to take any judicious group of studies from any well-organized and well-managed high school, and accept them as preparation for college" (M1, 292). Critics of Dewey and modern schooling argue that, to the detriment of university studies, this is precisely what has happened. Others might press for greater specification of a "judicious group," noting that when discussing the admission requirements for the School of Education at the University of Chicago in 1903 Dewey himself specified "the same amount of work required for admission to the Junior College of the University, viz., 15 units," studies requiring a unit in history, two in English, two and a half in mathematics, one in physics, two in a foreign language and the rest "selected from the official list already provided with reference to admission to a Junior College" (M3, 329-330). Still others may accept Dewey's general conception but doubt that he adequately explained or illustrated how a student's transition from a relatively interdisciplinary elementary school to a secondary school where the possession of the "organized subject-matter of the adult" (EE, 83) can be achieved in time for a person to be prepared for university studies.

Despite these misgivings, we can discern two typical lines in Dewey's thinking: first, that "general training and general culture is the function of the secondary school" (M1, 311) rather than specialist or vocational training; and second, that we must consider both the student's experience and understanding and the "systematized and defined experience of the adult mind...in interpreting the child's life" (M2, 279). The latter helps the teacher with her educational responsibilities to understand the student's needs, design appropriate learning experiences, and promote growth. Both ideas help guide curriculum planners and policy makers.

Therefore, Dewey called for a broad curriculum, more reflective of students' interests, backgrounds and future plans, and a more comprehensive high school offering more students a way of meeting a wider range of social goals than did the traditional academic high school. Such new subjects as commercial and manual but also aesthetic studies should be a part of the curriculum (M1, 295), and students should be free to take the same courses, and often the traditional courses, for different reasons: "algebra and geometry are their own justification" for some students while for others these courses are "dead and meaningless until surrounded with a context of obvious bearings—such as furnished in manual-training studies" (M1, 296). "The latter, however, are rendered unduly utilitarian and narrow when isolated," he continued, drawing attention to two further curricular considerations. First, training simply to conform to social roles and expectations avoids the educationally crucial cultivation of a student's powers or of an inquiring and reflective, socially responsible spirit. Second, such studies have educational potential once we recognize that work and occupations and related subjects can be successful only to the extent that they embody scientific principles and have relevant functions within a society. It is the business of the educator to help the student see this relevance (M1, 296).

This reference to the individual and to society brings us to a problem for the science of education, for

> We are no longer concerned with the abstract appraisal of studies by the measuring rod of culture and discipline. Our problem is rather to study the typical necessities of social life, and the actual nature of the individual in his specific needs and capacities. Our task is on one hand to select and adjust the studies with reference to the nature of the individual thus discovered; and on the other hand to order and group them so that they shall most definitely and systematically represent the chief lines of social endeavor and social achievement (M1, 299).

So, for Dewey, the two properly important questions became which groupings of studies will "most serviceably recognize the typical divisions of labor, the typical callings in society...[and which will] secure for [the student] the full use and control of his own powers" (M1, 295). If the former guarantees the relevance of the education, the latter guarantees its *being* education. While "it goes without saying that the organized subject-matter of the adult and the specialist cannot provide the starting point [for formal schooling]....it represents the goal toward which education should continuously move [as students proceed through their formal studies]" (EE, 83). The secondary student who enjoys this kind of experience and who receives the type of guidance Dewey envisioned would, then, participate in pursuing the ideal, "the active process of organizing facts and ideas" in the "ever-present educational process" (EE, 82). This ideal must be pursued for, as Dewey noted,

> No experience is educative that does not tend both to knowledge of more facts and entertaining of more ideas and to a better, a more orderly, arrangement of them. It is not true that organization is a principle foreign to experience. Otherwise experience would be so dispersive as to be chaotic (EE, 82).

If the high school is a time of transition for students, such that it cannot realistically expect simply to transform their more elementary, child-like understandings into those of the mature adult, much less presuppose an adult understanding—"the educator cannot start with knowledge already organized and proceed to ladle it out in doses" (EE, 82)—there should nevertheless be a progressive organization in the high school curriculum to achieve an "orderly development toward expansion and organization of subject-matter" (EE, 74). While these guidelines, like those for elementary education, are general, Dewey pointed out that

> finding the material for learning within experience is only the first step [for educators]. The next step is the progressive development of what is already experienced into a fuller and richer and also more organized form, a form that gradually approximates that in which subject-matter is presented to the skilled, mature person. That this change is possible without departing from the organic connection of education with experience is shown by the fact that this change takes place outside of the school and apart from formal education (EE, 73-74).

Therefore, the educator must become sophisticated in selecting

> those things within the range of existing experience that have the promise and potentiality of presenting new problems which by stimulating new ways of observation and judgment will expand the area of further experience. He must constantly regard what is already won not as a fixed possession but as an agency and instrumentality for opening new fields which make new demands upon existing powers of observation and of intelligent use of memory. Connectedness in growth must be his constant watchword (EE, 75).

Dewey realized that progressive schools—unfortunately but understandably—sometimes neglected to pursue this continuity:

> It is a cardinal precept of the newer school of education that the beginning of instruction shall be made with the experience learners already have.... I am not so sure that the other condition, that of orderly development toward expansion and organization of subject-matter through growth of experience, receives as much

> attention. Yet the principle of continuity of educative experience requires that equal thought and attention be given to solution of this aspect of the educational problem (EE, 74).

If we take the traditional curriculum question then—What subjects are of most worth?—and add the typically Deweyan question—For what ends?—we can appreciate his wish to recast the problem of how much time to allot to mathematics, classical and modern languages, history, English, and the various sciences in order to recognize larger social and general educational responsibilities. Thus he predicted that

> In the future it is going to be less and less a matter of worrying over the respective merits of...languages; or of the inherent values of scientific vs. humanistic study, and more a question of discovering and observing certain broader lines of cleavage, which affect equally the disposition and power of the individual, and the social callings for which education ought to prepare the individual. It will be...less...a question of piecing together certain studies in a...mechanical way...and more...a question of grouping studies together according to their natural mutual affinities and reinforcements for the securing of certain well-marked ends (M1, 295).

We can easily see this position as a rationale for conceiving general secondary education (especially during our current "explosion of knowledge") in terms of individually guided, representative selections from groupings of like subjects. A student proceeds less in terms of "election vs. prescription" or selections from an all-you-can-eat smorgasbord, "the untried and more or less capricious choice of the individual." Rather, it would be better for a student to enjoy "a region of opportunities large enough and balanced enough to meet the individual on his every side, and provide for him that which is necessary to arouse and direct" (M1, 297). Such an experience broadens and empowers by leading toward a more mature and adequate understanding—that is, toward genuine intellectual growth.

Steering clear of the dichotomous reefs of a fully prescribed or a completely elective curriculum, Dewey's ideas lead rather to a consideration of the means and the ends of genuine intellectual growth. They provide the conceptual criteria for educators and students to design programs of study that achieve the goals of students who are in control of their developed abilities for personal and social well-being. Individual whim and caprice should be put aside in the selection of studies. As students complete secondary school, we may expect the general education of prospective teachers to lead ideally to individuals who are increasingly independent in thought and choice, committed to the well-being of society, responsible in planning their future university and professional studies, and imbued with foresight in evaluating the consequences of their decisions and behavior.

UNIVERSITY EDUCATION. Referring "to knowledge of more facts and entertaining of more ideas and to a better, a more orderly, arrangement of them" (EE, 82), we can now imagine Dewey wishing to reconcile talk of a changed, broadened and varied university curriculum (and of education in general) as responsive to social and occupational problems with his conception of the traditional disciplines as "funded knowledge" distilled from experience and his fairly conventional admission requirements. If a revolution is to take place in university teaching and in the experiences of future teachers, then it may begin in our approach to knowledge and our conception of it. Such a revolution would, however, emphasize and give precision to some fairly traditional values. University study, Dewey said, should be more than a mere "survey of the universe." Instead studies and experiences should introduce and initiate the student into that broader universe of experience by "stimulating and liberating, aiming at ability to inquire, judge and act for one's self" (M1, 303). The university experience, he believed, would not be liberal in being defined by a particular subject matter studied—say, the classics or the seven liberal arts—and still less in being an education for a leisure class. Instead, it would be defined by how the subject matter is studied and the attitudes the student acquires, such as "[h]ospitality of mind, generous imagination, trained capacity of discrimination, freedom from class, sectarian and partisan prejudice and passion, faith without fanaticism" (M15, 201).

> The kind of liberal education an aspiring teacher needs, then, is one that will liberate his capacities and thereby contribute both to his own happiness and his social usefulness.... Theoretically any type of education may do this. As a matter of fact, all of them fall much short of accomplishing it, some in one respect and some in another (M7, 275).

What mattered to Dewey was that "the pupil shall be touched, shall be stimulated,...coming to know both himself and the universe, [and that] he may get his orientation—his placing of himself in the larger world" (M1, 312). Falling short of this, studies "fall short of being an education in any worthy sense of the word" (M7, 275).

Nowadays we recognize a similar-sounding objective: Education should help people think for themselves. This goal is so self-evident, in fact, as to appear trite and vague. But for Dewey, thinking and the love of thinking are central to education, and doubly so then for prospective and practicing educators who must gain this ability and this love through their own education and cultivate the same qualities in others. So Dewey could only conclude that

> No one gets far intellectually who does not "love to think," and no one loves to think who does not have an interest in problems as such. Being on the alert for problems signifies that mere organic curiosity, the restless disposition to meddle and reach out, has become a truly intellectual curiosity, one that protects a person from hurrying to a conclusion and that induces him to undertake active search for new facts and ideas (L4, 182).

Nowhere is this love more evident than in the ideal university with its commitments to research and teaching.

Thinking for Dewey, of course, begins with a genuine problem, genuine in that it hinders a person's advancement or growth. This point suggests that the kind of teaching that helps students—and especially future teachers—practice, cultivate and come to love thinking must involve them actively in the study of such problems, both in their universities and later in their classrooms. Moreover, this love of solving problems explains that love of the discipline that characterizes the university scholar. For while problems that seem genuine generally arise in immediate experience, the traditional academic disciplines have developed around solving problems whose intractable nature may not be so immediately evident. But what else are the great questions of philosophy, literature and science if not manifestations of a love of thinking and thereby finding solutions to problems?

Genuine thinking has for an educator additional interesting traits, some of them requiring a maturity and emotional stability that escapes many younger children. Because it calls settled ideas into question, it may not comfort or reassure: "Every time you think, you place a piece of the world in jeopardy" (Howard and Scheffler, 1995, 85). Or as Dewey put it,

> if we once start thinking no one can guarantee where we shall come out, except that many objects, ends and institutions are doomed. Every thinker puts some portion of an apparently stable world in peril and no one can wholly predict what will emerge in its place (Ratner, v).

When thinking does occur in universities, they probably become like the schools Dewey described—namely both "dangerous outposts" and "supremely interesting places" (M13, 334). Previously learned opinions, beliefs, thoughts and values may have to change; with new insights and new questions may come corrections of prior misunderstandings still accepted in the neighborhood, playground, living room, grocery store, library, club house, tavern, street corner, classroom, school corridor, church, synagogue or mosque. The excitement, and sometimes the danger and jeopardy, occurs because

> All thinking whatsoever—so be it is thinking—contains a phase of originality. This originality does not imply that the student's conclusion varies from the conclusions of others, much less that it is a radically novel conclusion. His originality is not incompatible with large use of materials and suggestions contributed by others. Originality means personal interest in the question, personal initiative in turning over the suggestions furnished by others, and sincerity in following them out to a tested conclusion. Literally the phrase 'Think for yourself' is tautological: all thinking is thinking for oneself (L8, 324).

Moreover, "[t]he fuller and richer the experience of the [intending or current] teacher, the more adequate his own knowledge of 'traditions,' the more likely is he, given the attitude of participator... to use them in a liberating way" (L2, 61)—that is to present them as quests and inquiries, as occasions for reflection, rather than as facts and formulas to be accepted, memorized, and unthinkingly repeated. Such a teacher is likely to cultivate in students an open and inquiring rather than uncritical and accepting spirit so as to empower and educate them. With this liberal background, the future teacher is then ready for any additional "special training which is needed to equip him for the particular calling in life which he finds adapted to his powers" (M1, 312). University professors today who criticize aspiring and present-day teachers for their inadequate and illiberal educations will find an ally in Dewey. On the other hand, it is easy to believe that Dewey would be inclined to hold many of these same critics responsible for the inadequate and illiberal education of prospective and practicing teachers, since these persons come to teacher education largely from programs in the arts, sciences and humanities.

Incidentally this conception of culture and tradition implies that, while universities, schools and other institutions have an obligation to maintain the culture, culture is always open to question—not sacred, valuable per se, or an invariably correct interpretation of human thought, habits, traditions and needs. As a result, in keeping with his ideas of community, experience and education, Dewey concluded that culture cannot be "a protected industry, living at the expense of the freedom and completeness of present social communication and interaction [for] the sole reason for maintaining the continuity of culture is to make that culture operative in the conditions of modern life, of daily life, of political and industrial life, if you will" (M1, 302).

Thus could Dewey argue that the university should prepare students for their vocations not by abandoning liberal education—which would be to leave them ignorant of the humanistic, artistic and scientific roots of civilization—but by immersing them in their intellectual heritage and their traditions in a lively, questioning, thoughtful way that does justice to the nature of those disciplines as "modes of inquiry" and quests for meaning. To provide experiences for students devoid of these emphases was for Dewey either noneducative or miseducative, and probably both.

Conclusion

When Dewey began writing about the education of future teachers, most practicing teachers had no more than a high school education or a limited amount of preparation in a normal school. Many had less. This historical perspective leaves one impressed by the vision Dewey had for teacher education. He envisioned families engaged deliberately in educative activities and communities keenly interested in the growth of children. He saw kindergartens and elementary and secondary schools nurturing, cultivating and guiding children and youth until they became personally responsible for themselves and for making contributions to the development of others in their communities. Out of these families, communities, kindergartens, and elementary and secondary schools he expected to come a stream of aspirants who would select and be selected for careers in teaching. Once in university, he hoped to see their growth furthered with each becoming a thinker who would ensure the doom of "many objects, ends, and institutions"—in particular those characterized by undemocratic, anti-scientific, authoritarian, individualistic and intolerant propensities.

By his own admission, Dewey was a visionary and a person of *faith*, a term he intentionally employed, asserting that "in the long run democracy will stand or fall with the possibility of maintaining the faith [in human nature, intelligence, community, and action] and justifying it by works" (L13, 152). If he can be accused of social, political and educational naiveté, he could often be a resolute realist:

> It is no easy matter to find adequate authority for action in the demand, characteristic of democracy [and its institutions], that conditions be such as will enable the potentialities of human nature to reach fruition. Because it is not easy the democratic road is the hard one to take. It is the road which places the greatest burden of responsibility upon the greatest number of human beings. Backsets and deviations occur and will continue to occur. But that which is its weakness at particular times is its strength in the long course of human history. Just because the cause of democratic freedom is the cause of the fullest possible realization of human potentialities, the latter when they are suppressed and oppressed will in time rebel and demand an opportunity for manifestation (L13, 154).

Dewey also recognized an urgent need for the forces of education—those described throughout this chapter—to come together (RP, 186) to nurture and release the best of ourselves and our institutions. In the end, then, he believed that

> The best thing that can be said about any special process of education, like that of the formal school period [and, as he also noted, the informal periods and influences], is that it renders its subjects capable of further education: more sensitive to conditions of growth and more able to take advantage of them. Acquisition of skill, possession of knowledge, attainment of culture are not ends:

> they are marks of growth and means of continuing (RP, 183).

But Dewey never completely forgot the Cimmerian side of human nature for he was aware of its perversity if all the forces of education did not work together:

> Law, state, church, family, friendship, industrial association, these and other institutions and arrangements are necessary in order that individuals may grow and find their specific capacities and functions. Without their aid and support human life is, as Hobbes said, brutish, solitary, nasty (RP, 188).

Dewey's faith seemed to be at its strongest when he considered the possibilities of families, communities, schools and universities. Appropriately, then, we return to the university to discover its proposed role in the transformation of teacher education and its contributions to the growth of future educators and the reform of schools.

CHAPTER SIX

The Professional Education of Teachers

> Education that takes as its standard the improvement of the intellectual attitude and method of students demands more serious preparatory training, for it exacts sympathetic and intelligent insight into the workings of individual minds and a very wide and flexible command of subject matter—so as to be able to select and apply just what is needed when it is needed (L8, 164).

> All other reforms are conditioned upon reform in the quality and character of those who engage in the teaching profession (M3, 234).

Except for those that come from within the profession, educational reform agendas seldom praise the contributions of teacher educators, the policies in place, the standards created, the programs developed, the courses taught, or the experiences planned for aspiring teachers. Hence we hear teacher educators' ideas described as out of date, their policies as self-serving, their standards as too low, their programs as fragmented, their courses as irrelevant, and their planned experiences as inconsequential.

Accordingly, prescribed university curricular reform tends to subordinate teacher education to the dictates of legislators, policy makers or school practitioners, regardless of whether the results show more coherence, consistency, logicality or compatibility. Quite often, the directives require more courses in one's teaching field, fewer courses in pedagogy, more in-school activities and higher admission standards. Simultaneously, we may encounter efforts to create alternative licensing routes using private enterprise, school districts, state and provincial agencies, and educational service centers. Waivers and exceptions to licensing regulations covering earned degrees and programs of study occur, inviting people with little or no pedagogical or content preparation to enter classrooms to teach children and youth in difficult settings with the most to gain from good teachers and the most to lose from incompetent ones.

Occasionally, laws and regulations allow anyone with a university degree who is not a convicted criminal or a suspected child abuser to teach any subject at any age level provided an influential official believes that person has the qualifications to teach. The idea that a person needs a particular kind of professional preparation to become a licensed educator has yet to be established in many jurisdictions, and in times of crisis the temptation to appoint ill-qualified persons arises still more frequently.

Dewey lived most of his life in a different time; yet at least one striking parallel between his time and ours appears in the area of teacher preparation: A strong sense exists that teacher preparation needs to be greatly improved or drastically altered. Unlike Dewey, however, most contemporary policy makers who call themselves reformers have neither considered nor proposed the reformation of a seamless educational fabric that extends from earliest experience to death. Instead, they—functionally, if not conceptually—think of teacher preparation as beginning in the first term of university or at the moment a student enters a preparation program. This separation of informal education, general education, content preparation and professional preparation disturbs anyone who understands the connectedness of learning, whether in Dewey's terms or not. In either case, an understanding of Dewey's views of the professional education of aspiring teachers only intensifies the sense of amazement at the current educational malaise and the prescience of Dewey's suggestions over fifty years ago. His theory of teacher education, then, promises an interesting contrast to modern thinkers both inside and outside the profession, offering a point of comparison that takes unexpected turns while making some predictable assaults.

Dewey's general orientation follows from his ideas on general education. To begin, he found no dichotomy between formal and informal education. There is or should be a continuity of experience making both domains merely different aspects of the same educative process. Further, just as no dichotomy exists between these two aspects of education, no sharp division exists between general education and professional preparation. The two spheres form part of a single educational gestalt and a single preparation program. Thus, the general and pedagogical dimensions of his teacher preparation program intersect, interact and mingle. Moreover, if a person is educated in the communities of the family, neighborhood, and town or city as well as in the park, supermarket, museum, theater, bank, and hospital—before and while in school and university—in the way Dewey envisioned, the would-be teacher stands ready to start systematic study and reflection on education and practical field experiences in school settings. This person also needs a special kind of study and experience to enable her to think, behave and create as a professional educator, as the artist of all artists. So while all of a teacher's formal and informal knowledge and education becomes an inseparable part of her professional education, Dewey distinguished professional knowledge from other realms of understanding (HWT, 275-276). We can usefully separate his discussions of this professional understanding further into the realms of subject-matter preparation, pedagogical preparation, practical preparation, educational theory and practice, and professionalism in teaching.

Subject-Matter Preparation

Whether or not Dewey himself included subject-matter knowledge as a formal part of professional understanding, we find no doubt about the importance he attached to preparation in the subject matter, despite frequent simplistic misunderstandings and popular misstatements of his views as child-centered learning and learning from immediate experience. We need only recall his belief that a good teacher demonstrates an excitement about a field of knowledge, depth of understanding in at least one branch of knowledge, and a love of sharing what is known with others to lay some of these false impressions to rest.

These three qualities arise from more than just ethereal circumstances or environmental osmosis: They result partly from formal study, particularly at university. A specific illustration of how a university may foster these qualities appears in an early essay. In 1903, a time when almost no one earned a degree from a university in order to become a teacher, Dewey described the teacher preparation programs offered in the new School of Education at the University of Chicago, a consolidated academic unit that arose out of the Chicago Institute (formerly the old Cook County Normal School) and the University's Department of Education. Presumably, since he was director of the

School of Education, he supported these programs and considered them appropriate for prospective kindergarten, elementary, secondary, and arts and technology teachers. In each program, three-quarters of the upper-level studies, the third- and fourth-year university courses, focused on the candidate's field of specialization, with nearly half these required specialization studies being electives (M3, 328-341). Interestingly, this configuration prevailed in all areas, not just the secondary and all-level licensure programs.

For example, we read that students seeking admission to kindergarten and elementary preparation programs, the "General Course," had to take the following *prerequisite studies*: four "majors" in science; one major in art; and two majors each in philosophy (including psychology and ethics) and educational theory and practice; English; history; a modern language; mathematics; and three major electives selected from any "subjects named" above or from an "Ancient Language" (M3, 329-331). In this academic credit scheme, where nine majors constituted a full year of university study, a total of 18 majors were prerequisites. In these prerequisite studies, psychology and ethics or philosophy did not count in the education majors (M3, 333). Hence, perhaps one major in education—"educational theory and practice"—was required in the first two years of university. *Once admitted to the program of study,* students were required to take the following additional courses: three majors in both education and science (including geography), and a total of three in history, English and oral reading; two majors in arts; and one major in mathematics. In addition, six electives in these subjects were required and could be selected from a single area of specialization or distributed across these fields (M3, 331). A planned combination of prerequisite studies, programmatic studies, and elective studies could easily lead then to a focus on one branch of knowledge—for example, science, mathematics, history, English or art.

This pattern of studies correlates with Dewey's belief that "the functions of elementary education have been seriously impaired by the lack of adequate training in subject-matter on the part of many of its teachers" (M2, 69) and was an effort to address the problem. Even today, at a somewhat different level, the debate over the subject-matter preparation of early childhood and elementary teachers continues to rage with either-or thinking common. "Good" is defined *either* as understanding children, materials, and methods *or* as understanding subjects, modes of inquiry and conceptual networks, while the disputants often seem to forget the twin evils of denying the truth in each position while combining the errors of both.

Future secondary teachers in the programs Dewey described were required to complete the first two years of university much the way prospective kindergarten and elementary teachers did, with studies in philosophy (including psychology and ethics) and educational theory and practice, English, history, a modern language, mathematics, and science together with electives. These first two years of university study, therefore, were devoted largely to scientific, humanistic, and language courses with, perhaps, a "major" in only the theoretical and practical aspects of education. *After students entered* the specific secondary preparation program, a course in pedagogy (related to teaching history and civics, Latin or mathematics) was sometimes included in the content-preparation program but more commonly not, its place being taken by Greek, French, German, English language and literature, physics, chemistry, geology, biology or home economics. During these third and fourth years, the equivalent of one modern university semester, four "majors," was devoted to both general and special pedagogical studies. Although it is difficult to be certain, the equivalent of student teaching appears not to have been included in these four majors. The subject matter or content pattern of studies during these two years, then, included approximately one and a half years or 13 or 14 "majors" in one's teaching field. Most graduates of the secondary programs, then, would have had the equivalent of approximately two full years of study in their teaching fields in addition to other non-professional courses.

Apparently Dewey and his colleagues were less prescriptive than many contemporary education critics, teachers, teacher educators, policy makers and university faculties. This greater freedom probably reflected an emphasis on preparing future educators to think for themselves, make evaluative decisions, and learn throughout their lives. University studies were only one valuable means to the continuing goal of personal and professional growth. More specifically, perhaps this freedom reflected Dewey's belief that if intending teachers are involved in curricular decisions throughout their formal studies as children and youth and plan one day to face the problem of selection for their own students, university is no time to discontinue or interrupt the habit. Perhaps too, this freedom allowed university advisors to adapt programs to an individual student's interests, strengths, needs and future employment.

These curricular requirements contrast strikingly with many current practices in undergraduate teacher education, especially those for students preparing to be early childhood and elementary teachers. One may object that our pedagogical knowledge base has expanded and the social challenges facing the school have changed tremendously in recent decades, but so too has our understanding of the disciplines taught in elementary school become more sophisticated. Thus Dewey's emphasis on solid subject-matter preparation remains no less applicable. Nor does the objection silence those who complain that teachers are inadequately prepared in their teaching fields. Ironically those responsible for the "academic" preparation of future teachers often blame inadequate subject matter preparation on "Deweyan" and "progressive" tendencies. Meanwhile, they forget to acknowledge Dewey's complementary visions of teachers who love knowledge, possess a depth of understanding in their fields, and love sharing what they know. Five-year and fifth-year teacher education programs—common now in some institutions and jurisdictions—are often designed to provide just the academic space and time aspiring teachers need to pursue various understandings, attitudes, habits, skills and experiences.

For the moment, though, let us return to the past to form a clearer picture of Dewey's thinking about the university studies of prospective teachers. Dewey came to his vision of subject-matter preparation from at least four related considerations. First, an abundance of knowledge beyond that in textbooks and lesson plans—to "the point of overflow"—gives the teacher flexibility, enabling her to see the educational potential of experiences and so to construct new educational experiences and to turn unanticipated questions and events to educational purposes (L8, 338). Second, familiarity with the subject matter frees the teacher to concentrate on the students, watching their reactions so that she can encourage the right kinds of attitudes to knowledge, like inquiry and active and alert mental dispositions, in their learning. These first two ideas suggest Dewey's strongly held belief that the teacher's knowledge should be so rich and full that she can focus on students instead of on what she is going to say or do next, and they deserve further consideration.

Some of the reasons the teacher needs a wealth of information and understanding may be obvious, but the central reason here sometimes goes unrecognized. *The problem of the pupil is found in subject matter; the problem of the teacher is what the minds of pupils do with the subject matter*. The teacher must have her mind free to observe the mental responses and movements of the student members of the recitation group or learning community. Unless she has mastered the subject matter in advance and is thoroughly comfortable with it, she will not be free to give her full attention to observing and interpreting pupils' intellectual reactions. The teacher must be alive to all forms of bodily expression of mental conditions—to puzzlement, boredom, mastery, the dawn of an idea, feigned attention and tendencies to show off or to dominate discussion because of egotism. She must be sensitive, as well to the meaning of all expressions in words (HWT, 275).

On the other hand, specializing in a single subject fails to bestow all the knowledge the average teacher must have. Dewey's argument that future teachers need to immerse themselves in a particular field of inquiry (AE, 53) was not a suggestion that each educator should simply become a specialist in one area. Leading to a contrast between the specialist and the expert, he offered this third consideration:

> The special teacher has arisen because of the recognition of the inadequate preparation of the average teacher to get the best results with these newer subjects [art, gardening, music, manual training, etc.]. Special teaching, however, shifts rather than solves the problem. As...indicated, the question is a twofold one. It is a question not only of what is known, but of how it is known. The special instructor in nature study or art may have a better command of the what—of the actual material to be taught—but be *deficient in the consciousness of the relations borne by that particular subject to other forms of experience in the child,* and, therefore, to his own personal growth (M1, 274, italics added).

This third consideration also merits explication.

Some educational reformers, in opposition to the specialist orientation, advocate special disciplinary courses designed exclusively for prospective teachers. They contend that the understanding of the disciplines teachers need is not that of the typical honors student, major or prospective graduate student in the discipline nor that of the specialist. Dewey was probably not addressing this idea per se and likely would not agree with the special courses approach. Nevertheless, he did mention in 1902 that "a considerable group of studies," such as "geography, history, nature study"—in the School of Education, University of Chicago—were for future teachers so that they might study "topics in the light of the selection and organization of subject-matter which, upon one side, is adequate from the side of scholarly information and training and, upon the other, is adapted to children's needs and powers at a given age" (M2, 71). This thought regarding dual preparation in some courses is missing, as are a number of other programmatic emphases, in the revised curriculum in Dewey's 1903 essay. These deleted emphases may have been a part of the Chicago Institute when it merged with the University of Chicago in 1901 (M2, 67).

The real issue before Dewey though was another matter, not a question of special courses, nor

> a question of the *specialist*, but of the *expert*. When manual training, art, science, and literature are taught, it is impossible that one person should be competent in all directions. Even if it were desirable it is a physical and mental impossibility. Superficial work is bound to be done in some direction and the child, through not having a model of expert workmanship to follow, acquires careless, and imperfect methods of work. The [University of Chicago's laboratory] school, accordingly, is endeavoring to put the various lines of work in charge of experts, and yet maintain unity through continued consultation and cooperation, and through controlling the different studies and occupations by reference to the same general principles. The undue separation [of forms of understanding and creativity] which often follows teaching by specialists, is not inherent in the method, but is the result of lack of supervision, cooperation and control by a unified plan (M1, 334, italics added).

Attempts to prepare either "the so-called all-round teacher" or "the specialist" are equally a waste of time, Dewey thought, nullified either by too limited a human capacity or by too one-sided a development (M1, 275, 334). Conversely, the expert teacher needs expertise for teaching—that is, both a depth of understanding in a field and studies in related areas—an integrated program of studies that allows her to see into other fields of inquiry, because

> without intellectual organization, without definite insight into the relation of these studies to one another and to the whole of life, without ability to present them to the child from the standpoint of

> such insight, we simply add an over-burdened and confused teacher to the over-burdened and confused child (M1, 275).

The importance Dewey gave to this idea appears in his observation that "each member of the Faculty, being familiar with the plan and work of the entire School [of Education, University of Chicago], is able to present his courses so that the relationship of his subject to the other subjects in the curriculum clearly appears" (M3, 345).

So we come to the fourth consideration. This same expertise for teaching led Dewey to the kind of understanding he wanted children to acquire in school. Referring to the predominantly utilitarian way many schools introduced experiences and studies in such newer subjects as manual training, school gardening and graphic arts (but probably having also in mind the rote mastery common to an earlier, more narrowly academic curriculum) he noted,

> Perhaps the most pressing problem of education at the present moment is to organize and relate these subjects so that they will become instruments for forming alert, persistent, and fruitful *intellectual* habits. That they take hold of the more primary and native equipment of children (appealing to their desire to do) is generally recognized; that they afford great opportunity for training in self-reliant and efficient social service is gaining acknowledgment. But they may also be used for presenting *typical problems to be solved by personal reflection and experimentation and by acquiring definite bodies of knowledge leading later to more specialized scientific knowledge* (L8, 290-291).

Taken together, these four considerations suggest that the subject-matter preparation of the aspiring teacher, then, should further a person's love of learning, enhance or deepen understanding, and be accompanied by related studies that provide the opportunity to see into several realms of knowledge and establish their relevance to the whole of life. Excessive studies in one field, therefore, would counter Dewey's argument that future teachers need to see into other branches of understanding and apply all of their studies to later learning and personal and societal problems. The well-educated teacher is not a narrow specialist but an expert in a field of knowledge with insight into related fields.

Pedagogical Preparation

Human nature and the dispositions cultivated by a person's own education make it difficult to draw sharp lines separating a distinct domain of pedagogy. Likewise, being part of learning communities throughout life and reflecting on the learning processes they entail prepare the intending teacher in the area of pedagogy. But understanding these invaluable insights into pedagogy, especially when the learning remains largely unconscious and unreflective, is insufficient to distinguish or clarify the field of pedagogy. Thus Dewey thought it possible to take a special scientific and reflective interest in the problems of learning and schooling—pedagogy—and he recognized this domain as an important field of inquiry and area of preparation for the future teacher.

For Dewey, love of knowledge, love of sharing knowledge, the transformation of ideas into moving forces, the scientific attitude toward problems, love of children, involvement with other members of one's community, and a commitment to personal educational growth and democratic social growth transform education into activities of caring and sharing. But this caring and sharing can be well or badly done; wise caring and sharing call for reflection and understanding; and these qualities define a realm for a pedagogy that can grow out of the true teacher's four loves: of knowledge, of sharing knowledge, of thinking and of children. The gifts of nature need to be awakened, stimulated, developed and guided; so Dewey became concerned with "the inadequate preparation of the average teacher to get the best results" (M1, 274) and the "pressing" need "to organize and relate [in pedagogically sound and powerful ways] these [school] subjects so that they will become instruments for forming alert, persistent, fruitful *intellectual* habits" (L8, 290).

Dewey's emphasis on "moving ideas" and the "scientific attitude" make the image of the cloistered scholar inappropriate to teaching. Such a person would lack the dispositions required of a teacher or an educator. A commitment to education is a democratic social commitment, for both commitments promote growth and the conditions which foster it. For this reason, apparently narrow pedagogical competencies assume larger social connotations: (1) students must be understood in their social, psychological, economic and historical context, not merely as individuals with personal pasts, presents, and emerging futures; (2) curriculum fields—disciplines—and their methods of discovering and assessing information and ideas must be understood in terms of social needs and interests as well as individual pursuits; (3) the means and methods of facilitating students' growth must see them as members of a community as well as individuals; and (4) the other goals of education—like reflection, critical thinking and problem solving—are personal, social, communitarian and democratic. Education, in a critically important way, becomes civic education.

In view of this understanding of education, Dewey recommended that prospective and practicing teachers and teacher educators understand and nurture the broader dimensions of citizenship, the social implications of being a productive worker, and the productive use of leisure. A good and useful citizen, Dewey argued,

> is not simply the man who can vote and use his influence to get good government. He is not the man alone who can render useful service in the profession which he carries on. A really useful citizen is one who can enjoy life and employ his leisure in a socially profitable way. He is a person who has capacity for appreciation of art, science, history, and literature for their own sake (M15, 167).

To the wise and appropriate cultivation of natural dispositions and a vision of the individual as a member of a community, Dewey added a third, modern-sounding pedagogical consideration, echoing recent discussions of teachers as reflective practitioners: The complex interactions of the elements and personalities involved in schooling and education require that a successful classroom teacher or school administrator be prepared for more than the job. Judgment—we might say "professional judgment"—not the mechanical application of rules, will inevitably come into play in one situation after another. According to Oakeshott (1956), judgment is a possible fruit of experience; but it can be fostered too because it is also

> the act of selecting and weighing the bearing of facts and suggestions as they present themselves, as well as of deciding whether the alleged facts are really facts and whether the idea used is a sound idea or merely a fancy (L8, 210).

Because it involves selecting, weighing and focusing, judgment must be developed in the planned activities of the prospective teacher. She needs to be involved in situations that lead her to understand experientially, not just intellectually, that

> no hard and fast rules for this operation of selecting and rejecting, or fixing upon significant evidential facts, can be given. It all comes back, as we say, to the good judgment, the good sense, of the one judging. To be a good judge is to have a sense of the relative indicative or signifying values of the various features of the perplexing situation; to know what to let go of as of no account; what to eliminate as irrelevant; what to retain as conducive to the outcome; what to emphasize as a clew to the difficulty. This power in ordinary matters we call *knack, tact, cleverness*; in more important affairs, *insight, discernment* (L8, 213).

To say that the cultivation of judgment cannot be identified exclusively with training is not to say that one cannot learn to make better judgments. Dewey identified a number of fields he thought would prepare intending teachers to think for themselves and make professional judgments about the appropriateness of certain kinds of activities and experiences for their students. Early in his career (1897), in a "Letter and Statement on Organization of Work in a Department of Pedagogy" for the President of the University of Chicago, Dewey wrote that undergraduate studies in education should include four courses, essentially in what we now think of as foundations subjects and educational administration: the history of educational doctrine, theoretical educational psychology, child development and study, and school administration (E5, 442-447). In clarifying this list, he added that "These four are general in character and to be taken by those interested in education, apart from specialization along any particular line" and that the list said "nothing...about work in the actual training of teachers," constituting "the cultural side" rather than "the professional side" of their preparation (E5, 446).

We should remember when interpreting this comment about *cultural* and *professional* studies that Dewey initially saw the main role of the Department of Education and the Laboratory School at the University of Chicago as preparing leaders for schools and districts and professors for normal schools. In preparing educational leaders to reform schooling and improve teacher and administrator preparation, he seems to have been commending the importance of studies in educational thought, educational psychology, child psychology and educational administration. He intended this "cultural side" of their preparation to take them beyond the "professional side"—for example, studies pursued in normal schools—they had already acquired while preparing to become classroom teachers earlier in life.

Even though Dewey did not delineate in detail what he understood by the difference between the cultural and the professional, we should also recall his distinction between philosophy, ethics and psychology, and educational theory and practice, on the one hand, and general and special studies in teacher preparation, on the other (M3, 327-341). Likewise, his belief—mentioned over a decade after his comment regarding the two sides of study—in the value of "an early acquaintance with psychology [still a branch of philosophy early in Dewey's career], history of education, the methods found helpful by others teaching various subjects" (L8, 339) appears to be consistent with the cultural (psychology and history of education) and the professional (methods) dimensions he mentioned.

In addition to the cultural side of teacher preparation, then, we can understand Dewey's wish to underscore—but also limit—the importance of experience for both practice and theory. His talk of "procedures [methods] that others have found useful" (L8, 339) illustrates the respect he had for the understanding that comes from practice and experience. He was quick to note that the teacher needed to be prepared in observation, interpretation and intervention methods—"equipped to note what would otherwise go unheeded in the responses of the students...quickly and correctly interpret what pupils do and say; [and]...give proper aid when needed because of his knowledge of procedures that others have found useful" (L8, 339). Therefore, aspiring teachers require a certain sensitivity to situations, and it is reasonable to expect some similarity in their responsibilities. These conditions imply the generality of a theoretical understanding informed by judicious practice: It is insufficient that "certain materials and methods have proved effective with other individuals at other times. There must be reason for thinking that they will function in generating an experience that has educative quality with particular individuals at a particular time" (EE, 46).

Thus, though individuals bring to education distinct personalities, talents, backgrounds and learning characteristics, they need the assistance of others in learning about teaching and learning. As Dewey observed,

> Those who have already studied these matters are in possession of information which will help teachers in understanding the responses different pupils make, and help them in guiding these responses to greater efficiency. Child-study, psychology, and a knowledge of social environment supplement the personal acquaintance gained by the teacher. But methods remain the personal concern, approach, and attack of an individual, and no catalogue can ever exhaust their diversity of form and tint (DE, 173).

In Dewey's opinion, then, while judgment may derive in part from experience, both judgment and experience, like invention, seem to favor the suitably prepared mind.

In fact, the artistry of the teacher finds a place in this discussion:

> In brief, the method of teaching is the method of an art, of action intelligently directed by ends. But the practice of a fine art is far from being a matter of extemporized inspirations. Study of the operations and results of those in the past who have greatly succeeded is essential. There is always a tradition, or schools of art, definite enough to impress beginners, and often to take them captive. Methods of artists in every branch depend upon thorough acquaintance with materials and tools (DE, 170).

Dewey saw art in teaching in activities as varied as teachers' diagnosing "the intellectual state" of pupils (L8, 326), questioning them in order to "form in them the independent habit of inquiry" (L8, 331), sharing in the act of creating culture (Archambault, 1964/74, 294) and forming students' minds and character (197). This "perfect and intimate union of science and art" in the field of education, then, led Dewey to see teachers as "the best of artists," people who engaged in "the supreme art" of "giving shape to human powers and adapting them to social service" (E5, 94).

But while judgment, experience, reflection and artistry are important, Dewey believed that a science or philosophy of education would emerge from these various reflective and experimental inquiries of educators and professors. It seemed to matter little to him whether the emerging perspective was called a science or a philosophy as long as it embodied an appropriate intellectual organization of the work and thought of teachers—"a body of verified facts and tested principles which may give intellectual guidance to the practical operating of schools" (L3, 259). But he was quick to point out that the teacher should be more interested in the "quality of activity and consequence... than any quantitative element" (L3, 261). While he knew very well that traditional schools with their interest in norms would value "tests and measurements," "marks, grading, classes, and promotions"—not to mention "measurement of I.Q.'s"—he persisted: "[W]hat has all this to do with schools where individuality is a primary object of consideration, and wherein the so-called 'class' becomes a grouping for social purposes and wherein diversity of ability and experience rather than uniformity prized" (L3, 260-261)?

At one point Dewey talked of sciences of education, fearing "pretense" and the imposition of "a rigid orthodoxy, a standardized set of beliefs to be accepted by all," for, he claimed, "until society and hence schools have reached a dead monotonous uniformity of practice and aim, there cannot be one single science" (L3, 259-260). Yet in reality, and despite his concern about how a bad pseudo-science of education could easily develop, he observed that

> such a statement goes contrary to the idea that science by its very nature is a single and universal system of truths. But this idea need not frighten us. Even in the advanced sciences, like those of mathematics and physics, advance is made by entertaining different points of view and hypotheses, and working upon different theories. The sciences present no fixed and closed orthodoxy (L3, 259).

One might wonder then what about education led Dewey to his suspicion that pretense and orthodoxy might prevail.

However we distinguish philosophy, science and principles of education—and his general conception of the scientific method discourages any such distinctions—what concerned Dewey was that teachers should have a solid knowledge base, including a carefully considered conception of the school and the society, and the disposition and skills needed to reflect thoughtfully on their practice and the ends toward which they work and to exercise judgment and artistry in their teaching. What matters is the development of "general principles" so that teachers are empowered as artists and as professionals and the study of education "rises above the level of recounting and cataloguing relevant phenomena" (M7, 302), affording

> the basis for a critical comparison of the various processes that are currently employed. As teachers are put in intelligent possession of it, their own work becomes less blind and routine; the science, as in other cases, develops a corresponding art which lifts its practitioners from artisans into artists (M7, 302).

Significantly for Dewey, the foundations disciplines of sociology, history, psychology and philosophy are very important in teacher preparation: They are needed both for the factual knowledge they provide and for their interpretive power and their concern with values and meaning—the perspectives they make possible. These perspectives would be important in any age but especially in a period that values competencies and objectively measurable success and talks of accountability without reflecting upon the broader dimensions of professionalism.

Dewey believed too that:

> the life which men, women and children actually lead, the opportunities open to them, the values they are capable of enjoying, their education, their share in all the things of art and science are mainly determined by economic conditions. Hence we can hardly expect a moral system which ignores economic conditions to be other than remote and empty (L4, 225).

So we find that Dewey connected his view of a moral system of education with the need for future and current teachers to possess a "knowledge of social conditions, of the present state of civilization," a knowledge

> necessary in order properly to interpret the child's powers. The child has his own instincts and tendencies, but we do not know what these mean until we can translate them into their social equivalents. We must be able to carry them back into a social past and see them as the inheritance of previous race activities (E5, 85).

Dewey considered psychology and child study, both still deeply rooted in their parent discipline of philosophy, particularly valuable for the aspiring teacher, helping her understand children and youth, diminishing any tendency to overemphasize facts and information, and cultivating habits of observation, discrimination and concentration—traits characteristic of clear thinking. Psychology, like philosophy, he believed, leads to a kind of reflection, which helps to

> resolve a complex subject into its component parts, seizing upon the most important and holding them clearly defined and related in consciousness; to take, in a word, any "chaos" of experience and reduce it to harmony and system. The analytic and relating power, which is an essential mark of the clear thinker, is *the prime qualification* of the clear teacher (PN, 3, italics added).

In bringing together these varied and scattered discussions of the pedagogical understanding a professional teacher needs, we see Dewey identifying and integrating five themes important to his understanding of education and so teacher education: (1) social, psychological, and historical knowledge; (2) mastery of the field to be taught; (3) knowledge of instructional methods; (4) philosophical, social, and ethical principles; and (5) an understanding of classroom management. Dewey synthesized these themes in one sentence:

> The educator is responsible for a knowledge of individuals and for a knowledge of subject-matter that will enable activities to be selected which lend themselves to social organization, an organization in which all individuals have an opportunity to contribute something, and in which the activities in which all participate are the chief carrier of [classroom] control (EE, 56).

To this conception of the theoretical understanding future teachers require, though, we must add an account of the practical experiences they should gain from their formal preparation programs.

Practical Preparation

In a significant sense, all aspects of teacher preparation are or should be practical or of value—intellectually and behaviorally—to the prospective teacher. But some aspects of the preparation are practical in that they are immediately concerned with classroom practice. Dewey's concern for the latter dimension of preparation is well known since his name has long been associated with laboratory schools. He also favored what he called the *laboratory* approach to field experiences over what he called an *apprenticeship* approach, the latter having as its objective using schools merely to pass on to future teachers tools, techniques, skills and proficiencies (M3, 249ff). By contrast, the laboratory approach—which Dewey did not limit to field experiences in laboratory schools—uses "practice work as an instrument in making real and vital theoretical instruction; the knowledge of subject-matter and of principles of education" (M3, 249). As was typical of his approach to dichotomies, though, Dewey noted both models of field experience had value, so one should decide carefully about the weight one gave to each (M3, 250-255). Three ideas come together here: the relation of theory and practice previously noted, the scientific attitude to problem solving, and the nature of a modern profession. What, then, did Dewey see in a modern profession that he considered an essential part of the teaching profession? His answer was explicit:

> the professions...are becoming less and less empirical routines, or technical facilities acquired through unintelligent apprenticeship. They are more and more infused with reason; more and more illuminated by the spirit of inquiry and reason. Theory depends upon science, in a word (M1, 310).

It followed then, Dewey noted, that "there is a *fundamental difference* in the conception and conduct of the practice work [and] the amount of time given to practice work, the place at which it is introduced, the method of conducting it, of supervising, criticising, and correlating it" depending upon which approach one selects (M3, 250, italics added). Time available and efficiency in achieving the aim of the program and a clear choice of aim are the crucial considerations. To what end is effective preparation being designed?

The laboratory model Dewey envisioned for the preparation of teachers probably grew out of his observations of other professional training programs because he believed "the problem of training teachers is one species of a more generic affair—that of training for professions" (315). Having explained some of the differences between the laboratory and apprenticeship approaches, he pointed to the aims of each, beginning with the latter:

> From one point of view, the aim is to form and equip the actual teacher; the aim is immediately as well as ultimately practical. From the other point of view, the immediate aim, the way of

> getting at the ultimate aim, is to supply the intellectual method and material of good workmanship, instead of making on the spot, as it were, an efficient workman. Practice work thus considered is administered primarily with reference to the intellectual reactions it incites, giving the student [or the aspiring teacher] a better hold upon the educational significance of the subject-matter he is acquiring, and of the science, philosophy, and history of education (M3, 249-250).

A merely practical training then is inadequate to the intellectual challenges or problems the teacher faces as a professional. Consequently, studies in educational theory—"the science, philosophy, and history of education"—are invaluable in developing the reflective professional. Yet there is a sense in which the theoretical or intellectual is practical: "There are times when the most practical thing is to face the intellectual problem, and to get a clear and comprehensive survey of the theoretical factors involved" (M1, 280), times to understand, as did Justice Holmes, "that theory is the most practical thing, for good or for evil, in the world" (RP, xli). *Reflective practice* is a term we have since come to use.

Indeed, given his conception of the scientific attitude, for Dewey there could be no sharp division between the practical, the theoretical and the intellectual. His discussion of this issue in terms of time, efficiency and aim illustrates this very point. The key lies in the aim of the practical work, which is

> *control of the intellectual methods* required for personal and independent mastery of practical skill, rather than...turning out at once masters of the craft. This arrangement necessarily involves considerable postponement of skill in the routine and technique of the profession, until the student, after graduation, enters upon the pursuit of his calling (M3, 251).

Since one can, if necessary, learn the skills, techniques, proficiencies and tools through experience on the job—even after graduation, though most of us expect teachers to start with a set of skills that enables them to handle the immediate problems of the classroom (M3, 256-257)—the question of the aims for preservice field experience becomes this: What can university studies contribute to the future teacher that she might not otherwise learn or gain? The issue is a question of priorities for a university preparation program with limited time, rather than a deliberate advocacy of delaying the learning of useful special skills. As Dewey reasoned,

> relatively speaking, the wise employ of this short time [in university preparation programs] is in laying scientific foundations. These cannot be adequately secured when one is doing the actual work of the profession, while professional life does afford time for acquiring and perfecting skill of the more technical sort (M3, 251-252).

Moreover the practice universities provide is seldom particularly realistic but rather "a somewhat remote and simulated copy of the real thing" whether in education, law or medicine (M3, 252), making the experience of limited practical value in any case. In what must seem like strange logic to those who consider public schools "the only way to the real world," Dewey contended that even field experiences in practice schools—roughly an early equivalent of contemporary professional development schools or associate schools—failed to provide truly realistic experiences for future educators:

> some of the most fundamentally significant features of the real school are reduced or eliminated. Most "practice schools" are a compromise. In theory they approximate ordinary conditions. As a matter of fact, the "best interests of the children" are so safeguarded and supervised that the situation [for the prospective teacher] approaches learning to swim without going too near the water (M3, 252).

In reality, these approximations can be both artificial and counter-productive. For example, the attention paid to the aspiring teacher's need to learn particular teaching skills and classroom management techniques—the "survival skills"—leads to ignoring "the more delicate and far-reaching matter of intellectual responsibility" (M3, 253). Slighting one's intellectual responsibilities focuses *"the attention of the student teacher in the wrong place, and...in the wrong direction*—not wrong absolutely, but relatively as regards perspective of needs and opportunities" (M3, 253). This misdirection of attention results in ignoring genuinely educational objectives calling for the development of professional judgment by focusing the would-be teacher on the external behavior of the students, their compliant behavior, instead of on their inner attention that is "a fundamental condition of mental growth" (M3, 252).

Dewey considered a student's thinking crucial to successful education and so to successful teaching. It follows, then, that the would-be teacher needs to learn how to study the thinking of children and youth. We have already seen this ability to follow students' thinking associated with the responsibility of the teacher as physician. Dewey observed:

> To be able to keep track of this mental play, to recognize the signs of its presence or absence, to know how it is initiated and maintained, how to test it by results attained, and to test *apparent* results by it, is the supreme mark and criterion of a teacher. It means insight into soul-action, ability to discriminate the genuine from the sham, and capacity to further one and discourage the other (M3, 254).

Thus the special responsibility of the university is to prepare teachers who "continue to be students of subject-matter, and students of mind-activity" (M3, 256). Learning to understand the minds of students can be a complicated undertaking, including a larger range of social considerations than those that arise in the classroom. It can include trying to find

> out what the children are thinking about and talking about outside of school, the kind of thinking they want to do, what games they are playing, why their activities are passing from one thing to another, and watch[ing] the development of these spontaneous activities (L17, 223).

Only by studying students this way can a teacher individualize the educational activities for each student. Without this kind of individualization, genuinely educative activities threaten to disappear from the classroom much of the time.

Pursuing this aspect of the continuity of experience, particularly the continuity of school with learning in the home and community and asking whether it is even necessary "immediately and simultaneously" to reinforce educational theory with teaching activities (M3, 257), Dewey noted that intending teachers bring all kinds of experiences to their own theoretical studies. In fact, to resist this continuity of learning simply "throws away or makes light of the greatest asset in the student's [or intending teacher's] possession—his own direct and personal experience" (M3, 258). The prospective teacher loses this valuable and relevant resource, and the separation of ordinary learning experience from psychological theories of learning—this dichotomy—simply encourages the future teacher to assume that in-school learning differs from out-of-school learning, a tragic error in much thinking about learning.

The laboratory setting makes the opportunity for distance and critical reflection explicit and possible, explaining the importance of the reflective seminar that sometimes accompanies student teaching experiences and making clear the professional goal of becoming a reflective practitioner. For as critical pedagogy and theories of the social construction of knowledge specify, we see in our experiences what we have learned to look for, and we question only that which we perceive as problematic. Without such an opportunity to gain "psychological insight—which enables...[the teacher] to judge promptly (and therefore almost automatically) the kind and mode of subject-matter which the pupil needs at a given moment" (M3, 255), the apprenticeship model alone is likely to form

> *habits of work which have an empirical, rather than a scientific, sanction.* The student adjusts his actual methods of teaching, not to the principles which he is acquiring, but to what he sees succeed and fail in an empirical way from moment to moment: to what he sees other teachers doing who are more experienced and successful in keeping order than he is; and to the injunctions and directions given him by others. In this way the controlling habits of the teacher finally [get] fixed with comparatively little reference to the principles in the psychology, logic, and history of education (M3, 255).

Empirical or ad hoc rather than scientific thinking provides the aspiring teacher with no tools for reflective inquiry or else those that are provided—principles of psychology, logic, and history of education—appear to lack immediate utilitarian value. The intending teacher thus becomes a mindless perpetuator of the status quo, not a reflective, questioning and professional educator. Even though the particular practices of certain teachers may be successful, no one who takes this empirical approach to learning acquires an understanding of success and failure. Nor does she acquire understanding of either what would constitute success or why or when some approaches work while others do not. *New teachers risk being socialized to the existing beliefs, values and practices of the profession or of particular schools and communities uncritically and without an incentive to reflect, question or improve existing practices.* In such circumstances, the notion of being an educator and educating students weakens significantly, the words becoming honorific rather than truly descriptive.

Moreover, for Dewey, without the laboratory approach, thought and action—theory and practice—separate. Both suffer as a result, with teachers often despising the former as purely theoretical and believing it is worthless to the teacher as an educator (M3, 255-257). Consequently, they devalue their own reflection, their own thinking and reasoning behind their successful practices. This separation of theory and practice, on the other hand, may also produce a situation where a teacher's ideas are lofty enough or good, defensible and workable while her practices are harmful or indefensible. In such a case, the teacher's ideas remaining removed from practice, we have the obverse situation of a teacher failing to understand her own success. In the latter instance, she cannot apply her successful strategies to other situations where they might also work. Here, Dewey lamented,

> we have the explanation, in considerable part at least, of the dualism, the unconscious duplicity, which is one of the chief evils of the teaching profession. There is an enthusiastic devotion to certain principles of lofty theory in the abstract—principles of self-activity, self-control, intellectual and moral—and there is a school practice taking little heed of the official pedagogic creed. Theory and practice do not *grow together out of and into* the teacher's personal experience (M3, 255, italics added).

Drawing together several of these points, Dewey noted that to avoid this harmful dualism and to facilitate the growth of theory and practice out of and into the teacher's experience, the intellectual and professional habits of the intending teacher must be developed

> under the inspiration and constant criticism of intelligence, applying the best that is available. This is possible only where the would-be teacher has become fairly saturated with his subject-matter, and with his psychological and ethical philosophy of education. Only when such things have become incorporated in mental habit, have become part of the working tendencies of observation, insight, and reflection, will these principles work automatically, unconsciously, and hence promptly and effectively. And this means that practical work [in teacher education programs] should be pursued primarily with reference to its reaction upon the professional pupil [the student teacher or intern] in making him a thoughtful and alert student of education, rather than to help get immediate proficiency (M3, 256).

Yet unlike some who place little value on field experiences, Dewey saw the value of practical preparation or experience if its role is rightly understood, noting for example that "an ounce of experience is better than a ton of theory." But he continued, it is better

> simply because it is only in experience that any theory has vital and verifiable significance. An experience, a very humble experience, is capable of generating and carrying any amount of theory (or intellectual content), but a theory apart from an experience cannot be definitely grasped even as theory. It tends to become a mere verbal formula, a set of catchwords used to render thinking, or genuine theorizing, unnecessary and impossible (DE, 144).

Indeed, what could a theory be about—how could we know what the theory means or whether it is false—if it is not formed and reformed by experience? If it is educative, an experience can be the source of theory, the realm in which theory is tested, verified and revised, and the theater where one uses it to guide practical activities and debate.

Still, not all school activity qualifies as genuine experience. Only that activity reflectively connected to consequences that bring about learning is experience (DE, 139-140). That is to say, an activity in a school may be nothing more than a crude or clumsy encounter, producing no insight or, worse, leading to ill-informed ideas and habits. Activities may be misinterpreted or misconstrued because the future teacher has insufficient experience and understanding to judge them properly. Learning experiences themselves can be educative, noneducative or miseducative, depending upon whether they involve and lead to further growth (EE, 25ff). If activities do not involve or lead to growth and a consideration of their consequences, Dewey concluded that they were neither practical nor valuable. One should, therefore, avoid taking the selection of practical activities lightly, for they have the potential to form or to misform the future teacher's theory and practice of education. The problem of selection, then, exists in the realm of field experiences as much as it does in the area of content and pedagogical preparation.

Educational Theory and Practice

To advocate a laboratory approach to field experiences is not then to deny the value of the practical, but to assert that its value lies in its integration with the concerns of theory in teacher education. So this question arises: "What must be the aim and spirit of theory in order that practice work may really serve the purpose of an educational laboratory" (M3, 257)? To answer Dewey's question, we begin by examining his thoughts about the relation of theory and practice and then analyzing further his thoughts about the purpose of an educational laboratory. Both dimensions of our answer bear upon the roles universities and schools play in the preparation of teachers.

THE RELATION OF THEORY AND PRACTICE. The problem of the relation of theory to practice is hardly unique to teaching. It characterizes such other professions as law, medicine, engineering and nursing too—and indeed the whole of education (L17, 67-68). For example, Dewey noted considerable dissatisfaction with the training of nurses in hospitals where many physicians believed that intending nurses became "over-practical [and lacked] enough training in the principles of nursing" (L17, 68). A commitment to the "immediate" and the "practical" may be an understandable reaction to a mechanical and insensitive application of rules, procedures and principles when the concerns and needs of individuals (students and patients, for example) get lost—when "common sense" would seem to dictate another, simpler course of action and a more "caring" response. Perhaps too, in view of Dewey's commitment to the importance of the student's experience in learning and in setting the conditions for further fruitful learning experiences, we can understand an antipathy to the "outside expert" or the newly graduated student full of "book learning" who arrives with little knowledge of the immediate, practical situation. The reaction might, in fact, be an appropriate critique of "one shot" professional development that seeks to impose ideas foreign to the thinking and experience of practitioners or fails to take as its point of departure their own sense of the problematic in their situation. Whatever its roots, Dewey conceded that the viewpoint is warranted at times but concluded that

> depreciation of theory does not contain the whole truth, as common or practical sense recognizes. There is such a thing, even from the common-sense standpoint, as being "too practical," as being so intent upon the immediately practical as not to see beyond the end of one's nose or as to cut off the limb upon which one is sitting. The question is one of limits, of degrees and adjustments, rather than one of absolute separation (L8, 296).

He stressed too that the issue is more complex than is sometimes thought, for those interested in educational practice may undermine their own interests if they continually neglect the theoretical for the useful. Educational theory or thinking frees the mind from the routine and custom of everyday educational practice for new ideas:

> Truly practical men give their minds free play about a subject without asking too closely at every point for any advantage to be gained. Exclusive preoccupation with matters of use and application narrows the horizon and in the long run defeats itself. It does not pay to tether one's thoughts to the post of use with too short a rope. Power of action requires largeness of vision, which can be had only through the use of imagination. Men must at least have enough interest in thinking for the sake of thinking to escape the limitations of routine and custom. Interest in knowledge for the sake of knowledge, in thinking for the sake of the free play of thought, is necessary to the *emancipation* of practical life—to making it rich and progressive (L8, 296).

The right use of theory in education, as elsewhere is to provide a conceptual framework for practical action, one that helps the teacher identify "the causes for conflicts that exist and then, instead of taking one side or the other, to indicate a plan of operations proceeding from a level deeper and more inclusive than is represented by the practices and ideas of the contending parties" (EE, 5).

Practice is more than just the application of theory, then, for Dewey believed that practical conflicts in education "set a problem" (EE, 5) in the first place. *The work of educational theory or philosophy* then is to clarify practical conflicts about methodology, curriculum, administration, students and facilities so as to show that they can only be solved at a broader theoretical or philosophical level in the context of underlying assumptions about the nature and interaction of children, adults, society and knowledge. Without such a philosophy or theory of education, teachers cannot be professionals. Instead, they remain "at the mercy of every intellectual breeze that happens to blow" (EE, 51), every social and professional fad or fashion. As we might expect, then, Dewey did not see a dichotomy of theory and practice. He explained that laboratory work is "effective just in the degree in which it develops a sense of the great ideas that lie behind it, the practical work serving to make real the meaning of theories and to test their value" (L17, 69).

If one assumes with Dewey that both theory and practice are important in the preparation of teachers, it does little to solve the problem of teacher preparation to presume that *practice alone,* learning on the job, can suffice. Such preparation is liable to neglect philosophical and theoretical issues, leaving teachers without the critical reflective framework they need to become professionals and, in effect, leaving them disempowered in the face of practical, political and social pressures or ideologies. Nor is it any solution to provide them only with theory, leaving practice as merely a matter of application. Studying *theory alone* would be untrue to the idea that theory arises from and has its value in relation to practice. In short, this stance would be pedagogically unpromising and violate all that Dewey's educational thought represented. No more promising is a third approach—*the denial of a relation* between theory and practice—which would isolate learning of the practical in the school and the theoretical in the university. Apart from denying the possibility of a solution, this approach cultivates a tendency, particularly among beginning and insecure teachers, to accept the routine of the school (since it "works," at least after a fashion, and it minimizes professional disagreements) and to resist theory and critical professional reflection. Even *the simple addition to theory* of a supposed laboratory experience may be unhelpful if the aspiring teacher merely masters certain techniques without seeing their "bearing upon the problems of subject-matter" (L17, 68).

This insight—that theory and practice both have a "bearing" upon pondering and then solving the problems of education—presents the key to the solution: Their integration, rather than their co-existence, is what matters. This coordination of the two, while respecting their distinct natures, integrity and contribution, also explains much of the difference between a genuine laboratory and an apprenticeship approach to field experiences:

> the mere fact of taking some kind of a subordinate position...even supposing it gave a man an experience valuable for practical purposes, would not necessarily be of any great educational or intellectual advantage to him. It is not enough, in other words, that a man should be carrying on theoretical work and practical work, either side by side or successively, either at the same time or one after he has done the other. What is wanted is that there should be some definite and active coordination between the theory and the practice (L17, 69).

For this coordination to succeed, "the practical work must be of a kind really to illuminate the theoretical instruction" (L17, 68). There must be "cross-fertilization between theory and practice" (L17, 70). Laboratory work is, then, "effective just in the degree in which it develops a sense of the great ideas that lie behind it, the practical work serving to make real the meaning of theories and to test their value" (L17, 69). The "coordination and correlation between the theoretical instruction and the field work" (L17, 69) is the way to make understanding of both domains intellectually and professionally informative.

Moreover, if we act on this approach to theory and practice, we can reflect on the theories, ideas and hypotheses we need to reform our schools, then test and make them understandable, and, finally, use them to advance us beyond the level of routine (SSCC, xxv ff)—an important consideration if future educators are to be prepared for the full range of their professional roles in schools and in society. Perhaps we can see here why theory so often takes the role of leading and directing practice. Theory indeed arises from practice and its problems, has its value and meaning in relation to practice, and is meant to solve the problems of practice. But to solve is to make choices, decisions and judgments—to see that practice could be other than it is, to have a vision of something better and to act. Dewey certainly saw the Laboratory School at the

University of Chicago as existing to establish the feasibility of other, better ways of educating children (SSCC, 94). The need for laboratories shows that the cross-fertilization of theory and practice requires effort and is not automatic: It requires people ready to try new ways and curious about finding better ways.

We require as well genuine collaboration, a requirement we see called for in certain kinds of research and education projects, identifying people on both "sides who are actively interested in this possibility and willing to cooperate with each other in seeing that connections are really made [with people] willing to see to it that...students shall get something intellectual out of their work, and not merely perform certain routine processes" (L17, 70). In keeping with his social philosophy and his views about the difficulties of achieving teacher professionalism, Dewey placed a great deal of responsibility for this cross-fertilization or integration on school administrators and teachers. If they are appropriately attuned to "the needs and possibilities of the social situation," he wrote, there is a "union of theory and practice [and] the philosophy of education will be a living, growing thing" (L13, 283). In another sense, Dewey may have expected school practitioners to provide leadership, uniting the two realms and making their union clear to aspiring teachers, because he believed that theory and practice "grow together out of and into" the experiences of practicing educators (M3, 255).

This simultaneous growing together—"out of and into"—occurs in the experience of the practitioner, not the researcher or teacher educator (or the university-bound future teacher). But the university can help by investigating and clarifying the growth of theory and practice together. The teacher as learner, then, may play a critical role in reflecting upon her own growth as she comes to understand the interaction of theory and practice in her daily activities and shares this information with other prospective educators and teacher educators. The teacher as engineer, too, may help unite and integrate theory and practice as she moves from "ideas" to "concrete life-experiences" (M13, 324) in an effort to reform or improve schooling.

Although Dewey remained silent on the topic, parallel thoughts seem to apply to the aspiring teacher when she is in the school and other learning environments: Her experience in the school and classroom enable her to bring theory and practice together in her mind if she reflects upon these experiences, whereas the two domains would remain separate and sterile without reflective field experiences and formal theoretical studies. Field experiences and practicing educators who nurture this kind of simultaneous growing together of theory and practice in the preservice assignments of aspiring teachers can make the difference between an intending teacher who becomes a truly professional educator and one who merely becomes a member of a profession.

Meanwhile, professors who join practitioners and would-be teachers in these activities, discussions and research serve both as agents for improving the understanding of practitioners and the preparation of prospective teachers and as vehicles for shaping and reshaping educational theory and the development of future generations of teachers and teacher educators. More important still perhaps is this learning with others gives the professors themselves new insights into theory, research, practice and teacher education that would otherwise be difficult to acquire.

THE PURPOSE OF OBSERVATION. The relation of theory to practice and of these two factors to an educational laboratory helps explain Dewey's view of observation, an important recurring theme in his philosophical orientation: To observe intelligently we need to know what to look for and what to make of what we see. The aspiring teacher, for example, should "observe with reference to seeing the interaction of mind, to see how teacher and pupils react upon each other—how mind answers to mind" (M3, 260), not naively or clouded by the conventions of everyday experience. So the observations of students should be less practically oriented than guided from the viewpoint of psychological theory that promotes an "ability to see what is going on in the minds of a group of persons who are in intellectual contact with one another" (M3, 260). Experience does not carry its interpretation on its face: rather, through observation,

> the subject-matter of science and history and art serves to reveal the real child to us. We do not know the meaning either of his tendencies or of his performances excepting as we take them as germinating seed, or opening bud, of some fruit to be borne (M2, 281).

So too, theory-laden observation helps us identify the inclinations, interests and behaviors of the child, some of which are "symptoms of waning tendency, [others] signs of a culminating power, [and still others] prophetic" (M2, 279-280). For those who pay serious attention to the study and use of observational skills, Dewey's statement that "all that the wisest man can do is to observe what is going on more widely and more minutely and then select more carefully from what is noted just those factors which point to something to happen" (DE, 146) may seem unsophisticated. But those who deplore the lack of serious study and attention paid to children today in many schools may find his words instructive. At any rate, his confidence in the scientific method was as pertinent to being a child watcher as to any other problem-solving situation.

Any conception of the theory-laden nature of interpretation raises problems of subjectivity, error and bias; so the teacher must avoid misinterpreting a child's activities—for example, taking an isolated incident out of context or failing to situate the action historically and socially. The significance of an action like a child's "individuality cannot be found in what he does...at a given moment; it can be found only in the connected course of his actions" (L3, 264). Today we might say that an aspiring teacher should be prepared to observe and interpret a child's patterns of behavior "in a social context." In keeping with Dewey's emphasis on the scientific method, the patterns, consequences and probable results of our actions are especially important. This is particularly true when the observations of experiences have educational potential and may lead to the "transformation of impulse into a purpose" (EE, 68). Yet the intending teacher must realize that "observation alone is not enough. We have to understand the significance of what we see, hear, and touch. This significance consists of the consequences that will result when what is seen is acted upon" (EE, 68). We need, in other words, some theory to provide an interpretative structure that determines the meaning of consequences. Thus, when the teacher understands the impulse and the desire of the student, she can work with that student to develop "a plan and method of action based upon foresight of the consequences of acting under given observed conditions in a certain way" (EE, 69).

Though theory's usefulness may appear in promoting an understanding and interpretation of our observations, we cannot rightly turn "psychological principles into rules of teaching" (M3, 261). In education, we have a decision and a choice to make about the potential to be realized—"the subordination of the psychological material to the problem of effecting growth and avoiding arrest and waste [being] a distinguishing mark of educational psychology" (M3, 261). Nor would an individualistic psychology be adequate to the social and mental considerations. The other distinguishing mark of educational psychology, Dewey argued, is the social factor, "the ways in which one mind responds to the stimuli which another mind is consciously or unconsciously furnishing" (M3, 261). While his psychological views have often been called functionalist, Garrison (1995) contends that Dewey's position is better understood as that of a *social behaviorist*, though it departs on significant points from the views of positivistic behaviorists. Recall that when these words were written in 1904 the disciplinary boundaries between psychology, sociology and philosophy were not so clearly defined as they are today (M3, 261).

Thus, Dewey believed that observational and theoretical child study, like all educational theory, is a means to understanding each student so that the teacher may better guide his or her development as a reflective and scientific thinker. "The more a teacher is aware of the past experiences of students, of their hopes, desires, chief interests," Dewey wrote, "the better will he understand the forces at work that need to be directed and utilized for the formation of reflective habits" (L8, 140-141). Educational theory then, like its applications, is concrete, historical and situated. The more a future teacher learns how to recognize the relevant in the past experiences of students and how to recognize students' present and emerging interests and abilities, the better she will be at guiding their everyday classroom experiences into a progressive organization of personal experience and expert knowledge. In the teacher's education, as in education generally, the transformation of specific bits of learning into mental attitudes and dispositions becomes crucial—especially those dispositions characteristic of the scientific approach and, in this case, an ability to recognize and respond appropriately to the educational potential in what students bring to school and do there.

Professionalism in Teaching

Dewey's account of theory and practice helps inform another aspect of teacher education, the development of a future teacher's professional judgment, a topic we encountered earlier. Like the wise mother, Dewey said, a teacher "draws upon past experiences of experts as well as her own for the light that these shed upon what experiences are in general most conducive to the normal development" of children and youth (EE, 42). Yet, the "funded experience of the past," "the advice of competent...others," "special study," and generally "the body of knowledge" she understands should not be viewed as "a fetish" (EE, 42-43). Even funded, tried-and-true experience, as much as theory, may be misleading—and so miseducative. In short, we can rely on the practical experience of educators no more than on their theoretical understanding. We must approach both reflectively, using our personal judgment. While using both experience and theory, judgment is a function of intelligence, an informed estimate of the most appropriate action to take. Professional judgment always, then, contains an element of flexibility:

> Unfortunately...professional knowledge is sometimes treated, not as a guide and tool in personal observation and judgment—which it essentially is—but as a set of fixed rules of procedure in action. When a teacher finds such theoretical knowledge coming between him and his own common-sense judgment of a situation, the wise thing is to follow his own judgment—making sure, of course, that it is an enlightened insight. For unless the professional information enlightens his own perception of the situation and what to do about it, it becomes either a purely mechanical device or else a load of undigested material (L8, 339).

If we take the teacher's need for judgment along with the need to be able to exercise it as the key to understanding Dewey's account of teaching as a profession and of the concept of professional spirit, then his notion of professionalism rises above a concern for achieving the prestige, independence, salary and status of such professions as law, medicine and dentistry. We can say so despite his work to promote teacher unions, recognition for the profession, and the achievement of working conditions that encourage the teacher's ability to exercise just this professional judgment. In fact, his social commitments make it far more important that a teacher's attitudes and working conditions be appropriate to her responsibilities than that she belong to a privileged social group—one of the prestigious professions—in any way divorced from the masses or a democratic philosophy of life. The adjective, *professional*, matters more than the noun. In passing, we note that Dewey also referred to teaching as a "calling" and a "vocation."

In learning, thinking, judging, deciding and acting, the teacher cultivates her professional knowledge and lives up to her responsibilities; she also emerges, grows and thrives educationally as a person, becoming an autonomous, reflective and scientific thinker. Thus, "two marked features [characterize] the teachers who have a distinctly professional spirit" (M7, 109): (1) a sense of responsibility to study the factors related to being a successful educator, and (2) a sense of responsibility to provide leadership in influencing the opinions of the public for the well-being of society, especially children. The first feature follows naturally from one of his criteria for selecting students for teacher education, a love of sharing knowledge:

> the teacher [should be] possessed by a recognition of the responsibility for the constant study of school room work, the constant study of children, of methods, of subject matter in its various adaptations to pupils. The professional spirit means that the teachers do not think their work done when they have reasonably prepared a certain amount of subject matter and spent a certain number of hours in the school room attempting in a reasonably intelligent way to convey that material to the children (M7, 109).

This attitude leads the teacher to avoid "aimless drift" and "sticking literally to the text" in favor of "special preparation for particular lessons" (L8, 339). Such professionalism is the basis for other important traits as well:

> Flexibility, ability to take advantage of unexpected incidents and questions, depends upon the teacher's coming to the subject with freshness and fullness of interest and knowledge. There are questions that he should ask before the recitation commences. What do the minds of pupils bring to the topic from their previous experience and study? How can I help them make connections? What need, even if unrecognized by them, will furnish a leverage by which to move their minds in the desired direction? What uses and applications will clarify the subject and fix it in their minds? How can the topic be individualized; that is, how shall it be treated so that each one will have something distinctive to contribute while the subject is also adapted to the special deficiencies and particular tastes of each one (L8, 339-340)?

The second feature of professionalism, "a recognition of responsibility of teachers to the general public," may follow from the love of sharing knowledge or commitment to it. Regardless of its source, it leads to teachers who bear "a responsibility as leaders, as directors in the formation of public opinion" (M7, 110). This feature may strike us now as a little odd, for we are not so accustomed to thinking of the teacher as playing a central role in either a democracy or a democratic and educative community. Recalling Dewey's assertion that we can view education as a form of social engineering may help us sense his meaning (L5, 20). He saw this role as a natural outgrowth of the teacher's special interests, knowledge and competencies:

> Now I am going to say in passing that it is a somewhat striking fact...a somewhat humiliating fact that in...these matters, teachers and professional educators have not been especially active. The larger questions about the protection of childhood, the movements for the abolition of child labor, movements for playgrounds, for recreation centres, even for the adequate use of the school plant, these and the thousand and one problems relative to children that have come forward with the great congestion of population in cities in the last generation—the initiative in the agitation of these questions and the formation of public opinion has to a surprisingly small extent proceeded from the teachers (M7, 110).

Teachers can take the lead in these matters because they know the problems, understand their importance, and have the education to envisage and implement appropriate, promising solutions. They may also be better able than most to explain how the components of the experiential continuum—non-school life and school life—are connected and support one another in bringing about desired educational outcomes.

If teacher professionalism and its consequences follow so naturally from the nature of the teacher's work, then, Dewey asked, "Why is it necessary to harp so continuously upon the formation of a professional spirit among teachers with respect to the ordinary affairs, the subject-matter, the methods and discipline in the classroom" (M7, 111)? Here we might remember his concern earlier about the unattractiveness of the profession, especially in certain school districts: A "system which makes no great demands upon originality, upon invention, upon the continuous expression of individuality, works automatically to put and to keep the incompetent teachers in the school" (M3, 234). Similarly, a system that faces public disrespect generally and where both schools and boards leave teachers "at the mercy of personal intrigue, political bargaining and the effort of some individual or class to get power in the community through manipulation of patronage" (M1, 276) can hardly expect to attract and retain large numbers of truly professional educators because

> the best minds are drawn to the places where they can work effectively. The best minds are not especially likely to be drawn where there is danger that they may have to submit to conditions which no self-respecting intelligence likes to put up with; and where their time and energy are likely to be so occupied with details of external conformity that they have no opportunity for free and full play of their own vigor (M3, 234).

Preaching to teachers about professionalism, then, is not the answer; instead, the solution lies in concerned persons addressing "the lack of adequate impetus" for teachers to be professional and in an examination of "the very nature of the work which makes the thing [professionalism] desirable" for students, teachers and society (M7, 111):

> There is not a single body of men and women in the world... among whom the development of professional spirit would not be hampered if they realized that no matter how much experience they got, however much wisdom they acquired, whatever experiments they tried, whatever results they obtained, that experience was not to count beyond the limits of their immediate activity; that they had no authorized way of transmitting or of communicating it, and of seeing it was taken account of by others (M7, 111).

Yet he considered this deplorable state to be the norm in his day (M7, 112), a pattern that remains in far too many schools and districts. The battle for professionalism then, like Dewey's battle for teacher unions, was against various ways of inhibiting and destroying professional spirit; against working conditions that strip teachers of their responsibility and incentive to think, conditions teachers resent just as keenly today. Here we have the crux of professionalism and its appeal for those who hope their work will matter: to be involved in the solution of educational problems by selecting, forming and arranging the environmental stimuli that enhance educative learning. Here too we see that both *the opportunity and the power produce an on-going educational reformation*: well-educated, experienced and reflective professionals with daily influence on the direction of schooling and society.

In fact, educational growth among teachers—and that is precisely what professionalism involves—leads to an "intellectual responsibility [that] has got to be distributed to every human being" (M7, 112) for personal, social and professional reasons. Dewey considered the rejection of this article of faith "the unforgivable sin," and we can see his career as its promotion through lectures, writing, experiment, and political and social action. Although he sometimes sounded like a naive and incurable optimist, he was a meliorist who believed in the potential of education and believed in democracy and in democracy as "an educative process" (L17, 86). He based his faith in the educative process of democracy on "human good sense and human good will as it manifests itself in the long run when communication is progressively liberated from bondage to prejudice and ignorance" (L17, 86).

The promotion of professional growth, then, amounts to the development of people (in this case, educators) who can think effectively (scientifically, in Dewey's terms) for themselves and act democratically. Thus, in contrast to the "empiric" or ad hoc thinker who is "helpless in the face of new circumstances," the scientific thinker has "power in grappling with the new and untried; he is master of principles which he can effectively apply under novel conditions. The one is the slave of the past, the other is director of the future" (PN, 9) because he is master of the past. Rather than being a "machine teacher" programmed to respond to anyone's directives (9)—and unsure whose to follow—the genuine educator characterized by professional spirit is not "at the mercy of every sort of doctrine and device" (11) but has "his own standard by which to test the many methods and expedients constantly urged upon him, selecting those which stand the test and rejecting those which do not, no matter by what authority or influence they may be supported" (11). Autonomy, then, is a major aspect of professionalism: Rejection of authoritarian prescriptions and proscriptions sometimes becomes necessary for the professional teacher, for she is unwilling to surrender her personal intellectual responsibilities and understands the wisdom of relying upon "good judgment, personal experience, and a knowledge of the ideas and practices of others" (E5, 209).

We see professionalism now as a set of dispositions to be cultivated throughout life, throughout education, and notably during university studies. They must certainly remain at the forefront during the career of the teacher who is, Dewey believed, "the only real educator in the school system" (M1, 272). Professionalism is captured in part in the ten analogies of the teacher—as learner, intellectual leader, partner and guide, wise parent, social servant, prophet, physician, engineer, pioneer and artist. The complexities of roles require thinking and learning and choosing and do not yield readily to mandates, legislation and prescriptions. In the end, professionalism represents one's integrity and a sincerity of commitment to one's beliefs and the process that led to their acquisition. This reflective disposition and professional spirit in the teacher is vital for the educator's own well-being, for the health of "the system," and especially for the student because

> in the degree in which the teacher's understanding is mechanical, superficial, and restricted, the child's appreciation will be correspondingly limited and perverted. If this be true, it is obviously futile to plan large expansions of the studies of the curriculum apart from the education of the teacher (M1, 273-274).

In fact, it seems futile to reform a school system so unattractive that it appeals primarily to a teaching corps characterized by docility and unreflectivity.

Conclusion

To take seriously his program of teacher preparation and the reform of preparation programs, Dewey believed, would be to commit oneself to a massive reconstruction of society and its institutions. Such a reconstruction would result in redeveloping those informal educational emphases that extend from birth to death and those institutional experiences from kindergarten through doctoral studies and beyond in further professional development. This reconstruction could also entail committing oneself to a view of life and purpose that unsettles traditions, customs, beliefs, habits and practices, including those that exist in university departments, colleges and professional schools. The potential for the reform of our schools and teacher preparation in this philosophy of life and learning is staggering if we take human intelligence seriously:

> To investigate truth; critically to verify fact; to reach conclusions by means of the best methods at command, untrammeled by external fear or favor, to communicate this truth to the student; to interpret to him its bearing on the questions he will face in life—this is precisely the aim and object of the university (M2, 55).

Given this meliorist view of the university and a complementary conception of human nature, one that seeks liberated rationality for teaching and teachers, "no one need be troubled for a moment about other educational reforms, or the solution of other educational problems." But one must make certain that this liberation includes a strategy to "draw to the calling of teaching persons of force of character, of sympathy with children, and consequent interest in the problems of teaching and of scholarship" (M3, 234).

Conversely, Dewey's world-view necessitates another commitment, a commitment to a particular kind of democratic society. In essence, his philosophy is based on the hypothesis that the human personality is inevitably social:

> The ideal of democracy demands the fullest possible development of personality in all—irrespective of birth, wealth, creed, or race—through cooperative association with others, and mutual understanding and consent. The ideal further demands that all the institutions, customs, and arrangements of social life shall contribute to these ends, that is, that they shall be educative (L11, 538).

Some may welcome an educational atmosphere and an outlook promoting pervasive caring and growth in schools, homes, hospitals and the community. They may be attracted to a conception of individual life as fulfilling, enriching and improving because it is always growing. They may also welcome educator preparation programs that cultivate growing, thinking, caring and understanding classroom teachers who nurture these same qualities in others, particularly their students, and thereby in communities. Others may be attracted by the participatory, emancipating promise of an active social role, the joy of learning, and even the excitement of toppling traditional icons and erecting fresh ones.

But some, of course, may find this pervasive educational

commitment stifling, limiting any real possibility of choosing, or even intrusive. Certainly, one may argue that Dewey's conception of reform and of the good society—a vision of the moral society that some might link with remnants of his early religious background—and a corresponding obligation on rational citizens to promote this vision might conceivably promote aggressive and sanctimonious implementation. Dewey, at least, expected educators to promote this inspiration among the young and in the schools, with the universities having precisely defined responsibilities. He also expected society to promote it both among the young and among its citizens and its teachers. Every person and institution plays an educational role in forming other members of the community, not just the young. In view of the informal, general and professional education that Dewey proposed for progressively democratic and scientific learning communities, where every institution contributes according to its proper role, one might even feel uncomfortable with his claim that the "teacher [and obviously other educators] in the free society of the future can surpass the typical teacher today" (L11, 545).

Has Dewey replaced a paternalistic or priest-ridden vision of society with—in the broadest Deweyan sense of the term—an *educator*-ridden vision? After all, not everyone enjoys happy memories of homes and parents or schools and teachers or universities and professors. Not everyone would wish to model society on them, and not everyone wishes to be continuously reconstructed or improved by neighbors. Could this be why the Deweyan image troubles those who live in present-day liberal societies—including those who hold diverse beliefs ranging from radically different democratic notions to deeply rooted religious commitments to passionately held existentialist beliefs? Does Dewey's social construct offend our image of what it means to be no longer a child but a free and independent adult? Could it be that Dewey's common faith is too communitarian, naturalistic and intentional—too Deweyan—to be common and accessible?

If so, we should remember that Dewey himself never intended people to change their minds on an issue unless they were convinced by facts, argument, reasons and reflective thinking. He also encouraged in the educational marketplace the inclusion of unorthodox as well as orthodox ideas (however they may be reflected and reversed on occasion) lest a fundamentalist mindset or subculture infect our associations and institutions. Indeed, any uneasiness over what may result from an application of Dewey's philosophy seems to run counter to the intent of his most basic thinking, his ideas of democracy, education, experience, art and growth. So, any sectarian, cultic or dogmatic ethos or community that grows out of Dewey's thought seems, at least to some, oxymoronic. On the one hand, we may want to remember the historical extremes and excesses of a variety of *isms*, including progressivism. On the other hand, we should also recall Dewey's forceful criticism of all *isms*, that "any theory and set of practices is dogmatic which is not based upon critical examination of its own underlying principles" (EE, 22).

CHAPTER SEVEN

Schools in Transition

> The system is a system only by courtesy. In fact, it is more like a patchwork, and a patchwork whose pieces do not form a pattern. It is a patchwork of the old and the new; of unreconstructed survivals from the past and of things introduced because of new conditions (L11, 162).

> [T]he fundamental issue is not of new versus old education nor of progressive against traditional education but a question of what anything whatever must be to be worthy of the name *education* (EE, 90).

Having examined Dewey's approach to thinking about educational reform, the educational concepts he employed to develop a coherent theory of education and experience, his theory of a series of overlapping and complementary democratic communities, his view of the complexities inherent in understanding and pursuing the aims of education, his picture of the roles and responsibilities of the reflective teacher, his notion of the role of the school in helping to build a good society, his portrait of growth as both the means and the end of education, and his formulation of the desirable preparation of aspiring teachers, we now seek insight into his thinking about "good and bad schools." The literature is filled with research and polemics focused on good and effective schools, desirable institutional outcomes, model practices, technological discoveries and so forth. We may wonder, then, if Dewey analyzed the schools he knew and said much about how to design them to promote the growth and development of children, youth and educators.

In fact, Dewey spoke and wrote a great deal about schooling and many of the efforts occurring today would hearten him just as many did in his own day. On the other hand, some contemporary approaches to educational reform may be seen as parts of the problem. We want to legislate specific procedures for districts and schools when a cultural transformation seems more appropriate. We want to isolate the school and educational responsibility from the broader communities when mutual responsibility is essential. We want to evaluate the school and teachers as educational islands when society forms the critical environment. We want to prescribe for schools as if they have a rare disease when a social plague seems to exist. We want to paint the little red schoolhouse green when it needs to be refurbished or reconstructed. Or, to phrase the matter more positively, we often content ourselves with encouraging some fleeting or superficial cooperation, collaboration or association with business partners, community people or institutional affiliates.

By contrast, Dewey would have explained that we are attempting to treat the problems of education without understanding them, isolating partial causes and consequences from broader concerns and issues, identifying educational effects as pedagogical causes, and attacking perceived and partial causes without a defensible interpretative framework or philosophy of education and society. In short, he claimed in the 1930s that "schools are a drift rather than a system" (L11, 163). Today he might similarly say that reform, at least in many quarters, is adrift without a philosophical rudder and a democratic compass.

Amid the intense criticism of schools today, we can usefully examine schooling as Dewey saw it, criticized it, and wished it to be. His perspective on school issues can help us evaluate our own schools and our opinions of them. In pursuing his understanding of schools, we must answer a number of questions: What kinds of schools would result from an implementation of his theory of schooling? What are the desirable and undesirable traits of schools he envisioned? How will such schools be administered and managed? What will their curricula look like? How is the student conceived in a Deweyan school? What roles can schools play in the on-going reform of education? What contributions should they make to the preparation of future educators? How can the schools, the universities and the greater community complement one another or cultivate an experiential continuity? While we have alluded to these issues in earlier discussions, the next two chapters examine them directly and comprehensively. In this chapter, "Schools in Transition," we examine the traditional school and the progressive school, using Dewey's lenses to analyze the desirable and undesirable features and practices of schools in general. The schools of the future—the ones Dewey described in more positive and ideal terms, including the laboratory school, the practice school, the school of tomorrow and the utopian school—receive a thorough examination in Chapter 8.

As we seek to observe the strengths and weaknesses of the schools "in transition," we should remember that from Dewey's point of view every growing school is in transition: changing for the better or into a different kind of institution; transforming beliefs, policies and practices; moving toward personal, community and institutional maturity; enjoying the present progress toward a life-long trip of growth. This idea acknowledges one of Dewey's fundamental principles: Schools that do not constantly form themselves most need reform. This idea also suggests a different interpretation of Horace Mann's remark Dewey admired so much: "Where anything is growing, one former is worth a thousand reformers" (M1, 5). One teacher's on-going formation of desirable habits in a student may be worth more than a thousand others attempting to reform undesirable habits already in place. Similarly, the school that continually forms desirable learning-community habits expends much less effort than a school faced with reforming. If we believe Dewey, the formation of personal and school habits is a momentous matter:

> Repeated responses to recurrent stimuli may fix a habit of acting in a certain way. All of us have many habits of whose import we are quite unaware, since they were formed without our knowing what we were about. Consequently they possess us, rather than we them. They move us; they control us. Unless we become aware of what they accomplish, and pass judgment upon the worth of the result, we do not control them (DE, 29-30).

Although Dewey criticized the traditional school severely and deplored some features and excesses of the progressive school, an examination shows what he found defensible and indefensible in each and, by inference, what he recommended for those schools of the future he found headed in the right direction. Dewey naturally hoped the indefensible elements of both traditional and progressive schools would either pass away or be rejected while the schools of the future built upon the defensible features and the more forward-looking principles and practices being discovered.

The Traditional School

In Chapter 1, we examined the criticisms Dewey leveled against the old education or traditional schools. Given the characteristics of the traditional schools of his time, he could hardly be blamed for recommending their transformation into more democratic, scientific, humane and educative environments. Yet, we should not consider his expression "traditional school" to denote so-called contemporary traditional schools. Contemporary traditional schools may or may not be traditional in the sense Dewey meant. To the degree they have a sufficiently large philosophical and pedagogical gestalt of traditionalism as Dewey viewed it, schools today may well be traditional. Of course, in Dewey's time, the term *traditional* was more appropriate in some cases than in others, for traditional education, like progressive education, was and is a matter of degrees rather than all-or-nothing. But degrees of *what*? Briefly, the what—or characteristics of the traditional school—may be found in two realms: traditional philosophical views and traditional educational practices.

THE PHILOSOPHICAL TRADITION. In the history of Western thought, Dewey saw a number of diverse positions that to varying degrees coalesced around a uniform set of beliefs, a collection of epistemological, ethical and metaphysical ideas that evidenced a search for certitude in all areas of life, a notion suggested by the title of his work *The Quest for Certainty* (1929). In different periods, this quest took the form of superstition, mythology and religion; later philosophy and then science became the forms of meaning in which people sought certainty. Indeed, at one time Dewey said the thirst for a "defense from social attack and the motive of glorification of a specialized calling conspired together [with the result that science] became a kind of sanctuary [and a] religious atmosphere, not to say an idolatrous one, was created" (L4, 176). The search for certainty has been endless largely, Dewey thought, because we live in a world of physical, economic, emotional and social hazards; thus the manifestations of the quest have been diverse, ranging from economic beliefs to nationalistic ideologies to cultural dogma to religious teachings to artistic theories to moral assumptions to political doctrines and—coming immediately to the point—to educational traditionalism. The perfect certainty that throughout history human beings have craved has been accommodated by one viewpoint or another, making it easy for beliefs, habits, traditions and laws to gain allegiance and difficult for them to be abandoned.

Although the intellectual roots of the amorphous general philosophical tradition Dewey identified were diverse and led back to ancient rational, eternal, spiritual and absolute emphases in Greece and Israel, the search became most evident in the varieties of idealism and realism ascendant in the decades immediately before and during Dewey's lifetime. In the forefront of Dewey's mind were political developments, especially in Europe, undergirded by "a whole system of philosophical conclusions" (L4, 17), including a belief these diverse views held in common: that the "Being, Nature or the Universe, the Cosmos at large, Reality, the Truth [was] fixed, immutable, and therefore out of time; that is, eternal" (RP, xii).

Moreover, he saw the connection between reality and truth as clear-cut:

> there is complete correspondence between knowledge in its true meaning and what is real. What is known, what is true for cognition, is what is real in being. The objects of knowledge form the standards of measures of the reality of all other objects of experience (L4, 17).

The search for certitude, then, determined "basic metaphysics" and led to the presupposition that "only the completely fixed and unchanging can be real" (L4, 18). The theory of knowledge, epistemology, was based upon this presupposition, leading to the conclusion that for knowledge to be certain it must be related to "that which has antecedent existence or essential being" or prior being, God or an absolute mind (L4, 18). Dewey saw here a philosophical web with an accompanying influence on knowledge, theory, practice and action, reaching "into practically all important ideas entertained upon any philosophic question" (L4, 19-20), including those affecting work, education, social classes and science (RP, xv ff). He saw a connection as well between the philosophical affirmation of rationality, immutability and eternity and the disparagement of sense data, changeability and temporality.

In the process, education became identified first with the affirmed intellectual values, then with the leisure classes, and then inevitably with the plans of the politically powerful. Appropriately enough, schools promoted the dominant belief systems and promulgated symbols of learning, literary studies and abstract understanding. The more matters stayed the same or became fixed, the better schooling was considered. Thus, new studies (music and art), empirical studies (science) and manual studies (vocations) often met opposition or were at least considered inferior to traditional studies. In the general culture, corresponding dichotomies developed and persisted between theory and practice, mind and body, culture and utility, the rational and the empirical, and leisure and labor. They also invaded the schools, institutions designed largely for the children of the possessing classes (DE, 136ff; 251ff). But as the world moved into the twentieth century, these intellectual and educational traditions attracted challenges.

As these challenges emerged, classical, medieval and reformation forms of thinking and practices were undercut by modern scientific, religious and philosophical studies. These studies, based upon naturalistic assumptions and explanations, often questioned absolutist traditions and raised serious questions about the origins of life, human nature, moral theory and belief in God. Consequently, frontal assaults on traditional philosophies ended up disturbing

> every aspect of contemporary life, from the state of the family and the position of women and children, through *the conduct and problems of education,* through the fine as well as the industrial arts, into political and economic relations of association that are national and international in scope (RP, xx, italics added).

The developments during this time encouraged the educational community, especially universities, to shift from "pre-scientific," "unscientific" and "anti-scientific" thinking to scientific inquiry (RP, xxvi ff). New explorations across the branches of knowledge occurred when they were "liberated from the incubus imposed on them by habits formed in a pre-scientific, pre-technological-industrial and pre-democratic political period" (RP, xxxvii). In particular, "the old spectator theory of knowledge," inimical to a view of knowledge as constructed and open to revision, became dislodged (L4, 163), and the certainty offered by "empiricism, rationalism and Kantianism" was demolished (L4, 137). As a result, "theoretical certitude" was eliminated and a "practical certainty [and] trustworthiness of instrumental operation" took its place (L4, 103). Additionally, demographic and occupational changes called for new skills and attitudes and created new social problems requiring attention. An accompanying philosophical shift in certain segments of the population resulted in attempts to effect "a more general equitable distribution of the elements of understanding and knowledge" (L4, 65).

In an interesting synopsis of some of these intellectual shifts, Dewey explained how many of these changes fueled the conflict between scientific and religious beliefs and altered presuppositions in the academic community and the disciplines, ultimately replacing supernatural explanations and interpretations with naturalistic ones:

> The impact of astronomy not merely upon the older cosmogony of religion but upon elements of creeds dealing with historic events—witness the idea of ascent into heaven—is familiar. Geological discoveries have displaced creation myths which once bulked large. Biology has revolutionized conceptions of soul and mind which once occupied a central place in religious beliefs and ideas, and this science has made a profound impression upon ideas of sin, redemption, and immortality. Anthropology, history and literary criticism have furnished a radically different version of the historic events and personages upon which Christian religions have built. Psychology is already opening to us natural explanations of phenomena so extraordinary that once their supernatural origin was, so to say, the natural explanation (L9, 22).

From an educational viewpoint as well as his own interpretation of the importance of these philosophical, scientific, religious and cultural revolutions, Dewey observed that,

> The significant bearing...of all this is that new methods of inquiry and reflection have become for the educated man today the final arbiter of all questions of fact, existence, and intellectual assent. Nothing less than a revolution in the "seat of intellectual authority" has taken place (L9, 22-23).

THE EDUCATIONAL TRADITION. Out of this early, general philosophical tradition, Dewey saw a steady flow of economic, political, religious and, more immediately relevant for our purposes, educational thought and practice. He tended to attribute every pedagogical evil to this absolutist philosophical tradition, rather than to mindlessness, caprice or ignorance. The educational tradition he saw gradually passing away, grounded in this philosophical heritage, did not welcome the new "seat of intellectual authority," resisted innovations in curriculum and pedagogy, objected to democratic ideas of administration and organization, and rejected scientific theories of child development. In this context, Dewey wrote, "It is radical conditions which have changed, and only an equally radical change in education suffices" (M1, 8).

Candid in his critique of traditional educational thought and practice, Dewey pronounced himself unwilling to issue a "wholesale condemnation of the old education" (EE, 27), but if he were allowed to speak "without the qualifications required for accurate statement" (EE, 17), he would say that the "three [main] characteristics" (EE, 18)—curriculum, standards of conduct and organization—of traditional education could be summarized as follows:

> The subject-matter of education consists of bodies of information and skills that have been worked out in the past; therefore, the chief business of the school is to transmit them to the new generation. In the past, there have also been developed standards and rules of conduct; moral training consists in forming habits of action in conformity with these rules and standards. Finally, the general pattern of school organization (by which I mean the relations of pupils to one another and to the teachers) constitutes the school a kind of institution sharply marked off from other social institutions (EE, 17-18).

He promptly added that subject matter, habits of action and school organization in the traditional school had come to determine the aims and means of schooling and that books and teachers had become, respectively, the representatives of past wisdom and agents and organs of that wisdom:

> The main purpose or objective is to prepare the young for future responsibilities and for success in life, by means of acquisition of the organized bodies of information and prepared forms of skill which comprehend the material of instruction. Since the subject-matter as well as standards of proper conduct are handed down from the past, the attitude of pupils must, upon the whole, be one of docility, receptivity, and obedience. Books, especially

> textbooks, are the chief representatives of the lore and wisdom of the past, while teachers are the organs through which pupils are brought into effective connection with the material. Teachers are the agents through which knowledge and skills are communicated and rules of conduct enforced (EE, 18).

In his discussions, Dewey deliberately highlighted the attitudes of students as manifesting "docility, receptivity, and obedience," the ordinary classroom as characterized by "time-schedules, schemes of classification, of examination and promotion, of rules of order" (EE, 18), and arranged with

> its rows of ugly desks placed in geometrical order, crowded together so that there shall be as little moving as possible, desks almost all of the same size, with just space enough to hold books, pencils, and paper, and...a table, some chairs, the bare wall, and possibly a few pictures (M1, 21).

This organization reminded him of a philosophy of absolutism, the philosophy that had emerged out of a mistaken search for certainty, a philosophy that led to schools designed as places for the recitation and acceptance of the unquestionable truth (M1, 21). Even reading and studying a book was just another form of listening and suggested the "dependency of one mind upon another. This attitude of listening means...passivity, absorption; that there are certain ready-made materials...of which the child is to take in as much as possible in the least possible time" (M1, 22).

This way of listening was no doubt attributable in part to traditional education that tended to neglect "the dynamic quality, the developing force inherent in the child's present experience, and therefore to assume that direction and control were just matters of arbitrarily putting the child in a given path and compelling him to walk there" (M2, 282). Dewey (for unexplained reasons) spent little time acknowledging that certain traditional educational practices made more sense in an era when printed books and materials were scarce, that almost everyone associated learning with acquiring ideas from others, and that in less affluent times schools and society can ill afford to experiment with new ideas and practices. He seemed content, perhaps too content, to think of causation in terms of a narrow socio-philosophical explanation in terms of political, religious and social absolutism.

Dewey sometimes summarized progressive thinkers' criticism of the traditional school without always indicating precisely if or when he differed with these critics. He usually agreed with their denunciations of the traditional school, but not with their reactive pedagogical theory-building tendencies, their either-or thinking about educational issues, and their misinterpretations and misapplications of fundamental educational principles. One summary of the progressive critics' evaluation of the traditional school, which he deemed "a product of discontent with traditional education" (EE, 18), includes insight into traditionalism's ideas of authority, its confusion of adult standards with children's capabilities, and its bent toward imposition:

> The traditional scheme is, in essence, one of imposition from above and from outside. It imposes adult standards, subject-matter, and methods upon those who are only growing slowly toward maturity. The gap is so great that the required subject-matter, the methods of learning and of behaving are foreign to the existing capacities of the young. They are beyond the reach of the experience the young already possess. Consequently, they must be imposed; even though good teachers will use devices of art to cover up the imposition so as to relieve it of obviously brutal features (EE, 18-19).

Dewey also observed that progressive critics believed that, in the traditional school, the curriculum reflects a static, absolutistic philosophy of knowledge and society, resulting in a curriculum that

> means acquisition of what already is incorporated in books and in the heads of the elders. Moreover, that which is taught is thought of as essentially static. It is taught as a finished product, with little regard either to the ways in which it was originally built up or to changes that will surely occur in the future. It is to a large extent the cultural product of societies that assumed the future would be much like the past, and yet it is used as educational food in a society where change is the rule, not the exception (EE, 19).

Dewey himself criticized the traditional school forthrightly, identifying a number of miseducative and noneducative experiences. The issue regarding experience was not, he maintained, that the traditional school failed to provide a variety of experiences while the progressive school did provide them. The issue was the detrimental and limiting consequences of the experiences in traditional schooling upon the desire to learn, make judgments and act intelligently—to grow and keep growing:

> The proper line of attack is that the experiences which were had, by pupils and teachers alike, were largely of a wrong kind. How many students, for example, were rendered callous to ideas, and how many lost the impetus to learn because of the way in which learning was experienced by them? How many acquired special skills by means of automatic drill so that their power of judgment and capacity to act intelligently in new situations was limited? How many came to associate the learning process with ennui and boredom? How many found what they did learn so foreign to the situations of life outside the school as to give then no power of control over the latter? How many came to associate books with dull drudgery, so that they were "conditioned" to all but flashy reading matter (EE, 26-27)?

While Dewey admitted that the undesirable and counterproductive features of the traditional school might sometimes be "exaggerated," he insisted that the typical characteristics of the school came close to producing an educationally lethal uniformity with "its passivity of attitude, its mechanical massing of children, its uniformity of curriculum and method" (M1, 23). Worse still was its placing "the center of gravity...outside the child. It is in the teacher, the textbook, anywhere and everywhere you please except in the immediate instincts and activities of the child himself" (M1, 23). Dewey, then, found the traditional school—with its lack of emphasis on the child, its inadequate understanding of a children's learning community, and its requirement that children spend most of their time in desks neatly situated in rows designed for docile listening—pedagogically and ethically abhorrent (M1, 21-23). He made it clear that he considered the traditional school dominated by "the medieval conception of learning" (M1, 18). That is to say, the traditional school's view of learning

> appeals for the most part simply to the intellectual aspect of our natures, our desire to learn, to accumulate information, and to get control of the symbols of learning; not to our impulses and

> tendencies to make, to do, to create, to produce, whether in the form of utility or of art (M1, 18).

This comment, by the way, provides a critically important illumination of what Dewey meant by *natural impulses and tendencies*: They are propensities toward *making, doing, creating and producing*. Moreover, it specifies another element of traditional schooling that troubled Dewey: the excessive stress placed upon "the symbols of learning" or the written and oral abilities connected to learning mathematical and language skills. He thought these skills important, but he also believed them better learned by utilizing the natural making, doing, creating and producing tendencies of children and that learning in this fashion should precede or at least accompany purely abstract and theoretical discussions of the skills. Moreover, the "excessive emphasis on symbolism" had a detrimental impact on the development of the child's imagination (M1, 85) and promoted a schooling that failed to distinguish between "having something to say and having to say something" (M1, 35). So pervasive was the influence of this emphasis in the traditional school, that Dewey resorted to hyperbole:

> The child comes to the traditional school with a healthy body and a more or less unwilling mind, though, in fact, he does not bring both his body and mind with him; he has to leave his mind behind, because there is no way to use it in the school. If he had a purely abstract mind, he could bring it to school with him, but his is a concrete one, interested in concrete things, and unless these things get over into school life he cannot take his mind with him (M1, 49-50).

In addition to the concept of natural tendencies so vital to his own theory of schooling, he explained some of his objections to the curricular and methodological emphases of the traditional school and the assumptions on which they were based. He argued that the "predigested dosage" approach to curriculum also encouraged a teacher to blame the student for anything amiss in the learning process and to dismiss the possibility that something was wrong with the conceptions of teaching, learning and schooling:

> The notion that some subjects and methods and that acquaintance with certain facts and truths possess educational value in and of

> themselves is the reason why traditional education reduced the material of education so largely to a diet of predigested materials. According to this notion, it was enough to regulate the quantity and difficulty of the material provided, in a scheme of quantitative grading, from month to month and from year to year. Otherwise a pupil was expected to take it in the doses that were prescribed from without. If the pupil left it instead of taking it, if he engaged in physical truancy, or in the mental truancy of mind-wandering and finally built up an emotional revulsion against the subject, he was held to be at fault. No question was raised as to whether the trouble might not lie in the subject-matter or in the way in which it was offered (EE, 46).

Even so, Dewey admitted the value of much in the traditional curriculum, the alternative being society's "relapse into barbarism." But he wished these studies had retained their social context and meaning and been approached as if they were more than just abstract skills and useless information: "The essential point of a social conception of education...is that these subjects be taught *in* and with definite reference to their social context and use" (L8, 59).

In addition to criticizing the traditional school for selecting and arranging studies that ignored young people's social bearings, disregarded their experiences, and relied exclusively on "the judgments of adults" (EE, 76), Dewey was especially critical of the similarly misconceived view of authority, rules, control and classroom management he saw undermining a school's ability to establish any real sense of community, much less a genuine democratic community:

> I think it is fair to say one reason the personal commands of the teacher so often played an undue role and a reason why the order which existed was so much a matter of sheer obedience to the will of an adult was because the situation almost forced it upon the teacher. The school was not a group or community held together by participation in common activities. Consequently, the normal proper conditions of control are lacking. Their absence was made up for, and to a considerable extent had to be made up for, by the direct intervention of the teacher, who, as the saying went, "*kept* order." He kept it because order was in the teacher's keeping, instead of residing in the shared work being done (EE, 55).

The traditional school, Dewey lamented, lacked not only an authentic sense of community that might develop the traits of a healthy society but also a sense of how to develop those commonalities so critical to a community. Instead of looking back to an obsolete philosophy that attributed an essential human nature to everyone, it should look forward to a philosophy that recognized that we are all in the process of creating ourselves (DE, 351-352). In the philosophy of the traditional school, this failure to see the child as in the process of self-creation led Dewey to descry the "extreme depreciations of the child morally and intellectually" (M2, 279). To provide freedom for self-creation and the creation of community, the school that moves away from traditionalism must recognize that

> There is more than a verbal tie between the words *common*, *community*, and *communication*. Men live in a community in virtue of the things which they have in common; and communication is the way in which they come to possess things in common. What they must have in common in order to form a community or society are aims, beliefs, aspirations, knowledge—a common understanding—like-mindedness as the sociologists say. Such things cannot be passed...like bricks; they cannot be shared...by dividing into...physical pieces. The communication which insures participation in a common understanding is one which secures similar emotional and intellectual dispositions—like ways of responding to expectations and requirements (DE, 4, italics added).

Dewey was troubled too that the traditional school lacked an appreciation for democracy, especially since it was supposed to develop children and youth for a productive and useful life in democratic communities: "Upon the ethical side, the tragic weakness of the present school is that it endeavors to prepare future members of the social order in a medium in which the conditions of the social spirit are eminently wanting" (M1, 10). Dewey attributed this failure of the traditional school in large part to the fact that it failed to provide either an environment in which a social spirit had the freedom for intellectual and moral growth or a setting with an intelligent respect for and study of students' personal impulses and desires (EE, 70). In this respect, the traditional school was deficient, and the deficiencies began with a limitation of physical freedom that extended to intellectual and moral freedom:

> The limitation that was put upon outward action by the fixed arrangements of the typical traditional schoolroom, with its fixed rows of desks and its military regimen of pupils who were permitted to move only at certain fixed signals, put a great restriction upon intellectual and moral freedom. Straitjacket and chain-gang procedures had to be done away with if there was to be a chance for growth of individuals in the intellectual springs of freedom without which there is no assurance of genuine and continued normal growth (EE, 61).

Still, the school of the future, or any school that plans to operate on the basis of sound pedagogical theory, should avoid the opposite end of the continuum. The progressive school, for example, often saw physical or external freedom as an end rather than a *means* to the "only freedom that is of enduring importance [which is] freedom of intelligence, that is to say, freedom of observation and of judgment exercised in behalf of purposes that are intrinsically worth while" (EE, 61). Instead of thwarting freedom, as the traditional school tended to do, or abandoning guidance, as the progressive school often did, the school of the future should provide an external freedom so that *the teacher* can engage in serious child study and *the child* can become seriously engaged in educative experiences (EE, 62).

The traditional school also "badly distorted" the notion of curriculum when it taught that by developing "certain skills and by learning certain subjects which would be needed later (perhaps in college or perhaps in adult life) pupils are as a matter of course made ready for the needs and circumstances of the future" (EE, 47). But, Dewey maintained, learning material in isolation from everyday life and disconnected from other branches of knowledge just to pass an examination did little to prepare a person for the analysis and resolution of personal and social problems, a much higher priority of schooling (EE, 48). The curriculum of the traditional school, however, disconnected knowledge in other ways, especially when it took steps to subdivide "each topic into studies; each study into lessons; each lesson into specific facts and formulae [and let] the child proceed step by step to master each one of the separate parts" (M2, 276). Subject matter, therefore, dictated both the "end" and the "method" of the traditional school (M2, 276).

Subject matter based upon an absolutist viewpoint, Dewey believed, also served a teacher's inclinations to inculcate "fixed conclusions" rather than develop the thinking abilities of students (L4, 201). The collateral learning that occurred in the traditional school then was perhaps more deadly in its influence, because students lost or failed to gain the most important attitude they can form, namely, the desire to go on learning throughout life (EE, 48). So Dewey, echoing Matthew 16, asked the traditional school:

> What avail is it to win prescribed amounts of information about geography and history, to win ability to read and write, if in the process the individual loses his own soul: loses his appreciation of things worth while, of the values to which these things are relative; if he loses desire to apply what he has learned and, above all, loses the ability to extract meaning from his future experiences as they occur (EE, 49)?

Dewey also expressed strong objections to the traditional practice of isolating knowledge from its human and social contexts and from the intrinsic but directed interests of the student. He considered the separation of knowledge from its social creation—ignoring its personal applications and slighting its inherent appeal—a major problem. Instead of keeping learning in its natural setting and maintaining a continuity of growth, the teacher was obliged to get students to learn isolated "facts, laws, information" (M1, 71) and managed to do so, if at all, by providing an artificial set of "encouragements, admonitions, urgings, and devices" (M1, 70). The emphasis on linguistic and mathematical symbols in the elementary school took up entirely too much time in the traditional school and left too little time for free development, exploration and contextual learning (M1, 70-71).

Obviously, Dewey saw little promise of the traditional school becoming a school of the future. On the contrary, he saw it rooted in a past characterized by medieval views, authoritarian organization and aristocratic curricula tied to undemocratic class interests. He acknowledged that the traditional school could be conducted more effectively and in ways more inspiring to educators and enjoyable and educative for students. But he had little interest in improving traditional schools along their current lines of practice and philosophy, established as they were on an undemocratic philosophy of society and schooling, designed as they were to perpetuate the values and problems of an inappropriate past into the future (M8, 388). He could only wish that these schools, which were a part of "the old social order," would pass quickly with that social order instead of lingering as a relic of the past (L14, 278). If the traditional school was unwilling to abandon its philosophical and political foundation, Dewey appeared ready to abandon any hope of its reformation.

The Progressive School

In view of the oral and written tradition that Dewey was a progressive, it may come as a surprise to find *the progressive school classified here as a school in transition*, as a school that would or should pass from the scene or should be transformed into a different kind of institution. We need some explanation of this claim. To begin with, we might recall this comment: "[T]he phrase 'progressive education' has been and is frequently used to signify *almost any kind* of school theory and practice" that parts company with traditional education (L17, 52, italics added). Dewey had no interest in becoming identified with this kind of reactionary, ambiguous progressivism because, in his mind, it was not genuinely progressive and was in need of transformation much like traditionalism:

> Many of these [so-called progressive] procedures, when examined, are found to be innovations, but there seems to be no sound basis for regarding them as progressive. For progress is not identical with mere change, even when the changes may accidentally here and there involve some casual improvement over what previously existed. Still less is it identical with a happy-go-lucky process or flashy, spur-of-the-moment improvisations (L17, 52).

Considering the so-called progressive practices and schools blooming all around him, Dewey undoubtedly felt uncomfortable with the label progressive. On the other hand, he did feel comfortable with educators in these schools working to transform or reform their institutions into the kinds of schools reflecting the philosophy he espoused.

Beyond this general reason for resisting the progressive label, Dewey had a particular reason: The progressive school was often identified with "the one-sidedness [of] child-centered education" (L17, 53). Again despite tradition, Dewey was clearly much less child-centered than community-centered: "the *process* of mental development is essentially a social process, a process of participation" (L11, 206). He had a profound respect for children, but insisted that they must be guided appropriately by educators. Furthermore, he objected vigorously to the misinterpretations of this respect that led many progressive schools to allow children to do as they pleased and to abandon any sense of community and responsibility.

Moreover, the fact that progressive education was based in part at times upon dichotomous, compromissorial, reactionary and dogmatic thinking and the misapplication of sound pedagogical principles is another reason that Dewey wanted progressive education to change and develop into a positive philosophy of education (EE, 17ff, 22). In fact, Dewey stated essentially the same objection to progressivism in 1938 he had made in 1898: "[T]he New Education, as it exists today, is a compromise and a transition: it employs new methods; but its controlling ideals are virtually those of the Old Education" (E5, 269).

Ultimately for Dewey the real issue was neither traditional nor progressive education but education itself (EE, 90). He appears to have been ready to welcome a great educational transition, the passing of both traditionalism and progressivism so that only education remained. If it can be said that all Dewey wanted was to make early and so-called progressive schools genuinely progressive, the fact remains that these schools were the very schools Dewey wanted to disappear, preferring however that they disappear by transformation or reformation. This is not to say that he wanted to leave behind every feature of the progressive school any more than he wished this for the traditional school. In his synthesis of the defensible elements of the old and the new education, he would have carried forward those features from each that were consistent with his scientific and democratic philosophy of society and education, creating a school of the future.

From Dewey's point of view, there are neither purely traditional schools nor completely progressive ones, only different kinds of schools we can classify as largely traditional or essentially progressive. The classification of schools, then, was not necessarily an either-or matter. Moreover, with a reflective understanding of schools, we recognize that Dewey saw diverse schools within these two general categories. Furthermore, he considered this diversity, especially on the part of progressive schools, healthy:

> In developing anything new, it is a good plan to have different methods working side by side, to experiment, to compare. This

> kind of difference has nothing whatever to do with whether a particular school is a good school or a bad school, with whether children learn what they are taught and are happy and successful at school and home. Nor does this mean that all progressive schools just by the fact of being labeled "progressive" are good schools. It simply means that progressive education has not one formula, is not a fixed and finished thing about which it is legitimate and safe to make generalizations (L9, 152).

While Dewey had these reservations about the merits of progressive schools, he saw additional problems as well: He considered them theoretically inadequate and practically defective, manifesting these inadequacies, among other ways, in their views of freedom and teaching. In his mind, the theoretical problems exacerbated the practical problems, and both infected everyday classroom beliefs and routines. In short, he saw the progressive school as a product of an incomplete, incoherent and unclear philosophy of education.

THE PROGRESSIVE PHILOSOPHY OF EDUCATION. While Dewey became associated in the public mind with the progressive school or the new education, his complete works then show him openly critical of it as "a product of discontent with traditional education" (EE, 18) and a "philosophy which proceeds on the basis of rejection, of sheer opposition" (EE, 21). As a result, the progressive school sometimes neglected crucial questions and often took an either-or stance on educational issues, defining itself by what it was not. For instance, progressive educators are inclined to think, Dewey suggested, that since "the old education was based on ready-made organization [of adult knowledge] ...it suffices to reject the principle of [curricular] organization *in toto*, instead of striving to discover what it [the organization of knowledge] means and how it is to be attained on the basis of experience" (EE, 21). Dewey considered such a reactionary philosophy unprofitable at best and wasteful at worst, blinding educators to the problems of progressive education. He also saw the weaknesses of this dichotomous thinking reflected in other oppositional claims and practices of progressivism:

> To imposition from above is opposed expression and cultivation of individuality; to external discipline is opposed free activity; to learning from texts and teachers, learning through experience; to

> acquisition of isolated skills and techniques by drill, is opposed acquisition of them as means of attaining ends which make direct vital appeal; to preparation for a more or less remote future is opposed making the most of the opportunities of present life; to static aims and materials is opposed acquaintance with a changing world (EE, 19-20).

Thus Dewey believed that many supporters of the progressive school had yielded to a reactionary philosophy and consistently examined pedagogical questions through either-or lenses. This being the case, he said, the danger in the progressive school movement is that in "rejecting the aims and methods of that which it would supplant, it may develop its principles negatively rather than positively and constructively. Then it takes its clew in practice from that which is rejected instead of from the constructive development of its own philosophy" (EE, 20). He believed that rejecting an indefensible philosophical belief or pedagogical practice of traditionalism solves no problem; it merely identifies the problem. The next step is to decide what beliefs and practices are intellectually meritorious. So too, rejecting a traditionalist position and proposing a position built upon agreeable terms or fashionable phrases solves no problems. One solves problems as one clarifies and defends concepts and justifies and implements the pedagogical implications (EE, 22-23). Moreover, Dewey warned that the abstract principles associated with progressivism, while perhaps defensible in principle, must also be examined from the point of view of how they are *interpreted* and *applied* and what their *consequences* are as they are "worked out in practice" (EE, 20). For him, "everything depends upon the interpretation given [abstract principles] as they are put into practice in the school" (EE, 20).

Today, to select examples of historical and contemporary interest, Dewey might ask what certain educators mean by such terms as *democratic schools* (Apple and Beane, 1995), *learner-centered schools* (Texas Education Agency, 1994), and *student-centered classrooms* (Zemelman, Daniels, and Hyde, 1993), and he would want to know where he could see these ideas operationalized. He would also be interested in determining whether schools based on these concepts demonstrate a clear understanding of what constitutes educative activities, democratic communities, community-centered schools, and personal and social growth. In essence, he would want a clear understanding of the philosophy of education behind these concepts.

Dewey added to his criticism of the progressive philosophy noting that while it found unity in "the idea that there is an intimate and necessary relation between the processes of actual experience and education," it was seriously weakened by its failure to develop "a correct idea of experience" (EE, 20). The fact that Dewey entitled his final major educational work *Experience and Education* is widely thought to imply that he believed the supporters of the progressive school had so far failed to develop a correct view of experience. In this connection, it is instructive to review our discussion of his concept of experience described in Chapter 1. Dewey wanted it clear that having explained the idea of experience in terms of the connected term *experiment*,

> Mere activity does *not* [italics added] constitute experience. It is dispersive, centrifugal, dissipating. Experience as trying involves change, but *change is meaningless transition unless* [italics added] it is consciously connected with the return wave of consequences which flow from it. When an activity is continued *into* the undergoing of consequences, when the change made by action is reflected back into a change made in us, the mere flux is loaded with significance. We learn something. It is not experience when a child merely sticks his finger into a flame; it is experience when the movement is connected with the pain which he undergoes in consequence (DE, 139-140).

Moreover, even if genuine education comes about through experience, this "does not mean that all experiences are genuinely or equally educative. Experience and education cannot be directly equated to each other" (EE, 25). To be sure, the educator in the school of the future should select experiences that ideally are "enjoyable," "interesting," or at least "agreeable" (EE, 26-27), but more importantly she should "select the kind of present experiences that live fruitfully and creatively in subsequent experiences" (EE, 28). And, Dewey insisted, it was critical that "no experience is educative that does not tend both to knowledge of more facts and entertaining of more ideas and to a better, a more orderly, arrangement of them" (EE, 82). So the teacher who follows Dewey is not interested just in student activity but in engaging students in "*intelligent* activity" (EE, 69).

THE PROGRESSIVE PHILOSOPHY OF THE CURRICULUM. In the light of this need for a positive philosophy of progressive education and a correct understanding of experience, Dewey obliged the curriculum planner in the progressive school to answer a series of questions:

> What is the place and meaning of subject-matter and of organization *within* experience? How does subject-matter function? Is there anything inherent in experience which tends towards progressive organization of its contents? What results follow when the materials of experience are not progressively organized (EE, 20-21)?

For Dewey, these were not just rhetorical questions; they were questions he addressed much of his life and which he expected others to address. Unfortunately, the progressive schools appeared to resist these and similar curricular questions.

Nevertheless, Dewey was greatly pleased to note elementary schools responding to the idea that "anything which can be called a study, whether arithmetic, history, geography, or one of the natural sciences, must be derived from materials which at the outset fall within the scope of ordinary life-experience" (EE, 73). He insisted, on the other hand, that using the material of everyday life experiences was only the first, easy step. "The next step," he argued, "is the progressive development of what is already experienced into a fuller and richer and also more organized form, a form that gradually approximates that in which subject-matter is presented to the skilled, mature person" (EE, 73-74).

This second step, Dewey believed, had received less attention than it deserved in the progressive school because of the school's inadequate notion of experience and because it confused the notion of experience with mere activity. Indeed, Dewey claimed "the weakest point" of schools that claimed to be progressive fell into the area of selecting and organizing subject-matter (EE, 78). In short, Dewey accused the progressive school of neglecting the problems of both curricular selection and curricular organization. Thus, if the progressive educator was to do his job responsibly, he must see "the office of the educator"* as being involved in the selection, not just of anything that is different and advanced, but (while planning for the future and using the past and present) the selection of those

> things within the range of existing experience that have the promise and potentiality of presenting new problems which by stimulating new ways of observation and judgment will expand the area of further experience. He must constantly regard what is already won not as a fixed possession but as an agency and instrumentality for opening new fields which make new demands upon existing powers of observation and intelligent use of memory. Connectedness in growth must be his constant watchword (EE,75).

THE PROGRESSIVE PHILOSOPHY OF FREEDOM. Dewey saw additional problems in the progressive school, however, requiring special attention if it was to focus on the personal growth of each student and the growth of the school as a learning community. For example, some of the misinterpretations and misapplications of the sound abstract principles many progressive educators subscribed to were based on little more than a reaction to the traditional school. Moreover, Dewey found it particularly disturbing when these views resulted in defective educational practice and noneducative and miseducative student activities. He lamented some of the tendencies of the progressive school and pointed toward appropriate considerations:

> When external control is rejected, the problem becomes that of finding the factors of control that are inherent within experience. When external authority is rejected, it does not follow that all authority should be rejected, but rather that there is need to search for a more effective source of authority. Because the older education imposed the knowledge, methods, and the rules of conduct of the mature person upon the young, it does not follow, except upon the basis of the extreme *Either-Or* philosophy, that the knowledge and skill of the mature person has no directive value for the experience of the immature. On the contrary, basing education upon personal experience may mean *more* [italics added] multiplied and *more* [italics added] intimate contacts between the mature and the immature than ever existed in the traditional school, and consequently *more* [italics added], rather than less, guidance by others. The problem, then, is: how these contacts can be established without violating the principle of learning through personal experience. The solution of this problem requires a well thought-out philosophy of the social factors that operate in the constitution of individual experience (EE, 21).

Dewey concluded that the tendency in some progressive schools to reject authority promoted the misleading idea that freedom for activity is "an end in itself," a mistake that could hardly be greater (EE, 63). On the contrary, the progressive school should value free activity as "a means to a freedom which is power: power to frame purposes, to judge wisely, to evaluate desires by the consequences... power to select and order means to carry chosen ends into operation" (EE, 64). The purpose of free activity, then, was principally to supply a means to the goal of growth that opened up a still greater variety of freedom for individuals in society.

Likewise, the progressive school erred in thinking that freedom from restraint or freedom for children to express their "natural impulses and desires" was an end in itself, rather than a "starting point" (EE, 64). Instead, Dewey said, the progressive school should engage in *reconstructing* and *remaking* original impulses and desires in an effort to promote intellectual growth. The conduct of students in the progressive school should not be guided by "the illusion of freedom" or "dictated by immediate whim and caprice; that is, at the mercy of impulses into whose formation intelligent judgment has not entered" (EE, 64-65). The reconstruction of a student's impulses and desires was critical, Dewey thought, because it is the only path to developing self-control and a self-determination based upon reflection:

> This remaking involves inhibition of impulse in its first estate. The alternative to externally imposed inhibition is inhibition through an individual's own reflection and judgment. The old phrase "stop and think" is sound psychology. For thinking is stoppage of the immediate manifestation of impulse until that impulse has been brought into connection with other possible tendencies to action so that a more comprehensive and coherent plan of activity is formed. Some of the other tendencies to action lead to use of eye, ear, and hand to observe objective conditions; others result in recall of what has happened in the past. Thinking is thus a postponement of immediate action, while it effects internal control of impulse through a union of observation and memory, this union being the heart of reflection. What has been said explains the meaning of the well-worn phrase "self-control." The ideal aim of education is creation of power of self-control (EE, 64).

Conversely, Dewey saw no more solid point in the progressive school than its emphasis on "the participation of the learner in the formation of the purposes which direct his activities in the learning process, just as there is no defect in traditional education greater than its failure to secure the active co-operation of the pupil" (EE, 67). The cooperative process in constructing educational purpose, however, was no simple matter, for it required teachers and students to work together to reconstruct original *impulses,* especially as they encounter obstacles, and to convert them into *desires* that must be postponed until observation and memory unite to weigh the consequences of pursuing these converted desires. The formation of *purposes* lies in identifying those justifiable desires that are ends in view. These purposes, in turn, receive the reflective judgment of individuals as they develop and eventually pursue *plans of action* (EE, 67-72). In all of these activities and decisions, the teacher is no passive observer allowing students to "do their own things" but is a well-informed guide, an intellectual leader and a wise parent.

Dewey saw a related problem in the progressive school when the spoiled child or the pampered child is allowed to act without regard for personal consequences or the impact of such individualism upon others. Any child provided this sort of pseudo-freedom or taught to see freedom as an opportunity for the expression of personal caprice and whim, rather than learning to transform impulses into intelligent, reflective desires and purposes, may well become spoiled. Dewey claimed further that the results of spoiling a child are ongoing because a habit, an outlook, or an attitude

> which operates as an automatic demand that persons and objects cater to his desires and caprices in the future [is established]. It makes him seek the kind of situation that will enable him to do what he feels like doing at the time. It renders him averse to and comparatively incompetent in situations which require *effort* and *perseverance* in overcoming obstacles (EE, 37, italics added).

THE PROGRESSIVE PHILOSOPHY OF TEACHING. If ill-conceived progressive schools sometimes fostered spoiled children, their distorted notion of the freedom of the child also promoted a false notion of teaching, viewing the teacher as largely inactive. The simple-mindedness of this concept of *non-teaching*—that teachers should *not* share what they have learned and were learning for fear of imposing adult standards upon children and thereby inhibiting their natural development—struck Dewey as more than silly and pointless:

> The greater maturity of experience which should belong to the adult as educator puts him in a position to evaluate each experience of the young in a way which the one having less mature experience cannot do. It is the business of the educator to see in what direction an experience is heading. There is no point in his being more mature if, instead of using his greater insight to help organize the conditions of the experience of the immature, he throws away his insight (EE, 38).

As we would expect, then, Dewey deplored any school that claimed to be progressive but depreciated the teacher's maturity and tended "to make little or nothing of organized subject-matter of study; to proceed as if any form of direction and guidance by adults were an invasion of individual freedom" (EE, 22) or one that acted "as if the idea that education should be concerned with the present and future meant that acquaintance with the past has little or no role to play in education" (EE, 22). The progressive schools that *suppressed* the knowledge, experience and understanding of their teachers by denying them the roles of intellectual leaders, guides and wise parents were forcing them to abandon their moral responsibility to help others in educative ways (EE, 38). In the end, this kind of suppression was no better than the suppression of the talents and abilities of teachers in traditional schools when they were stripped of their freedom to think and act accordingly.

Dewey saw moral and ethical implications in the possibility that teachers might be denied the right or fail to use their experiential maturity (including their informal and formal education) and their professional preparation and judgment to encourage their students' growth and, thereby, cultivate spoiled children. First, he said the teacher has no moral "right to withhold from the young on given occasions whatever capacity for sympathetic understanding his own experience has given him" (EE, 38). In fact, the opposite is the case: The teacher has a moral responsibility to foster the intellectual and moral capacities of children in a democratically oriented micro-community.

Second, he observed that visitors to some "progressive schools are shocked by the lack of manners they come across" (EE, 59-60). Perhaps, he admitted, some of these behaviors were attributable to the freedom and enthusiasm children show in a progressive school. Even so, he said, the lack of manners also represented in part "a failure in education, a failure to learn one of the most important lessons of life, that of mutual accommodation and adaptation [necessary in forming valuable] attitudes and habits" for future learning (EE, 60). The fact that manners are "minor morals" (DE, 18), "differ from place to place and time to time" (EE, 59), and could become "empty ritualistic forms" (EE, 59) did not keep Dewey from his basic position, for he believed that "the existence of some form of convention is not itself a convention. It is a uniform attendant of all social relationships. At the very least, it is the oil which prevents or reduces friction" (EE, 59). Given the friction that exists in society and schools, learning minor morals or manners became an important consideration growing out of the daily interaction of students in learning communities.

For Dewey, then, progressive schools, as conceived and operating in his time, did not necessarily "solve any of the problems" facing educators (EE, 21). Rather then as now they "set new problems which have to be worked out on the basis of a new philosophy of experience," a philosophy Dewey thought too often lacking (EE, 21-22). Departing from the traditional school, therefore, solved no problems; it merely established new problems or issues to be pursued intelligently: "What does freedom mean and what are the conditions under which it is capable of realization?" and "How shall the young become acquainted with the past in such a way that the acquaintance is a potent agent in appreciation of the living present" (EE, 23)? Unless progressive thinkers can answer inquiries and questions like these and develop plans of action that help them move beyond a "planless improvisation" (EE, 28), unless

> experience is so conceived that the result is a plan for deciding upon subject-matter, upon methods of instruction and discipline, and upon material equipment and social organization of the school, it is wholly in the air. It is reduced to a form of words which may be emotionally stirring but for which any other set of words might equally be substituted (EE, 28).

The plan a progressive school develops must come down out of the air and consider the "external conditions" of experience, notably, since Dewey's philosophy of education is community-centered, the community (EE, 39). If we ignore the external aspects or wider environmental influences of experience, we fail to recognize that

> we live from birth to death in a world of persons and things which in large measure is what it is because of what has been done and transmitted from previous human activities. When this fact is ignored, experience is treated as if it were something which goes on exclusively inside an individual's body and mind. It ought not to be necessary to say that experience does not occur in a vacuum. There are sources outside an individual which give rise to experience. It is constantly fed from these springs. No one would question that a child in a slum tenement has a different experience from that of a child in a cultured home; that the country lad has a different kind of experience from the city boy, or a boy on the seashore one different from the lad who is brought up on inland prairies (EE, 39-40).

While the traditional school had overemphasized the external world of the environment and underemphasized the internal world of the students' "powers and purposes" (EE, 45), the progressive school had a tendency to yield to the opposite extreme (EE, 42). Thus, the educator must concentrate on building an external, educative environment continuous with the various environments of all students.

Conclusion

In conclusion, Dewey noted that, while the traditional school could manage reasonably well without "any consistently developed philosophy of education" (EE, 28), the progressive school must have a coherent philosophy of education to be defensible and effective (EE, 29). The traditional school could continue to ride the waves of tradition. The progressive school had no such tradition to propel it and, therefore, needed an educational philosophy to guide its development. Dewey appears to have seen the rudiments of such a philosophy of education in progressive schools and noted these rudiments when he described two features worthy of praise:

> one thing which has recommended the progressive movement is that it seems more in accord with the democratic ideal to which our people is committed than do the procedures of the traditional school, since the latter have so much of the autocratic about them.

> Another thing which has contributed to its favorable reception is that its methods are humane in comparison with the harshness so often attending the policies of the traditional school (EE, 33-34).

We should, therefore, reflect a "hospitality to progressive education" (EE, 35) and prefer those characteristics of schools that "promote a better quality of human experience"—what we now might call a better quality of life both in school and in society—by promoting freedom, decency, kindliness, mutual consultation and persuasion over "repression and coercion" (EE, 34).

Dewey also praised the progressive school for "shifting the center of gravity" from a morally, socially and epistemologically reprehensible absolutism. Comparing this shift to the Copernican revolution, he asserted that "the child becomes the sun about which the appliances of education revolve; he is the center about which they are organized" (M1, 23). Children are, nevertheless, social animals, members of several learning communities, and must remain within these contexts if we are to understand and address their needs and interests. Fortunately, no longer will children have to leave their minds behind, as in the traditional school, now that children and their experiences are respected (M1, 50). Yet, he confessed that the many complaints about progressive schools neglecting the traditional school studies provided "sufficient evidence that the exact balance is not yet struck" between the old curriculum and the new (M1, 78). Much more attention needed to be given to building a curriculum that began with children's experiences in life and their developing interests and proceeded to refine those experiences and interests in the light of everyday occupations into adult modes of thinking.

While Dewey had a stronger affinity for the progressive school than the traditional school, he criticized those reactionary, either-or, excessive and thoughtless tendencies that impaired its ability to develop an intelligent philosophy of experience, education, schooling, curriculum and instructional practices. Yet he held out hope for the progressive school *if* progressive educators practiced adequately conceived fundamental concepts and the principles, aims and means stemming from these key concepts (EE, 89-90). In the final analysis, however, Dewey concluded that "the fundamental issue" has more to do with what is worth being called education, not whether we call ourselves traditionalists or progressivists (EE, 90). With Dewey, we hold that our progress as educators will be greater when we focus on understanding the nature of education and the conditions intrinsic to genuine education and move beyond the progressive-traditional debate (EE, 90-91). Understanding that both traditionalists and progressives have badly misconstrued education, however, provides insight into what education is and is not, a beginning to understanding other kinds of schools, including schools important in any scheme of educational reform faithful to Dewey's vision.

CHAPTER EIGHT

Schools of the Future

> In this school the life of the child [which is essentially social in nature and lived in community with others] becomes the all-controlling aim. All the media necessary to further the growth of the child center there. Learning? certainly, but living primarily, and learning through and in relation to this living (M1, 24).

> We want that type of education which will discover and form the kind of individual who is the intelligent carrier of a social democracy—social indeed, but still a democracy (M11, 57).

> The motto must be: "Learn to *act* with and for others while you learn to *think* and to judge for yourself" (L6, 98).

Schools of the future are seldom just schools of the future. They embody the best thinking and practice of the present and are already in operation in many cases. They are presently developing, but they are also close enough to our ideals, especially compared with other institutions and with schools we can imagine, for us to see them as part of the future.

Yet if they are truly schools of the future, we expect them to have more than a part in the future: We count on them to play major roles in introducing the educational future and in modeling what our future schools could or should be like, how they should be staffed, organized, managed, administered, designed, arranged and operated. We also expect schools of the future to provide us with insight into the roles and responsibilities of administrators and teachers, the emphases of the curricula, and the activities and experiences of students. In short, these schools of the future are usually currently operating institutions that provide the best educational environments and experiences we can imagine and resources can provide. While they are already genuine schools of the future, that is not a settled, realized future: They only reach their full potential as constantly growing learning communities after having been operationalized and evaluated and adjusted and are continually reforming and transforming themselves.

If we are parents—or simply interested members of the community—we may want to know what value schools of the future place upon languages, technology, science, mathematics, the arts, social studies and other branches of inquiry, creativity and understanding. Some of us are interested in such co-curricular activities as debating teams, athletics and drama. We sometimes wonder if the teachers are effective, particularly in such basic subjects as reading and languages, mathematics and science, music and theater and art. We may ask how the test scores of the students in one school compare with those in other schools. We may wonder where the former students find their higher education or work after they leave or graduate. Are they accepted by prestigious public or private institutions? Do they find secure jobs with good pay with reputable companies? What kinds of awards do they receive? What roles do the alumnae and alumni play in their communities?

In keeping with Dewey's criticisms of traditional and progressive thought and practice, we would expect him to provide a vision of possible schools incorporating the best of traditional practices and innovations into realistic, realizable projects. We would also expect him to use his imagination and serve as a pedagogical pioneer, suggesting what the future might include if we are creative. Interestingly, however, our prior list of questions did not include one that is distinctively Deweyan. If these questions accurately reflect our values, we are manifesting a traditional academic interest in future schools and a concern for a social life our children find as a result of their education. Of course, we might interpret some of these concerns from Dewey's viewpoint, but that is different from their being the questions Dewey would have raised. *We neglected to ask* how the schools intend to foster the intellectual, social and ethical growth of our children or how they plan to nurture moral, communitarian and democratic sympathies in our students. We neglected to ask about the kinds of thinking—scientific, reflective, independent—the schools plan to cultivate. Did we ask about the quality of students' lives in the school, or whether the atmosphere was supportive, open and encouraging? Where did we suggest that we wanted the schools to further reflective and productive workers and citizens, people who are creative in their work and who encourage democratic work habits and lifestyles? Did we ask whether the school leaders and policy makers think schools have a responsibility for shaping certain kinds of people and cultures? Were we interested in whether the schools see a proper role for themselves in helping to form and reform schooling, teacher preparation and society? Do we want our children to attend schools that intend to nurture children and youth who will help improve their communities, provinces, states and nations?

To understand future schools from Dewey's perspective, we can usefully recall what we have learned about his views of education, thinking, experience, community, freedom, authority, democracy, science, curriculum, pedagogy, children, learning, teaching, teachers, theory, practice and schools. These concepts, all intrinsic parts of his idea of the ideal school, provide a useful interpretative scheme for understanding his hopes for the future. Dewey himself never used the words *schools of the future* to express his thoughts about the roles a variety of schools should play. Nevertheless, we use the phrase to refer to four different kinds of schools important to him, including the (1) laboratory school, (2) practice school, (3) school of tomorrow, and (4) utopian school.

A discussion of these four kinds of schools illuminates various aspects of the responsibilities of their teachers to the profession, aspiring educators, children and society. The analogy of the teacher as pioneer comes immediately to mind when we think of the responsibility to help create schools of the future. But the other roles and responsibilities are relevant too. The Laboratory School Dewey helped develop at the University of Chicago still has many implications for on-going educational reform. It illustrates both the role of a laboratory school in international, national, regional and local educational reform and the roles of other schools, especially the practice school, that prepare future educators. The third type of school, the school of tomorrow or the schools discussed in *Schools of To-Morrow*, existed in the early part of the twentieth century; but from Dewey's standpoint, it could realize its greater potential only as more people became convinced of the full implications of what it means to build, nourish, sustain and extend the influence of democratic schools in a democratic society. The fourth kind of school, the utopian school, represented Dewey's ideal school—less a school in the customary sense than a school founded upon a full application of natural learning theory in a fully functioning democratic community. In spite of a cryptic description of the latter, both the school of tomorrow and the utopian school point us in the directions Dewey wanted to see schools move, suggesting ideas and practices that all schools could profitably examine and evaluate, and possibly adopt for their own use.

Above all, however, Dewey's view of change and the importance of a school's responding to the needs of its community ensured that schools of the future will be neither identical nor uniform. Instead, they will continually change as new knowledge relevant to schooling and society becomes available. They will adapt to and incorporate the local needs and interests of communities, and they will change as these needs and interests evolve; they will use the past and present experiences of students as they come to think and solve personal and societal problems; and they will be grounded in the belief that imaginative and creative teachers need freedom for themselves and the children in their learning communities. Yet these schools will retain common concerns and aims: developing reflective, productive and useful citizens for a democracy and a community of mutually concerned citizens. The schools of the future, therefore, will differ even within communities even though we will find commonalities—shared values or means or qualities or concerns or problems—in each.

While Dewey was at the University of Chicago (1894-1904), the School of Education created a "system of schools" it described as "Connected Schools" (M2, 77). The system included the University Laboratory School, University Elementary School, University Secondary School, and the Chicago Manual Training School. Designed from the start as either laboratory schools or practice schools, they helped shape Dewey's educational thinking. Through them university students came into "contact with problems of educational method, subject-matter, organization, and administration, and [were] enabled to test, interpret, criticize, and verify the principles...[they had] learned" (M2, 78). We return shortly to these connected schools Dewey considered invaluable in both the preparation of intending educators and the professional development of practicing educators. For the moment, the important point is the purpose he envisioned for field experience in those schools, for it is the opposite of what we might now expect: the future teacher was to "test, interpret, criticize, and verify the principles *he had learned*" (M2, 78, italics added), not imitate, much less criticize, the techniques and principles the regular classroom teacher displayed. If the standard of excellence and the test of theory resided with anyone and occurred anywhere, it rested with the teacher and in the school, not the professor and the university (unless of course the laboratory and other schools were a part of the university). Of course, this is only part of the story about theory and practice. We will soon examine the relationship of theory and practice in greater detail.

The Laboratory School

While Dewey criticized both traditional and progressive schools harshly, his observations about the school he helped establish at the University of Chicago were quite different, even though the school was new, evolving and lasted only from 1896 to 1903 (HWT, v). Dewey saw the Laboratory School as a vital, dynamic institution for encouraging ongoing interest in educational reform. In fact, he asserted in 1898 that if "experiment stations," an expression referring to any school experimenting with "the New Education" and also applicable to his view of the experimental function of the Laboratory School (M1, 56), "which represent the outposts of educational progress" can be supported for "a number of years" and allowed to work out "carefully and definitely the subject-matter of a new curriculum...the problem of the more general educational reform will be immensely simplified and facilitated" (E5, 269).

Supporting a variety of experimental schools, including his Laboratory School, then, was a wise and economical practice as well as a means of engaging in systematic educational experimentation that would lay the foundation for and speed up the process of broader educational reform. In one sense, therefore, Dewey thought that those schools that were experimenting on the basis of new beliefs about children, society and education were the places likeliest to initiate educational reform. Yet, we have seen his expectations for laboratory schools realized only rarely. Laboratory schools as a group have yet to accomplish much in the way of teacher preparation, much less educational reform (Goodlad, 1990). Failure to realize the potential of the laboratory school movement is, however, no reason to reject its potential for educational reform any more than the failure of public schools to maximize their potential is grounds for rejecting their potential role in educational reform.

On the other hand, there have been and are experimental schools that are not laboratory schools that are serving as centers of reform much in keeping with Dewey's wishes (though they rarely seem to survive the departure of their founders or principals or turnovers in the central offices of school districts). As exemplars of courage, experimentation and creativity, they continue to influence local and sometimes national reform agendas positively. Indeed, we see signs that even laboratory schools are awakening to the responsibility to be reform agents although it is too early to tell whether they can establish a professional rapport with other school and university communities (Klag, 1994). Meanwhile, in the spirit of Dewey, we may wish to ask what their ends or purposes have been for the past century or so.

A COMMUNITY-CENTERED PHILOSOPHY. In 1895, the year before the Laboratory School opened, Dewey wrote that the University Primary School was a means of addressing the "ultimate problem of all education," namely the coordination of the "psychological and social factors" relevant to education (E5, 225). "The co-ordination demands, therefore," he wrote, "that the child be capable of expressing *himself*, but in such a way as to realize *social* ends" (E5, 224). Thus, he implied early in his career that the community-centered approach, not the child-centered approach favored by many progressivists, was the position he wished to promote. He already saw the school as a community in which young children could grow emotionally, socially and intellectually in ways that have unity and continuity with their prior and current home lives. Briefly, Dewey claimed that,

> The end of the institution must be such as to enable the child to translate his powers over into terms of their social equivalencies; to see what they mean in terms of what they are capable of accomplishing in social life. This implies:
> 1. Such *interest* in others as will secure responsiveness to their real needs—consideration, delicacy, etc.
> 2. Such knowledge of social relationships as to enable one to form social ideas or ends.
> 3. Such volitional command of one's own powers as to enable one to be an economical social agent (E5, 225).

In the same essay, Dewey wrote of the Laboratory School,

> Attention may again be called to...having the school represent a genuine community life; and to...a study of the individual child,

> with a view of having his activities properly express his capacities, tastes and needs. Attention may again be called to the principle of *indirect* training, and the consequent necessary emphasis upon initiating the proper *process* rather than securing any immediate outward *product*, in the faith that the proper process, once obtained, will determine, in its due season, its own products; while any attempt to force the result apart from first securing the proper psychological process can result only in undue forcing and gradual disintegration of power (E5, 232).

He displayed his confidence in natural child development, indirect training, and the value of proper process more hyperbolically later in 1899, again in biblical language:

> If we seek the kingdom of heaven, educationally, all other things shall be added unto us—which, being interpreted, is that if we identify ourselves with the real instincts and needs of childhood, and ask only after its fullest assertion and growth, the discipline and information and culture of adult life shall all come in their due season (M1, 37).

A TWOFOLD MISSION. In June of 1896, Dewey clarified the two essential sides of the School's work: "the one for the children, the other for students in the University taking up pedagogical work" (E5, 244). But, he said the School was not "a school of practice in the ordinary sense; nor is the main object...to train teachers." In fact, the Pedagogical Department and, therefore, the Laboratory School had been designed to work with experienced teachers, normal school teachers, administrators and others. In particular, the School was to serve a role connected with theory and practice and the testing and developing of instructional methods—that is, to be a genuine laboratory like those in science departments (E5, 434), with as its

> focus to keep the theoretical work in touch with the demands of practice, and also [make] an experimental station for the testing and developing of methods which, when elaborated, may be safely and strongly recommended to other schools. It is believed that there is nothing which our common schools need more than wise guidance in this respect—the presentation of methods which are the offspring of a sound psychology, and have also been worked

out in detail under the crucial tests of experience (E5, 244).

In September of 1896, Dewey called the Laboratory School a part of the Pedagogical Department's intent to prepare not "the rank and file of teachers [but] the leaders of our educational systems—teachers in normal and training schools, professors of pedagogy, superintendents, principals of schools" who had *already* studied the rudiments of teaching, completed an apprenticeship, and studied educational theory (E5, 281). The Laboratory School was also important to the Pedagogical Department's faculty and students who devoted "themselves more directly to the work of pedagogical discovery and experimentation" (E5, 282). Ideally, Dewey wanted them to study "present practice, to test it scientifically, to work it out into shape for concrete use, and to issue it to the public education system with the imprimatur...of scientific verification" (E5, 283).

The School was, in this sense, a place of "practice, experiment and demonstration" (E5, 285) as well as a place to "test and exhibit in actual working order the results of the theoretical work" (E5, 288). As such, the Laboratory School was based upon the thought that there must be "a continual union of theory and practice" where practice is understood in the university context or "enlarged sense [and refers] to the principles which are tested and demonstrated." The university could be effective in its pedagogical offerings only

> in proportion as the theory of the class room is accompanied by actual school work. Only in this way can the student get the real force of what is advanced in the lecture or text-book; only in this way can there be assurance that the teaching of the class room is not vague and impracticable (E5, 288).

In an early conceptualization of the Laboratory School prepared for William Rainey Harper, the president of the University of Chicago in 1896, Dewey described it as "a school of demonstration, observation and experiment in connection with the theoretical instruction [and] *the nerve* [italics added] of the whole [Department of Pedagogy's] scheme." Without a laboratory school, Dewey thought that no pedagogical department was capable of commanding "the confidence of the educational public it is seeking to lay hold of and *direct*; the mere profession of principles without their practical exhibition and testing will not engage the respect of the education profession. Without it, moreover, the theoretical work partakes of the nature of a farce and imposture" (E5, 434). This phrasing suggests that he believed one means of reforming education was through the graduate preparation of the leaders of school districts and teacher education programs, a promising idea seldom realized or at least documented. Further, the school was to furnish the impetus for its own on-going development or reform: "[I]t tends of itself to arouse the interest needed for its own development" (E5, 434). Moreover, Dewey saw it providing "as nearly as possible an ideal education" for the children who attended the school and "a model school" (E5, 434-435), the latter notion of being a model seemingly contradicting other denials.

By October of 1896, in an address to the Pedagogical Club of the university, Dewey distinguished two main purposes of the university side of the School's mission (excluding presumably the education of children in the School): "(1) to exhibit, test, verify, and criticize *theoretical statements* and principles; (2) to add to the sum of *facts and principles* in its special line" (E5, 437, italics added). Once again he seemed compelled to clarify what was not within the mission of the Laboratory School, denying that it was focused on immediate practicality and on presenting approved "standards and ideals" for the profession (E5, 437).

By contrast, he thus compared the Laboratory School with the practice schools frequently affiliated with normal school teacher training programs:

> It is the function of some schools [practice schools] to provide better teachers according to present standards; it is the function of others to create new standards and ideals and thus to lead to a gradual change in conditions. If it is advisable to have smaller classes, more teachers and a different working hypothesis than is at present the case in the public schools, there should be some institution [laboratory schools] to show this. This the school in question hopes to do, and while it does not aim to be impractical, it does not aim primarily to be of such character as to be immediately capable of translation into the public school (E5, 437).

A RESEARCH LABORATORY. By 1899, after three years of working with the Laboratory School, Dewey's view of it appears to have become clearer and more comprehensive, perhaps as a result of the evolution of his philosophy of education and teacher preparation. The problem of the School, he wrote, is to "unify, to organize, education, to bring all its various factors together, through putting it as a whole into organic union with everyday life" (M1, 55). Thus, the school was to serve again as a "model for such unification" (M1, 55). More was involved, however, for the school was to serve as a research laboratory in which "the student of education sees theories and ideas demonstrated, tested, criticized, enforced, and the evolution of new truths" (M1, 56).

Thus, defending the School against a critic who dismissed the Laboratory School because it was an "experimental school" working under conditions unlike those in most public schools, Dewey claimed that an experimental school is deliberately different and is partially special in that it conducts experiments so that other schools will not have to do so (M1, 56). The differences were intentionally planned, Dewey maintained, just like the differences in research laboratories specializing in chemistry, biology, physics and business:

> Laboratories lie back of all the great business enterprises of today, back of every great factory, every railway and steamship system. Yet the laboratory is not a business enterprise; it does not aim to secure for itself the conditions of business life, nor does the commercial undertaking repeat the laboratory. There is a difference between working out and testing a new truth, or a new method, and applying it on a wide scale, making it available for the mass of men, making it commercial. But the first thing is to discover the truth, to afford all necessary facilities, for this is the most practical thing in the world in the long run. We do not expect to have other schools literally imitate what we do. A working model is not something to be copied; it is to afford a demonstration of the feasibility of the principle, and of the methods which make it feasible. So...we want here to work out the problem of the unity, the organization of the school system in itself, and to do this by relating it so intimately to life as to demonstrate the possibility and necessity of such organization for all education (M1, 56).

He developed this view of the role of laboratory experimentation much later in terms of his conception of research when he discussed factory research and its relationship to business: "laws and facts...do not yield *rules of practice*. Their value for educational practice...is indirect; it consists in provision of *intellectual instrumentalities* to be used by the educator" (L5, 14). When public school educators, like manufacturers, think with and apply the scientific research of the laboratory, they should not expect results identical to those in the scientific settings. Instead, they ought to be interested in the *"improvement"* of practice or partial resolution of problems, not their complete dissolution. The manufacturer and the educator are aware that

> factory [or school] conditions involve more variables, and variables harder to control, than are found in the conditions of laboratory experiment. The divergence of actual results from strictly scientific results is, therefore, a direction to him to observe more exactly and, upon a larger scale, all the conditions which affect his result. He notes...he discovers...he modifies his practical procedures. Thus he hopes to better his practice, each step calling attention to the influence of subtler and more obscure conditions which affect results, so that improvement is reasonably progressive (L5, 14).

A CURRICULAR AND CHILD-STUDY FOCUS. In 1899, Dewey explained that when the School started, the staff had "certain ideas in mind" or, better, "questions and problems" to address (M1, 58). The four key questions were (1) How can the school be brought to a closer relationship with the external life of the child? (2) How can the study of history, science and art be accomplished so that the inquiry results in worthwhile attainments in knowledge of genuine value and significance for the child? (3) How can an appealing study of reading, writing and computing be tied to current adult occupations and the everyday experience of the student? and (4) How can the individual child's intellectual interests, physical needs, social development and overall growth be the center of the school's focus (M1, 59-61)? Securing answers to the second question concerning curricular matters appropriate for children, Dewey observed, was the chief educational interest of the school and the realm in which he expected the school to make the greatest "contribution to education in general" (M1, 60). Answering these and related questions concerning administration was "almost entirely in the hands of the teachers of the school" (M1, 58).

As far as Dewey was concerned, we should think too of the occupational emphasis of the Laboratory School when we look for an answer to the second question, for

> The great thing to keep in mind, then, regarding the introduction into the school of various forms of active occupation, is that through them the entire spirit of the school is renewed. It has a chance to affiliate itself with life, to become the child's habitat, where he learns through directed living, instead of being only a place to learn lessons having an abstract and remote reference to some possible living to be done in the future. It gets a chance to be a miniature community, an embryonic society. This is the fundamental fact, and from this arise continuous and orderly streams of instruction (M1, 12).

By 1915, it was more than clear to Dewey, now a professor at Columbia University, that the most important feature of the Laboratory School was its scientific emphasis or the contributions it made in "educational thinking"—a reference to strengthening the knowledge base of teacher preparation in the areas of child study and curriculum development and thereby the thinking ability of professional educators:

> The aim of educating a certain number of children would hardly justify a university in departing from the tradition which limits it to those who have completed their secondary instruction. Only the scientific aim, the conduct of a laboratory, comparable to other scientific laboratories, can furnish a reason for the maintenance by a university of an elementary school. Such a school is a laboratory of applied psychology. That is, it has a place for the study of mind as manifested and developed in the child, and for the search after materials and agencies that seem most likely to fulfil and further the conditions of normal growth (M1, 67).

Again, Dewey evidently felt compelled to make a series of denials about the Laboratory School—for instance, it was not a normal school, a model school, or a demonstration school if from that label one infers an intent to "demonstrate any one special idea or doctrine" (M1, 67). Instead, its duty was "the problem of viewing the education of the child in the light of the principles of mental activity and processes of growth made known by modern psychology" (M1, 67). As Philip Jackson (1990) points out, the so-called modern psychology Dewey admired was neither new nor a specific theoretical orientation that explained scientific research in a narrow sense. Rather, it was a view of human nature that went back to Rousseau, Pestalozzi and Froebel, including the belief that human beings are propelled by their natural needs, inclinations and interests as they strive to examine their environments (SSCC, xxi-xxiii).

In pursuing a synthesis of Dewey's thinking about the Laboratory School, questions of interpretation arise: How are his various comments to be understood? Are there changes of mind, even vascillation? Or is there simply the rewording of underlying ideas? Or can we discern an evolution of his concept? Is there, perhaps, a combination of these explanations? In approaching these questions, we can begin with what was clearly outside the school's mission: It was not a normal school, or an early teacher training school, or a practice school where aspiring teachers had many of their field experiences, or a model school which simply represented the best *current* practice in teaching, or a demonstration school based upon a particular philosophy.

Yet, the Laboratory School was a working model or a school where practitioners and others tested new ideas and their theoretical feasibility. So too it was a place to demonstrate the success of the principles and methods upon which the School itself was based, including its affiliation with the University of Chicago (SSCC, 93). Here it is important to understand that Dewey was impressed with the possibility that the University of Chicago could "do something significant and important in the way of providing the working model of an economic and efficient unification of the various parts of the education system" (M2, 69), meaning he thought the university could connect kindergarten, elementary, secondary, junior college, senior college, graduate and professional school education and then connect all these with life before schooling and university studies began and while they were being pursued (M2, 67-69). So having a working model of a school and a university assisting each other, Dewey appears to have wanted to experiment with and demonstrate his conception of the continuity of experience and education.

Clearly, the Laboratory School also had two immediate missions: providing a good education for a small number of children and serving as an educational laboratory. In the former capacity, it was to provide an ideal education and be a model school. Educational experiments with children, at least in this aspect of the School's mission, could hardly be allowed to fail. In the latter capacity, it was a laboratory of applied psychology for studying and testing the education of children in view of their developing intellectual capabilities and general psychological and social growth. As such, it was also a place for developing materials, methods and devices to facilitate the normal growth of children. In addition, the Laboratory School was an embryonic community where children learned the values of democracy through directed living, and one of its chief educational problems was finding the appropriate curricular or experiential matters for developing children, such as how much is worthwhile for a child to learn of "the world about him, of the forces of the world, of historical and social growth, and in capacity to express himself in a variety of artistic forms" (M1, 60).

In pursuing its mission and meeting all these other responsibilities, the Laboratory School had to be involved—in order to be theoretically sound and practically relevant—in demonstrating, testing and criticizing theories, ideas, principles and practices as well as in creating new knowledge for the profession. Moreover, it had to avoid presenting this new knowledge in a predigested form or as rules to be followed. As a place of scientific inquiry and discovery, the School was intended to discover ways of seeing and doing and testing and thinking and judging "intellectual instrumentalities"—that would indirectly enable educational leaders to improve their work. In the end, the Laboratory School—at least in Dewey's mind—had to be involved in this way, academically and theoretically, if it was to make a serious claim to preparing educational leaders, professors, principals and superintendents for the mission of educating children and youth, supervising other educators, preparing aspiring educators, and reforming schooling, educator preparation programs and society. Only this way could it claim for its proposals a scientific foundation and justification.

The Practice School

While the Laboratory School was not a practice school, having a somewhat different role and function, Dewey considered the practice school important in a teacher education program and indeed one of the factors of the "complete educational scheme" in the School of Education at the University of Chicago (M2, 68). In an essay published the year after the Laboratory School at Chicago was closed (1904) and shortly before Dewey moved to Columbia University, Dewey had a great deal to say about the connection of educational theory to pedagogical practice and how the two of them are appropriately included in a teacher preparation program and connected in practice schools.

In particular, it appears that he had increased his understanding of how universities and schools could work together to prepare aspiring teachers, especially when they were students who had no prior experience as educational practitioners and needed to understand the relation between educational theory and classroom practice. In keeping with the nomenclature of his time, he referred to these schools as "practice schools" (M3, 252ff). Today we call similar schools—sometimes with fine and significant conceptual distinctions —clinical schools, associate schools, professional practice schools, partner schools, or professional development schools (Colburn, 1993; Darling-Hammond, *Professional Development Schools* 1994; David et al., n.d.; Holmes Group, 1990; Levine, 1992; and Osguthorpe et al., 1995). Goodlad's (1994) discussion of these schools is rooted in a Deweyan perspective and reflects a sensitivity to problems and opportunities few writers on the subject manifest. Thus to the list of different kinds of schools that Dewey considered important and, in a broad way, a school of the future, we may add the practice school.

The mission of a practice school, however, was significantly different from that of a laboratory school; its purpose was primarily to educate the children and youth who attended, not to serve as a university laboratory. Practice schools also followed an apprenticeship approach to teacher education—a tradition that Dewey thought should be reconsidered—and were often affiliated with normal schools. As we saw in Chapters 5 and 7, Dewey thought the field experiences of intending teachers should be designed largely in keeping with a laboratory approach to learning. No doubt, his experiences in the Laboratory School and his examination of other teacher training practices in normal schools influenced his opinion. Most likely, then, his views regarding the practice school were an extension of his ideas about the Laboratory School.

As was often his habit when writing, Dewey skipped over the procedural and mechanical aspects of university-school collaboration —issues that may have held less importance for him given the "connected schools" at the University of Chicago—and went immediately to a core question: What is the purpose of practical experiences for aspiring teachers in a practice school? This question, of course, is different from an inquiry into the fundamental mission of a practice school. The primary mission of a practice school is to educate the children and youth who attend it; a secondary purpose though is to help prepare a better or, in Dewey's opinion, *a different kind of teacher*. In this context, therefore, Dewey's views about the practice school should be understood and evaluated.

THE PROBLEMS IN THE PRACTICE SCHOOL. Dewey began his discussion of the practice school by pointing out problems that existed in his time, several of which still exist. First, he identified problems that might be seen from *the practical or school side*. He said that the role of "a room critic-teacher"—or "cooperating teacher" for us—alters the environment of the classroom in such a way that "some of the most fundamentally significant features of the real school are reduced or eliminated" (M3, 252). Instead of the practice school being "the real world," as many contemporary reformers argue, Dewey thought it an artificial simulation in important details: The educational needs of children are "so safeguarded and supervised that the situation approaches learning to swim without going *too* near the water" (M3, 252). Learning about teaching and how to teach without venturing too near the water, Dewey maintained, occurs in various ways. For example, an unreal environment is created by the "deprivation of responsibility for the discipline of the room; the continued presence of an expert ready to suggest, to take matters into his own hands; close supervision; reduction of size of group taught" (M3, 252) and keeps the would-be teacher from becoming both pedagogically and intellectually responsible for the classroom and the activities of the students.

In addition to coming to think of the unreal world of the practice school as a genuine educational setting, the future teacher in a practice school is, as an apprentice, liable to focus prematurely upon learning skills and techniques, principally how to manage classroom behavior, and is inclined to ignore how subject matter may be applied or examined in such a way as to form the basis of discipline (M3, 252-253). Too early an immersion in the practical and pressing aspects of teaching and classroom management, therefore, would hinder, in Dewey's opinion, the aspiring teacher from learning about the internal thinking or attention of individual students and about using that attention to assist the students in their development (M3, 252-255).

Beyond these problems but partially as a consequence of learning in an artificial school setting to attend to immediately pressing demands of classroom control, the aspiring teacher develops an attitude and habits that have *"an empirical, rather than a scientific, sanction"* or what we might term an unmethodical, unreflective, uninquiring rather than systematic orientation (M3, 255). The future teacher, Dewey believed, thus comes to adopt teaching strategies in the light of what works from *instant to instant* rather than from a theoretical approach grounded in scientific inquiry about practice. The prospective teacher attempts to employ

> what he sees other teachers doing who are more experienced and successful *in keeping order* than he is; and...the injunctions and directions given him by others. In this way the controlling habits of the teacher finally [get] fixed with comparatively little reference to principles in the psychology, logic, and history of education. In theory, these latter are dominant; in practice, the moving forces are the devices and methods which are picked up through blind experimentation; through examples which are not rationalized; through precepts which are more or less arbitrary and mechanical; through advice based upon the experience of others (M3, 255, italics added).

Rather than an empirical or unreflective experiential accumulation of what we might roughly call teaching folklore, Dewey wanted the future teacher to develop habits "formed under the inspiration and constant criticism of intelligence, applying the best [knowledge] that is available" (M3, 256). For him, this meant that "practical work should be pursued primarily with reference to its reaction upon the professional pupil [future teacher] in making him a thoughtful and alert student of education, rather than to help him get immediate proficiency" (256). He explained that "unless a teacher is a student [especially of subject matter and student thinking], he may continue to improve in the mechanics of school management, but he can not grow as a teacher, an inspirer and director of soul-life" (256). Focusing on classroom survival and management skills, therefore, jeopardized the development of the teacher as physician of the soul.

Dewey saw at least two other overlapping evils in the apprenticeship method as the dominant way of preparing future teachers. First, it established habits and inclinations that are reflected in some teachers who are professionally stagnant—that is, lacking "intellectual independence" and "intellectual vitality" (M3, 256-257). Second, it encouraged the willingness of teachers to "accept without inquiry or criticism any method or device which seems to promise good results," the tendency to "flock to those persons who give them clear-cut and definite instructions as to just how to teach this or that," and the inclination to "swing over to some new educational gospel" (257). The latter inclination is especially noticeable, he thought, in the willingness of some teachers, particularly those who accept administrative positions, to become "submerged in the routine detail of their callings, to expend the bulk of their energy upon forms and rules and regulations, and reports and percentages" (257). After criticizing teachers who manifest these two evils, he delivered this goad: "If teachers were possessed by the spirit of an abiding student of education, this spirit would find some way of breaking through the mesh and coil of circumstance and would find expression for itself" (257).

THE PROBLEMS IN THE UNIVERSITY. Next, Dewey mentioned several problems that relate to *the theoretical or university side of teacher preparation* or the joining of the university and the practice school. Initially, he criticized some teacher educators and school practitioners for subscribing to the belief "that instruction in [educational] theory is merely theoretical, abstruse, remote, and therefore relatively useless to the teacher as a teacher, unless the student is at once set upon the work of teaching" (M3, 257). He argued that practical matters and concerns already existed in "theoretical instruction of *the proper sort*" (258, italics added). Using educational psychology as an example of the practical being *present in* the theoretical, he claimed that the subject can be taught so that the professor conveys the erroneous opinion that all of the intending teacher's prior learning is irrelevant to and different from the learning theory examined in the university and pertinent to future teaching.

This dichotomy of learning out of school and learning in school is both "unnecessary and harmful" (M3, 258), and it perpetuates some of "the greatest evils" of present-day school practices (258)—namely that the "psychology of the schoolroom [is] different from that of the nursery, the playground, the street, and the parlor" and thus the pedagogical potency of the materials and methods studied in university is significantly greater than that of the larger, external environment (259). Continuity of learning, particularly in the field of learning theory, Dewey believed, was especially important for future teachers to understand. The separation of would-be teachers from their past is a part of "the great cause in education of wasted power and misdirected effort" (259). The apprenticeship approach to field experiences, therefore, implicitly and explicitly contributes to the misinterpretation of educational theory in its various forms.

The apprenticeship approach has other negative consequences

according to Dewey. Observations in school settings are aimed at learning the techniques of teaching instead of learning about the thinking of students and teachers, and aspiring teachers often seek to find a one-to-one correlation between psychological principles and methodological procedures. Instead of attempting to turn psychology into pedagogical maxims, university professors and cooperating schools should lead the aspiring teacher to be become "an independent judge and critic of...[psychological thought and its] proper use and adaptation" (M3, 260).

Dewey moved from pedagogy to subject-matter preparation to continue his criticism of those who believed theoretical studies were inferior to practical ones. Subject matter, he maintained, "when properly presented is not...*merely* theoretical, remote from the practical problems of teaching" (M3, 262). Good university professors and good elementary and secondary teachers who have had neither pedagogical preparation nor practical teaching experience, according to a study Dewey had read, may well have been good because the material or subject matter they studied and taught was itself "a most effective tool for training and turning out good teachers" (263). The intellectual method critical to both understanding and teaching a field of knowledge is not, as some in his day argued, something that has to be extracted, separated and applied independent of that "body of knowledge" but forms instead the organizing or "controlling intellectual principles" of the branch of knowledge and may be broadly described as the scientific method (263).

Dewey insisted that "this scientific method is the method of mind itself [and that] there is something wrong in the 'academic' side of professional training, if by means of it the student does not constantly get object-lessons of the finest type in the kind of mental activity which characterizes mental growth and, hence, the educative process" (M3, 263). So, he concluded,

> Only a teacher thoroughly trained in the higher levels of intellectual method and who thus has constantly in his own mind a sense of what adequate and genuine intellectual activity means, will be likely, in deed, not in mere word, to respect the mental integrity and force of children (M3, 264).

Of course, plenty of present-day critics are willing to say with Dewey that there is something wrong with how the arts and sciences are taught, especially in those universities and colleges that rely primarily upon the lecture method. Dewey added there must have been something wrong with the instruction of teachers who lack both genuine intellectual preparation and respect for the intellectual potential of their students. While arguing for good or proper preparation in pedagogical theory and subject matter, Dewey offered this acknowledgment:

> We have here, I think, the explanation of the success of some teachers who violate every law known to and laid down by pedagogical science. They are themselves so full of the spirit of inquiry, so sensitive to every sign of its presence and absence, that no matter what they do, nor how they do it, they succeed in awakening and inspiring like alert and intense mental activity in those with whom they come in contact (M3, 265).

THE ROLE OF THE PRACTICE SCHOOL. In Dewey's time, much teacher preparation took place in normal schools that taught both pedagogical science and subject matter. Thus, we may wonder what the proper study of the arts and sciences had (or has) to do with the practice school. We need to start at the beginning of Dewey's argument to observe its development on this subject. First, he seems to have been attempting to force the institutions that prepare future teachers in the branches of knowledge, whether normal schools or universities, to understand that they have a critical role in getting future teachers to *think scientifically* (for example, historically, mathematically, philosophically, aesthetically, psychologically and so forth) in the areas where they seek depth of understanding.

Second, he thought elementary and secondary schools, including practice schools, should also be part of the on-going educational culture that nurtures scientific thinking from the beginning and throughout life. Consequently, the practice school should be "engaged in work of an adequate educational type [not in] a certain triviality and poverty of subject-matter, calling for mechanical drill, rather than for thought-activity, and [not in] technical mastery of certain conventional culture subjects, taught as independent branches of the same tree of knowledge" (M3, 267). Speaking to the university as well as the practice school, Dewey wrote,

> The great need is convergence, concentration. Every step taken in the elementary and the high school toward intelligent introduction

> of more worthy and significant subject-matter, one requiring consequently for its assimilation thinking rather than "drill," must be met by a like advance step in which the mere isolated specialization of collegiate subject-matter is surrendered, and in which there is brought to conscious and interested attention its significance in expression of fundamental modes of mental activity—so fundamental as to be common to both the play of the mind upon the ordinary material of everyday experience and to the systematized material of the sciences (M3, 267).

In view of these criticisms of and reservations concerning the university, teacher preparation programs and the practice school, it is reasonable to ask what specific roles one might play in a university-school collaborative relationship. What positive roles could the practice school play in the preparation of intending teachers and the reform of education? Dewey answered this question but feared that his answer could result in "a scheme with more appearance of rigidity than is desirable" (M3, 268), a recipe for those continually in search of an unthinking panacea for educational problems. He would *not* have wanted anyone or any institution to implement unreflectively the five basic steps of his proposal.

In the first stage, he stated, the practice school should primarily serve the purpose of observation, but such observation ought to focus less upon seeing how teachers teach or learning how to teach than on understanding the overall educational operations of the school and the working of the minds of both students and teachers (M3, 268). He elaborated on this point and its connection to his conception of the continuity of experience:

> What is needed is the habit of viewing the entire curriculum as a continuous growth, reflecting the growth of mind itself. This in turn demands, so far as I can see, consecutive and longitudinal consideration of the curriculum of the elementary and high school rather than a cross-sectional view of it. The student should be led to see that the same subject-matter in geography, nature-study, or art develops not merely day to day in a given grade, but from year to year throughout the entire movement of the school; and he should realize this before he gets much engaged in trying to adapt subject-matter in lesson plans for this or that isolated grade (M3, 267-268).

In the second stage, Dewey said, the progressive involvement of the intending teacher

> would then be [a] more intimate introduction to the lives of the children and the work of the school through the use as assistants of such students [aspiring teachers] as had already got psychological insight and a good working acquaintance with educational problems. Students at this stage would not undertake much direct teaching, but would make themselves useful in helping the regular class instructor (M3, 268).

The help of the would-be teacher should be real "to the school, to the children" and related, on occasions, to understanding and helping special population children as well as developing an understanding of curricular materials: "Special attention to backward children, to children who have been out of school, assisting in the care of material, in forms of handwork, suggest some of the avenues of approach" (M3, 268).

In the third stage, after future teachers have had adequate educative experiences in the previously mentioned areas, they can move from the "more psychological and theoretical insight to the observation of the more technical points of class teaching and management" (M3, 269) and can also assist in the "selection and arrangement" of subject matter and supplementary materials and problems. At first, these assignments might involve several grades so prospective teachers may better understand their students' development (269). Later, these activities might include "finding supplementary materials and problems bearing upon the work in which the student [intending teacher] is giving assistance," and still later the future teacher might develop curricular materials or alternative lessons for particular students (269).

In the fourth stage, as quickly as is advisable, would-be teachers receive "actual teaching" assignments. The prerequisite for this experience is adequate previous preparation "in subject-matter, in educational theory, and in the kind of observation and practice already discussed" (M3, 269). At this juncture, prospective teachers should be allowed "the maximum amount of liberty possible" (269), instead of being corrected meticulously and repeatedly:

> They should not be too closely supervised, nor too minutely and immediately criticised upon either the matter or the method of their teaching. Students should be given to understand that they

> not only are *permitted* to act upon their own intellectual initiative, but that they are *expected* to do so, and that their ability to take hold of situations for themselves would be a more important factor in judging them than their following any particular set method or scheme (M3, 269).

At this stage of the future teachers' practical experience, expert educators should provide critical analyses of both the activities of the future teachers and the results of their activities. Sufficient time should be allotted to ensure that "the shocks" of the experience are adequately absorbed and that the prospective teacher sees "the *fundamental* bearings of criticisms upon work done." Those involved in mentoring the intending teacher should concentrate on getting the aspiring teacher to make professional judgments about

> his own work...,to find out for himself in what respects he has succeeded and in what failed, and to find the probable reasons for both failure and success, rather than to criticising him too definitely and specifically upon special features of his work (M3, 270).

Experts or supervisors, in Dewey's opinion, should concentrate on building the appropriate reflective disposition and avoid the "travesty" of being overly critical, of inspecting and criticizing each feature or activity of the emerging teacher.

About the student's experience of "actual teaching" (M3, 269), Dewey argued it ought to be extensive, intensive and consecutive:

> [It] should be *extensive* or continuous enough to give the student time to become at home and to get a body of funded experience, it ought to be *intensive* in purpose rather than spread out miscellaneously. It is much more important for the teacher to assume responsibility for the *consecutive* development of some one topic, to get a feeling for the movement of that subject, than it is to teach a certain number (necessarily narrower in range) of lessons in a larger number of subjects. What we want, in other words, is not so much technical skill, as a realizing sense in the teacher of what the educational development of a subject means, and, in some typical case, command of a method of control, which will serve as a standard for self-judgment in other cases (M3, 270, italics added).

In the fifth stage, if the period of preparation is sufficiently long and the schools are sufficiently large (M3, 270), intending or aspiring teachers who have completed the prior experiences should be prepared to complete the equivalent of an apprenticeship (271). This apprenticeship, Dewey stressed, should follow all of the previous kinds of preparation and experience and should be calculated to facilitate "an individual mastery of the actual technique of teaching and management" (271). Even so, it is "important that the student should be given as much responsibility and initiative as he is capable of taking, and hence that supervision should not be too unremitting and intimate, and criticism not at too short range or too detailed" (271). In particular, supervisors should *not* aim at reproducing "their own notions and methods" in would-be teachers but at fostering inspired and enlightened new teachers through "prolonged contact with mature and sympathetic persons" (271).

If the plural "persons" is taken literally—and it probably should be—Dewey recommended that future teachers be nurtured by two or more cooperating teachers or practicing educators. Future teachers nurtured by two or more practicing educators may be likelier to learn to think about their experiences and decisions than those supervised by only one. This apprenticeship time, Dewey believed, also had the advantage of making it easier to identify aspiring teachers who need to be excluded ("eliminated more quickly") from teaching as poorly fitted for the profession (M3, 271). In essence, then, Dewey recommended both the laboratory and the apprenticeship approach to field experiences whenever possible.

Dewey did not believe that his five stages of field experiences represented a utopian philosophy (M3, 271), but he did note that the conditions he described required at least two other factors, one of schools and the other of universities, if his view of theory and practice were to be operationalized (272). First, practice schools needed to be carefully chosen to "represent an advanced type of education properly corresponding to the instruction in academic subject-matter and in educational theory given to training classes" (272). He seems to have based this requirement upon the assumption that education in universities and educator preparation programs was more current, reflective and imaginative than that in schools, a sometimes debatable assumption. Second, the work in "psychology and educational theory [must] make concrete and vital the connection between the normal instruction in subject-matter and the work of the elementary and high schools" (272). This requirement appears to place upon teacher educators the responsibility of seeing that the forms of inquiry and creativity and the everyday life of practice schools are brought together in clear, lively and definite ways, a formidable challenge that requires, among other ingredients, talented and dedicated teacher educators who understand and appreciate the importance of theory and practice.

The School of Tomorrow

If the family, community, university, educator preparation program, laboratory school and practice school have done their jobs well and have nurtured well-educated, reflective, democratic aspiring educators who love to learn and communicate with students they understand, what kinds of schools would emerge? What types of *Schools of To-Morrow* (1915) would students attend? Many schools of tomorrow were playing roles in the transformation of education and society in Dewey's day. They were emerging as examples of educational practices that reflected the democratic philosophy of life and education he expected to become more prevalent as individuals, educators, communities and society grew. Yet he rightly observed, in *Schools of To-Morrow*, that educators frequently forget that

> what is learned in school is at best only a small part of education, a relatively superficial part; and yet what is learned in school makes artificial distinctions in society and marks persons off from one another. Consequently we exaggerate school learning compared with what is gained in the ordinary course of living. We are, however, to correct this exaggeration, not by despising school learning, but by looking into that extensive and more efficient training given by the ordinary course of events for light upon the best ways of teaching within school walls (M8, 211).

The school of tomorrow, therefore, was not a prototype. In his reference to "training by the ordinary course of events," Dewey implied a better model of learning than the one existing in the traditional school or discussed in the traditional educational courses or even seen in the progressive school. Indeed, he saw a model behind the school of tomorrow and identified this model of learning with the ordinary learning experiences of life in noninstitutional settings:

> If we want, then, to find out how education takes place most successfully, let us go to the experiences of children where learning is a necessity, and not to the practices of the schools where it is largely an adornment, a superfluity and even an unwelcome imposition (M8, 212).

He added that perhaps "the greatest and commonest mistake that we all make is to forget that learning is a necessary incident of dealing with *real situations*" (M8, 212; italics added).

THE GENERAL TREND OF NEW SCHOOLS. *Schools of To-Morrow* was written mainly by Dewey's daughter, Evelyn, and fits into Dewey's works as largely a descriptive rather than evaluative piece on school practices (M8, 208). In explaining the selection of schools, Dewey noted that they were ones he knew about, conveniently located, and typical of general trends but not necessarily the best or representative of everything available. Notably, he omitted agricultural education and the reorganization of rural schools (M8, 208, 388). The schools he selected were not attempting to be better conventional schools but to make "more fundamental" changes (M8, 388). More precisely, these schools were "working away from a curriculum adapted to a small and specialized [social, economic, political] class towards one...truly representative of the needs and conditions of a democratic society" (M8, 389).

We may say, therefore, that while the descriptions in *Schools of To-Morrow* illustrate "the general trend of education" in Dewey's time, they do not necessarily and certainly do not always represent his best thinking, as a careful reading of his other pedagogical writings demonstrates. In the absence of a basic understanding of Dewey, one could easily misinterpret the descriptive statements and the practices selected as representing his ideas. Instead, one should understand the schools as examples of where schools, generally speaking, should be headed at the time he wrote. He recognized in these schools three characteristics or tendencies he accepted: "tendencies towards greater freedom and an identification of the child's school life with his environment and outlook; and, even more important, the recognition of the role education must play in a democracy" (M8, 208).

Our discussion of the school of tomorrow, therefore, proceeds along these three lines. Obviously, they overlap and appear in both discrete and integrated ways. Moreover, we can hardly overemphasize the interconnectedness of school freedom, the child's life and democratic schools for Dewey. Both the integration of these domains and the weight Dewey gave them resonate in the phrase "even more important, the recognition of the role education must play in a democracy." Any attempt to discuss separately these three realms, therefore, is, though necessary and useful, somewhat artificial.

THE PRACTICE OF FREEDOM. Given Dewey's view of the nature of the child, the importance of the practice of democracy in schools, the need for professional autonomy, the desirability of the school and classroom being communities, and the utilization of the immediate community for educative purposes, we would expect him to have selected schools attempting to provide a greater freedom for students and educators. Of the selected schools, Dewey spoke approvingly of the diversity that freedom allowed:

> While these schools are all alike in that they reflect the new spirit in education, they differ greatly in the methods that have been developed to bring about the desired results; their surroundings and the class of pupils dealt with are varied enough to suggest the influence that local conditions must exercise over methods even when the aim is identical (M8, 389).

On another occasion, Dewey expressed his displeasure with the lack of freedom he saw in some schools, and he no doubt would have banished them from the future he wished for:

> Exorbitant desire for uniformity of procedure and for prompt external results are the chief foes which the open-minded attitude meets in the school. The teacher who does not permit and encourage diversity of operation in dealing with questions is imposing intellectual blinders upon pupils—restricting their vision to the one path the teacher's mind happens to approve. Probably the chief cause of devotion to rigidity of method is, however, that it seems to promise speedy, accurately measurable, correct results. The zeal for "answers" is the explanation of much of the zeal for rigid and mechanical methods. Forcing and overpressure have the same origin, and the same result upon alert and varied intellectual interest (DE, 175).

Freedom for diversity of pedagogical methodology, use of educational surroundings, and spontaneity in student activities were only a few of the manifestations of freedom that interested Dewey. Freedom is also invaluable in allowing children to discover what they can and cannot do, and in encouraging this liberty Dewey believed that the teacher would find "the spontaneity, the liveliness, and initiative of the pupil aids in teaching, instead of being...nuisances to be repressed" (M8, 298). This freedom for the student, Dewey held, is essential since education is designed to help "the growing of a helpless young animal into a happy, moral, and efficient human being, [and] must allow enough liberty to promote that growth" (M8, 296). Thus, instead of teachers stressing the "negative virtues of obedience, docility, and submission" they should emphasize the "positive virtues—energy, initiative, and originality" (M8, 394-395) in the emerging schools of tomorrow.

Consistent with the roles and responsibilities of the teacher discussed in Chapter 4, Dewey believed that the teacher played a vital role in cultivating an environment of freedom in the class. The teacher does not create an atmosphere in which the student can do just anything, but guides the "natural growth" of each student while avoiding the imposition of strictly adult interests, norms and curricula (M8, 218). In order to guide each student, the teacher must understand "the home conditions of each child" (M8, 349) as we have noted previously; and given an understanding of home, neighborhood and community environments, Dewey said the teacher can introduce the student to greater degrees of knowledge regarding the world of nature:

> The modern teacher takes as a starting point anything that is familiar to the class[:] a caged canary, a bowl of gold fish, or the dusty trees on the playground[;] and starting from these she introduces the children to more and more of nature, until they can really get some idea of "the country" and the part it plays in the lives of every one (M8, 267-268).

Additional understanding of and freedom for the student may be gained when the teacher provides

> conditions for wholesome, natural growth in small enough groups for the teacher (as a leader rather than an instructor) to become acquainted with the weaknesses of each child individually and then

> to adapt the work to the individual needs. It [the selected school] has demonstrated that it is possible for children to lead the same natural lives in school that they lead in good homes outside of school hours; to progress bodily, mentally, and morally in school without factitious pressure, rewards, examinations, grades, or promotions, while they acquire sufficient control of the conventional tools of learning and of study of books—reading, writing, and figuring—to be able to use them independently (M8, 235).

A primary concern of the Deweyan teacher in selecting appropriate learning conditions is each student's development of personal independence and so the acquisition of learning tools, skills, dispositions and attitudes. Yet Dewey made it clear that he disagreed with Maria Montessori's view of the teacher, rejecting it as too simple and her account of the teacher as too passive, too conducive to the conclusion that the teacher should cease teaching so that children can educate themselves (M8, 307). He also found her theory of the student asocial or individualistic (M8, 307). By contrast, Dewey thought that because educative experiences are

> social, they require that children work more together in common pursuits; because they are social they permit and often require the teacher's aid, just as one gains assistance from others in the ordinary affairs of life. Help from others is not to be feared as an encroachment upon liberty, but [what should be feared is] that kind of help which restricts the use of the children's own intelligence (M8, 311-312).

Teacher assistance and group activities, therefore, need not limit individual freedom but can establish both the grounds and the environment for developing and sustaining personal freedom. In the context of a learning community then, the child becomes both a reflective questioner and an experimenter, and teachers "instead of having...classes read and then recite facts from text-books ...[change their] methods." Significantly, teachers recognize that:

> Facts present themselves to every one in countless numbers, and it is not their naming that is useful, but the ability to understand them and see their relations and application to each other. So the

> function of the teacher must change from that of a cicerone and dictator to that of a watcher and helper (M8, 318).

The teacher as *watcher and helper* is, of course, hardly passive, but active as she learns what she needs to know about students and plans how to assist them as they grow. Here, the teacher as learner, partner and guide comes to mind, for understanding facts, seeing relationships and applying knowledge are abilities a student develops best in social interaction with the teacher and other students. Ideally, the student will come to see "the connection between [himself] and his environment" and recognize the relevance of what he understands for both his own well-being and the betterment of the community (M8, 389).

For this freedom to thrive, Dewey concluded that we need to surrender "our feverish desire to lay out the whole field of knowledge into various studies, in order to 'cover the ground'" (M8, 219). Instead we should adopt "the better ideal of dealing thoroughly with a small number of typical experiences in such a way as to master the tools of learning, and present situations that make pupils hungry to acquire additional knowledge" (M8, 220-221). *"To find out how to make knowledge when it is needed,"* he wrote, "is the true end of the acquisition of information in school, not the information itself" (M8, 221). "[R]eading, writing, arithmetic and geography will always be needed, but their substance will be greatly altered and added to," then, in a school of the future (M8, 317). As well, he stressed the importance of studying nature both to learn science and to "cultivate a sympathetic understanding of the place of plants and animals in life and to develop emotional and aesthetic interest" (M8, 272).

The child who studies in the freedom of a democratically oriented school of the future should learn about ordinary matters, occupations and tools like "the scissors, knife, needle, plane, and saw, and...the artists' tools, paint and clays, [knowledge] which lasts the rest of his life" (M8, 232). So, too, the student should be involved in vocational studies covering cooking, sewing, gardening and so forth. But these studies are not to prepare students for "any trade or profession, but to train them to be capable, happy members of society" (M8, 232). Though students "need to be intelligent in the conduct of households, the care of children, the management of farms and shops, and in the political conduct of a democracy where industry is the prime factor, [the] aim is not to prepare bread-winners" (M8, 364). No doubt today, he would update certain aspects of this curriculum because studies should always be shaped by the actual community, and communities have changed dramatically since he wrote these words. Still, his warning seems as pertinent as ever: "[T]here is great danger...the really educative type of work that is being done...may be overlooked in favor of trade training" (M8, 401). Consequently, "educators must insist upon the primacy of educational values, not in their own behalf, but because these represent the more fundamental interests of society, especially of a society organized on a democratic basis" (M8, 402).

Ultimately, Dewey thought schools of tomorrow ought to prepare children and youth to move beyond the studies just mentioned toward an understanding of organized bodies of knowledge. They should take childhood's

> crude experiences and organize them into science, geography, arithmetic, or whatever the lesson of the hour is. Since what the child already knows is part of some one subject that the teacher is trying to teach him, the method that will take advantage of this experience as a foundation stone on which to build the child's conscious knowledge of the subject appears as the normal and progressive way of teaching (M8, 254).

So, Dewey believed schools should help students develop a "deep and vital interest in subject-matter" (M8, 361). Moreover, a reversal in learning is equally valuable. That is to say, not only should the experiential learnings of life be developed into systematic branches of knowledge but also the learning of systematic branches of knowledge should be connected to life or "human activity" (M8, 363). All this learning depends in part, of course, on the future school examining "fewer subjects and fewer facts" and providing "more responsibility for thinking the material of those subjects and facts through" (L8, 138). Unless schools stress scientific, reflective and independent thinking, they will fail to find free people growing in them.

The connection Dewey made between evaluation and freedom is an interesting one. Like some contemporary educational reformers, he valued both quantitative and qualitative evaluation for obtaining a full picture of the development of students and schools. He clearly preferred the latter, however, because he saw it as concerned with gaining insights into the student's life and thinking and so with evaluating the student's understanding, seeing and applying knowledge. Understanding, seeing and applying are the concepts that identify what is important in "so-called activity programs" and explain how they go beyond the activities themselves (L9, 171). As a result, he observed that

> the more mature and experienced the teacher, the less will he or she be dependent upon tangible, directly applicable, external tests, and will use them, not as final, but as guides to judgment of the direction in which development is taking place. The more fully the processes of long-term growth are studied, the more objective will be estimates of what is going on in particular individuals, while too much reliance upon special tangible tests tends to prevent attention to the conditions and laws of general growth (L9, 171).

Other measures may measure precisely but measure precisely what is not important.

Just as schools can use standardized examinations to diminish—even eliminate—the pedagogical freedom and professional judgment of the teacher, so too textbooks frequently make teaching more difficult for the professionally minded teacher (M8, 255). Dewey had little respect for *the way* the traditional school employed textbooks to limit the freedom of both the teacher and the students. Indeed, he castigated prescribed textbooks, both because they limited the immediate freedom of the teacher and the students and because they eliminated much of the provocative character of education and the excitement of personal learning. Yet, textbooks, if used reflectively, can retain a role in school learning:

> For the specialist in any one subject the material is all classified and arranged, but before it can be put in a child's text-book it must be simplified and greatly reduced in bulk. The thought-provoking character is obscured and the organizing function disappears. This does not mean that the text-book must disappear, but that its function is changed. It becomes a guide for the pupil by which he may economize time and mistakes. The teacher and the book are no longer the only instructors; the hands, the eyes, the ears, in fact the whole body, become sources of information, while the teacher and text-book become respectively the starter and the tester. No book or man is a substitute for personal experience; they cannot take the place of the actual journey (M8, 255).

The teacher as *starter*, then, leads and guides students, especially in the early stages of their journeys, as they travel toward greater independence and freedom and acquire a more mature understanding and application of the branches of knowledge. The practice of freedom, therefore, is both a means and an end in schooling.

THE LIFE OF THE CHILD. Intimations of Dewey's view of the life of the child at school appear in the previous discussion of freedom and the school as a community. Yet much remains to be said, notably about interests and play. If we recall Dewey's view of the natural world as an artist, of the teacher as a distinct aspect of nature and an artist above nature, and of the child, also a distinctly human part of nature and also an artist, we can interpret the explicitly stated "reverence for childhood" that compelled his concern for the full development of students, including their physical maturation during the school years (M8, 214). In this context of revering, understanding and facilitating the natural development of each student, Dewey stressed the importance of developing a science of education connected to the artistic assignments of the teacher:

> A truly scientific education can never develop so long as children are treated in the lump, merely as a class. Each child has a strong individuality, and any science must take stock of all the facts in its material. Every pupil must have a chance to show what he truly is, so that the teacher can find out what he needs to make him a complete human being. Only as a teacher becomes acquainted with each one of her pupils can she hope to understand childhood, and it is only as she understands it that she can hope to evolve any scheme of education which shall approach either the scientific or the artistic standard (M8, 297).

Dewey's personal study of childhood convinced him that children develop differently in different settings and that the release of their natural tendencies is a positive experience if the teacher recognizes a responsibility to guide and transform these propensities. He believed further that adults should not overemphasize the future of the child but instead recognize the present as the best route to the future. Further, he thought that a true believer in children would change schooling in important ways:

> If we could really believe that attending to the needs of present growth would keep the child and teacher alike busy, and would also provide the best possible guarantee of the learning needed in the future, transformation of educational ideals might soon be accomplished, and other desirable changes would largely take care of themselves (M8, 213).

So the natural experience of each present facet of child development, guided by the teacher, the artist above nature, is the best preparation for future needs and contains meaning and enjoyment for each student (M8, 222). The student, therefore, should be allowed to continue "the natural course" begun

> at home of running from one interesting object to another, of inquiring into the meaning of these objects, and above all of tracing the relation between the different objects. All this must be done in a large way so that he gets the names and bearings of the obvious facts as they appear in order. Thus the obscure and difficult facts come to light one after another without being forced upon the child's attention by the teacher. One discovery leads to another, and the interest of pursuit leads the child of his own accord into investigations that often amount to severe intellectual discipline (M8, 224).

This approach to child life—when followed in the school—leads to the acquisition of appropriate skills and dispositions (M8, 224). A critical feature of Dewey's thought arises at this juncture. Of one of the schools of the future, it was observed that "each pupil may do as he pleases as long as he does not interfere with any one else" (M8, 226). One should not mistake this descriptive comment for Dewey's imprimatur, for he observed in a later section that liberty should not be confused with "doing as one pleases" even if it does not hurt anyone else (M8, 306). He added that schools must go beyond teaching noninterference to nurture the development of cooperative and intelligent activity among students: "It is desirable not merely that the child should learn not to interfere with others as they execute their own ends, but also that he should learn to work with them in an intelligent way" (M8, 312).

The dogma of the absolute supremacy of student interests, therefore, never infiltrated Dewey's idea of the life of the child at school

(M8, 395). On the contrary, at times he found it appropriate to "object that interest cannot serve as a [much less *the*] criterion, either. If we take interest in its narrowest sense as meaning something which amuses and appeals to the child because of its power of entertainment," we easily see the fallacy of the interests doctrine (M8, 396). He amplified this position by stating we should invest little in *making tasks interesting* to a student but rather in selecting "work on the basis of the natural appeal it makes to the child. Interest ought to be the basis for selection because children are interested in the things they need to learn" (M8, 396). Developmental interest, then, appears to have been an important Deweyan idea, but a concept to be distinguished from misinterpretations that cater to "the whim of children" and activities designed to make school easy for them. Dewey strenuously objected to such misunderstandings of developmental interests and allied pedagogical theory in a passage that summarizes his key concerns:

> But the work is not made easy for the pupils; nor yet is there any attempt to give the traditional curriculum a sugar coating. The change is of a more fundamental character and is based on sound psychological theory. The work given to the children has changed; the attempt is not to make all the child's tasks interesting to him, but to select work on the basis of the natural appeal it makes to the child. Interest ought to be the basis for selection because children are interested in the things they need to learn (M8, 396).

In the context of Dewey's complete theory of education, then, the developing interests of students play a key but liberating role: "[T]he range of the [curricular] material is not in any way limited by making interest *a* standard for selection" (M8, 397, italics added). One cannot dismiss the additional standards of curricular selection just discussed by appealing to developmental interests alone, much less by referring to momentary whims and sporadic impulses. In the end, any factor considered in the selection of school experiences must be gauged by the ways in which it contributes to a student's ability to grow intellectually and to learn new ways of contributing to that growth. As in accounts of individual growth and of children becoming happy members of society, part of his theory of education includes understanding that each person, including students and teachers, lives in a society—ideally a community, at least "a social world—where since even the simplest act or word is bound up with the words and acts of his neighbors, there is no danger that this liberty will sacrifice the interests of others to caprice" (M8, 297). Thus, liberty seen in its social or community context

> does not mean the removal of the checks which nature and man impose on the life of every individual in the community, so that one individual may indulge impulses which go against his own welfare as a member of society. But liberty for the child is the chance to test all impulses and tendencies on the world of things and people in which he finds himself, sufficiently to discover their character *so that he may get rid of those which are harmful, and develop those which are useful to himself and others* (M8, 297, italics added).

Dewey obviously resisted both the practice of pampering the whims of students and any effort to introduce such harmful educational ideas and practices as a philosophical distrust of children into the school of the future:

> No proper system of education could tolerate the common assumption, that the mind of the individual is naturally averse to learning, and has to be either browbeaten or coaxed into action. Every mind, even the youngest, is naturally seeking for those modes of active operation within the limits of its capacity. The problem is to discover what tendencies are especially seeking expression at a particular time and just what materials and methods will serve to evoke and direct a truly educative development (L9, 196).

Given that he found these beliefs a part of modern psychology, Dewey thought the school of tomorrow should be rooted in past learning, the present propensities of students and well-defined future goals. He also thought these schools should be characterized to a large degree by "learning by doing" (M8, 253). Describing one school of tomorrow, he connected this idea to the role of the teacher as a partner:

> Not only were the children "learning by doing" in the sense that nearly all the school work centered around activities which had intrinsic meaning and value to the pupils, but most of the initiative for the work came from the children themselves. They

> made their own number problems; suggested the next step in the work on the house; criticised each other's compositions, and worked out their own dramatizations (M8, 258).

Continuing he observed, "The children themselves do all the work. The teacher steps in with advice and helps only when necessary to prevent real errors, but the pupils are given the problem...and are expected to solve it for themselves" (M8, 260). Dewey frequently used such transitive verbs as *use, mold, build, put, float, study, construct, count, decide, go into, do, express, make, see, notice, find out, walk,* and *write* to describe the children in schools of the future who engaged in thought and action (M8, 260-261, 263ff). Another word, *play*, suggested several other significant concepts for Dewey, and he saw play as a form of learning by doing:

> Abstract ideas are hard to understand; the child is never quite sure whether he really understands or not. Allow him to act out the idea and it becomes real to him, or the lack of understanding is shown in what is done. Action is the test of comprehension. This is simply another way of saying that learning by doing is a better way to learn than by listening—the difference of dramatization from the work already described lies in the things the child is learning (M8, 286).

Drama too was important to Dewey from yet another perspective, for it had the power to attract the community to schools and served as a means of introducing subject matter from several fields of understanding. Seeing many possibilities for various forms of drama, he envisioned this particular kind of learning by doing as a means of acquiring skills and understandings in such diverse subjects as spelling, reading, geography, history and literature (M8, 293). Of course, he found the educational value of play self-evident:

> It teaches the children about the world they live in. The more they play the more elaborate becomes their paraphernalia, the whole game being a fairly accurate picture of the daily life of their parents in its setting, clothed in the language and bearing of the children. Through their games they learn about the work and play [and democratic characteristics] of the grown-up world (M8, 278).

THE SCHOOL IN A DEMOCRACY. Since Dewey's view of democracy is a life-encompassing concept, the notion of democracy—as we have seen repeatedly—permeated his thinking about schools and society—for example, in his comments about the practice of freedom and the life of the child in the school and in his view of the relationship between democracy and schooling. Now we can relate this thought to his overall theory of society and schooling and, in particular, his conceptions of the curriculum and the administration of the school of tomorrow.

Since Dewey believed that the "educational end and the ultimate test of the value of what is learned is its use and application in carrying on and improving the common life of all" (L9, 202)—that the ends of education are social and that the ideal social life is the democratic community—he naturally thought as well that "schools exist for a democratic purpose, for the good of citizenship" (M8, 339) and that a "society of free individuals in which all, in doing each his own work, contribute to the liberation and enrichment of the lives of others is the only environment for the normal growth to full statue" (L9, 202-203). Further, Dewey believed both that the school of tomorrow has a democratic purpose and that it must itself be *characterized by democracy*. Schools are both a means to and a manifestation of democracy. But in contrast to what he wanted, he saw beliefs and practices that undermined democracy in all segments of society and in school practices that prevented its development and even its learning:

> Our state is founded on freedom, but when we train the State of tomorrow, we allow it just as little freedom as possible. Children in school must be allowed freedom so that they will know what its use means when they become the controlling body, and they must be allowed to develop active qualities of initiative, independence, and resourcefulness, before the abuses and failures of democracy will disappear (M8, 398).

If Dewey was correct, the basic business of the school of tomorrow can be said to be *in this sense* to teach the student "to live in the world in which he finds himself, to understand his share in it, and to get a good start in adjusting to it. Only as he can do these things successfully will he have time or inclination to cultivate purely intellectual activities" (M8, 315). In adjusting education to help create schools of tomorrow, Dewey became convinced that "three general moral principles" needed to guide decisions (M8, 361). The first was that all people should be prepared to engage in "self-respecting, self-supporting, *intelligent* work" that enabled them to provide the necessary material needs for themselves and their families (M8, 361). This is not to say that all work is rewarding or valuable. But it should be such that it has a worthwhile social function. The second moral principle Dewey recommended for guiding education was an understanding of how much one's own work influenced the well-being of others in society (M8, 361) and of the network of social activities that "bind people together" (M8, 362). Thus work serves to build a sense of community and to undercut and reduce social divisions. The third guiding moral principle was that students should come to understand that life, work and occupations depend upon a "knowledge of facts and laws of natural and social sciences [and] upon intricate mathematical, physical, chemical, and biological insight" (M8, 362). This general knowledge and a knowledge of the academic disciplines lie at the root of both education and the possibility of social progress.

Dewey's philosophy of schooling for tomorrow would provide the average person or worker an understanding of "the *physical* and *social* facts behind and ahead of the material and appliances with which they are dealing" (M8, 362, italics added). Even so, the emphasis of schooling should not be upon "amassing more information, but [on] the formation of certain attitudes and interests, ways of looking at things and dealing with them" (M8, 362). That is, one should understand everything one learns about work and other fields to have a bearing upon the common social life of a community (M8, 362). These themes run through much that Dewey wrote, including this statement:

> If schools are to recognize the needs of all classes of pupils, and give pupils a training that will insure their becoming successful and valuable citizens, they must give work that will not only make the pupils strong physically and morally and give them the right attitude towards the state and their neighbors, but will as well give them enough control over their material environment to enable them to be economically independent (M8, 400).

As we would expect, Dewey saw in the schools of tomorrow he selected a movement away from an aristocratic curriculum toward an understanding of knowledge and life suitable for a democratic society

(M8, 389). The purpose of these schools included giving "the child an education which will make him a better, happier, more efficient human being, by showing him what his capabilities are and how he can exercise them, both materially and socially, in the world he finds about him" (M8, 247), not providing him with a sterile knowledge founded upon the symbols of learning. The school of tomorrow, then, ought to aim "to help the *whole* society by helping the *whole* individual" (M8, 247, italics added).

The school of tomorrow then has a demanding task: "The hardest lesson" a student has to learn is "a practical one" that cannot be compensated for by any "amount of book knowledge." It is the critically important matter of intelligent adjustment to one's neighbors and one's job (M8, 253-254). The hardest lesson may also be the most important lesson, for every aspect of democracy depends "upon the ability of people to work together successfully. If they can do this a well-balanced, happy and prosperous society results" (M8, 314). Introducing occupational and social activities in the school in this spirit, therefore, provided a way for Dewey to promote democracy as well as a natural basis on which to expand children's learning, a means of getting them to understand "social life" or "human life." When work and occupations are disconnected from school, community and democracy,

> Work...is isolated, selfish and individualistic. It is based on a conception of society which no longer fits the facts, an every-man-for-himself society which ceased to exist a hundred years ago. The ordinary school curriculum ignores the scientific democratic society of to-day and its needs and ideals, and goes on fitting children for an individualistic struggle for existence (M8, 314).

Consequently, Dewey believed each community should help its schools understand that they play vital roles in the "welfare of the whole" and turn out citizens who contribute to the growth of "community spirit and interests" (M8, 320). If school and community leadership fail to press this purpose, it will be nearly impossible for schools to prepare a student to be "successful as [both] a human being and an American citizen" (M8, 322). Ultimately neither society nor the individual student is well served if schools fail to teach neighborly adjustment and mutual respect, the hardest lesson, for "Society *is* individuals-in-their-relations. An individual apart from social relations is a myth—or a monstrosity" (L8, 80). In view of Dewey's concept of the school as a democratic community, we may safely say: "School *is* individuals-in-their-relations. A student apart from social relations is a myth—or a monstrosity."

In what now appears to be an overstatement from one perspective and an understatement from another, Dewey pushed his democratic agenda of a classless society and schools promoting the social good:

> The only fundamental agency for good is the public-school system. Every American is proud of what has been accomplished in the past in fostering among very diverse elements of population a spirit of unity and of brotherhood so that the sense of common interests and aims has prevailed over the forces working to divide our people into classes. The increasing complexity of our life, with the great accumulation of wealth at one social extreme and the condition of almost dire necessity at the other makes the task of democracy constantly more difficult. The days are rapidly passing when the simple provision of a system in which all individuals mingle is enough to meet the need. The subject-matter and the methods of teaching must be positively and aggressively adapted to the end (M8, 404).

Later, Dewey employed the term *fellowship* to describe part of what he meant by community. During the Second World War, he argued that

> The present state of the world bears witness also to the fact that any desirable new education must express and must create fellowship. Fellowship is more than the opposite of war, discord, hatred, and intolerance. It provides the only sure and enduring guarantee that these evils will not continue to plague mankind. Education in and for and by fellowship, through cooperation and with a cooperative society as its aim, is an imperatively required factor in an education that will arise in contrast to the world now engaged in destroying itself (L14, 278).

In his lifelong avoidance of dichotomies, Dewey saw the dangers in the "false antithesis" (L9, 172) that many claim for individuality and community in society and school. Individuals, he argued, have innumerable preferences and interests. Both *the child and the teacher* must therefore select as development occurs within a community of learners. If not, *the student can* make "an arbitrary imposition on himself when, in response to an inquiry as to what he would like, he, because of ignorance of underlying and enduring tendencies and interest, snatches at some accidental affair" (L9, 173). "The problem is, therefore," Dewey said, "to discover *within* present experience those values that are akin to those which the community prizes, and to cultivate those tendencies that lead in the direction that social demands will take" (L9, 172-173). So again, from Dewey's perspective, the educator should "study the tendencies of the young so as to be more consciously aware than are the children themselves what the latter need and want. Any other course transfers the responsibility of the teacher to those taught" (L9, 173).

In a democratic classroom, community or school, Dewey believed students learn by practicing a variety of values that are intrinsic parts of a democratic way of life and government. For example, a democratic learning community naturally develops the character of its students, forming their "desires, purposes, and habits" in such a fashion that the well-being of others becomes a factor in decision making (L9, 186). Yet, the school should not be seen as the moral corrective of society, for "at best the schools can be but one agency among the very many that are active in forming character" (L9, 187). Character, then, is something that is "*formed* rather than something that can be taught" although certain "things about character can be taught, and such teaching is important" (L9, 187-188).

While the role of the school in forming character is important and should proceed through concrete social experiences and positive student involvement in the life of the institution, Dewey identified three larger influences on character development that were more important than and necessary supporters of character development in schools (L9, 192). First, Dewey believed an economic setting promoting "useful work, security for old age, and security of a decent home and of opportunity for education of all children" was the "most important factor" in developing character—a belief perfectly consistent with his social activism and promotion of economic reform. Second, he maintained that the role of parents in developing character is more significant than the role of the school. Third, he believed that positive social and recreational settings and activities are invaluable because the "two dominant impulses of youth are toward activity and toward some kind of collective association" (L9, 192).

Thus, character formation and moral education in the school—despite his other claims of the importance of the school as an agency for good—ranked no higher than fourth on Dewey's list of influential factors in moral growth. Logically, no character education program, he believed, however important its contribution, could overcome a powerful counter-force of the three stronger formative influences. Yet there remained a tension if not an inconsistency in Dewey's thinking. Dewey—the prophet, the usher and the social engineer—writing just two months later than the passages cited, failed to resist the temptation to blame schools for what he termed "the present unprecedented wave of nationalistic sentiment, of racial and national prejudice, of readiness to resort to force of arms" (L9, 203). He lamented that schools had neglected to do more to develop character:

> For this spirit [of nationalism, racism and warmongering] to have arisen on such a scale the schools must have somehow failed grievously. Their best excuse is maybe that schools and educators were caught unawares. But that excuse is no longer available. We know the enemy; it is out in the open. Unless the schools of the world can unite in effort to rebuild the spirit of common understanding, of mutual sympathy and goodwill among all people and races, to exorcise the demon of prejudice, isolation and hatred, they themselves are likely to be submerged by the general return to barbarism, the sure outcome of present tendencies if unchecked by the forces which education alone can evoke and fortify (L9, 203-204).

If the school of tomorrow is to become democratic in the activities of teachers and children, its mission and its curriculum, a democratic orientation must also exist in the way the school is administered. The practice of a democratic community "should extend to administration so that oligarchical management from above may be abolished" (L9, 184). One indication that an oligarchical management team is yielding to democratic practices occurs when every teacher has "some regular and organic way in which he can, directly or through representatives democratically chosen, participate in the formation of the controlling aims, methods and materials of the school of which he is a part" (L11, 222). We see here the Dewey who advocated teacher unions and professionalism. Here too the Laboratory School experience may help illuminate Dewey's view of one possible way democracy can influence school administration, for he reported that the administrative side of the school was "almost entirely in the hands of the teachers" (M1, 58). Mayhew and Edwards (1966) provide further insight into the operations and administration of the Laboratory School and into its effects on Dewey's beliefs, providing examples of what Dewey often described in his writings.

When compelled, Dewey could harshly criticize schools, teachers and administrators—but his criticism often implicated society too. For instance, he referred to urban schools as "big scholastic factories" and rural schools as "dead, dispirited, poorly equipped" (L2, 116). The explanation for these deplorable conditions Dewey found in "the old saying: As is the teacher, so is the school" (L2, 116). Deplorable teachers make deplorable schools. Yet, of course, Dewey knew the problem to be far more complicated: "Teachers are *an effect* of social conditions before they are *a cause* of schools" (L2, 116, italics added). Why, Dewey asked, are teachers—especially elementary teachers—as bad as they seem to be and what keeps them that way? His answer was that

> The responsibility is found in the community; we can not unload it on the teachers, they are symptoms, products of our own beliefs, desires, ideals, and what we are satisfied with. To find out what is the matter with the schools, we have to make an examination of teachers; to find out what is the matter with the teachers, we have to examine ourselves (L2, 116-117).

What do we find when we examine the facts? First, we find that we are unwilling to pay well enough to attract and keep the kind of "teachers who alone can make our schools be what they should be" (L2, 117). Implicit in this statement we find the notion that a group of teachers can or should have a profound influence on the direction and operation of a school. Second, we find that we are not adequately interested in cultivating desirable levels of "esteem, respect, social prestige, hearty backing" for teachers (L2, 117). Obviously, the lack of support in these areas affects not only instructional activities but other leadership roles for teachers too. Instead of adequate salaries, expenditures on schools, and support for educators, Dewey saw political manipulation, personal favoritism and a society guided by "the old belief that anybody who is in possession of his five senses and who has himself or herself learned to read, write and figure" can be a teacher

(L2, 119). Thus, we have not "a profession [but] an improvised occupation [that can be] easily taken up and easily laid aside" (L2, 119). Under these conditions, even the best teachers would find it difficult to provide the leadership good schools require.

Moreover, the social conditions that create teachers and schools appear within the school: The teacher is forced to instruct large classes, experience constant emotional stress and suffer from exhaustion. Furthermore,

> The teacher is compelled to instruct in batches and on a basis of uniformity. Everything tends automatically to lockstep treatment in teaching and discipline. To cover so much ground with every pupil, to have each one go through as nearly as possible the same motions as every other, is the same thing as to discourage originality and depress individuality (L2, 121).

Teachers had, therefore, assumed "the status of upper-class servants," not professionals (L2, 122). Expected to have no thoughts of their own, teachers were called to work in an environment that demands "colorless intellectual conformity, blank vacuousness" (L2, 122). The lack of respect society has for teachers, then, goes beyond the simple matter of career or occupational status. At heart, it reflects the undemocratic structure of society, an orientation that devalues its most important public servants and prizes nearly every other career or occupation more than it does teaching. The manifested value system simultaneously devalues professional behavior and judgment, democratic leadership and reflective educational experiences. The administration of the schools in his day, Dewey believed, was more than just anti-teacher. It was also anti-democracy and anti-education.

The undemocratic social conditions that produce teachers who produce undemocratic school environments also produce administrators who foster organizational and administrative circumstances that compound the ineffectiveness and humiliation of classroom practitioners. With as much anger as insight, the prophet Dewey (he referred to himself as Jeremiah) spoke of the field of administration as "that professional mystery" responsible for the "ever-thickening wall which divides the classroom teacher and the administrative officer" and which demands that teachers abandon teaching if they wish to gain any respect and a proper salary. His derogatory comments occasionally turned acerbic, notably when he wrote of "the irritable vanity of that petty tyrant, the educational administrator" (M11, 56) and referred to school administration as "a mass of ritualistic exercises" when it is not based upon scientific thinking (M13, 321). With a remarkable show of passion, Dewey wrote what could be an editorial in a contemporary teachers' magazine:

> The further away one is from children and from the only place where education takes place, the direct contact of mind and mind, the greater is the probability that one will be an educational authority and looked up to with respect and envy. In the name of scientific administration and close supervision, the initiative and freedom of the actual teacher are more and more curtailed. By means of achievement and mental tests carried on from the central office, of a steadily issuing stream of dictated typewritten communications, of minute and explicit syllabi of instruction the teacher is reduced to a living phonograph. In the name of centralization of responsibility and of efficiency and even science, everything possible is done to make the teacher into a servile rubber stamp. After we have either scared away intellectual creativeness and originality, or else segregated it in offices remote from fertilizing contact with child life which is touched only through statistics and standardized tests, we wonder why all the energy and zeal expended upon education bears so little fruit (L2, 122-123)!

When we want to reform schools, Dewey concluded, we are inclined to "tinker" with nearly anything and avoid asking what social and institutional conditions, including undemocratic beliefs and repressive practices, keep "mature, rich, free, independent personalities" out of teaching (L2, 123). More specifically, he asked, "What can be done to liberate teachers, to free their personalities and minds from all the petty economic, social and administrative restrictions which so frequently hem them in and repress them" (L2, 123)?

Dewey considered this question crucially important. Democracy could hardly be learned by students as long as teachers were virtual slaves in both their schools and their districts. This insight led him to allege that public schools are characterized by "much more autocracy" than are universities and that they are "ridden by 'administrators'; they are administrator mad. An arm's-length efficiency, conducted by typewriters from central offices, reaches into the class-rooms where all the educational work is done, and produces there the inefficiency of irresponsibility and routine" (L3, 279). Instead, administrators, Dewey urged, must see that "the controlling force" in schools is the "desire to work with others, for mutual advantage" (L6, 97).

Yet, Dewey found too little of this desire for him to conclude that schools were becoming centers of cooperative work and learning for the advantage of everyone—centers, that is, of democratic learning. His descriptions of teachers as repressed, ridden, living phonographs, servile rubber stamps, upper-class servants, and possessors of no more than their five senses—the antithesis of the ten analogies that expressed his dreams for teachers—vividly portray the anger he felt about the abuse and undemocratic treatment teachers received in his lifetime, and in various venues still receive today.

Beyond his fiery condemnation of society, principals, central office personnel, superintendents and board members, Dewey moved to provide further understanding of democratic administration by talking positively and concretely of teacher liberation. Obviously, he thought the school of tomorrow should operate as a cooperative community organized on a philosophy that includes a respect for and guidance by teachers, staff members, students and administrators "so that oligarchical management from above may be abolished" (L9, 184). He thought teachers should definitely be involved in decisions regarding curricular and policy matters. Likewise, he believed they should be prized for their imagination and creativity as well as respected for their thorough knowledge of a field. He saw his selected schools of tomorrow "*directed by sincere teachers* trying earnestly to give their children the best they have by working out concretely what they consider the fundamental principles of education" (M8, 207, italics added).

Elsewhere, returning to the notion of not losing sight of one's purposes, he explained his underlying insight: "[O]rganization is never an end in itself. It is a means of promoting *association*, of multiplying effective points of contact between persons, directing their intercourse into the modes of greatest fruitfulness" (RP, 206-207). If organization is not an end in itself, then school districts should be willing to modify it as necessary to obtain the collective wisdom of practicing professionals. At the very least, they must free themselves of the habit or tradition of treating knowledgeable educators as "servile rubber stamps."

Yet other comments on democracy and the administration of school districts and schools in Dewey's essays illustrate a more sympathetic understanding of the challenges practicing administrators face. For example, in an essay entitled "Toward Administrative Statesmanship," he acknowledged the difficulty and complexity of administrative responsibilities, noting three "obscure and conflicting factors" (L11, 345). The first dimension concerns the curricular and methodological decisions made in a district and school and how administrators involved in "the development of minds and character" (L11, 345) can defeat their own purposes by imposing these matters upon teachers, precluding them from employing their own *minds*. The second dimension of the work he described as dealing with "personal relations in the family" and the "divided personality" that can result from attempting to create harmony and effectiveness among teachers, other administrators, board members, taxpayers and politicians. The divided personality problem manifests itself when an administrator is "diplomatic" with one group but "arbitrary" with another (L11, 345-346). The third dimension of the administrator's work centers on dealing with "detail and routine" which could influence a person to become "impersonal," work in "isolation," and regard teachers much like "employees in a factory" (L11, 346).

His recommendation to administrators contained three elements. First, they should unify these responsibilities and related problems under a fundamental decision regarding the social function of the school, deciding whether the school was to help "perpetuate existing conditions [or to] take part in their transformation." If the choice is the former, the administrator will conform to community expectations. If the latter, life will be more difficult, but the administrator will be making decisions in the light of what is educationally best for students and society and supporting the teachers in their roles as social servants, social engineers and democratic pioneers.

The second element of his recommendation was that the administrator should treat "the school itself as a cooperative community," providing leadership via "intellectual stimulation and direction" with others rather than being "aloof." Third, the administrator ought to become involved in the education of the neighborhood community in an effort to facilitate education within the school and to enhance opportunities for "the transformation of society" (L11, 347). Dewey considered this tie with the community important because "it is necessary that the public school system should become more and more the harmonizing centre and clearing house, concentrating and unifying all...educational activities of the community, forcing them, stimulating them, and seeing to it that they are really made useful to the people" (L17, 74).

In a futuristic article projecting the success of a society in both "preserving and extending democracy" (L11, 537), Dewey said that in this future free society "factories and offices will take over some of the functions of the school" (L11, 539) and the teacher will be "*mediator* and *interpreter* of what other vocations may contribute to the development of [the student's] personality" (L11, 540, italics added). The community—as seen "in doctors' offices, in museums, newspaper plants, farms, forests, steamboats, buses, art studios, factories, stores, government offices, civic concerts, theaters, public discussions and in the thousand other enterprises of living" (L11, 541)—and the teacher—as "a *student* of child development, a friendly *guide* to individual children, an *organizer* of harmonious group activities, and a *'generalist'* in thinking about the effects of the social order upon personal growth" (L11, 542, italics added)—will be the two main sources of instruction in a democracy.

But the teachers will need the freedom to interact with community businesses and agencies in order to know and use the educational resources needed by each student (L11, 540). As well, they will need the professional autonomy to visit homes, "play groups or studios or clinics [and] conduct excursions" (L11, 543). In this kind of advanced democracy, people will become "increasingly intolerant of practices which irk, confine, humiliate, and breed hypocrisy in teachers," resulting in a society were teachers are "fairly secure and truly free" (L11, 546). In this kind of society, we will have schools with a genuine community and professional spirit and

> the kind of administration which exalts the free and intelligent personality and does not depend upon rules, regulations, formal procedures, and prescriptions. Under these conditions teaching can become the high art [where the teacher is "*a great orchestral conductor*" (L11, 544; italics added) of the classroom and the extramural activities] that it rarely is today. Teachers individually and in their organizations can develop standards for professional work and can work in accord with those standards without being hampered by external worries, limited economic resources, impossible working conditions, military-minded executives, and popular misunderstanding of the function and work of the schools (L11, 546).

Dewey's hypothesized school in an ideal democracy of the future leads us conveniently into an analysis of the school he described as suitable for his Utopia. Revealingly, he neglected to mention administrators or administration in this essay.

The Utopian School

If Dewey could have had his political and pedagogical way and the world had adopted his philosophy of life and learning, he would have radically altered education in Utopia. In fact, he bluntly and happily stated, "The most Utopian thing in Utopia is that there are no schools at all" (L9, 136). But if the concept of having no schools at all is so radical as to be incomprehensible to many, Dewey said he would modify his position and be satisfied to see that the schools in Utopia were "nothing of the sort" that we currently know (L9, 136). In the ideal world, then, Dewey believed that it would be best to have "children...gathered together in association with older and more mature people who direct activity" (L9, 136). His thinking, in a few respects, may call to mind Plato's "symposium."

The gathering or assembly place—the utopian school—would be characterized by "large grounds, gardens, orchards, greenhouses and none of the buildings...will hold much more than 200 people...[since this number has] been found to be about the limits of close, intimate personal acquaintance" (L9, 136). In these "open-air schools" there would be none of the furnishings we currently associate with schools, such as rows of desks (L9, 136). On the contrary, there would be "rather something like a well-furnished home of today, only with much greater variety of equipment and no messy accumulations of all sorts of miscellaneous furniture; more open spaces than our homes have today" (L9, 136). Inside the open-air structures, Dewey would have "workshops with their apparatus...[and] all kinds of material—wood, iron, textiles" (L9, 136). Likewise, the structures would contain "historic museums and scientific laboratories, and books everywhere as well as a central library" (L9, 136-137). (It would be necessary for us to translate some of his dated industrial elements into contemporary technological components if we were to formulate a present-day application of his thought.)

The people in Dewey's utopian school constitute an interesting configuration with some qualifications that raise eyebrows today. For instance, those *adults*—people we might call teachers—who direct the activities of the children must be "married persons and, except in exceptional cases, must have had children of their own" (L9, 137). Even so, younger, *unmarried persons* may "serve a kind of initiatory apprenticeship" in an assembly place (L9, 137). It is unclear whether Dewey was alluding here to would-be teachers doing apprenticeships in utopian schools after they had completed their university preparation as teachers.

Since there are no classes and grades in the assembly place, older children participate in directing the activities of younger children. Those *youth* aged 13 to 18 have the opportunity to direct younger children under the observation of adults after undergoing a type of self-selection process. That is, those "who are especially fond of younger children are given the opportunity to consort with them." As they work with younger children, Dewey thought it would become "evident who among them have the taste, interest and the kind of skill which is needed for effective dealing with the young" (L9, 137). Those youth who demonstrate this taste, interest and skill to work would be able to center their further education on "the study of processes of growth and development" (L9, 137). Dewey believed that people "we would call teachers" should be selected in a similar manner. *Parents*, too, who are "taken out of the narrower contact with their own children in the homes and are brought forward in the educational nurture of a larger number of children" may prove to be good teachers through "a very similar process of natural selection" (L9, 137).

The educational group—teachers, apprentices, teens, parents, and children—would operate much as a colony of artists or painters. The "adult leaders" or "older people" would combine their interest in children, their knowledge of them and their particular "gifts" to direct studies in certain areas. They would engage in the work in which they were "competent, whether painting or music or scientific inquiry, observation of nature or industrial cooperation in some line" (L9, 137). "Younger people" would learn somewhat as apprentices, at first observing and later moving from the simpler to the complex activities of adults. "Younger children" would likewise observe and listen before participating in simple matters and eventually cooperating in more complex matters as they learned greater responsibility for themselves and others.

What, we may wonder, is the purpose of the activities of these educational centers or assembly places? Dewey's answer may appear less than precise. Since "the whole concept of the school, of teachers and pupils and lessons" would have been completely forsaken in the utopian school, the answer is not easily stated (L9, 138), but part of it is found in the conception of the assembly as the place to make the lives of children and youth worthwhile and to help them grow and develop. The purpose of an assembly place is simply to promote "the process of a developing life" by refining natural community processes. Moreover, the processes or means in the learning activities themselves would naturally be important in a utopian school. The purpose of an assembly place is stated in somewhat more modern terms as

> the discovery of the aptitudes, the tastes, the abilities and the weaknesses of each boy and girl, and then [the development of] their positive capacities into attitudes and [the arrangement and reinforcement of] the positive powers so as not to cover up the weak points but to offset them (L9, 138).

We may wonder too how the learning of subject matter is handled in a utopian school. How do the adults ensure that children learn to "read and write and figure" and master, for example, "geography and arithmetic and history"? Questions of this sort are, Dewey claimed in language anticipating a later Ivan Illich, largely irrelevant in a utopian school because "the whole concept of acquiring and storing away things [is] displaced by the concept of creating attitudes by shaping desires and developing the needs that are significant in the process of living" (L9, 139). Just as children learn to walk and talk in the process of living, so too they learn such other matters as geography, biology and history in the process of living in an assembly place. Yet, *we should interpret Dewey's position here in view of the fact that Utopia itself would be a fully functioning democratic educational community and would not depend primarily upon schools to educate children and youth.* When we ignore or forget this idea, Dewey's view of a utopian school becomes decontextualized and consequently misinterpreted.

Some of the attitudes to be learned in a utopian school are diametrically opposed to those learned in the schools of our times but overlap with social and intellectual attitudes already discussed. In the process of acquiring certain attitudes, "personal acquisition" and "private possession" would disappear as ideals. The "acquisitive system of society" would no longer exist, and the enjoyment of creation and productivity would be emphasized. Competition, rivalry, rewards, punishments, examinations and promotion would be banished from an assembly place, for they conflict with the goal of natural learning in a democratic community. These changes—"the great educational liberation" of society and schools, ultimately resulting in the arrival of Utopia and utopian schools—would achieve dominant force in Dewey's imaginary world when:

> the concept of external attainments was thrown away and when...[people] started to find out what each individual person had in him from the beginning, and then devoted themselves to finding out the conditions of the environment and the kinds of activity in which the positive capacities of each young person could operate most effectually (L9, 139).

The various attitudes developed in a utopian school are difficult to rank, but one thing Dewey definitely wanted students to achieve was "a sense of positive power" (L9, 140). The attitude that would produce this sense, Dewey claimed, would lead to an "elimination of fear, of embarrassment, of constraint, of self-consciousness; [and]...the conditions which [create]...the feeling of failure and incapacity" (L9, 140). On the other hand, a sense of positive power would lead to "the development of a confidence, of readiness to tackle difficulties, of actual eagerness to seek problems instead of dreading them and running away from them" (L9, 140).

In another context, Dewey spoke of the importance of adopting the "attitudes of open-mindedness, intellectual integrity, observation and interest in testing...opinions and belief that are characteristic of the scientific attitude" (L9, 99). No doubt these attitudes too would be highly valued along with habits "which are more intelligent, more sensitively percipient, more informed with insight, more aware of what they are about, more direct and sincere, more flexibly responsive than those now current" (M14, 90). In this setting, Dewey reiterated an old theme when he affirmed that "the scientific inquirer is above all else a continuing and persistent learner" (L9, 99).

For Dewey, then, the utopian school or assembly place is a radical extension of his comprehensive social and educational philosophy, including his democratic ideals, natural learning theory, and discovery-oriented pedagogy. Anything less would be far removed from any Utopia he could envision. Thus, because the learning community was natural, the "feeble stimulus" of instruction (M14, 20) and the sometimes despicable art of schooling or "taking advantage of the helplessness of the young" (M14, 47) would come to their ends in Utopia.

Conclusion

Through Dewey's eyes, we have seen the weaknesses of the traditional school, the mixed features of the progressive school, the experimental agenda of the laboratory school, the professional role of the practice school, and the promise of the school of tomorrow, the democratic school and the utopian school. Dewey's analyses of past, present and future schools, however old, seem alive and still applicable, with challenging and rewarding implications for the reconstruction of our own schools and societies along democratic and educative lines. His criticism of the traditional school and guarded praise for the progressive school remain sufficiently relevant to raise questions about the directions we take in the next century. If we are reflective, his comments can influence us to seek a balanced attention to the child and the curriculum, neglecting neither and prizing both. His thoughts about laboratory and practice schools call to mind recent proposals for professional development schools and cause us to wonder whether some of our current goals and objectives and outcomes are in part attributable to the discontinuities that exist in our teacher preparation programs as a result of superficial relationships between our universities and schools. Perhaps we also will be influenced to utilize these schools to further our knowledge of theory and practice and, accordingly, revise our preparation programs for aspiring educators.

Our discussion of the laboratory and practice schools may remind us of Dewey's conviction that field experiences, theory, research and practice went far beyond preparing future teachers for the current needs and standards of schools and communities to open the possibility of a true science of education. He saw that they represent an opportunity for schools and universities to collaborate in nurturing future educators and thereby providing "educational leadership"—teachers who will go beyond "doing better" what is currently being done to alter the very nature of schooling and society "by changing the conception of what constitutes *education*" (M3, 272, italics added). Educator preparation programs that deal merely with the existing realities of education, according to Dewey, fail to fulfill their complete responsibilities and are derelict in their duties (272). They should help create a world in which the school of tomorrow and the ideal school emerge and flourish, eventually to be replaced by the utopian school.

The school of tomorrow, the school in a thriving democracy and the utopian assembly point us toward Dewey's explicit recommendations. Taken together, Dewey's criticisms and recommendations can help us develop and sustain a variety of schools or assembly places that would be complementary centers of learning—democratic communities that thrive on the intellectual vitality that surrounds and permeates active, open community life. On the other hand, his ideas of the school in an ideal democracy and the utopian school may imply that nearly all schools, as we know them today and as Dewey spoke of them in *Schools of To-Morrow,* would vanish in a future democratic society where all societal segments fully understood and carried out their educational responsibilities.

In the light of these suggestions and proposals, we may usefully reflect on Dewey's observation that what we need "above all else is the creatively courageous disposition. Fear, routine, sloth, identification of success with ease, and approbation of others are the enemies that now stand in the way of educational advance" (M13, 328). In the past, rather than using what we knew to understand and address our problems,

> We have depended upon the clash of war, the stress of revolution, the emergence of heroic individuals, the impact of migrations generated by war and famine, the incoming of barbarians, to change established institutions. Instead of constantly utilizing unused impulse to effect continuous reconstruction, we have waited till an accumulation of stresses breaks through the dikes of custom (M14, 73).

Perhaps even today—perhaps especially today—Dewey would raise the question, "Shall we continue to allow war, revolution, heroic individuals, migrations and barbarians to break open the customs of education or shall we reconstruct our communities and environments and, thereby, our impulses and purposes through intelligence?" If our answer affirmed what he would call the intelligent option, where would the choice lead us?

CHAPTER NINE

The Spirit of Deweyan Reform

> Genuine ignorance is more profitable because it is likely to be accompanied by humility, curiosity, and open-mindedness; whereas ability to repeat catchphrases, cant terms, familiar propositions, gives the conceit of learning and coats the mind with a varnish waterproof to new ideas (L8, 307).

> The ideal of democracy demands the fullest possible development of personality in all—irrespective of birth, wealth, creed, or race—through cooperative association with others, and mutual understanding and consent. The ideal further demands that all institutions, customs, and arrangements of social life contribute to these ends, that is, that they be educative (L11, 538).

> The fundamental factors in the educative process are an immature, undeveloped being; and certain social aims, meanings, values incarnate in the matured experience of the adult (M2, 273).

In the Preface, we identified some of the conflicting claims people make about schools and educational reform and suggested a more modest approach to what we can profess to know. Education is a complex and complicated endeavor that involves a plethora of judgments and policy choices affecting diverse people and the "meanings" they place on their experiences, lives and institutions. Education, in addition to being a complex undertaking, is an immensely important affair that is made clear in the frequency of philosophical arguments, ethical debates, legal controversies and legislative action.

The role of the school in society is hotly contested in part because we debate social, economic and political matters—what Dewey called "social aims"—views of the kind of society we would like to build and choose to live in. Similarly, the responsibilities of the teacher are always open to argument, debate and discussion, for they entail choices related to the selection of values or worthwhile ideas, activities and experiences—both ends and means—as well as about the distribution of attention, encouragement, support, assistance and rewards. The "immature, undeveloped being" adds to the pedagogical drama, or perhaps tragedy, for the child or youth can be cared for or ignored, educated or miseducated, and actualized or frustrated as "the matured experience of the adult" is brought into her or his life.

Education, including its offspring educator preparation programs and schooling, involves judgments, decisions and actions about science, art, ethics, religion, philosophy, law and politics and the importance of these choices for the present and future lives and development of children, youth and adults. Indeed, these judgments involve nearly all forms of understanding and touch all social and personal development. Thus there is the need for at least a reasonable degree of modesty on the part of everyone. Recognizing our limitations, as Hare (1993) observes, is a much needed virtue. To claim knowledge across all of the branches of inquiry involved in educational decision making is one thing. To assert that one understands largely how all of this knowledge is to be weighed and applied in a diverse and dynamic society and its institutions is another. To hold that one has little of importance to learn about education by listening to the ideas and examining the arguments of other equally and legitimately concerned individuals is a third matter. To contend that one's position on the myriad details involved in education is completely correct is still another. To claim that everyone concerned with educational choices should immediately concede that one's own opinions should be followed explicitly is yet another matter, one that appears to undercut the fabric of Deweyan democracy and "the fullest possible development of personality in all." Anyone who consciously or unconsciously accepts this progressively stronger string of claims, no doubt, risks being appropriately described as having a "conceit of learning" that coats her or his mind with "a varnish waterproof to new ideas."

If an admission of "genuine ignorance" is not merited occasionally as we face educational issues, if "humility" is not warranted as values are discussed, if "curiosity" is not well-advised as opinions are argued, if "open-mindedness" is not fitting as the development of children, youth and society is examined, if explaining our "catchphrases, cant terms, familiar propositions" is not desirable as we seek to communicate with others, then it is not likely that we are entering into the spirit of Deweyan reform. For that spirit entails, as an absolute minimum, our being interested in learning and thinking for ourselves. Such a minimum Deweyan spirit, however, is insufficient because thinking may be selfishly or destructively employed. Others must be encouraged and allowed to do so too. Dewey wanted a society of individuals who act for one another, people concerned to promote the well-being and growth of their families, neighbors, colleagues and other human beings. Thus the intellectual, social and moral dimensions of the Deweyan spirit are largely encapsulated in the motto "'Learn to *act* with and for others while you learn to *think* and judge for yourself'" (L6, 98).

The strength of Dewey's account, then, lies less in its detailed suggestions for precise reforms than in the approach—reflective and comprehensive—he suggests and the way it integrates core educational values and larger social concerns. Indeed, many currently controversial issues were unknown in his day while others are now better understood and viewed in different ways. Yet at times, of course, his proposals remain interesting, insightful and provocative.

THE ROLE OF DEBATE. Given this spirit of Deweyan reform, we may ask where it would lead us as we think for ourselves and act with and for others. What kinds of questions and considerations have we learned from Dewey that are worthy of further reflection? What have we learned from Dewey that merits our reflective use and, ideally, will lead to personal and social action and growth?

We might well begin with Dewey's idea that it "would not be a sign of health if such an important social interest as education were not also an arena of struggles, practical and theoretical" (EE, 5). First, was he not correct, in other words, in thinking that debate about social concerns such as education is healthy? Would ours really be a better society and have improved schools if we all agreed on educational questions and there were no issues? Second, if he is incorrect, how would we go about dealing with his views? Would it be through educational means, such as seeking to refute his assumptions and arguments? Or would we seek to prohibit the reading of his books and the discussion of his ideas? Our responses to these questions illustrate several considerations that are important in understanding the spirit of Deweyan reform: Reform should be based upon respect for reasoned arguments, freedom of thought, open debate and participation by interested parties.

Perhaps we are not convinced that his views of democracy and education are necessarily in the best interest of society: There are risks and disadvantages as well as advantages in his proposals. We may have mixed feelings, being unsure how our values fit together and should be operationalized and what to make of the good and bad consequences we observe. We may even find that Dewey's ideas conflict with other deeply held values (related, for example, to competition and free enterprise).

Dewey, of course, would welcome our uncertainty and the opportunity for discussion of these values and their implications for school and society, for he believed that

> Thinking begins in what may fairly enough be called a *forked-road* situation, a situation that is ambiguous, that presents a dilemma, that proposes alternatives. As long as our activity glides smoothly along from one thing to another, or as we permit our imagination to entertain fancies of pleasure, there is no call for reflection. Difficulty or obstruction in the way of reaching a belief brings us, however, to a pause. In the suspense of uncertainty, we metaphorically climb a tree; we try to find some standpoint from which we may survey additional facts and, getting a more commanding view of the situation, decide how the facts stand related to one another (L8, 122).

While Dewey would not be troubled by our uncertainty, he would be troubled if we stopped thinking, for he believed that real educational reform—indeed all aspects of a worthwhile life—can only emanate from thinking and acting in the light of evaluating alternatives. But how would he have us think? Manifestly, he would want us to go beyond the formalities of hearings, committee meetings and task force sessions and to avoid going to them with a blind determination to get across our positions and to ignore the views of others. Instead, he would have us "weigh, ponder, deliberate," for he believed that "the thoughtful person...scrutinizes, inspects, examines...probes...reckons, calculates, casts up an account...searches" (L8, 175). He would have us take thinking seriously. He would have us reevaluate our thinking processes themselves because he was convinced that some ways of thinking, especially "scientific" ones, are better than others (L8, 113) and that scientific thinking—as a thoughtful, reasoned and reflective approach to problems—is both a part of the democratic ethos and based in a respect for public evidence and argument. He would encourage us to become thoughtful persons who are liberated from the dead hand of unselected habits and obsolete conventions and empowered to recognize, analyze and act on the challenges that face us. As educators, he would have us cultivate these traits in ourselves and move beyond the thoughtful person to become a reflective practitioner who is able to critique her or his own educational practice and theory and views of reforming schooling and society.

Metaphorically speaking, we might say that the other fork in the road, the alternative to the thoughtful person, is the pre-, un-, or anti-scientific person whose limited thinking and decisions are controlled primarily by dead traditions, whimsical impulses, stifling beliefs and unreflective habits. The alternatives to the democratic society are rather clear from Dewey's point of view. Society and individuals are either shaped and controlled by a few people or sets of people who have power over others through their ownership of material, cultural and human resources or by the forces of barbarism that are released in the absence of enlightened humane influences or centralized control. Dewey was convinced that no self-respecting person would really want to select an intellectual fork that would increase dependence for thought and life upon others who had little interest in her or his own well-being. Yet, he did not believe the decision to be a thinker would be an easy one. Struggles are involved because thinking is hard work, emotionally, psychically and physically.

THE REFORM ISSUES. If we move forward in the Deweyan spirit, then, our guiding values will be those of democracy, education and thinking: a respect for the rights of others to argue their views, a willingness to consider alternative positions on their merits, a curiosity about the reasons why interested parties think differently, a humility in the face of complexity and controversy, and a commitment to the well-being of all parties and segments of society. The Deweyan spirit takes us further, however, for it raises a set of questions that we seem well-advised to consider when we enter discussions and debates. Some of these questions fall neatly into two domains, the philosophical and the practical. These two domains overlap significantly since thinking philosophically and addressing philosophical questions is practical and has implications for practice, just as practice and experience are the source of philosophical problems. As we approach these questions, it is helpful to remember that the key question for Dewey was: What is it we can or should expect of educational discussions and decisions, and how can they help us in determining what we can and should expect of schools, the community and the university? In the end, the spirit of Deweyan reform lies in adopting this attitude, not in specific practices and changes.

In the philosophical domain, we have already seen how important it is that we think carefully and clearly. Yet there are precise questions and concerns that face educators and policy makers as they consider educational reform. Among the many questions that may arise, no doubt we should ask:

- What are the roots or causes of the educational conflicts? What do we, the various parties involved, assume or believe that keeps us divided and debating but not deciding how to move forward?

- What are the merits of these sources or causes of conflict? Are our assumptions and beliefs consistent with solid research, reflective experience and reasoned arguments?

- What are the strengths of the various positions before us that we want to preserve in any reconstructed educational proposal? Are the partial truths in the conflicting opinions we have studied acknowledged and included in the resulting consensus? Is justice done to the partial truths that are contained in the views we find generally ill-considered and repugnant?

- Is the reform proposed coherent or a patchwork of potentially inconsistent, counter-productive or conflicting remedies? Does an interest in attending to the ideas of everyone result in a hodgepodge of incompatible ideas?

- Are the proposed educational changes based upon an understanding of the seriousness of the notion of change itself—on-going evolutionary change and social change—and the ways of understanding, thinking about and coping with change?

- Does the recommended reform include a self-correcting component that encourages an examination of the consequences of the revised educational program? How does this element in the plan recognize the importance of rethinking both ends and means, revising them as warranted?

- Do the proposed solutions or reforms move from one philosophical, pedagogical, or paradigmatic extreme or position to another without policy makers and educators debating and deciding upon the strengths and weaknesses of the proposed reform agenda? Does the debate alter practice or is it purely ideological?

- Are reform efforts largely a reaction to what people dislike about current educational practices or are they based upon a positive and coherent philosophy of education?

- Does the plan for school reform make surface changes or substantive ones? Will a little tinkering with the status quo here and there suffice? Has the possibility been considered that neither minor patching nor uncoordinated programs of reform will be sufficient to produce wanted changes? Is a comprehensive rethinking of education, its institutions and values, and its place in society warranted?

- Is the school in the business of creating complete people and personalities or just inquiring minds and intellectual dispositions? Is it understood that studying ideas and engaging in experiences partially form the personality of students? Are the underlying values truly educational?

- Is our theory of learning founded upon the ways children and youth learn in everyday life or is it an artificially conceived one? How is school practice based upon the theory?

- Is the proposed agenda founded upon an explicit philosophy or theory of education that is open to public scrutiny and debate?

In the practical domain, there are also many questions. There is the atmosphere of the school; there are questions of organization, authority and responsibility. There are values, attitudes and dispositions to be selected, taught, expressed and reflected. Reflecting our objectives and mission, there are issues of evaluation, assessment and accountability.

Questions regarding the curriculum for general education in the primary, elementary and secondary grades and beyond arise. Questions of education for the workplace and for civic responsibilities occur as well. Moreover, there is the matter of appropriate programs for teacher preparation and certification; of standards; of teachers' status, responsibility and professionalism; and of the assessment of innovative practices. Questions that Dewey might raise in this realm are along the following lines:

- Are both children and knowledge truly important in the reform proposal? How does the proposed reform agenda respect the importance of children and forms of inquiry, creativity and understanding?

- How are children and youth viewed in the reform agenda? Are they treated as active learners who need to engage in developmentally appropriate and educationally relevant activities? Are they guided in their educational experiences by teachers who love children, learning, thinking and communicating?

- Whose interests are being served by the school or the reform agenda? Are the students being empowered, being liberated and growing? Are teachers able to think and act on their own as professionals? Do parents have a say? Is the welfare of the entire community being considered?

- How does the proposal reflect the connection of school to society? Are the roles and limitations of the school and the importance and contributions of society understood and taken into consideration? Are the history and the resources of the community understood, appreciated and utilized? In what ways does the reform proposal recognize, emphasize and cultivate the idea that all social institutions and individuals are educators?

- Are the concepts of education and growth understood and appreciated? Do fundamental beliefs and values in this realm need to be reconsidered, priorities identified, and policies and strategies developed to respect and achieve them? Is it evident why without clear fundamental concepts we are unable to set priorities, see their rationale, and protect ourselves from arbitrary decisions and actions? Is it evident how proposed reforms follow from fundamental beliefs and values?

- Is it evident that all learning and experiences are not equally worthwhile? Is the educational value of an experience determined by its present and future potential for students' growth?

- How does the proposal support the on-going growth of educational personnel in the areas of subject matter, educational theory, school practice, child study and neighborhood heritage? What resources, programs, opportunities and time are provided for these kinds of growth?

- Do the goals, activities and experiences of children and youth focus upon creating just skills and competencies or, in addition, attitudes and dispositions?

- Does the reform proposal support the idea that somewhat different kinds of schools are needed for distinctive purposes and communities? How is the need for experimental schools addressed? In what ways are schools that collaborate with universities for the purposes of experimentation, research and educator preparation specifically planned, supported and promoted? Is there artificial or unproductive uniformity?

- How do issues of quality of life and experience influence discussions about and decisions regarding the school and the classroom as a community of learners?

- Are educational means (administration, buildings, books, materials, equipment, methods and experiences) and ends (skills, understandings, attitudes and dispositions) viewed as fixed or flexible? Is it understood that ends—skills, understandings, attitudes and dispositions—are also means to further growth, the progressive development of the thoughtful person? Is a new way of conceptualizing ends and means needed? Would success be a static state? In what ways do the school assessment and evaluation plans accommodate the notion of changing means and ends?

- How does the school reform include changing the school ethos into that of a democratic community where everyone is prized and treated with equal respect? Is it clear that learning and experiencing democracy at school is a key educational and moral experience?

- Does the reform agenda as it relates to assessment and evaluation focus on understanding the individual child and the teacher in order to enhance each person's growth? Are the plans and procedures consistent with respecting each child as a learner and each teacher as a professional? How does school assessment include an analysis of its democratic ethos and community atmosphere?

- Is the complexity of the roles and responsibilities of the teacher understood and appreciated? Are teachers employed for their ability to handle these complexities or for their willingness to conform to site or district prescriptions? What provision is made for teachers to exercise professional judgment and discretion?

- How are the educational experiences of children and youth designed to diminish class, gender, ethnic and economic inequities? Do proposals show an awareness that schooling is intrinsically a moral endeavor and connected to the development of ethical attitudes, dispositions and behavior?

JUDGING REFORM PROPOSALS. From such questions, it is possible to identify at least seven themes which ought to inform educational reform and its assessment: school-community relationships; university-school collaboration; the centrality of educational priorities; an inquiry-based orientation to curriculum; a constructivist epistemology and ethics; a purpose-based account of professionalism, authority and social organization; and a democratic conception of the school as a learning community. But merely repeating these phrases or clichés will fail to keep the Deweyan spirit, creating a Dewey who bears little more resemblance to the reality than the one Neatby and others castigated decades ago.

Because these Deweyan themes have their roots in a conception of learning and knowledge, they in turn imply an active learner, a curriculum for freedom and power, and a commitment to democratic values and a spirit of fraternity. They also create a basis for understanding teachers' responsibilities and authority, and, thereby, suggest a conception of teacher preparation and professionalism, a new respect and independence for the classroom teacher, and a social role for the teacher as a former of the ideas and attitudes of new citizens. They also create a role for the community.

It is in the light of these thoughts, then, that detailed and specific proposals for educational change should be judged in a Deweyan spirit. At their most basic level, these themes talk of the responsibilities of teachers and learners. They define an educationally legitimate sense of teacher responsibility, identifying the kind of learning and growth for which teachers should be accountable but also for which they have rightful claims to the necessary resources. They enable us to pose relevant and perceptive questions about, for example, proposals for national testing of student achievement and lists of expected educational outcomes. They also urge a realistic sense of the limits of the power of the school and a wider recognition of the impact of other "schoolhouses" scattered throughout the neighborhood, broader community and world.

Reflection on the use of schools to foster economic competitiveness or a national economic strategy or to wage "war on poverty" illustrates the potential power of these seven themes to identify and refine relevant issues for analysis and so to frame educational policies which address them in terms of educationally legitimate objectives and strategies. No school should be oblivious to the working and living conditions in the community which surrounds it, but it does not follow that the school would necessarily be doing its students a service by attacking these problems directly any more than it would be by simply preparing students to adapt themselves to them. The former approach might tempt us in the case of poverty, as the latter, on the contrary, might in the case of employment skills—and in both cases for reasonable, noble motives. Yet the critic who wonders whether acquiring "necessary workplace skills" or even factual knowledge or competencies needed to demonstrate "mastery" of the curriculum really constitutes an education is raising the question of educational priorities and so whether we are diverting attention to other worthwhile, but not educational, matters. Those who talk of inquiry, building understanding and questioning raise appropriate epistemological, ethical and institutional considerations. The critic who talks of empowerment and growth or providing students with the tools they really need in all aspects of life (or at least an education which does not stifle individuals' development and limit their life chances) is perhaps closest of all to a Deweyan perspective. Those who say that the quality of life in school, the learning community, matters as much as the "amount" learned may be pointing to yet another important consideration.

For these reasons, then, a *comprehensive* view of educational reform matters. Schools can become more effective in what they do, yet achieve nothing that truly matters. Equally, changes can be cosmetic. Neither a change of principal nor a new program in reading or science or mathematics nor the establishment of a mission statement nor even a commitment to a philosophy of excellence or accountability will itself transform schools (though some changes may remedy specific problems and others may incorporate helpful developments). Nor will simply adding or removing course requirements, examinations or hours of field experience automatically change the preparation of teachers in significant or relevant ways.

It is not then a tautology to say that real reform in addition to being *fundamental* and *comprehensive* takes place only in the *transformation* of individuals and in the day-to-day relationships within the school and between the school and its various communities. Much depends on the education, judgment, independence and responsible exercise of authority of the persons involved, notably teachers and principals; much depends on the relationship of the specific school to its community, including the university. For this reason then educational reform can never be completed. Nor can completion be a viable aim of reform movements. Structural, curricular and personnel changes, as important as they may be, by themselves will not have the necessary and desired effects: What is most important lies in the characteristics of the people involved—and so their education, their work environment, and their freedom and capacity to be truly professional educators. The reflective practitioner or "the thoughtful person" who has become an educator, in short, is the key to genuine educational reform; and reflective practice, like judgment, is a disposition which involves considering the particularities—the individual district, school, teacher, child and community. Thoughtful people are needed too in the principal's office, central administration, board room and legislative chamber as well as in the home, bank, park, theater, hospital, business, university and factory. But we must never forget Dewey's point about society creating teachers: They are to a large degree what the community will tolerate. They are also what the profession, district and school will tolerate.

We conclude, then, by extracting a Deweyan thought from another context: No learning community—classroom, school, university, neighborhood, district or nation—"gets far intellectually [that] does not 'love to think,' and no one loves to think who does not have an interest in problems" (L4, 182). If societies, communities and educators are genuinely interested in addressing the problems of school and society, Dewey believed they could do so—and successfully. And, for him, to choose to become or remain in an unthinking state or educational ghetto where reflection, social action and growth are minimally pursued is personally wasteful, socially destructive and moraliy irresponsible.

Selected Bibliography

Primary Sources

Archambault, R. D. (Ed.). (1964/1974). *John Dewey on education: Selected writings*. Chicago: The University of Chicago Press.

Boydston, J. A. (Ed.). (1967-1972). *The early works of John Dewey, 1882-1898*. (Vols. 1-5). Carbondale: Southern Illinois University Press.

Boydston, J. A. (Ed.). (1976-1983). *The middle works of John Dewey, 1899-1924*. (Vols. 1-15). Carbondale: Southern Illinois University Press.

Boydston, J. A. (Ed.). (1981-1991). *The later works of John Dewey, 1925-1953*. (Vols. 1-17). Carbondale: Southern Illinois University Press.

Dewey, J. (1900/1902/1915/1943/1956/1990). *The school and society* and *The child and the curriculum* (Expanded ed.). Chicago: The University of Chicago Press.

Dewey, J. (1909/1936/1975). *Moral principles in education*. Carbondale: Southern Illinois University Press.

Dewey, J. (1916/1966). *Democracy and education: An introduction to the philosophy of education.* New York: The Free Press.

Dewey, J. (1920/1948/1957). *Reconstruction in philosophy* (Enlarged ed.). Boston: Beacon Press.

Dewey, J. (1925/1929/1958). *Experience and nature*. New York: Dover Publications, Inc.

Dewey, J. (1927). *The public and its problems*. New York: Henry Holt and Company, Inc.

Dewey, J. (1929). *The quest for certainty*. New York: Minton, Balach and Co.

Dewey, J. (1933/1960). *How we think: A restatement of the relation of reflective thinking to the educative process* (New ed.). Lexington, MA: D. C. Heath and Company.

Dewey, J. (1934/1980). *Art as experience.* New York: Perigee Books.

Dewey, J. (1934/1962). *A common faith.* New Haven, CT: Yale University Press.

Dewey, J. (1938/1963). *Experience and education.* New York: Collier Books.

Dewey, J. (1939/1989). *Freedom and culture.* Buffalo, NY: Prometheus Books.

Dworkin, M. S. (Ed.). (1959). *Dewey on education: Selections with an introduction and notes.* New York: Bureau of Publications, Teachers College, Columbia University.

McLellan, J. A., & Dewey, J. (1908). *The psychology of number and its applications to methods of teaching arithmetic.* New York: D. Appleton and Company.

Ratner, J. (Ed.). (1939). *Intelligence in the modern world: John Dewey's philosophy.* New York: The Modern Library.

Secondary Sources

Books and Chapters:

Anderson, J. (1988). *The education of Blacks in the South, 1860-1935.* Chapel Hill: University of North Carolina Press.

Apple, M. W., & Beane, J. A. (Eds.). (1995). *Democratic schools.* Alexandria, VA: Association for Supervision and Curriculum Development.

Archambault, R. D. (Ed.). (1965). *Philosophical analysis and education.* London: Routledge & Kegan Paul.

Benn, S. I., & Peters, R. S. (1959). *Social principles and the democratic state.* London: Allen & Unwin.

Brown, R. G. (1991). *Schools of thought: How the politics of literacy shape thinking in the classroom.* San Francisco: Jossey-Bass Publishers.

Buchmann, M., & Floden, R. E. (1993). *Detachment and concern: Conversations in the philosophy of teaching and teacher education* (Advances in Contemporary Educational Thought, vol. 11). New York: Teachers College Press.

Clifford, G., & Guthrie, J. (1988). *Ed school: A brief for professional education.* Chicago: The University of Chicago Press.

Cohen, D. (1989). Practice and policy: Notes on the history of instruction. In D. Warren (Ed.), *American teachers: Histories of a profession at work* (392-407). New York: Macmillan Publishing Co.

Colburn, A. (1993). *Creating professional development schools.* Bloomington, IN: Phi Delta Kappa Educational Foundation.

Cremin, L. (1961). *The transformation of the school: Progressivism in American education, 1876-1957.* New York: Alfred Knopf.

Cremin, L. (1988). *American education: The metropolitan experience, 1876-1980.* New York: Harper and Row.

Cuban, L. (1989). The Persistence of reform in American schools. In D. Warren (Ed.), *American teachers: Histories of a profession at work* (370-391). New York: Macmillan Publishing Co.

Cuban, L. (1993). *How teachers taught: Constancy and change in American classrooms, 1880-1980* (2nd ed.). New York: Teachers College Press.

Curtis, S. J., & Boultwood, M. E. A. (1970). *A short history of educational ideas* (4th ed.). London: University Tutorial Press.

Darling-Hammond, L. (Ed.). (1994). *Professional development schools: Schools for developing a profession.* New York: Teachers College Press.

David, D., Fracchia, T., Gangwer, T. P., Johnson, T. W., Lesley, B., Mullen, B., Palacios, R., Seifert, E., Simpson, D. J., Thompson, J. L., & Wagstaff, L. (n.d.). *The professional development school: A commonsense approach to improving education.* Fort Worth, TX: Sid W. Richardson Foundation.

Dill, D. D. (1990). *What teachers need to know: The knowledge, skills, and values essential to good teaching.* San Francisco: Jossey-Bass Publishers.

Dykhuizen, G. (1973). *The life and mind of John Dewey.* Carbondale: Southern Illinois University Press.

Flower, E., & Murphey, M. (1977). *A history of philosophy in America* (Vol. 2). New York: Capricorn Books.

Freire, P. (1970). *Pedagogy of the oppressed.* New York: Seabury Press.

Fullan, M. G. (with S. Stiegelbauer). (1991). *The new meaning of educational change* (2nd ed.). Toronto and New York: OISE Press and Teachers College Press.

Giroux, H. A. (1988). *Schooling and the struggle for public life: Critical pedagogy in the modern age*. Minneapolis: University of Minnesota Press.

Goodlad, J. I. (1990). *Teachers for our nation's schools*. San Francisco: Jossey-Bass Publishers.

Goodlad, J. I. (1994). *Educational renewal: Better teachers, better schools*. San Francisco: Jossey-Bass Publishers.

Goodlad, J. I., Soder, R., & Sirotnik, K. A. (Eds.). (1990a). *The moral dimensions of teaching*. San Francisco: Jossey-Bass Publishers.

Goodlad, J. I., Soder, R., & Sirotnik, K. A. (Eds.). (1990b). *Places where teachers are taught*. San Francisco: Jossey-Bass Publishers.

Greene, M. (1973). *Teacher as stranger: Educational philosophy for the modern age*. Belmont, CA: Wadsworth Publishing Company, Inc.

Greene, M. (1994). Epistemology and educational research: The influence of recent approaches to knowledge. In L. Darling-Hammond (Ed.), *Review of research in education*, Vol. 20 (Chap. 10, 423-464). Washington: American Educational Research Association.

Hare, W. (1979). *Open-mindedness and education*. Montréal: McGill-Queen's University Press.

Hare, W. (1993). *What makes a good teacher: Reflections on some characteristics central to the educational enterprise*. London, ON: The Althouse Press.

Herbst, J. (1989a). *And sadly teach: Teacher education and professionalization in American culture*. Madison: University of Wisconsin Press.

Herbst, J. (1989b). Teacher preparation in the nineteenth century: Institutions and purposes. In D. Warren (Ed.), *American teachers: Histories of a profession at work* (213-236). New York: Macmillan Publishing Co.

Holmes, M. (1990). The character and quality of Canadian education: Some contemporary issues. In J. Downey & D. McCamus (Eds.), *To be our best: Learning for the future* (4-9). Montréal: Corporate Higher Education Forum.

Holmes Group. (1986). *Tomorrow's teachers: A report of the Holmes Group*. East Lansing, MI: The Holmes Group.

Holmes Group. (1990). *Tomorrow's schools: Principles for the design of professional development schools.* East Lansing, MI: The Holmes Group.

Holmes Group. (1995). *Tomorrow's schools of education.* East Lansing, MI: The Holmes Group.

hooks, b. (1994). *Teaching to transgress: Education as the practice of freedom.* New York: Routledge.

Howard, V. A., & Scheffler, I. (1995). *Work, education, and leadership.* New York: Peter Lang.

Jackson, P. W. (1990) Introduction. In J. Dewey, *The school and society* and *The child and the curriculum* (Expanded ed.), ix-xxxvii. Chicago: The University of Chicago Press.

Johnson, T. W. (1995). *Discipleship or pilgrimage? The educator's quest for philosophy.* Albany: State University of New York Press.

Kincheloe, J. (1993). *Toward a critical politics of teacher thinking: Mapping the postmodern.* Westport, CT: Bergin and Garvey.

Kliebard, H. (1986). *The struggle for the American curriculum, 1892-1958.* Boston: Routledge & Kegan Paul.

Levin, R. (1990). Recurring themes and variations. In J. I. Goodlad, R. Soder, & K. A. Sirotnik (Eds.), *Places where teachers are taught* (40-83). San Francisco: Jossey-Bass Publishers.

Levine, M. (Ed.). (1992). *Professional practice schools: Linking teacher education and school reform.* New York: Teachers College Press.

Lovejoy, A. O. (1936/1964). *The great chain of being: A study of the history of an idea.* Cambridge, MA: Harvard University Press.

Mayhew, K. C., & Edwards, A. C. (1936/1966). *The Dewey school.* New York: Atherton.

Neatby, H. (1953). *So little for the mind.* Toronto: Clarke, Irwin & Company Limited.

Oakeshott, M. (1956). Political education. In P. Laslett (Ed.), *Philosophy, politics and society* (First series), 1-21. Oxford: Basil Blackwell.

Osguthorpe, R. T., Harris, R. C., Harris, M. F., & Black, S. (Eds.). (1995). *Partner schools: Centers for educational renewal.* San Francisco: Jossey-Bass Publishers.

Paringer, W. A. (1990). *John Dewey and the paradox of liberal reform.* Albany: State University of New York Press.

Perkinson, H. J. (1993). *Teachers without goals. Students without purposes.* New York: McGraw-Hill, Inc.

Peters, R. S. (1958). *The concept of motivation* (Studies in Philosophical Psychology). London: Routledge & Kegan Paul.

Peters, R. S. (1959). *Authority, responsibility and education.* London: George Allen & Unwin.

Peters, R. S. (1966). *Ethics and education*. London: George Allen & Unwin.

Peters, R. S. (Ed.). (1977). *John Dewey reconsidered.* London: Routledge & Kegan Paul.

Peters, R. S. (1981a). *Essays on educators* (Unwin Education Books). London: George Allen & Unwin.

Peters, R. S. (1981b). *Moral development and moral education.* London: George Allen & Unwin.

Phenix, P. H. (1964). *Realms of meaning: A philosophy of the curriculum for general education.* New York: McGraw-Hill Book Company.

Rury, J. R. (1989). Who became teachers? The social characteristics of teachers in American history. In D. Warren (Ed.), *American teachers: Histories of a profession at work* (27-48). New York: Macmillan Publishing Co.

Schlechty, P. C. (1991). *Schools for the twenty-first century: Leadership imperatives for educational reform.* San Francisco: Jossey-Bass Publishers.

Socket, H. (1993). *The moral base for teacher professionalism.* New York: Teachers College Press.

Spring, J. (1994). *The American school, 1642-1993* (3rd ed.). New York: McGraw-Hill.

Tyack, D. (1974). *The one best system: A history of American education.* Cambridge, MA: Harvard University Press.

Tyack, D. (1989). The future of the past: What do we need to know about the history of teaching? In D. Warren (Ed.), *American teachers: Histories of a profession at work* (408-421). New York: Macmillan Publishing Co.

Tyack, D., & Hansot, E. (1982). *Managers of virtue: Public school leadership in America, 1820-1980.* New York: Basic Books.

van Manen, M. (1991). *The tact of teaching: The meaning of pedagogical thoughtfulness.* Albany: State University of New York Press.

West, C. (1989). *The American evasion of philosophy: A genealogy of pragmatism.* Madison: University of Wisconsin Press.

Westbrook, R. B. (1991). *John Dewey and American democracy.* Ithaca, NY: Cornell University Press.

Zemelman, S., Daniels, H., & Hyde, A. (1993). *Best practices: New standards for teaching and learning in America's schools.* Portsmouth, NH: Heinemann.

Zilversmit, A. (1976). The failure of progressive education, 1920-1940. In L. Stone (Ed.), *Schooling and society: Studies in the history of education.* Baltimore, MD: Johns Hopkins University Press.

Journal Articles:

Burnett, J. R. (1979). Whatever happened to John Dewey? *Teachers College Record*, 82, 2, 192-210.

Burnett, J. R. (1988). Dewey's mature philosophy. *Educational Theory*, 38, 2, 203-211.

Cohen, A. (1980). Society and social education in Martin Buber's philosophy. *Educational Studies*, 10, 4, 335-356.

Covert, J. R. (1993). Creating a professional standard of moral conduct for Canadian teachers: A work in progress. *Canadian Journal of Education/Revue canadienne de l'éducation* 18, 4, 429-445.

Fraser, J. (1988). Who were the progressive educators anyway? A case study of the progressive education movement in Boston, 1905-1925. *Educational Foundations*, 2, 4-30.

Garrison, J. (1995). Deweyan pragmatism and the epistemology of contemporary social constructivism. *American Educational Research Journal*, 32, 4, 716-740.

Hare, W. F. (1990). Limiting the freedom of expression: The Keegstra case. *Canadian Journal of Education/Revue canadienne de l'éducation* 15, 4, 375-389.

Hawley, W. D., & Rosenholtz, S. J., with Goodstein, H., & Hasselbring, T. (1984). Good schools: What research says about improving student achievement [Special issue]. *Peabody Journal of Education*, 61, 4.

Johnson, W. R. (1987). Empowering practitioners: Holmes, Carnegie, and the lessons of history. *History of Education Quarterly*, 27, 221-240.

Klag, P. (1994). A message from the president: Ten reasons why lab schools are growing and becoming important agents for educational change and reform. *NALS/NEWS*, 35, 3, 1-2.

Lagemann, E. C. (1989). The plural worlds of educational research. *History of Education Quarterly*, 29, 185-214.

Lazerson, M. (1984). If all the world were Chicago: American education in the twentieth century. *History of Education Quarterly*, 24, 165-179.

Levin, B. (1995). Educational responses to poverty. *Canadian Journal of Education/Revue canadienne de l'éducation*, 20, 2, 211-224.

Madigan, T. (1993). Russell and Dewey on education: Similarities and differences. *Current Issues in Education*, 10, 1, 3-12.

McQuaide, J., & Pliska, A. M. (December 1993-January 1994). The challenge to Pennsylvania's educational reform. *Educational Leadership*, 51, 4, 16-21.

O'Neil, J. (1995). On lasting school reform: A conversation with Ted Sizer. *Educational Leadership*, 52, 5, 7.

Pratte, R. (1992). Reconsideration of John Dewey: *The Public and Its Problems*. *Educational Studies*, 23, 2, 139-151.

Smith, N. J. (1994). Reconsiderations: *Dynamic Administration: The Collected Papers of Mary Parker Follett*. *Educational Studies*, 25, 3, 199-209.

What the public wants. (1995). *Education Update* [Association for Supervision and Curriculum Development], 37, 5, 4-5.

Technical and Research Reports:

Darling-Hammond, L. (1994). *The current status of teaching and teacher development in the United States*. (National Commission on Teaching and America's Future). New York: Teachers College.

For the love of learning: Report of the Royal Commission on Learning. A short version. (1994). Toronto: The Queen's Printer for Ontario.

Ministry of Education and Training. (1993). *The Common Curriculum*. (Working Document). Toronto: Author.

Province of British Columbia. (1993). *Improving the quality of education in British Columbia: Changes to British Columbia's education policy*. Victoria: Author.

Province of British Columbia. (1994). *Guidelines for the kindergarten to grade 12 education plan: Implementation resource, Part 1.* Victoria: Author.

Texas Education Agency. (1994). *Learner-centered schools for Texas: A vision of Texas educators.* Austin, TX: Author.

U.S. Department of Education. (1994). *Changing education: Resources for systemic reform.* Washington: Author.

U.S. Department of Labor. (n.d.). *What work requires of schools: A SCANS report for America 2000.* Washington: Author.

Index